Pop-Culture Pedagogy in the Music Classroom

Teaching Tools from *American Idol* to YouTube

Edited by
Nicole Biamonte

THE SCARECROW PRESS, INC.
Lanham • Toronto • Plymouth, UK
2011

Published by Scarecrow Press, Inc.
A wholly owned subsidary of The Rowman & Littlefield Publishing Group, Inc.
4501 Forbes Boulevard, Suite 200, Lanham, Maryland 20706
http://www.scarecrowpress.com

Estover Road, Plymouth PL6 7PY, United Kingdom

British Library Cataloguing in Publication Information Available

Library of Congress Cataloging-in-Publication Data

Pop-culture pedagogy in the music classroom : teaching tools from American
idol
to YouTube / edited by Nicole Biamonte.
     p. cm.
  Includes bibliographical references and index.
  ISBN 978-0-8108-7736-8 (cloth : alk. paper) — ISBN 978-0-8108-7663-7
(pbk. : alk. paper)
  1. Music—Instruction and study. 2. Popular music—Instruction and
study. 3. Popular culture--Study and teaching. I. Biamonte, Nicole.
  MT1.P638 2010
  780.71—dc22

                                                        2010020715

∞™ The paper used in this publication meets the minimum requirements of
American National Standard for Information Sciences—Permanence of Paper
for Printed Library Materials, ANSI/NISO Z39.48-1992.

Printed in the United States of America

Contents

Introduction

Nicole Biamonte

The essays collected in this volume offer a broad range of ideas and techniques for teaching music classes using elements of popular culture that resonate with students' everyday lives: popular songs and genres, video games, music videos, television shows, mixes, mashups, MP3s, turntables, and online resources. Each chapter provides a pedagogical model for incorporating pop culture and its associated technologies, encompassing a wide variety of music courses. This volume is designed for use by college and secondary-school music teachers, although many of the methods and materials detailed herein can be adapted to any educational level. It can serve as a teaching resource, a primary textbook for music pedagogy courses, or supplemental reading for courses in criticism, analysis, or cultural studies.

Assimilating elements of popular culture into classroom music teaching both acknowledges their prevalence and takes advantage of their potential to enrich course content and promote interactive learning. Students' cultural identification with these media makes them powerful tools for fostering classroom engagement. In the digital age, recorded music, video, and other multimedia materials have become ubiquitous commodities, easily accessible at little or no cost, which can reinforce the learning of music concepts and techniques in the verbal, auditory, visual, and kinesthetic domains.

The three essays in the first section, "General Tools," explore practical applications that can be implemented in almost any music class: sound-mixing techniques, iPods and other portable media storage devices, and YouTube and other online video sources. The middle section, "Teaching Musicianship and Music Theory," comprises essays that call upon popular songs or other aspects of pop culture to demonstrate music-theory topics or to develop musicianship skills. Classes in theory and aural skills lend themselves particularly well to the inclusion of examples or paradigms drawn from popular music since these courses focus on concepts and methodologies that are not necessarily tied to a particular repertoire. In contrast to this top-down model of incorporating content into an established framework, the essays in the final section, "Teaching Music Analysis and Criticism," follow a bottom-up model, in which the examination of musical, lyrical, or visual content serves as a point of departure for addressing broader issues and contexts.

In "Appreciating the Mix," Benjamin Bierman argues compellingly for the development of enhanced listening skills through an understanding of the sound-mixing process, presented within the context of a music appreciation course. The first part of the chapter explains how to manipulate a stereo field using panning and volume, creating (or subverting) aural analogues to the physical placement of sound sources, and offers sample assignments. The second part surveys sound-production techniques and aesthetic values in jazz, classical, and popular music genres through interviews with producer-engineers and scholars. While the chapter is focused on teaching music appreciation, the sound-mixing unit could be incorporated into many other types of music classes.

The following two chapters explore the full functionalities of portable media players and streaming Internet video, both of which are powerful and flexible teaching tools that can be integrated into classes in any discipline. Kathleen Kerstetter's essay, "Pod-Logic," describes the capabilities and teaching potential of the iPod beyond music playback, elucidating its lesser-known functions, such as sound recording, video playback, data storage, and (for the iPhone and iPod Touch) software applications. In "Global Connections via YouTube," Hope Munro Smith surveys the landscape of Internet video and discusses using YouTube in the context of an ethnomusicology class, although the techniques and issues considered are, again, more generally applicable to any classroom setting.

The next three chapters suggest models for incorporating popular music into traditional undergraduate theory classes. All three authors advocate demonstrating new concepts within the context of a familiar genre and for granting students agency by including student-selected examples. Nancy Rosenberg's chapter begins with a solid grounding in the philosophy of music education, followed by a wide spectrum of examples, activities, and resources for teaching aspects of rhythm and meter. The chapter by Heather MacLachlan is similarly grounded in learning theory and offers numerous sample lessons and musical examples of chord types, progressions, motives, and other pitch-based structures. A mathematical perspective is presented by James R. Hughes, who treats several of the same topics—chords, progressions, melodies, and rhythms—as transformations of musical space and relates them to notational conventions and patterns through a transcription exercise.

In a chapter focused on formal analysis, Keith Salley asserts the importance of comprehending structures aurally through active listening, which he compares to a kind of vicarious composition. The chapter integrates approaches to form, hypermeter, and phrase structure in jazz standards and musical theater repertoire and provides examples of expository, developmental, cadential, and connecting phrase functions. My own chapter considers the simplified forms of notation used in the video games Guitar Hero and Rock Band, surveys the formal terminology used in the games, and reimagines the sparser note cues at easier levels of difficulty as implicit analytical reductions. This chapter also serves as a pivot between the pedagogical applications of the formal issues discussed in the preceding chapter and those of the video game technology investigated in the following chapter.

The pair of chapters that conclude the book's middle section suggest new technologies for developing students' musicianship, with a focus on rhythm skills. In "DDR at the Crossroads," Brent Auerbach, Bret Aarden, and Mathonwy Bostock present a detailed study of the potential of the video game Dance Dance Revolution for rhythmic training. They describe the outcomes of a semester's classroom use of the game as a rhythmic component of an aural-skills lab and of a pilot experiment designed to measure the game's effects on rhythm sight-reading. In her chapter on turntablism, Karen Snell reports on her experiences with turntablism classes and explains the ways in which studying turntable techniques can help to develop students' rhythmic abilities, pitch discernment, improvisational skills, and a broad awareness of popular music styles and subgenres.

The third section of the book, like the first, begins with an essay on music appreciation. James A. Grymes discusses his adoption of *American Idol* as a tool for teaching music criticism and exploring a wide variety of issues related to performance studies, including vocal technique, interpretation and expressivity, stage presence, repertoire selection, and marketing and the music industry. Victoria Malawey's chapter provides an analytical model for cover songs, comprising a set of broad and specific musical parameters that serve as a basis for nuanced comparisons of different versions of a song, which might have in common only a generalized melodic, rhythmic, and lyric profile. Lori Burns, Tamar Dubuc, and Marc Lafrance delineate sets of both musical and visual interpretive parameters for interrogating the relationships between music and images between an original music video, or *sourcetext*, and a cover version, or adaptation. The authors designate this relationship as "cotextual" and offer a prototype for graphically representing the correlations between musical and visual events.

The following two chapters investigate stylistic elements of rap music. Alyssa Woods examines constructions of gendered, racial, and class identity in rap, situating new research on the expression of black masculinity through vocal quality, flow (rhythmic delivery of the lyrics), and production effects within the context of earlier work on lyrical and visual representations of masculinity. In "Crunkology," Ali Colleen Neff details a course that explores the Southern hip-hop subgenre of "crunk" from a cultural studies standpoint, unpacking a host of aesthetic, social, political, economic, racial, and gender issues through analysis of crunk music and lyrics. The final chapter, Wayne Marshall's "Mashup Poetics as Pedagogical Practice," is a trenchant consideration of mashups, not simply as clever juxtapositions or recontextualizations of existing material but as "musically-expressed ideas about music," whose new intertextual meanings constitute audible musical analyses and cultural critiques.

This book is intended as a broad and varied but not comprehensive survey of some possible uses of popular culture in music classes. Pop-culture tools whose music-educational potential is not examined here are blogs, podcasting, and other digital journalism; wikis and other collaborative information resources, social-networking sites such as Facebook and MySpace; and online environments such as Second Life. Perhaps these topics might be addressed in a future volume that includes explorations of new cultural tropes and technologies as yet unknown.

Since the essays in this book focus on the practical pedagogical applications of pop-culture elements and technologies, the vexed and thorny questions of what constitutes popular music, whether it has or should have a canon, and whether it can or should be addressed using paradigms originally developed for Western art music—all of which have been argued at length elsewhere—are addressed within this volume only implicitly, if at all. The underlying assumption of this collection, however, is that popular culture and popular music are vitally important both as teaching tools and as subjects for scholarly inquiry. Much can be taught with these materials, and much can be learned from them as well.

I

GENERAL TOOLS

1

Appreciating the Mix: Teaching Music Listening Skills through Sound-Mixing Techniques

Benjamin Bierman

Teaching music appreciation is a crucially important element of under-graduate liberal-arts programs. Many former students think back fondly and with great "appreciation" to this course that gave them new insight into music as well as a background in musical styles with which they would have otherwise been unfamiliar and, still more importantly, the development of basic listening skills. In the following essay, I suggest that along with teaching the fundamentals of music and providing a broad knowledge of genres and styles, instructing students in the fundamentals of sound recording will contribute to a deeper engagement with the music in the course and, more significantly, for the rest of their listening lives.

Many instructors feel strongly about the value of teaching music appreciation and dedicate a great deal of time, effort, and creativity to the endeavor. Naturally, as with any course that has a long-standing pedagogical tradition, there is the danger of a certain inertia that may keep us on a particular well-worn track—although there have been many recent advances. Many if not most new music-appreciation textbooks take care to include more popular music, jazz, world music, and a larger variety of 20th- and 21st-century music than earlier texts. Some are specifically geared toward addressing musical elements, such as melody, harmony, timbre, texture, and form, in all genres. A chronological approach is no longer assumed, and extensive multimedia resources are offered. This is all to the good, and we, of course, should continue to question our preconceived notions and search for new methods that address the needs and interests of our current students while also broadening their perspectives and giving them a foundation on which to build a life of learning and growth in musical understanding.

While some departments have a shared music-appreciation curriculum, in many instances we have a great deal of flexibility regarding the material we present and how we present it. For example, we can choose to focus on teaching elements of music, style conventions, music history, wider social and cultural contexts, or simple breadth of repertoire, and we can adjust the historical, geographical, and cultural compass of the repertoire. What we all have in common, however, is that we strive to deepen our students' awareness of music and help them to become better listeners.

For a variety of economic and cultural reasons (the state of the arts in our country, the lack of music education in many primary and secondary schools, etc.), our students frequently have little or no experience with live music and still less with live concerts of art music. We generally address this by having our students attend at least one concert and write a brief report about it. The concert report is a staple of most music-appreciation classes and should remain one. Some of us are lucky enough to have a wide variety of concerts available in the area, and some even manage to present live music in the classroom. But the rest of the time, we are presenting recorded music.

We are currently in the midst of a radical shift in the way recorded music is made and distributed that affects all aspects of music making and listening. Gone are the days of huge booming speakers (with the notable exception of cars in my neighborhood!) and, conversely, of tiny transistor radios. At our disposal are incredibly affordable, convenient, and sophisticated music players, headphones, and compact speakers, which give us a previously unheard-of accessibility to a fantastic array of music with excellent sound quality.

The new paradigm is complicated and fraught with difficult issues, however. The ubiquitous compressing of audio files, for example, has fundamentally changed the way we make and hear music. Audiophiles cringe at the "lossy" compressed sound of the MP3 format, which is typically at a resolution of 128 kbps, less than one-tenth the size of the original audio file. Nonetheless, for most of us, such compressed audio files have become the norm. Our students do much of their listening through headphones, which is another significant change in their involvement with the surrounding environment, as well as with the music. How many times have you seen a group of friends walking together, each with headphones on, listening to his or her own music? I also frequently see friends sharing earbud headphones with each other—a new method of listening together. Additionally, the convenience of buying music is unprecedented, and even more extraordinary is the fact that we can carry our entire music library to class on our laptops or a very small device.

Listening in our classes necessarily relies upon recorded music, and our students' listening experiences throughout their lives will primarily consist of recorded music. Consequently, I suggest that giving instruction early in the semester in some basic issues of sound recording can enhance our students' ability to listen well, increase their appreciation of music, musicians, and the recording process, and allow them to get one step deeper into the music of their choice. As in all of our teaching, we must make difficult choices regarding which issues we choose to tackle in our classes. My proposed unit on recorded sound would necessarily displace other course material; nevertheless, I believe the concepts and techniques will prove of lasting value to students. A condensed look at the mixing process provides an opportunity to examine some of the more basic and easily explained aspects of the recording process. Because of the wide availability of excellent, free software,[1] combined with today's students' generally high level of technical savvy with both computers and audio files, we can also create an environment that allows them to experience and participate in this process firsthand.

In this chapter, after briefly introducing some basic concepts, I present several expert viewpoints regarding the mixing process and its importance by offering the opinions and perspectives of three producer-engineers working in various musical genres. Different styles of music often have different sound-mixing goals, and even within genres, producers and artists can have radically different approaches, further illuminating the importance of these processes to our listening perceptions. Albin Zak, the author of numerous articles and books on the importance of recording to the music-making process, also contributes his perspective regarding the pedagogical impact of the unit I propose.

MIXING BASICS

There are several stages of the sound production process, and mixing is the penultimate phase. In advance of the recording, artists and producers discuss issues such as repertoire, arrangements, and personnel. Once these issues are settled, recording sessions are scheduled. It takes considerably more time to record than one might expect. Microphone choices and placement take time, and these are critical technical and aesthetic issues. Multiple takes are generally recorded, and time is often taken to listen back. Once recording is completed, the mixing process takes place. The final stage (other than pressing CDs, artwork, liner notes, distribution, etc.) is mastering the recording. This process varies greatly but generally includes equalization (adding or subtracting high, middle, and low frequencies), adjusting volume levels, adding digital or analog effects (such as reverb and delay), and spacing the tracks.

At its simplest, mixing entails combining and balancing all the musical elements of a given piece. Beyond this simplified concept, it can get quite

Figure 1.1. A typical digital audio workstation mixing board, with panning and volume controls. The row of knobs at the top control panning. Numbers below the knobs indicate left and right placement in the stereo field (zero position indicates center placement). The sliders control the volume. Numbers immediately below the sliders indicate decibels that are added or subtracted (zero position means nothing is added or subtracted).

complicated very quickly, as discussions with various producer-engineers will illustrate. I have chosen to present and have students experiment with the most basic issues of mixing: creating a stereo field through panning and volume (see figure 1.1). The stereo field is an aural image that in turn creates a visual image for the listener, whether consciously or unconsciously. Panning is the placement of musical elements in the left and right speakers that creates a sense of breadth in the stereo field (side to side), while the relative volume of different elements governs its depth (front to back). This leaves out many other important aspects of mixing, such as effects and equalization. It does, however, allow for a very focused and manageable discussion that provides students with great insight into the recording process and adds an analogous breadth and depth to their listening.

Mixing is an interpretive art that requires technical skill, and mixers are crucial partners in the process of communicating a performance. Unfortunately, the importance of the engineer-mixer to the final recorded product is generally overlooked, as is the importance of the mix to our listening experience.

LECTURE, CLASS ACTIVITY, PROJECT

I frequently begin the semester with the unit on sound recording and find that it quickly gets students listening more carefully to the mix. More importantly, it immediately encourages them to become active listeners. I have found that a participatory class activity illustrates the principles more clearly and quickly than a lecture, so after an introduction, I tend to move directly to a demonstration. The recordings you choose should be well mixed and have distinctive mixing styles. Providing examples of contrasting mixes is helpful. Examples from any genre of music can be used, but I have found that employing contemporary popular music is quite effective for two primary reasons. First, the mixes can be quite exciting and are often extremely sophisticated and thoughtful. Secondly, students are able to quickly grasp these concepts in the familiar context of pop music, and are immediately excited by the details that are present in the mix.

To establish the basic elements of a mix, I begin with a contemporary classical CD that I produced, composer Sean Hickey's *Left at the Fork in the Road*.[2] The stereo field is quite straightforward, and I use it to illustrate breadth and depth. In the title composition, "Left at the Fork in the Road," the clarinet and bassoon are panned to the left and right respectively, and the flute is in the center, sounding as if it is a bit set back. I contrast this with one of the great contemporary popular mixes, James Taylor's CD *October Road*.[3] The mix for "On the 4th of July" contains numerous subtleties that illustrate the importance of the mix to the overall musical fabric: the placement of Taylor's acoustic guitar amongst drums and electronic instruments that would normally drown it out and the immediacy of Taylor's voice. More subtle touches can be found as well, such as a synthesizer line panned to the right, which has to be focused upon to notice its importance, and the background vocals, which slowly sneak in without our noticing them until they are firmly established.

For both of these listenings, I employ a handout (see figure 1.2) that asks the students to map various sounds in the stereo field on the sheet as the music plays. I then ask a student to place other students, one by one, in the front of the room in the places where he or she heard each instrument in the mix. I ask the class for comments on the positioning and to suggest other interpretations, continuing to move the students around. We then replay the piece and assess our physical representation of the stereo field. In addition to illustrating the importance of the mix, the activity is physically active and creates an exciting learning environment.

After this lecture and activity, I give an assignment. The students download Audacity,[4] a free, multi-platform (Mac and PC) audio software program that has effective and straightforward panning and volume controls. I give instructions for importing a CD into the program and ask them to import a track of their choice and experiment with volume and panning. Next, I assign a project to be done in two parts and submitted online via Blackboard course-management software. The assignment employs a wonderful resource: the popular band Radiohead has made five individual

"Left at the Fork in the Road," Sean Hickey, *Left at the Fork in the Road*

Place the following in the stereo field: Flute, Clarinet, and Bassoon

---

"On the 4th of July," James Taylor, *October Road*

Place the following in the stereo field (in order of entrance): Guitar, Voice and Drums, Bass, Synthesizer pad, Chorus, Synthesizer lead, Whistler and 2nd guitar (optional).

Figure 1.2.   Activity worksheet for placement of instruments in the stereo field

instrumental and vocal component tracks, or "stems," for their hit song "Nude" available for download from iTunes. The students are asked to download these tracks and create a mix of their own (see figure 1.3).

MIXING JAZZ

Jim Clouse, the owner-engineer of Park West Studios in Brooklyn, New York, specializes in the recording of jazz groups ranging from mainstream to the avant-garde.[5] I asked Clouse what he thinks about when he is mixing a jazz CD. He responded quickly and with glee: "It's funny because I've thought about it, but I never got to tell anybody about it, so thanks. I think about the Vanguard." He refers to the Village Vanguard in New York City, certainly one of the most venerable and respected jazz clubs in the world. Most jazz musicians and aficionados that live in or have visited New York City have been to this club, and more than 100 live albums have been

Radiohead Mixing Assignment

Due date:
A first draft of the assignment is due on Monday, 9/15, by 11:59 pm. I will provide comments on your draft, and you will submit the final version by 9/22.

Directions:
For this assignment, you must download the five individual Radiohead "stems" for "Nude" from iTunes ("Bass Stem," "Drum Stem," "Guitar Stem," "String FX Etc. Stem," and "Voice Stem"). In Audacity, very carefully and thoughtfully set volume and panning levels for each track (or stem) to create your own mix that reflects your musical aesthetic and that showcases the various components of the song, as well as the overall mix, to the greatest degree possible.

To export your final mix:
Go to Audacity > Preferences. Click File Formats. OGG Export Setup, set quality slider all the way to the left to 0. Click OK.
Go to File > Export as Ogg vorbis. If a warning comes up, press OK.
Name the file FirstName_LastName_Nude_Mix.ogg and save to a convenient spot on your computer. This will create a stereo mix. Quit Audacity, and then double-click the saved file to make sure it works. It should open, and it should play your mix. When you open this file, you will see one stereo track with two waveforms, representing the left and right tracks of your stereo mix.

To upload the assignment:
Go to the Digital Dropbox in Blackboard. In File Information, enter your name. Click "choose file," navigate to your file, and then choose it. Click to submit.

Figure 1.3. A sample final project

recorded there, including important records by John Coltrane, Bill Evans, Wynton Marsalis, Dexter Gordon, the Thad Jones/Mel Lewis Orchestra, and more recently, Brad Mehldau.

The room has a small and irregularly shaped bandstand, the sound system is not particularly notable, and the room itself has quirky angles throughout. There are two levels, columns on one side create awkward sightlines, and the room narrows at the back where there is a bar along one side. Clouse explains: "I say that because of all the things I heard there. But getting to play there! The first time was with the Thad Jones/Mel Lewis Orchestra. There's something about sitting in front of that band that was very special, but there's also something that is unbelievable about sitting *in* the band. Something about that club! The way those funky old curtains, or whatever is. The uneven walls—there was just something about the way sound came out of it. It was pure—that's the simplest word."

It is the combination of the impressions that Clouse had as an audience member and a performer that he seeks to recreate as he mixes. In other words, his intention is to make the recording as close to a live performance at his favorite club as he can from both perspectives. His desire is to stay out of the way as he mixes. He finds that the musicians, most of whom are excellent and extremely experienced in both performing and recording, manage to actually mix themselves. As we spoke, Clouse was startled to realize that he makes almost no changes in many aspects of his recording settings from one recording project to the next. His goal with microphone choices and placement is to get as close to the players' sound as possible, with the least intrusion upon the actual playing experience.

This said, when it comes time to mix, making a mixer's mark on the music is necessary and inevitable. The sounds have to be placed left and right (panning) and front and back (volume). This is an artificial process, and a mixer must make choices that have a huge impact on how the listener perceives the music. Clouse's intention is to create a "natural" sound through this artificial process.

Regarding panning for a typical jazz recording of a quintet with two horns (e.g., trumpet and saxophone), piano, bass, and drums, he takes care to "spread the drums out exactly like they are" over the central area of the stereo field. The high-hat is to the left, ride cymbal to the right, snare slightly to the left, tom-toms spread across this span, and bass drum in the middle, just as most drummers set up their kit (from the drummer's point of view). He puts the bass directly in the center of the stereo field, as the bottom end needs to be equally distributed, and with the bass and bass drum in the middle, all aspects of the mix have a distinct and unique placement, allowing the mix "to breathe." The piano presents a bit of a dilemma. In live performance, it is generally off to one side or the other, and an "old school" recording approach might have it clearly in its physical spot, but Clouse adopts a more modern technique: he does not give it such a tight, specific location but slightly spreads it out over a portion of the stereo field, perhaps slightly to the left to reflect its actual position. The horns are panned slightly to opposite sides. The aural and visual picture thus presented is largely as we would see it in a club: drums in the center (slightly spread out), bass to the right, piano to the left but washing over to the right as well, and trumpet to the left and sax to the right (or vice versa). This is a pretty straightforward mix that clearly demonstrates the desire to recreate the live listening experience in both the timbre of the instruments and the aural and visual sound-image.

Some aspects of the depth of this picture are simple while others are more complicated. The horns should normally sound as if they are in the front of the band. This is accomplished with a combination of microphone placement and volume settings, which necessarily affect each other. For example, making the horns a bit louder will make them seem more up-front. The volume of the piano and bass should be slightly lower and the drums perhaps a bit lower still. Since the drums are spread out, they will have a strong presence despite being set back in the mix. A vocalist would be put even farther out front in the mix than the horns, both for clarity of text and because vocalists are generally "accompanied" by the band, as opposed to being part of a larger whole.

MIXING WESTERN ART MUSIC

I myself have produced a number of albums in the jazz and classical fields. As Clouse speaks to the jazz perspective, I will briefly discuss my general approach to mixing a classically oriented recording. In truth, my approaches to classical music and to acoustic jazz are quite similar since both are chamber-oriented musics and have a somewhat standardized concert setup. For example, string quartets generally sit in a standard order across the stage in a kind of semicircle (from left to right: violin 1, violin 2, cello, viola). Orchestras have more variation, but we generally know what to expect.[6] Subconsciously, experienced listeners expect this setup to be recreated in a recording. Our students do not have this knowledge (or baggage), and recordings can be used to help the students aurally visualize the standard stage settings common in classical music performances.

Like Clouse, my first concern is to capture the sound of the performer as much as possible. As is true for all recorded music, microphone choices and placement are the first and perhaps most important step. Experience tells an engineer what microphones are generally good for recording particular instruments, but only one's ear can make a final decision as to which microphone is best for recording an individual performer. Microphone placement, at its most basic, will determine if the sound of the recording is more present (with microphones close to the performer) or more remote (with microphones farther away). Close microphone placement makes the listeners feel as if they are quite close to the music, and sounds such as fingers on the instruments and the breathing of wind players become part of the music. A more remote placement creates the effect of being in a large hall listening to the music from some distance away.

These are important aesthetic decisions. I prefer an intimate environment and an immediate presence that allows the listener to feel close to the music and the musicians. I like the sound of keys and valves clicking and bows viscerally pulling strings. I find that this recording technique, as opposed to a more remote and reverberant sound, is also more conducive to an effective use of panning and volume to create a clear aural and visual picture in the stereo field.

Using the string quartet as an example, I would usually pan the first violin farthest left, the second violin slightly left of center, the cello slightly right of center, and the viola farther to the right, probably symmetrically balanced with the first violin. This creates a stereo field that replicates the concert experience of sitting in the middle of the concert hall and is a balanced sound as well. To create depth, I would use volume levels to place the second violin and cello slightly farther back in the stereo field while having the first violin and viola a bit forward. This is subtle and challenging as the volumes must be musically correct, and the inner voices of the second violin and viola can be obscured and difficult to pick out. A mixer must also subtly balance the volume of the second violin and cello, making them seem a bit farther back but still clear and appropriately musically present. These are very refined musical issues and are an indication of the subtlety that goes into the process of recording and mixing. These same types of subtleties also are important for deep listening and can lead to interesting discussions that can bring our students—and ourselves—into more intimate terms with the music, particularly in its recorded form.

MIXING ROCK, POP, AND R&B

Adrian Harpham,[7] an independent producer-songwriter-instrumentalist in New York City, offers a contrasting perspective on the mixing process. He generally works in the pop, rock, and R&B genres and has a very different approach to the specifics of mixing, although there are, of course, many underlying similarities of process. Rather than trying to recreate the aural or visual image of a live performance, Harpham stresses that he looks for the right sonic place for each instrument in the stereo field with no preconceived notion of where each is supposed to be, but tries to stay open to all possibilities. This is an intuitive process, and every song may call for an entirely different approach. He calls on his performance experience and attempts to bring improvisational spontaneity to the music and "make it sparkle and stand out as something truly unique."

Harpham thinks in metaphors: he works toward each instrument having "its own space in the mix" and looks to "create a large and weighty sound that still has air in it and is uncluttered." His sonic picture of a mix might at times be layers of frequencies, with the lowest frequencies at the bottom (the bass, for example) and the highest at the top (guitar or vocal). This arrangement does not reflect the band members as they might appear at a concert but instead highlights the various levels of sound organization. This is conceptually very different from Clouse's approach, underscoring the point that understanding a few intricacies of mixing can lead to deeper listening, ultimately changing the way we listen to music.

Harpham speaks of mixing as a creative activity and of the mixer as an independent artist who brings new dimensions to the music that the creators never dreamed of. The notion of employing the mix as a pedagogical tool appeals to him greatly, as he feels that mixes and mixers are underappreciated: "People overlook the intellectual and creative aspects of rock and soul. There is some deep stuff going on there. If they only knew what went into the recording. Mixing is a performance, just like cutting a great bass track or a trumpet solo in the recording studio. It's all performance. It is all based on whatever the music is telling you at that moment—I don't have any formula."

Harpham gives some specific illustrations:

In rock and in soul, it starts with the drums. The music needs to be from the bottom up—it has to have weight to it. Think of Led Zeppelin, the Beatles, or even Al Green. It's all got this bottom to it. It's about creating air, a space for each instrument, and a punch to the sound. Led Zeppelin is a really good example because they are recorded so well. There is an implied heaviness. Robert Plant [vocals] is on top in the high-highs [frequency range], Jimmy Page [guitar] is four inches below in the high-mids, John Bonham [drums] is in the entire mid-range and a bit in the low end, and John Paul Jones [bass] is below that in the low end. What you are hearing is this huge sound, but it is just three instruments and a voice. They are moving so much air because each instrument is in an exact slot sonically. It has this open quality, yet it is powerful and huge. You have to get the instruments out of the way of each other.

For example, in some modern rock, and this is a bad thing, they might put, say, nine guitars on the same part because it has to sound big. They are all distorted and over-driven, and panned across [the stereo field]. The drums are often close miked and high end [high frequencies are favored or embellished], the drums are eaten up by the guitars, and the track becomes harsh and unpleasant and loses its heaviness. The heaviness comes from the drums, so you have to give the drum kit its space to allow it to add its weight and power.

I'm really intrigued by mixing soul and rock because the more records I listen to and the more I mix, the more I feel it is done by instinct and that there are no rules or patterns. You are just reacting to what's happening. For example, if you think about Motown, you think about soft drums. The drums aren't prominent, but they're there. And then the bass is very loud—like it's the lead instrument. It would seem like it would be like breaking some kind of rule to put the bass that high in the mix—it might even be louder than the voices. So the mixer had to be very "in the moment" to allow himself to do something unorthodox, but that was right for the mix.

Harpham also spoke of Prince taking the opposite approach to the bass in his hit "When Doves Cry" from the album *Purple Rain*. At the point of completing the final mix, Prince spontaneously made the unorthodox and rather radical decision (for a 1984 dance hit) to eliminate the bass when on the verge of completing the final mix.

Harpham gives another example: "When you think of [the hard rock band] the Black Crowes, the first thing you think of is the singer. But when you listen carefully, you notice that he is pulled back in the mix, and the guitar and bass are more up-front. Yet you still come away with the impression that the singer is what stands out. The same with Led Zeppelin. The singer is perceived to be up-front, but he actually isn't." In these cases, the mixer has managed to create "sonic spaces" for the singers that allow the vocals to stand out, even though the guitars and basses are louder and pushed a bit forward. This is an example of a particular mixing aesthetic that does not necessarily recreate the concert experience. It also does not adhere to the more typical vocal setting that places the vocal well forward, both in position and volume.

In contrast to Clouse's notion of capturing a performance and staying out of the way of the musicians, Harpham might employ a wide array of sonic effects, perhaps even radical ones, to make something stand out in a mix or to clarify particular musical elements. Harpham speaks of making the track "come alive" and focuses on the track as something distinct from an actual performance. This leads us to the work of Albin Zak.

THE TRACK

Albin Zak is a musician, musicologist, and recordist.[8] In *The Poetics of Rock: Cutting Tracks, Making Records* (Zak 2001), he discusses the recording process and its importance to a final product extensively and in great detail. He argues convincingly that sound recording has changed our conceptions of music and points out that "records are often equated with their song or performance, but these are only aspects of what is actually a more comprehensive work, the track" (xiii). He also speaks of a conflation of writing, recording, and performance that "makes for a seamless process where song, sound, and musical performance flow together in a steady stream of raw creative expression" (31).

Zak describes why the writing of rock and pop and the recording of the music are inseparable. In relation to my proposed course unit, he equates discussing the mixing process with other elements of the music appreciation curriculum:

> I completely agree with your premise. When I teach music appreciation, it is mostly based on the concept of examining how music gets written. Once they start to grasp the idea of form, for example sonata form, which has a narrative

scheme to it, they get really excited. They look empowered as they can hear the music in a way that they feel a sense of authority: "I know where I am in the piece, and I know what is going on here."

The same goes for other idioms. For example, Led Zeppelin's "Whole Lotta Love" is a great example of how a mixer, very consciously, sets up the stereo space as if it's a stage for maximum dramatic effect.[9] It begins with a hint or a shadow of a guitar panned to the right, as opposed to the heavy guitar riff that is panned left, and when the guitar solo finally comes in, panned all the way right, the students kind of come out of their seats and say, "Yeah!" as they totally understand that this is an important moment that the song has been leading up to. It is all part of teaching people to listen in an informed way.

He sees understanding the mixing process and its intentions in the same light as understanding sonata form: they both enhance the listener's ability to hear and understand what is taking place in the music.

Zak continues: "There are certain principles we teach regarding classical music; it is the same with listening to jazz and understanding what they are doing with the [chord] changes or if you are listening to a rock mix and hearing what is going on. The more you know about it, the more you hear, the more fun you have, and the more you are engaged by the music. Being more informed is always a better thing."

Regarding differences in mixing approaches, Zak states:

In addition to genres, different historical periods handle mixing issues differently. For example, there was a time when all recordings were mono and panning was irrelevant. That is where the depth of the mix was so important. That is the whole point of Phil Spector's "Wall of Sound."[10] What's in there? Well, that's the whole point—you don't know what's there—and that's how he wants it. You hear the voices, you hear the beat, you hear the string line, and the rest is just a murky mess. He spent endless hours getting the balances just how he wanted so you would have the aural perspective that he was after. How you set up the volume—I like to refer to it as prominence—affects how the listener experiences the depth of the track and how deeply they are drawn in. And if there is some kind of inscrutable background—whether they want to do it or not—their ear is grasping for that background. It gets you back there behind the singer somewhere, and it's a cool effect.

Zak gives another example of depth in one of my all-time favorite records, Marvin Gaye's "What's Going On":[11]

He sets it up with voices just talking, and that's the foreground. Then the band comes in, and it's louder, and the voices are a step back, and the band is in front. Then finally, the lead vocal comes in and is even further out in front, and now the voices are really to the back. But because he started out with the talking, as they transition from talking to becoming backup singers, you are very aware of the voices and this sense of camaraderie ["Hey, what's happening brother. How you doin'? Groovy party, man."][12] In the middle of the song, the voices come back, and it is as if you are zooming in on this sort of man party in the middle. The sense of layering and just how deep that track is is part of the thrill of the listening experience.

Finally, Zak's experience speaking to engineers mirrored my own experience as I interviewed Clouse and Harpham:

> Engineers don't talk much about what they do—they just do it. They are usually self-effacing and will say things like "It was all feel," "You got to have a good song and good musicians," or "It's just a craft." But then they say, "I wanted it to sound like it sounded in the room," or "I wanted to catch the magic." So while they are hesitant to take much credit, they are responsible for turning an aural image into a mental image and then try to replicate that somehow electronically. It isn't their job to articulate it, and it is ours to unpack what is going on there. It is an aesthetic process, no matter how much they seek to replicate the real world. It still involves artifice and sleight of hand. It isn't the real world, it's still a record![13]

CONCLUSION

What I am suggesting is actually very simple (so why did it take so long to say it, you may ask) as well as practical and musically sound. At the core of music appreciation courses, no matter what our musical perspectives are, I believe we all agree that our most important job is to teach students how to listen to music. Since they are primarily listening to recorded music, both in this course and in their lives, we should be instructing them, and ourselves, how to listen to recordings in a more sophisticated manner. The basics of the mixing process, panning and volume, are possible places to start.

This basic concept can be employed for both non-music majors and music majors at the undergraduate level. In my experience, most music majors are inexperienced in this area, as are most instructors, so this unit can be an exploratory journey for all involved. Non-music majors' ability to listen critically and deeply to recordings will be improved. This is true for music majors as well, but in addition, understanding the basics of the recording process is essential for all contemporary musicians, as is fluency in basic audio-editing programs. Although I developed the unit for college-level classes, I believe it would be quite successful in the secondary-school music curriculum as well.

The unit on mixing techniques can also be incorporated into a wide variety of other courses. Discussions and exercises such as these can be extremely valuable, for example, as the first element in a course on electronic music, whether a survey course or a more technically oriented course for music majors. In world music, a discussion of mixing could illuminate recordings of a gamelan orchestra, exploring the stereo field and its relationship to the performance layout of the gamelan. A pop-rock survey course could also benefit greatly from this unit, as the mixing process is of primary importance in these genres: think of Phil Spector's "Wall of Sound," George Martin's work with the Beatles, Brian Wilson's experiments with the Beach Boys, the bass- and drum-heavy sounds of hip-hop, or the glossy orchestral sheen of a pop ballad. Considering the treatments of panning and volume and their relationship to the larger musical context can greatly enhance and deepen our students'—and our own—listening.

NOTES

1. Audacity is a free, open-source, multi-platform software program that is quite effective for basic recording and editing. Apple's GarageBand is an affordable program for audio and MIDI recording that is popular in educational settings but is not available for PC. A more full-featured program than GarageBand is Logic Express, and the next step up, Logic Studio, is an industry standard. Pro Tools, SONAR, and Digital Performer are other examples of full-featured, industry-standard recording programs.

2. Sean Hickey, *Left at the Fork in the Road*, Naxos, 2005.

3. James Taylor, *October Road*, Atlantic, 2002.

4. Audacity is available for free download at http://audacity.sourceforge.net.

5. Jim Clouse, interview by the author, October 5, 2009, Brooklyn, New York.

6. One typical arrangement of the orchestra places the strings across the stage (from left to right: violins 1, violins 2, violas in the center, cellos, and basses); behind the strings, centrally located, are the woodwinds; behind the woodwinds are brass (left to right: horns, trumpets, trombones, and tuba); and percussion and timpani are in the rear.

7. Adrian Harpham, interview by the author, October 9, 2009.

8. Albin Zak, telephone interview by the author, October 16, 2009.

9. Led Zeppelin, "Whole Lotta Love," *Led Zeppelin II*, Atlantic, 1969.

10. The influential producer Phil Spector (b. 1939) created a production technique, the "Wall of Sound," that was extremely dense and layered.

11. Marvin Gaye, *What's Going On*, Sony, 1971.

12. This is a loose transcription of several simultaneous voices that simulate party conversation at the beginning of "What's Going On."

13. For further reading on this subject, see Allan F. Moore's work on the "heuristic sound-box model" and his discussion of the stereo field from several perspectives. His publication website (http://www.surrey.ac.uk/Music/NewsGenInfo/AcademicStaff/Moore/MoorePub.htm) is an excellent resource; in particular, see Moore 2005.

REFERENCES

Gould, Glenn. 1984. *The Glenn Gould reader.* Ed. Tim Page. New York: Knopf.

Martin, George, ed. 1983. *Making music: The guide to writing, performing and recording.* Pan Books.

Massey, Howard. 2000. *Behind the glass: Top record producers tell how they craft the hits.* Backbeat Books.

———. 2009. *Behind the glass, volume II: Top record producers tell how they craft the hits.* Backbeat Books.

Moore, Allan F. 2005. The sound of popular music: Where are we? Unpublished paper given at Comparative Perspectives in the Study of Recordings, residential symposium at Royal Holloway, University of London, Egham, April 14–16. http://www.surrey.ac.uk/Music/NewsGenInfo/AcademicStaff/Moore/MoorePub.htm.

Moorefield, Virgil. 2005. *The producer as composer: Shaping the sounds of popular music.* Cambridge, MA: MIT Press.

Zak, Albin J., III. 2001. *The poetics of rock: Cutting tracks, making records.* Berkeley: University of California Press.

2

Pod-Logic: A Guide to Getting the Most out of Your iPod in the Music Classroom

Kathleen Kerstetter

One of the most influential pieces of hardware developed in the past decade has been the Apple iPod and similar MP3 players. These portable devices can be used in music classes for much more than their traditional purpose of music playback. However, many iPod users are unaware of the device's potential to aid in music teaching. The Duke University iPod First-Year Experience, in which the university issued iPods to all first-year students in 2004–05, cited five academic uses of the iPod: course content dissemination, classroom recording, field recording, study support, and file storage and transfer (Duke 2005). More general educational benefits included portability of course content and adaptability to individual learning styles and preferences. The Duke Digital Initiative continued a program of first granting and later loaning iPods to the faculty, who, as of 2007, reported using iPods for delivering instructional materials, such as Power-Point, images, and videos, for recording themselves and their classes, and for transferring large files (Belanger 2007).

In the 21st century, it is crucial for educators to include technology in their teaching methods. However, many obstacles prevent educators from this integration. Lack of formal technology training, lack of equipment and facilities, and lack of guidance in pedagogical applications for the music classroom are oft-cited barriers to technology inclusion (Barry 2004, 3). To use any technology efficiently, whether for classroom or personal use, one must understand the full range of its capabilities. Therefore, this chapter will address areas of iPod functionality outside of traditional music playback: recording, video playback, and interactive content (applications).

IPOD BACKGROUND

The Apple iPod was released to the public on October 23, 2001 (Miller 2007, 9), following the release of Apple's iTunes music player software earlier that year. In the nine years since its public debut, the iPod has become the dominant music playback device. According to Apple financial reports, as of 2005, more than 80 million devices had been sold to over 30 million customers (Miller 2007, 4). By June 2008, over 152 million iPod devices had been sold (Horwitz 2008, 4). It is reported that one-third of all teenagers own an Apple iPod (Harrison Group). Since its inception in 2001, the iPod has undergone several model changes, called "generations." Fifth-generation iPods, introduced in 2005, and later models include video playback.

As of January 2010, the most current full-sized iPod is the iPod classic, available with 160 GB (gigabyte) memory. Smaller iPods include the iPod nano, available with up to 16 GB of memory and a built-in video camera, and the iPod shuffle, available with up to 4GB of memory. Both the classic and the nano are equipped with a screen for video playback. The iPod Touch, which is available with up to 64 GB of memory, contains a larger screen and is, therefore, more suited to video playback, and incorporates a touch-screen interface and Wi-Fi capabilities. Since the release of the 2.0 version of the iPhone operating system in 2008, software applications can be downloaded for the iPod touch and the iPhone from the iTunes App Store. As of January 2010, there were more than 140,000 applications available for the iPod touch and iPhone.

A THEORY FOR INTEGRATION

One of the factors holding back teachers from embracing the integration of technology into their teaching is the fact that it constitutes a "wicked problem" (Rittel and Weber 1973). Wicked problems are unique and novel, with no direct or right answers. The diversity of teachers, students, settings, and the technology itself all contribute to the wicked problem of incorporating technology into teaching. The rapid rate of technological change, inappropriate design of software for the classroom, and the situated nature of learning all contribute to the mismatch between the goals of technology and those of education. What is needed to help the process of technology integration in education, then, is a framework for guidance.

If we look outside of the field of music education, Shulman (1986) introduced the concept of pedagogical content knowledge more than two decades ago. This knowledge is context-dependent and includes the understanding of what makes learning specific topics difficult or easy when individual learners and situations are taken into account. Developing from this theory, the concept of technological pedagogical content knowledge (TPACK) can be applied as a framework for incorporating technology into teaching (Mishra and Koehler 2006). TPACK takes into consideration the subject matter, grade level, student background, and types of technology available. Using TPACK as a foundation for technology integration, we can look at some of the nontraditional functions of the iPod as a framework for using technology in the music classroom.

IPOD RECORDING

One of the greatest advantages of the iPod is its recording capability, especially in light of its portability and high capacity for information storage. Several third-party attachments in a variety of price and quality ranges are available for recording on the iPod. Low-priced, portable microphones are available from many companies and include the Belkin TuneTalk Stereo for iPod (www.belkin.com), Griffin iTalk Pro (www.griffintechnologies. com), XtremeMac MicroMemo (www.xtrememac.com), Tunewear Stereo Sound Recorder (www.tunewear.com), Logictec Stereo Mic LIC-iREC01 (www.logictec.com), and Blue Mikey (www.bluemic.com/mikey). These microphones attach directly to the iPod and are designed for high functionality and portability. A quick search of YouTube will result in video clips of several artists demonstrating the use of iPod microphones to record a variety of instruments and genres on their iPods. When reviewing portable microphones, you should look for 16-bit, 44.1-kHz, CD-quality recording capability. Other additional features available include a line-in for external microphones, speaker capability for immediate playback, and a pass-through USB cable for simultaneous recording and charging.

In addition to portable recording devices, iPod workstations that provide higher quality direct-to-iPod recording are currently beginning to enter the market. These workstations allow for multichannel mixing when recording to the iPod. The Belkin TuneStudio (www.belkin.com) is a four-channel audio mixer that allows for high-quality digital recording of up to four different instruments or audio sources directly to an iPod. The Belkin GoStudio and Alesis MultiPort direct-to-iPod recorder (www. realaudiopro.com) offer gain and filter controls, internal microphones, and two-channel microphone inputs, allowing for the recording of two sources. Even newer models can provide rack integration of your iPod into any live music rig. Systems such as the Numark iDec, an iPod recording and playback system (www.numark.com), fit into any standard 19-inch frame enclosure for professional audio equipment and allow for quality audio recording to the iPod with a convenient interface. These products allow professionals and students alike to record live rehearsals and performances directly to the iPod.

There are many recording applications on the market for use with an iPod touch or iPhone. Applications such as FourTrack by Sonoma Wire Works and MultiTrack, a 16-track recorder by Harmonicdog, allow for the recording of multiple music tracks. By offering students the opportunity to create a multitrack recording, school-based music can more closely model professional music production.

iPod recordings are saved as .wav or Apple Lossless audio file formats and coded as voice memos, which are stored in a separate dedicated folder of the iPod. Using iTunes software to synchronize your iPod, voice memos will be automatically downloaded to your computer and removed from the iPod (although they can be re-synced if desired). To access these recordings in iTunes, select the Voice Memos playlist from the source pane on the left side of the screen. If you wish to upload files to the Internet or burn them to a disc, you may wish to compress them to a smaller size. The iTunes application has the ability to convert the original file to a number of other audio file formats, including MP3 and AAC (advanced audio coding).

APPLICATIONS FOR RECORDING

Performance-based music faculty have the greatest potential uses for direct-to-iPod recording capabilities. With the large popularity of iPods among students, many will likely own one. Studio teachers who are equipped with a recording workstation can invite their students to bring their iPods to lessons for recording and instant playback capabilities. Music students can be encouraged or required to purchase their own direct-to-iPod recorder or microphone for use in conjunction with applied music lessons. Teachers can easily model the advantages of recording and playback for assessment purposes through the use of a portable recorder or recording workstation.

In addition to recording students' practicing and performances on their personal iPods, faculty can use iPods to record events such as group performances, special lectures, and master classes for dissemination and review, either in class or by students individually. The digital audio files can be made accessible by uploading them to a course website or by using them as the basis for a podcast (the podcast creator, however, must be sure to observe all current copyright laws).

Another application of convenient and portable recording is the ability to reduce the in-class time needed for assessment. With an iPod recorder or workstation, students in ensemble-based classes can record performance assessment, seating assignment, or audition material without consuming rehearsal time. Individual recording stations can be set up in a small practice room, allowing the ensemble director to listen at a later time. Additionally, students can record performance directives or notes for review after rehearsal.

Another creative use of these recording applications is especially helpful in beginning instrumental instruction. For settings consisting of homogeneously grouped lessons with minimal large-ensemble rehearsal time, recording the different instrumental parts of the piece (e.g., flutes, clarinets, etc.) to virtually construct the full work provides an aural model to students. A technologically minded music teacher can take digital recordings of individual instrumental parts made with the iPod and mix them using a program such as GarageBand or Audacity to create realistic listening examples of how a full instrumental version of their repertoire will likely sound. This strategy is used in teaching lessons with speech therapy and English Language Learners (ELL) to produce fluency (McGuire 2007), where iPods are used to record students reading a story aloud. Using an audio editor, teachers edit out flaws and pauses in speech and then return the audio file to the students so that they have an aural model of what the story should sound like read in their own voice. This new recording models language fluidity and provides the student with an opportunity to hear the story as a whole for better understanding.

VIDEO PLAYBACK

Another nontraditional use of the iPod is large-scale video playback. Many music educators, both in K–12 and higher education, teach in rehearsal halls and other nontraditional classrooms. Having a compact portable device to transport large audio and video files can be extremely helpful. By reducing the need for an additional piece of hardware, such as a DVD player or laptop computer, the incorporation of large and varied media files can be used more frequently to enhance learning. Video-equipped iPods can be connected to televisions or computer monitors and video projectors to enable large-group viewing. You will need to purchase either an AV composite or AV component cable. A list of supported iPods and the corresponding cables required is available on the Apple website (www.support.apple.com). In order for still images or video to be viewed, select the TV Out option on your iPod.

There are several options for formatting videos to be played by the iPod. The iTunes Store offers numerous preformatted videos, many of which are free. iTunes U, the educational section of the iTunes store, offers free content from universities, museums, and other cultural institutions. iTunes also has a limited selection of commercially produced videos for purchase. If you would like to use a legally owned, commercially produced DVD that is not available through iTunes, there are several programs that will convert your video for the iPod. A free cross-platform conversion program, which has easy-to-follow directions, is HandBrake (www.handbrake.fr). The time needed for converting the file(s) will depend on your computing power. Videos recorded with a digital camera can also be edited and formatted for the iPod, where they can be stored and viewed.

Not only videos but also presentations created in PowerPoint or Keynote can also be displayed from the iPod. This reduces the need for an additional piece of hardware, such as a laptop, when preparing short multimedia presentations for classes. Presentations should be saved as a folder of images in .jpg format, with each slide representing one picture, and stored with the other images on the iPod. When synchronizing your iPod with iTunes, select the folder containing the presentation to be transferred to the iPod. You can now show your presentation slides using a TV or video projector, with the ability to go forward and backward in your presentation just as you would on a computer. Transitions from slide to slide can be incorporated through the Settings menu in the Photos section of your iPod. You can also save your presentations as QuickTime movie (.mov) files, which will include automatic slide transitions and timings. Coupled with a recording of your lectures, you can provide students with the necessary study tools to view multimedia course content on their personal iPods for one-on-one technology-enhanced experiences.

OTHER FEATURES

An often overlooked feature of the iPod is its capacity for large file storage. The iPod has the ability to act as an external hard drive for storage of large files, such as those from notation programs like Finale or Sibelius. Once you enable the iPod for disk use using the Preferences menu, you can drag files into the disk like any USB storage device. Other features of standard click-wheel iPods include clocks, calendars, contact lists, alarms, games, notes, and stopwatch features. Text files can be viewed using iPod Notes, which supports documents coded in hypertext markup language (.html) and plain text. There are also numerous software tools, many of them freeware, that will allow text or .pdf files to be read on the iPod. These tools can be used to provide students not only with lecture notes and handouts but also with listening guides or librettos that can be viewed while listening.

Educators can create or upload content and record on any traditional click-wheel iPod, many of which are inexpensive and provide large amounts of storage. However, if your students or school has access to iPod touches or iPhones, there are many potential pedagogical uses of professionally created interactive content or applications (also known as "apps").

APPLICATIONS OF APPLICATIONS

Since the introduction of the iTunes application store in late 2007 and the availability of third-party developers to create apps in 2008, several useful iPod applications for the music classroom have been developed. Several educational societies focused on music technology, such as the Technology Institute for Music Educators (TI:ME) and the Association for Technology in Music Instruction (ATMI), have investigated the use and availability of applications for the iPod in music education. While there are other portable devices that support similar applications, none has yet achieved the market saturation of Apple products. The following is just a sample of available applications and their potential usefulness in music-education settings. It is important to note that not all iPod touch generations have built-in microphones and that any application requiring a microphone may need an external, third-party microphone.

Productivity applications can enable music educators and students to efficiently handle daily tasks. The wide variety of productivity apps encompasses applications for travel, for transferring documents from a desktop computer to a mobile device, and for GPS-enabled applications, just to name a few. For teachers, there are applications to store and maintain grades (e.g., GradePad by Portage Interactive) and software for learning management systems such as Moodle (e.g., Educate by iKonstrukt).

There are several music reference applications, many of which include built-in visual and aural examples. Some of the currently available music dictionaries and encyclopedias are Almond by RoGame, Oxford Dictionary of Music by White Park Bay Software, Music Dictionary by Tomsoft, and Musictionary by Andreas Lindahl. There are applications that provide specific instrument references, such as Instruments In Reach by Westover, which provides visual fingering charts for all band instruments. Several applications provide visual diagrams for guitar chords as well, such as the Waterstone Chord Library (www.ModGuitars.com) or iRocker by Talking Panda, which includes scales, progressions, chords, and a tuner. *The Real Book*, currently published by Hal Leonard, provides lead sheets for hundreds of jazz standards. A virtual version, the application iReal Book by Massimo Biolcati, provides chord changes for more than 800 jazz standards available for view on the iPhone or iPod Touch.

Another category of applications available for the iPod focuses on musicianship instruction. Rhythm in Reach from Westover provides rhythm training using the touch-screen interface in a videogame model. Other skill-building applications include ear training (e.g., Karajan by appsolute GmbH), note recognition (e.g., iNote Trainer by Pokmis), and scale recognition (e.g., ScaleMaster by RoGame). These applications can provide one-on-one training for students who need remedial practice or who simply wish to further improve their musicianship skills.

For use during rehearsals or practice sessions, metronomes, tempo finders, and digital tuner applications are available. These range from very inexpensive or free, with basic functionality, to higher-priced, customizable applications. Peterson Tuners, a leader in music technology for over 60 years, now offers iStroboSoft, an application for a strobe tuner for the iPod touch or iPhone, and Cleartune by Bitcount provides a highly customizable tuner that can be set to different temperaments.

Finally, there are a variety of virtual instruments available as applications for the iPod touch or iPhone, which range from drum machines and sequencers to reproductions of acoustic instruments. Most applications use the touch-screen interface for music production (e.g., Pocket Piano by Better Day Wireless, Band by MooCow Music, BtBx by Pure Profit, and Thereminator by Synthtopia). Other applications use the accelerometer, the ability of the iPod touch to register its physical orientation in space, to trigger sounds. The accelerometer is used for instruments that respond to tilting or shaking to produce sound, such as Pocket Shaker by HappyAppy and Rain Stick by Frontier Design. The iPhone features a built-in microphone (although the iPod touch does not), and several virtual instruments respond to the microphone input as a wind controller. Ocarina by Smule is an iPhone instrument triggered by blowing into the microphone end of the device.

Virtual instruments have a number of potential educational applications in the music classroom. Several new ensembles, such as iBand (www.iband.at), have been created using instrument applications available for portable devices. Electronic-music ensembles featuring handheld media players are appearing on the horizon of music composition and performance. Additionally, virtual instruments can be used for students with special needs, especially for students with physical limitations. The multi-touch interface allows for a wide range of sounds to be created from minimal movement. Similarly, virtual instruments are an economical way to expand traditional ensembles and include world, historical, and avant-garde instrumental timbres.

While the iPod is not the only portable music technology device available, it is currently synonymous with music playback and must be acknowledged as the dominant apparatus on the market. The large popularity of the iPod for personal use enables music educators in the 21st century to engage students in multimedia-rich environments and to enhance one-on-one interactive learning. By comprehending the full range of capabilities of the iPod beyond traditional music playback, music teachers can fully embrace the integration of technology into their classroom, studio, and rehearsal hall teaching practices. Incorporating the use of additional features, such as recording, video playback, and interactive applications, will expand the possibilities of mobile learning in music education.

REFERENCES

Apple. 2010. iPad keynote presentation (video file), January 27. http://events.apple.com.edgesuite.net/1001q3f8hhr/event/index.html.

Barry, Nancy H. 2004. University music education student perceptions and attitudes about instructional technology. *Journal of Technology in Music Learning* 2 (2): 2–20.

Belanger, Yvonne. 2007. Center for Instructional Technology summary of DDI instructional programs, 2006–2007. http://cit.duke.edu/pdf/reports/ddisummary_0607.pdf.

Duke University. 2005. Duke University iPod First Year Experience final evaluation report. http://cit.duke.edu/pdf/reports/ipod_initiative_04_05.pdf.

Harrison Group. Quoted in Miller 2007, 4.

Horwitz, Jeremy. 2008. Download now: The free iPod + iPhone Book 4. iLounge. http://www.ilounge.com/index.php/news/comments/download-now-the-free-ipod-iphone-book-4/.

McGuire, Carol Anne. 2007. Reading fluency with iPods and GarageBand. Apple Learning Interchange. http://edcommunity.apple.com/ali/story.php?itemID=10804.

Miller, Michael. 2007. *iPodpedia: The ultimate iPod and iTunes resource.* Indianapolis, IN: Que.

Mishra, Punya, and Koehler, Matthew J. 2006. Technological pedagogical content knowledge: A framework for teacher knowledge. *Teachers College Record* 108 (6): 1017–33.

Rittel, Horst, and Webber, Melvin M. 1973. Dilemmas in general theory of planning. *Policy Sciences* 4 (2): 155–69.

Shulman, Lee S. 1986. Those who understand: Knowledge growth in teaching. *Educational Researcher* 15 (2): 4–14.

3

Global Connections via YouTube: Internet Video as a Teaching and Learning Tool

Hope Munro Smith

I became aware of Internet video websites, such as YouTube and Yahoo! Music, as part of the audience for this new form of popular culture. Like most people, I enjoyed watching the antics of the "Numa Numa Guy"[1] and the "Star Wars Kid,"[2] which circulated as viral videos just as YouTube was getting started, and experienced these videos as a source of entertainment. As I explored YouTube and similar websites with a more critical eye, however, I gradually realized that there were many possible uses for this technology in the classroom. I was especially excited about the potential sources of material for my courses in world music, particularly as video-sharing websites such as YouTube became increasingly accessible globally. Because of its temporal and performative nature, music is particularly congenial to the video format. One of the advantages of Internet video is that musicians can bypass traditional channels of distribution to reach their intended audience, and performers and audiences can find each other instantaneously. For educators, Internet video sites such as YouTube offer a broad spectrum of content for free and allow us to bring to life our subject material in ways we could not imagine previously. While there are disadvantages to Internet video, such as instability of content and copyright concerns, many of these can be addressed or overcome using the guidelines outlined in this chapter.

As most ethnomusicology professors will attest, videos in this subject area are expensive to acquire, become outdated quickly, and typically do not encompass the breadth of material desirable in a world-music survey course. For example, the most commonly used video series, the *JVC Smithsonian Folkways Video Anthology of World Music and Dance*, costs between $130 and $280 for each regional set as of this writing. The newest footage was produced 20 years ago, and some is far older. The image and audio quality reflect the technology of the time, and in certain cases, such as the Native American recordings, the sound and image were not synced correctly. Many educators in the field have been looking for an alternative to this series and other outdated ethnographic video sources for a number of years. When I discovered the growing online archives of music videos from around the world, available for free, I quickly integrated them into my classroom teaching and have been using YouTube and several other video-sharing websites as teaching resources since September 2006. I am not alone in this endeavor: on the Society for Ethnomusicology mailing list, participants share links to content that they have found particularly useful.[3]

Although the main focus of this chapter is using Internet video in the world-music classroom, many types of music classes can benefit from this resource. Over the past four years, I have used examples culled from YouTube for courses in world music, jazz and rock history, music appreciation, and every historical period of Western art music, including recreations of musical performances from the ancient world. The available videos include many useful examples for illustrating key concepts in music and bringing the performance context of many musical genres into the classroom. YouTube is useful for demonstrating music fundamentals, such as chords, scales, the difference between major and minor, and the basics of musical form. Many historical and modern performances are archived on YouTube, allowing for comparisons between different conductors, orchestras, opera companies, and so forth. There are interviews with musicians and composers from many vernacular and classical traditions, including rehearsals and performances of student works. There are lecture demonstrations and master classes with musicians working in a variety of genres. Music lessons abound, for every imaginable instrument and vocal style. Internet video is a valuable educational resource for a variety of teaching environments and provides information for many different types of learners, from amateurs to professionals.

However, as I have become more experienced with the pedagogical applications of the technology, I have realized that Internet video content is not merely the latest version of audio-visual educational aids. Because YouTube is one of the most popular websites and so deeply embedded in contemporary popular culture, students are already quite familiar with it, and many use it on a daily basis. Using it effectively as a teaching tool can make lectures livelier and more entertaining, as well as provide valuable resources to enhance student learning. This essay draws upon my own successes and failures with YouTube in the classroom, as well as comments from students (both in class and in written course evaluations), to reflect upon the potential of this technology and offer educational strategies. I also offer some suggestions for those without Internet access in their classrooms or who seek an alternative to the distracting YouTube interface while lecturing.

THE LANDSCAPE OF INTERNET VIDEO

The sheer volume of video material available online is astounding. Currently, YouTube is the dominant provider of Internet video content in the United States, with approximately 43% of the market share. Its closest competitors, Fox Interactive Media and Yahoo! Video, represent 3.7% and 2.5% of the market share respectively (comScore 2009). In January 2009, 100 million U.S. Internet users accessed YouTube, viewing 14.8 billion online videos. As of May 2009, 20 hours of video are uploaded to YouTube every minute (Junee 2009). Google CEO Eric Schmidt estimates that three-quarters of this content originates from outside the United States (Vitali 2009). Michael Wesch, a cultural anthropologist exploring the impact of digital media on society and culture, has observed that the most commonly uploaded videos on YouTube are created by individuals acting on their own and are intended for an audience of less than 100 viewers (Wesch 2008).

Much of the user-generated content on YouTube seems frivolous: young people updating their video blogs or dancing to their favorite songs in their bedrooms or tourists sharing holiday memories. Many amateur videos are of a very serious nature, however, such as the dozens of clips depicting the violent government crackdown on post-election protests in Iran that were uploaded to YouTube in June 2009 (Parr 2009). The technology allows citizens—or propagandists—to spread news and information (or misinformation) globally at a rapid pace. Major media outlets frequently rebroadcast the work of "citizen journalists" that document powerful testimonies of political and human-rights abuses (Naím 2007). The ability of YouTube to spread information quickly has caused the governments of a number of countries, including China, Pakistan, Thailand, Turkey, and Iran, to block access to it at various times.

Individual users of YouTube are granted their own "channels" on which to upload their own content or to share links to videos on the site with other users by creating lists of favorites or playlists organized around various topics. Since its acquisition by Google in 2006, YouTube has developed into a mainstream media outlet, with traditional news sources such as the *New York Times* and the Associated Press, the White House, and political candidates and groups maintaining YouTube channels, creating a valuable archive from which this material can be replayed and reviewed and shared and commented upon with others via email, blogs, social-networking sites such as Facebook, and, of course, one's own YouTube channel.

Musicians have been quick to adopt YouTube as a means to share their work with their intended audiences, thus bypassing traditional distribution channels. In recent years, "viral video" has launched the careers of a number of young artists, such as rapper Soulja Boy Tell 'Em (www.youtube.com/user/souljaboy) and Hawaiian ukulele virtuoso Jake Shimabukuro (www.youtube.com/watch?v=puSkP3uym5k). Currently, YouTube appears to be surpassing MySpace in popularity among musicians, which is most likely because MySpace only allows users to upload six audio clips to their accounts, while users are able to upload an unlimited number of videos to their YouTube channels. A number of solo musicians and groups now maintain YouTube channels that contain official versions of their music videos, live performance footage, demo versions of new material, and news and announcements. Some record companies have created YouTube channels, and Google has reached licensing agreements with corporations such as Sony Music, BMI, Universal Music, and various smaller record labels to share their content for free via YouTube. For the ethnomusicologist, both amateur and commercial videos contain material that is potentially interesting and useful in the classroom, particularly as experts in certain musical practices or enthusiasts of particular genres of music establish their own channels to share the material that they have created.

THE EDUCATIONAL VALUE OF INTERNET VIDEO

Much of the content on YouTube and similar websites is educationally valuable for a wide range of subjects, as well as for librarians teaching media and information literacy. However, a number of secondary schools, including many in the United States, have blocked access to YouTube on their networks to prevent students accessing or uploading content to the site while at school. There are various justifications for this, including preserving the limited bandwidth at many public schools for educational use and attempting to prevent students from using the site inappropriately, such as for cyber-bullying their classmates (Valenza 2008). Most colleges and universities in the United States do not block access to YouTube: even Brigham Young University recently decided to lift a three-year ban on YouTube because of the increase in educational material available on the site (*Huffington Post* 2009). In 2007, several high school teachers in Texas launched TeacherTube (www.teachertube.com), a video-sharing site based on YouTube but currently operated as an independent entity. This online community was developed specifically as a platform for sharing educational resources. Videos uploaded to the site must address specific learning objectives or provide professional development for educators. Teachers can use their channels to upload examples of student presentations and performances, and students can create their own accounts to share their work with teachers and classmates. One advantage of TeacherTube over YouTube is that the former allows an unlimited maximum file size and running time, whereas YouTube's maximum for individual users is 2 GB and 10 minutes.[4] Currently, TeacherTube's archive comprises less than 100,000 videos, and content is heavily weighted toward math and science, but there are a grow-ing number of music-related videos, including student performances. The site is quite useful for those working in the field of music education, par-ticularly as a tool for teacher training.

In order to get the most educational value from video websites like YouTube, they must be used as more than a way to liven up one's lectures (although they will typically have that effect). Frequently, I have heard col-leagues refer to showing traditional videos as "the teaching box," implying that showing a video recording fills up class time without the instructor having to expend much effort. Presumably, the students will passively absorb the content, and the instructor is relieved of a few hours of class preparation time. Although Internet videos can be used the same way since online video examples tend to be short, their classroom potential is more flexible than that of longer video forms. For example, during a class discus-sion, an instructor can present brief examples of musicians playing different types of instruments or short excerpts of a particular musical work, without negotiating the menus of a DVD or cueing up a VHS tape. Additionally, instructors can access many different types of materials for free—a develop-ment that is especially welcome in these days of shrinking library budgets. The main drawback of YouTube and other Internet video sites is the insta-bility of its content. Users may decide to reorganize their channels or delete their content at any time. YouTube reserves the right to remove content that contains copyright infringements or violates its community guidelines and terms of service (www.youtube.com/t/community_guidelines). Instructors should be aware that many students have their own YouTube accounts, and it is statistically likely that more than half of them have created their own media content (Jenkins 2007). Thus, students will regard their profes-sor's engagement with YouTube critically. As with any other type of teach-ing tool, instructors should become proficient with its features in order to avoid potential embarrassment in the classroom.

USING INTERNET VIDEO EFFECTIVELY

Getting started on YouTube and similar websites is fairly straightforward: simply go to the website (www.youtube.com), and type in some search terms. Potentially useful or interesting YouTube links can be bookmarked in one's web browser or embedded within PowerPoint presentations or lecture notes. As one's list of potential links grows into the dozens or hun-dreds, a more efficient way to make use of the YouTube interface is by creat-ing an account. Accounts are free, and being a registered user allows you to do a number of things that will save time and trouble during lectures and presentations. The most important of these is organizing and saving links to videos so that they are accessible from any computer once you log in to your YouTube account. You can also share your videos with your students or colleagues conveniently via the channel that an account provides.

YouTube favorites can be arranged in playlists by topic, genre, performer, or other criteria, and ordered for a particular lecture or presentation. Less useful examples can be moved to the bottom of a playlist as supplements. While there is no limit to the number of examples that can be saved to a playlist, I find that lengthy playlists are difficult to navigate when trying to find particular examples quickly during a lecture or classroom discussion. Periodically, you should do a "housecleaning," removing links to videos that are no longer available and searching for new links to replace them. Currently, YouTube allows users to mark their playlists as private or public. In my experience, it is most beneficial to make public the playlists that I have created for use in class so they are available to everyone, including my students. This has several advantages: if I run out of time in a given class period, I can ask my students to watch the remaining clips outside of class; students may want to revisit videos or share them with friends who are not currently taking the class; other users with similar interests can view them and use the site's messaging options to send me new links, thus increasing my library of material.

Once you have a YouTube account, you should take a critical look at the appearance of your personal channel. As with any other social-networking site, you should keep in mind how your students might perceive you based on what appears there and organize the information accordingly. Those who already have an established YouTube presence for personal entertainment, or for promoting artistic or commercial enterprises, may want to create a new account specifically for use in teaching. Before customizing your channel, make decisions about what personal information you want to share with your students. It is a good idea to keep your profile and "about me" details professional. You can subscribe to channels of other users that contain videos of interest, and when new videos are added to these channels, there are various ways you can be notified, including via email. While playlists can be made either public or private, at this time it is not possible to selectively hide subscriptions; for this reason, I recommend hiding the subscription module on your channel. You will still be able to see your list of subscriptions and thumbnails of new videos by clicking the subscription tab, but they will not be visible to your students or anyone else. You may want to customize other modules, such as friends, comments, recent activity, and so forth, in order to make your channel less cluttered in appearance and to hide things that you do not want to share publicly.

For classroom access, bookmark your channel rather than the YouTube home page to avoid the distracting promotional clips and featured videos there. Although I teach at a fairly liberal public university in Northern

California, occasionally students have commented that they found the promotions or featured videos on the YouTube homepage offensive or inappropriate for viewing in an academic setting. Also, I prefer to avoid the impression that I am endorsing particular forms of popular entertainment or commercial products.

YouTube's search feature is similar to that of its parent company Google: when a search query is entered, a box with a pull-down menu of suggestions appears. This is helpful for when there are several possible spellings of a search term. Search results are optimized so that the most highly-ranked links appear first. Videos are ranked by YouTube users, and the resulting score is a product of how many times the clip has been viewed and how many stars it has received from viewers, on a scale of one to five. Typically, this indicates the popularity of a particular video clip rather than its overall quality, which may not be helpful in searching for classroom examples. For example, as of this writing, the first result for the search term "uilleann pipes" (a type of Irish bagpipes) is Davy Spillane performing "Caoineadh Cú Chulainn" from *Riverdance: The Show*. The video has a rating of five stars and has been viewed 348,577 times.[5] However, further down the list are performances from BBC television by Seamus Ennis, one of the greatest players of all time. Three pages later, one finds tutorials on how to play the uilleann pipes, as well as pipers playing in traditional settings, such as pubs and dancehalls. These sorts of examples are far more useful for showing students how the musical instrument works and the typical traditional settings in which it would be played. In ethnomusicology, I have found that user-generated content is often more helpful for teaching purposes and more educational for students than professional productions created for commercial purposes.

GATHERING USEFUL INTERNET VIDEOS

Which Internet videos will be most appropriate depends on your student demographic and on how much knowledge you can assume on their part. At California State University at Chico, where I teach, the student population is more ethnically diverse than in some other parts of the United States. However, much of the student body comes from the surrounding regions of rural Northern California. A high percentage of these students are the first in their families to attend college; hence, my students tend to be less cosmopolitan, less aware of cultural diversity, and less musically sophisticated than students at more urban or more elite institutions might be. My class for non–music majors, in particular, requires remediation and strategies to convey very basic concepts. However, many of the examples I outline below could be adapted to apply to a variety of classes and student populations.

In all of my world-music classes, including the ones designed for music majors, we start with the perennial question, "What is music?" To generate discussion on this topic, I usually play contrasting audio examples of orchestral music, popular music, and music that most likely falls outside the experience of my students, such as Japanese gagaku or a Qur'anic recitation. After discussing the audio recordings, I then move on to video examples that challenge this concept further. A particularly useful example is the BBC Symphony Orchestra, conducted by Lawrence Foster, performing *4'33"* by John Cage.[6] While non–music majors tend to find this example baffling, music majors find it hilarious, and it becomes a good starting point for examining the conventions of classical-music performances and their settings. Another example that typically generates interesting discussions is an interview with David Byrne regarding his installation *Playing the Building,* in which he connected a keyboard to various activation devices within the Battery Maritime Building in New York City, essentially turning it into a very large musical instrument.[7] In addition to generating debates about what is music or what is art, the video is useful for demonstrating how sounds can be generated. It also gives students ideas on how they can create music using found objects, which is one of the projects that I assign early on in the semester.

Another fundamental question is whether humans are the only species that has the ability to create and enjoy music. YouTube has a number of videos depicting animals playing musical instruments, spurring the debate as to whether or not they are behaving musically. A personal favorite is "Nora the Piano Cat," which famously shows the musical endeavors of a gray tabby that belongs to a piano teacher in Philadelphia, Pennsylvania. There are videos of Nora playing solo, duets with piano students, and even a Piano "CATcerto" written by composer and artist Mindaugas Piečaitis and performed by his chamber orchestra in conjunction with a video montage of Nora performing.[8] Similar examples include videos of various songbirds and the famous Elephant Orchestra of Lampang, Thailand.[9]

Another aspect of teaching that is facilitated by Internet video is to demonstrate musical techniques that I have not mastered or am not capable of. For example, it is difficult for me to demonstrate falsetto effectively since I sing in the mezzo-soprano range. So I turn to the Expert Village channel, which contains a lesson by singer-songwriter Tom Kenaston in which he explains the concept of falsetto as well as how to find one's falsetto voice.[10] Yodeling and overtone singing are other vocal techniques that elude me, but there are numerous online examples of singers who can perform these techniques well and even tutorials on how to do them.[11] If neither you nor your students are particularly squeamish, you can show precisely how the human vocal chords work using videos made with a laryngoscope.[12]

When introducing the Sachs-Hornbostel classification system of musical instruments according to how sound is produced, I can only bring a small number of instruments from each of the four basic categories of idiophones, aerophones, membranophones, and chordophones to the classroom. Thus, I supplement this demonstration with video clips of various amateurs and experts from around the world who have filmed themselves playing their musical instruments. In many cases, they also explain the basis of how to play that instrument. These types of videos are also helpful when discussing specific genres of music. For example, when I am explaining bhangra music, I want students to be able to see musicians playing the various instruments used in that genre. Videos that I have found useful for this unit include a tumbi tutorial by "tumbiwalla," a Canadian student of Punjabi ancestry who also records himself in his dorm room playing along with electronic dance music.[13] While some might think that videos of "old masters" of traditional music would be preferable, I find that showing my students videos of musicians close to their own age helps them make connections between their own experiences and the global music we are studying in class.

Live performances are abundant on YouTube and represent a wide variety of musical genres and performance contexts. While there are many professionally produced videos, there are also amateur endeavors documenting special events in order to share them with fellow participants (much like the home movies of earlier generations) and video diaries recorded by observers. Several of the Ghanaian examples that I use in class were created by local videographers at the request of the performing groups appearing in the videos. Some are clearly intended for broadcast on music television in Africa and to interested audiences in Europe.[14] There are entire channels devoted to particular genres of music, with content created or compiled by talented enthusiasts. For example, there are several YouTube channels devoted to steelband music: the most extensive is connected to the website When Steel Talks and features steelpan rehearsals and performances from around the world.[15] A growing collection of videos and YouTube channels document the work of ethnomusicologists conducting research in their regions of interest; indeed, YouTube has become a quick and inexpensive way to share one's ethnographic materials with students and colleagues.[16]

Whenever possible, I choose specific examples of festivals and recitals that depict the ethnic diversity of California and emphasize to my students that they can easily encounter live performances of world music within a short distance of where they live. When we discuss Hindu devotional music, I use examples that were recorded at the Shiva-Vishnu Temple in Livermore, California. I show bhangra competitions that feature dance teams from the various University of California (UC) and California State University (CSU) campuses in addition to older styles of bhangra dance from India. Balinese music is illustrated by video recordings of the gamelan ensembles of UCLA, CalArts, and UC Davis as well as of Balinese ensembles. These examples also allow me to demonstrate how various groups portray and celebrate their cultural identities in their communities in the United States.

One of the problems with YouTube is that a considerable number of videos on the site have been uploaded without the approval of the copyright holders. I recommend setting a good example by showing official versions of copyrighted material, such as documentaries, movie musicals, and commercial music videos, which typically means relying on older forms of audiovisual materials. Additionally, both the image and sound quality of pirated materials is often substandard, which is another reason for avoiding their use in the classroom. Fortunately, there are other options to supplement expensive DVD recordings. As noted earlier, YouTube has reached licensing agreements with most of the major record companies. For some purposes, other Internet video sites may be more useful than YouTube. Yahoo! Music has a much wider selection of official versions of music videos, which are a great deal easier to find than on YouTube. In the latest beta version of Yahoo! Music (new.music.yahoo.com), it is possible to watch videos on their own or as part of stations organized around various musical genres. Like YouTube, users can create playlists; although at present, it is not possible to customize the order of selections within playlists; this may change in future versions of the Yahoo! Music user interface.

In my world-music classes, I find that professional music videos are useful for demonstrating popular-music genres such as highlife, soca, and reggae. They also provide evidence to my students that popular music and the means of sharing it via various forms of mass media are a global phenomenon. Audiences in Accra, Kingston, and Mumbai consume imported North American music as well as create exciting local popular music and music videos. One site that I have found useful for this purpose is Synergy TV, the music television station of Trinidad and Tobago, which, like YouTube and Yahoo! Music, allows registered users to create playlists of their favorite videos (www.synergytv.net). Of course, MTV and MTV2 host streaming music-video content, as do their native-language counterparts throughout Europe, Latin America, and Asia. Members of these sites can save online content to an archive called "my videos" for access at a later time. Unfortunately, a new account needs to be created for each MTV network, and switching between them can be somewhat cumbersome in the classroom.

Currently, it is also possible to view some full-length television programs and movies for free via Internet video. Only a minority of US television and cable channels are represented on YouTube because most of them have already reached a licensing agreement with the streaming video site Hulu.[17] Thus, a live performance from *The Tonight Show* or *Saturday Night Live* can be viewed legally on Hulu rather than YouTube. A handful of music documentaries and movie musicals are available on Hulu and YouTube, including *Buena Vista Social Club*, *Hair*, *Jesus Christ Superstar*, and several Bollywood films. Hulu also serves as a portal to independent channels that are not widely distributed by cable companies. One such example is Link TV, whose slogan is "Television Without Borders." This site contains a growing number of interviews and official world-music videos by performers such as Angélique Kidjo and Salif Keita, organized by region, in addition to documentaries and news reports from various parts of the world (www.linktv.org).

ALTERNATIVES TO STREAMING VIDEO IN THE CLASSROOM

Just as online video can enhance a lecture or presentation, it can detract from it by failing to perform as expected. Investing time outside of class to set up user accounts and playlists will facilitate smooth integration of Internet materials into a lecture or presentation to a certain extent. However, the popularity of sites like YouTube can interfere with their ease of use at critical moments: I have had videos fail to load or crash my browser just when I was trying to illustrate an interesting topic. Another issue is the increasing number of revenue-generating ads on video websites; this is especially problematic on YouTube. It is no wonder, then, that a number of third-party applications have been developed that allow users to download streamed videos and play them back using programs such as iTunes or Windows Media Player. These downloading applications, which generally cost less than $20 and in some cases are free, are marketed as a way to save online content for playback on iPods or similar devices without requiring Internet access. The classroom potential of this software is obvious: one can store video clips indefinitely, retrieve and play them at any time without waiting for the buffered video stream or even any need to be online, bypass distracting advertisements, and eliminate concerns about the material being removed from the site.

In this endeavor, I have had great success with the program TubeSock, which was developed for Mac OS X but is also available for Windows XP. The software enables users to download online videos to a computer, video iPod, or PlayStation Portable.[18] There are several different ways to convert and save videos using TubeSock. My preference is to store videos in my iTunes library, which allows me to sort them into playlists and copy them to a flash drive for classroom use. Currently, TubeSock can only download videos from YouTube, Dailymotion, and a few other websites; it is not compatible with premium content providers such as Yahoo! Music, MTV, or Hulu.

At present, Google allows some videos to be downloaded officially from YouTube and is experimenting with allowing content providers to sell downloads via Google Checkout. The iTunes Store includes music videos that can be purchased for $1.99 each, although their selection is limited to artists who have reached a licensing agreement with Apple. It is likely that in the near future there will be a number of options for users to pay to download various forms of online video content. As I mentioned earlier, official content features better sound quality than pirated versions and is often available in high-definition video. Instructors could potentially customize their selection of videos based on their classroom needs, which would be less of a financial investment than many educational DVDs currently on the market.

STUDENT REACTIONS TO THE USE OF INTERNET VIDEO IN THE CLASSROOM

As at most universities, students at my institution complete anonymous evaluations each semester. Although my evaluations did not ask specific questions about Internet video or other classroom technology, many students mentioned my use of YouTube. The most frequent comment I received was that students really appreciated my incorporation of short videos from YouTube and other sources, which I presented alongside static visual media, such as PowerPoint slides and photographs, as well as audio examples, to illustrate course concepts. In particular, the students in my class for non–music majors liked not only the entertainment value but also the extensive visual reinforcement of lecture topics since most of the material was new to them.

Some other student comments were more critical of my use of online video on the grounds that there were sometimes too many video examples, they were too long, or they were not an ideal use of class time since they could be viewed at home. This has made me more attentive to whether I might be using video examples to fill up lecture time rather than illustrate something important, and as a result, I have become more selective, using fewer and shorter examples in each class. I avoid illustrating every concept or musical genre with a video clip gleaned from YouTube when in-class demonstrations or participatory activities would be more effective. As with PowerPoint, even the most interesting online videos can bore the class if used without thought or self-reflection.

YOUTUBE AND ACTIVE LEARNING

Thus far, I have discussed using a new technology, online video, for the most part in a fairly old-fashioned way: the same kind of passive consumption that has characterized the use of audiovisual examples for decades. I must admit that I have been guilty of this myself during my first few years of using YouTube and similar websites in the classroom. If my student evaluations are any indication, however, students are hungry for more active, hands-on learning experiences rather than passively listening to lectures. Unlike older audiovisual materials, video-sharing websites like YouTube allow for new, interactive media engagements that increase the participatory possibilities for students (Trier 2007a, 5). As educators, our challenge is to fully realize the various pedagogical possibilities of Internet video websites—otherwise, we are simply updating older audiovisual formats with newer technology, much as CDs replaced cassettes and LPs.

As our students already know, YouTube is not just an archive of video clips; it is also a social-networking site. Users can create and upload their own content and link to it using other networking sites, such as Facebook, MySpace, blogs, and so forth. Students can be asked to find and share videos appropriate for class or a supplemental playlist. One activity I plan to implement, particularly in my class for non–music majors, is to require students to create playlists of music they enjoy as an alternative to traditional homework assignments, such as written essays.[19] As the semester progresses, I ask the students to compare the musical examples they have chosen to the ones we discuss in class and identify commonalities in terms of musical features and the role of the music in the different cultures represented. This gives me a better understanding of what types of music my students are listening to and which musical performers are important to them, and is a valuable way to stay current with popular musical styles and performers. It also helps to inform the content of future lectures and to make meaningful comparisons between music that is new to the students and music they already enjoy.

For music majors, online video sites are valuable platforms for sharing their performances or original compositions with their peers and the world at large. In fact, several colleges and universities are using YouTube, as well as competing sites such as iTunes U, to promote various programs, including those in music and other performing arts, to recruit new students, and to share lectures and performances.[20] In student presentations, my music majors have made extensive use of YouTube to illustrate their chosen topics just as I have in my classroom lectures. Other activities for music majors include the creation of YouTube channels for sharing their favorite videos and uploading original content such as performances, original compositions, or commentaries on specific works or more general class topics.

Obviously, I have not exhausted all the possibilities afforded by Internet video-sharing sites, but hopefully, I have conveyed the central role they play in contemporary popular culture and, hence, in the lives of our students. Using videos from YouTube and other websites can help make lectures more visually interesting and engaging and, thus, enhance students' learning outcomes. However, as I have discovered, this technology is not a time- or labor-saving device if used thoughtfully as a tool for active learning. This form of popular culture has vast potential for making teaching more interactive and learning more hands-on and participatory, thus enriching the university experience of our students.

NOTES

1. The "Numa Numa Guy" is Gary Brolsma. The original version of his video is archived on his YouTube channel at http://www.youtube.com/watch?v=KmtzQCSh6xk.

2. The "Star Wars Kid" is Ghyslain Raza. This Internet video is regarded as a case of cyber-bullying because the footage of him pretending to be Darth Maul was posted online without his knowledge and with the intent of public humiliation. The Raza family sued their son's school board and settled out of court. For more information, see Helene A. S. Popkin, "Survive your inevitable online humiliation" at http://www.msnbc.msn.com/id/20611439/.

3. For example, Michael Bakan has compiled a list of YouTube links that correspond with the content of his textbook *World Music: Traditions and Transformations.* They are available on his blog at http://mailer.fsu.edu/~mbakan/index.html.

4. Providers of premium content can upload full-length television programs and movies of unlimited length and file size.

5. Davy Spillane. "Caoineadh Cu Chulainn (Lament)," *Riverdance: The Show* (the Point Theatre, Dublin, 1995), http://www.youtube.com/watch?v=WSjmvU_8xLY.

6. John Cage. *4'33"*, BBC Symphony Orchestra, conducted by Lawrence Foster (the Barbican Centre, London, 2004), http://www.youtube.com/watch?v=ZHEZk6dSReI.

7. David Byrne. "Playing the Building," Boing Boing TV, June 10, 2008, http://www.youtube.com/watch?v=M1D30gS7Z8U.

8. "Nora the Piano Cat," http://www.youtube.com/user/burnellyow.

9. "The Elephant Orchestra," http://www.youtube.com/watch?v=k1NpvHsxjgw.

10. Tom Kenaston. "Singing and Songwriting for Beginning Pianists: How to Sing Falsetto," http://www.youtube.com/watch?v=Z6qaT56QdB4.

11. Bonnie MacDonald. "Learn How to Yodel with Bonnie," http://www.youtube.com/watch?v=i6s6NM5sYQs; Winton Yuichiro White. "Overtone Singing Tutorial," http://www.youtube.com/watch?v=a940YFaRI50.

12. Fauquier Ear, Nose, and Throat Consultants. "Video Stroboscopy of the Vocal Cords," http://www.youtube.com/watch?v=ajbcJiYhFKY.

13. "Tumbi," http://www.youtube.com/user/tumbiwalla.

14. Kpatchave Junior and his ensemble. "Evi Mawu Ye Nana," http://www.youtube.com/watch?v=KCuNeaAWUAM.

15. "When Steel Talks," Steelband Network, http://www.youtube.com/user/basementrecordings.

16. See, for example, the channel of ethnomusicologist Julian Gerstin at http://www.youtube.com/user/jgerstin.

17. Hulu is a joint venture of NBC Universal, Fox Entertainment Group, ABC, and Disney. The site also carries shows from other networks, such as Comedy Central, PBS, USA Network, Bravo, Fuel TV, FX, Speed, Syfy, Style, Sundance, E!, G4, Versus, A&E, Oxygen, and online comedy sources, such as Onion News Network.

18. TubeSock can be downloaded from the official site: http://stinkbot.com/Tubesock/index.html. The download is free, but a registration fee of $15 is required after the 30-day trial period.

19. This assignment is inspired by activities suggested in Trier 2007b.

20. See, for example, University of California at Berkeley's YouTube channel at http://www.youtube.com/ucberkeley.

REFERENCES

Bakan, Michael. Bakan World Music blog. http://mailer.fsu.edu/~mbakan/index.html.

Brolsma, Gary. Numa Network. http://www.youtube.com/user/NewNuma.

comScore. 2009. YouTube surpasses 100 million U.S. viewers for the first time. March 4. http://www.comscore.com/Press_Events/Press_Releases/2009/3/YouTube_Surpasses_100_Million_US_Viewers.

Gerstin, Julian. jgerstin's Channel. http://www.youtube.com/user/jgerstin.

Huffington Post. 2009. Brigham Young University lifts YouTube Ban. *Huffington Post*, June 27. http://www.huffingtonpost.com/2009/06/27/brigham-young-university-_n_221908.html.

Jenkins, Henry. 2007. From YouTube to YouNiversity. *Chronicle of Higher Education* 53, no. 24 (February 16): B9–B10. Full text is also available on Henry Jenkin's weblog at http://www.henryjenkins.org/2007/02/from_youtube_to_youniversity.html.

Junee, Ryan. 2009. Zoinks! 20 hours of video uploaded every minute! Broadcasting Ourselves, May 20. http://youtube-global.blogspot.com/2009/05/zoinks-20-hours-of-video-uploaded-every_20.html.

Naím, Moisés. 2007. The YouTube effect. *Foreign Policy* 158: 104–5.

Parr, Ben. 2009. Iran election crisis: 10 incredible YouTube videos. Mashable, June 20. http://mashable.com/2009/06/20/iran-youtube/.

Popkin, Helene A.S. 2007. Survive your inevitable online humiliation. MSNBC, September 6. http://www.msnbc.msn.com/id/20611439/.

Trier, James. 2007a. Cool engagements with YouTube: Part I. *Journal of Adolescent and Adult Literacy* 50, no. 5: 408–12.

———. 2007b. Cool engagements with YouTube: Part II. *Journal of Adolescent and Adult Literacy* 50, no. 7: 598-603.

Valenza, Joyce. 2008. When YouTube is blocked. *School Library Journal*, December 19. http://www.schoollibraryjournal.com/blog/1340000334/post/1410038141.html.

Vitali, Sarah. 2009. Eric Schmidt: The power of global connectivity. *WWS News Magazine* 32, no. 2 (Spring). http://wws.princeton.edu/wws-news-magazine/archive/spring-2009/colloquium-schmidt/.

Wesch, Michael. 2008. An anthropological introduction to YouTube. Presentation at the Library of Congress, June 23. http://www.youtube.com/user/mwesch.

II

TEACHING MUSICIANSHIP AND MUSIC THEORY

4

Popular Music in the College Music Theory Class: Rhythm and Meter

Nancy Rosenberg

The following chapter offers practical suggestions for including popular music in music theory classroom practice around the teaching of rhythm and meter. Reflecting their deep interrelatedness, these subjects are usually introduced in close proximity toward the beginning of the study of music theory and revisited repeatedly as students broaden their familiarity with repertoire and their understanding of other music theory topics. The goal of focusing on these two basic music theory concepts is twofold: to provide music theory instructors with specific ideas to enrich their classroom practices and to offer a starting point for the development of further popular music theory pedagogy. The ideas and activities put forth in this article neither delineate a beginning music theory curriculum nor comprise fully developed lesson plans. Rather, instructors may choose how and when to implement these suggestions into the theory curriculum as they deem appropriate, adapting the popular music materials and methods offered here to their own curricula, while utilizing their music theory classrooms as vibrant workshops for the continued creation of new methods and materials.

Prior to determining specific techniques for integrating popular music into music theory classroom practice, one question lingers among the numerous philosophical and practical issues surrounding the inclusion of popular music in the traditional theory curriculum, and it must be addressed: practically speaking, how can music theory educators identify materials from constantly evolving popular music trends to best serve the instructional purposes at hand? Aside from employing whatever examples of popular music might be included in the theory textbook in use, music theory teachers with expertise in the popular music repertoire can and do draw upon their personal knowledge of favorite bands or songs in choosing which material to feature. This neither solves the problem for those unfamiliar with the repertoire nor addresses the challenge of keeping pace with the rapidly changing popular music landscape.

This latter point, that a flood of past and current popular music remains ever and easily accessible, complicates efforts to include popular music at all levels of music education. Those growing up surrounded by the rock music of the 1960s and 1970s may share an implicit acknowledgement of a loosely defined canon of great popular music artists and works, and it is from this supposed canon that many theory textbooks draw their popular music examples. However, while decades-old examples of commercially successful popular music may serve as valuable illustrations of various theoretical concepts, in terms of remaining current, music educators can do better in choosing repertoire for study. Today's undergraduates experience popular music differently from past generations, particularly in their tacit presumption of the global breadth of its availability and variability. The popular music repertoire on which music theory education focuses should reflect this, but the difficulties of establishing a popular music canon complicates matters. A few scholars have examined canon formation in relation to modern popular music (Karja 2006; Hebert 2009), but if a current canon of popular music can be said to exist—and the assertion is arguable—its extent is vast, and its boundaries vague and mercurial. How then can music theory instructors realistically keep up with the various popular music trends to which students are continually exposed, and how can they effectively choose which music to feature?

The answer is straightforward: to supplement teacher-chosen examples from art and popular music, student-chosen works must become integral to the repertoire used in music theory education. Many of the following suggestions not only draw on students' knowledge of and preferences for specific popular-music artists, bands, and works, both current and past, but also presume students' input in determining the various musical activities to be explored. In a paradigm shift from traditional expository methods of teaching music theory, students are called upon to provide and replenish the cache of popular music source material used in the classroom. This method requires of music theory teachers both the willingness and the ability to undertake, sometimes on the spot, analyses of largely non-notated and often unfamiliar musical materials. For theory instructors willing to learn alongside students while offering their musical insight and expertise, the result in terms of classroom dynamic can be exciting indeed for both teachers and students.

For many of the suggested activities in this chapter, students are asked to compile popular music examples relating directly to specific music theory concepts. Allocating to students the responsibility of revisiting their known music to clarify and reinforce music theory concepts intersects with aspects of several important student-centered, experiential approaches. It aligns with the constructivist belief that learning is dynamic and active as opposed to passively absorbed,[1] links with problem- and inquiry-based learning approaches that stress self-direction as a primary motivator in learning, and reframes the role of the teacher toward that of a guiding tutor or facilitator.[2] Research on incorporating informal music learning processes into formal music education settings likewise supports student involvement in choosing popular music materials to illustrate music theory concepts. As Green and others note, the self-directedness characterizing the learning styles of popular music practitioners translates positively into classroom practice focused on popular music (Green 2001; Green 2008; Lebler 2007). As students mine their popular music libraries for audio examples of music theory concepts, the formal-informal dichotomy is recontextualized with formal music educational practices and concerns carrying over into their informal listening practices as opposed to the other way around. Numerous other connections will emerge between suggested means of including popular music in the music theory classroom and aspects of experiential teaching and learning approaches.

While many of the methods discussed below share the goal of notational literacy central to undergraduate music theory education, particular emphasis is given to the use of popular music as a focus of non-notation based aural training. Western popular music represents a tradition largely learned and taught by ear and, as such, holds special value as a central component in aural training. Furthermore, regardless of the specific musical tradition upon which music education focuses, many argue that musical learning is best fostered when aural/oral training precedes training in analytical and notational skills. Edwin E. Gordon based his music learning theory on the idea that music education should proceed from the primary objective of developing tonal and rhythmic *audiation*—the ability to "think music in the mind with understanding" (GIML 2009). Some of Gordon's proponents suggest rethinking the undergraduate music theory curriculum to more closely align with Gordon's music learning theory, especially in its focus on aural over notational aspects. In separate articles, music educators Bruce Dalby and Bruce Taggart propose devoting much of the first year of undergraduate music theory education to aural training, echoing Gordon's insistence that students build a foundation of aural skills through real-music experiences and sequenced pattern instruction prior to learning notation and music theory (Dalby 2005; Taggart 2005). The so-called rote methods of Kodaly, Suzuki, and Dalcroze likewise consider aural musical experience to be paramount within the sequential processes of music education.

There is room within music theory education to accommodate ample overlap of notational and non-notational methods, whichever tradition is involved, be it art or popular music. As popular music scholar Lars Lilliestam concedes, "The opposition between orality and literacy ought not to be seen as an opposition between two conditions, as a dichotomy, but rather as a continuum where cultures have different degrees (as well as types) of literacy" (Lilliestam 1996, 197). Many of today's music students straddle art and popular music cultures, learning and creating from within the great tradition represented by their well-worn classical instrumental scores, while simultaneously engaging in the computer-dominated popular music culture in which the significance of musical orality clearly outweighs that of notational literacy. For these students, an approach granting added emphasis on aural aspects alongside notation-based music theory is essential.

POPULAR MUSIC RHYTHMIC TRAINING

Rhythm, often one of the first subjects presented in the study of Western music theory, sometimes receives short shrift in the long term. Although practical training in rhythmic skills may continue throughout the academic year, either integrated into a single music theory course or as part of a separate aural training program, it is common for theory textbooks to quickly proceed from offering the basic mathematical foundations of Western rhythm and meter to subjects relating to tonality. Given the centrality of rhythm as a feature of popular music and that listeners often develop a strong conscious and/or unconscious familiarity with the rhythmic characteristics associated with various popular music styles, popular music can prove singularly effective for teaching written, aural, and performance aspects of rhythm and meter.

Using popular music as source material for rhythmic training has several other compelling advantages. For one thing, because of its presence in the daily lives of undergraduates, students are afforded the opportunity to reinforce what they are learning in the classroom through their personal listening experiences. For another, serious training in the rhythmic practices of popular music, including learning to recognize, play, and create varied popular music drumming patterns, can fully educate students in many of the salient rhythmic features of Western classical music. Additionally, emphasis on popular music rhythm in the theory classroom involves numerous different learning processes, both kinetic and intellectual. Drawing from Piaget, White notes that a multifaceted approach can best provide the range of physical and "logico-mathematical" learning opportunities essential for mastery of each of the components that combine to comprise musical expertise (White 2002, 13), and popular music rhythmic study provides a much-needed excursion into kinetic processes. Finally, while there is little argument that the rhythmic language of Western music can be taught with examples created for expressly pedagogical aims, it makes logical sense to offer musicianship training within the context of real music whenever possible. Popular music offers concise, real-music examples, often containing whole sections of consistent rhythmic patterns and, as such, provides a particularly effective resource for learning and practice purposes.

The uninitiated or unwilling listener might perceive popular music rhythm as simultaneously overpowering and simplistic. It is true that the rhythm section instruments that dominate rock texture—drums, bass, electric guitar, and piano or keyboard/synthesizer—emphasize the music's percussive elements and also that rock musicians often seek to create and sustain a pulsating, often loud, rhythmic force. In practice, the intensity of the rhythmic treatment in Western popular music varies from style to style, whether exhibiting the rhythmic relentlessness of heavy metal, grindcore, rap, and hip-hop, the relaxed rhythmic jauntiness of reggae, or the relatively freer rhythmic treatment associated with the work of many solo singer/songwriters. Much of popular music's apparent rhythmic simplicity stems in part from the frequent use of common meter, with backbeat accents on beats two and four. Actually, popular music repertoire offers countless examples of other metric schemes, including extensive use of asymmetrical meters, changing meters, and polyrhythms. Nonetheless, examples of popular music utilizing the most basic rhythmic techniques and patterns provide excellent material for beginning rhythmic studies, and closer examination of what initially seems to be metrically simple music often reveals a wealth of foreground and background rhythmic subtlety worthy of attention.

As with traditional rhythm study, popular music rhythmic training must include levels ranging from small, single-beat motives to phrase structure, periodicity, and larger rhythmic phenomena. Much popular music lends itself particularly well to a multilevel exploration of rhythmic features, as discrete aspects such as drum and bass patterns, collective rhythm-section treatment, and solo guitar and vocal lines can be readily perceived and analyzed, whether separately or within the context of the overall rhythmic texture. Related musical aspects, such as text setting, melodic rhythm, melodic shape, and harmonic rhythm, can also be effectively examined through a popular-music lens.

Let us consider how popular music might figure into the teaching of basic rhythmic principles. To begin with, music theory educators should explore the use of the drum kit as a tool in rhythmic training. Music students' understanding of popular music rhythmic treatment can be greatly enhanced through direct experience with drum kit usage, especially given the instrument's central role in popular music practice, but the benefits of elementary training in drum kit techniques extend to a general rhythmic understanding independent of style, whether popular or classical. Additionally, the spatial separation of drum kit components provides an opportunity for students to stretch their rhythmic abilities through engaging in relatively complex kinetic processes. Working on drum kit also serves as an excellent means of integrating collaborative learning approaches into the music theory classroom.[3] Music theory instructors who are not percussionists can learn alongside students, an experience that can prove enjoyable (and humbling) for the instructor, while furthering active student engagement with the material. This shift in the expert vs. student paradigm toward a more collaborative approach, even temporarily, can positively complement lecture-centered approaches to teaching music theory.

In many cases, a rock drummer can be solicited from among class members or the broader school community to demonstrate drumming basics. Even without the expertise of a drumming practitioner, a unit on rock drumming can be organized around one, several, or many of the online video tutorials that are available on YouTube.[4] For example, a beginner-level tutorial, "Learn to Play Drums," offered on YouTube as part of the online resource FreeDrumLessons.com, introduces students to a basic rock drum pattern: high-hat on every beat of a four-beat measure, bass drum on beats one and three, and snare on beats two and four.[5] A bird's-eye view familiarizes students with the drum kit layout, and the explanations and demonstrations offered by drummer and instructor Mike Michalkow are concise and easy to follow.

Whether or not a drum kit is available for demonstration and practice purposes, rock drum charts are readily available in print and online, providing excellent materials for developing rhythm sight-reading and performing skills. Online resources also include numerous sites that explain basic drum-kit notation, many of which offer downloads of rock and popular music drum patterns arranged by level of difficulty, which serve as excellent rhythm sight-reading material. High-hat, snare, and bass drum combinations in varied beat patterns or high hat, ride cymbal, and snare combinations (see example 4.1) offer countless coordination exercises in simple and compound meters that beginning music theory students would likely find both interesting and challenging. Transcribed drum patterns of specific songs, also widely available as free or payable downloads, allow students

Example 4.1.   Sample rock drum patterns

to follow the drum chart notation while listening to a particular song. A list of print and online resources featuring popular music drum patterns and charts that can be adapted for use in rhythmic training is provided in appendix A at the end of this chapter.

Rhythm activities designed around popular music are as limitless as their art-music parallels. As students learn to read, perform, and notate drum grooves, all manner of instruments can serve, whether drum kit, found percussion instruments, or desktops, hand clapping or vocalizing. Students can hone their transcription skills using popular music examples played in class or practice transcribing from memory known rhythms from specific popular songs. Karaoke-style drumming sessions, during which students read and play learned patterns along with existing popular music record-ings, provide a fun, cooperative learning experience. Bass patterns offer a vast reserve of material for rhythmic training, ranging from metric regularity to extended passages of syncopated and otherwise complex rhythm. As the syncopated refrain of Grandmaster Flash's "The Message" illustrates, sung and rapped vocal lines are also excellent material for memorization, per-formance, and dictation exercises, with the inclusion of lyrics often serving to highlight rhythmic patterns, potentially enhancing learning considerably (see example 4.2). Even at an elementary level, instructors may introduce basic rhythmic patterns by stylistic "feel," isolating examples from rock, Latin, disco, blues, and so forth for aural analysis and performance. Divid-ing popular music rhythm into separate styles also opens the door for a larger conversation on the musical and cultural significance of similarities and differences in popular music rhythmic treatment.

Granting students agency in the music-theory learning process requires that instructors relinquish a degree of control so that students can partici-pate more directly in determining the course and materials of their own study. To this end, homework assignments and classroom activities in-volving the identification, memorization, transcription, and performance of popular music rhythms directly link classroom and life experiences as students engage in a kind of musical treasure hunt within which their own personal listening choices comprise the playing field. A practical advantage

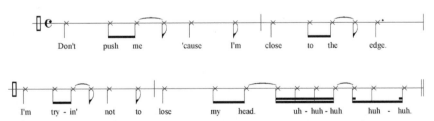

Example 4.2. Grandmaster Flash and the Furious Five, "The Message," syncopation. *The Message,* **Sugar Hill Records, 1982. International copyright secured. All rights re-served. Used by permission of Sugar Hill Records.**

to such assignments is that they enhance students' and teachers' collective knowledge of current musical trends. Toward this goal, notated excerpts, especially when completed on computer software notation such as Finale or Sibelius, can be compiled as part of a renewable library of rhythmic examples for use in present and future classroom exercises. Asking students to participate in compiling classroom materials increases their engagement in the subject matter, be it rhythmic training or other aspects of music theory education. Instructors can encourage student participation at all levels of course design and implementation in numerous other ways, often through simple means, such as giving students a choice of whether to focus on the music of an individual song, artist, or style or whether to work individually, in small groups, or as a whole class during project-based activities.

Focusing on Aural-Based Rhythmic Studies

Opportunities abound for using popular music as source material for rhythmic study outside of the context of notation, and there are many advantages to doing so. As previously discussed, many music educators focusing on popular music teaching and learning strategies stress the importance of learning and creating music by ear in popular music practice. Lilliestam notes that while classical musicians use notation as a method of storing music and as a kind of mnemonic aid to musical memory, popular musicians often use other means to remember music (Lilliestam 1996, 201). He cites four types of memory in popular music learning and performing processes:

1. *Auditive*, whereby we perceive music by hearing it and remember it with voice or instrument
2. *Visual*, which involves remembering, for example, what finger patterns look like on an instrument when a certain chord is played
3. *Tactile*, or the muscle memory of how certain movements on our instrument feel
4. *Verbal*, which includes our vocabulary for naming musical phenomena as well as nonverbal sounds musicians make to indicate rhythms (Lilliestam 1996, 201)

Classical musicians utilize the above kinds of memory as well, but Lilliestam implies that in the absence of reading and notating music, these avenues for memorization take on a greater importance for musicians working in popular styles.

Providing the opportunity for students to step away from the pursuit of notational mastery, even temporarily, serves to heighten memorization skills for art music as much as popular music as evidenced in the methods of Kodaly, Orff, Dalcroze, Gordon, and Suzuki.[6] It also aligns with learning theories advocating varied and individualized approaches to address students' personal learning styles.

The MP3 player (e.g., the iPod and similar devices) is an excellent resource for examining and comparing the rhythmic characteristics of different musical styles outside of notational contexts. The ease with which earphones can be adapted for use by multiple listeners facilitates cooperative small-group work, and a single set of speakers allows for larger-group listening. In a simple classroom exercise, students, working individually, in pairs, or in small groups, choose a song from their iPod libraries and learn and perform its primary rhythmic patterns, either vocally, on drum kit, or on separate percussion instruments. Limiting the allotted time for memorizing the parts adds an element of urgency and competitive play to the activity. Again, having students choose the music on which an activity is based both models mutual respect for individual musical preferences and also assures a comparative sampling of the rhythmic characteristics of varied popular music styles for class consideration.

Hip-hop, Beatboxing, and Turntablism

While popular music of all styles can be used in teaching fundamental rhythm concepts, certain musical styles lend themselves to specific purposes. For example, the use of looped "beats" in rap and hip-hop renders the music especially valuable in aural rhythmic study. Some music educators, scholars, and listeners, whether focusing primarily on classical or popular music, reject rap and hip-hop as musically unsatisfying or inferior; however, the rap and hip-hop repertoire provides a wealth of material for rhythmic study, much of which reflects a high degree of musical sophistication and inventiveness. Old-school rappers, such as Grandmaster Flash and the Furious Five, Afrika Bambaataa, and Run-D.M.C., expanded rap's horizons technically, musically, and in terms of its social consciousness. More recent hip-hop artists such as Nas, Jay-Z, Kanye West, Lauryn Hill, Eminem, Missy Elliott, and 50 Cent more than deserve their renown and are likely to be appreciated by today's music students as are groups such as the Fugees, Beastie Boys, Outkast, the Roots, and Wu-Tang Clan, to name just a few.

Hip-hop rhythmic loops can serve as the basis for numerous music theory classroom activities and assignments. As illustrated in example 1.2 above, the emphasis on rhythmic repetition in the style renders it an excellent source of material for memorization and dictation. Students can bring in recordings to use as the basis for improvised clapping and drumming exercises. In-class composition activities, perhaps presented within a limited timeframe to heighten the sense of urgency and fun, can center on the creation of hip-hop beat patterns, with students performing their "beats" for their classmates. Assigning the memorization of rapped excerpts or whole songs to small or large groups of students provides excellent practice in accurate rhythmic delivery, and learning the lyrics to faced-paced, rhythmically complex rapped passages adds to the challenge. Finally, students might be called upon to rap freestyle while others provide the beat, an activity that combines rhythmic dexterity, vocal presence, breath support, and imaginative flow and is likely to challenge musicians who have never attempted rapping in surprising and beneficial ways.

Evolving out of the hip-hop movement, beatboxing, a vocal technique in which performers imitate myriad percussion sounds, can be used to good effect in rhythmic training. Pioneered by Doug E. Fresh and others with hip-hop's emergence in the 1980s, contemporary beatboxing has reached a high level of sophistication and popularity, as evidenced by the 2005 international Beatbox Battle held in Leipzig as part of the Hip Hop World Challenge. Beatboxing's reliance on aurality, improvisation skills, and both gross and fine motor processes makes it an excellent tool among an array of popular music-based activities from which students working to master rhythmic concepts might benefit.

Collegiate a cappella, which frequently features beatboxing accompaniment in place of instrumental percussion, enjoys huge popularity on campuses across the US, and student beatboxers from campus a cappella groups can be asked to provide classroom demonstrations that are likely to generate curiosity and enthusiasm. Again, YouTube proves an invaluable resource, containing numerous excellent beatboxing tutorials to help students master some basic techniques, as well as amazing video clips of famous beatboxers, such as Rahzel, Kid Lucky, DJ Mesia, Bee Low, and many others. Working independently or in groups, students can use an array of recorded music as backdrop for beatboxing practice and performance, engaging a range of learning and thinking processes too often neglected in the music theory classroom. Asking students to develop notational symbols for beatboxing vocal techniques provides another interesting and unique learning opportunity.[7]

Turntablism is another aspect of rap and hip-hop with important implications for aural-based rhythmic studies. The term *turntablism* refers to the manipulation of vinyl LPs using phonograph turntables and a DJ mixer.[8] The tradition emerged out of the Bronx in the early days of rap when DJs, such as Kool Herc and Grandmaster Flash, sought ways to create a seamless stream of dance music by alternating between a pair of turntables. Grand Wizzard Theodore is credited with developing the earliest "scratching" techniques, involving moving records back and forth underneath the turntable stylus to create the complex rhythmic effects that eventually characterized the hip-hop of the 1990s and beyond, developed by individual turntable pioneers, such as DJ Qbert, DJ Quest, GrandMixer DXT, and DJ Krush, and DJ crews, such as Beat Junkies and the Allies. A class in "Introductory Turntablism" was introduced at University of California, Berkeley, as part of the university's DeCal (Democratic Education at CAL) program as early as 1998 (Dmitri 2002), although the subject remains a rarity among college music course offerings. Classical guitarist Stephen Webber, author of *Turntable Technique: The Art of the DJ*, now leads a highly successful turntablism program at Berklee College of Music, attesting to its emergence as a mainstay of practical popular music studies (Webber 2003).[9]

Turntable setups consisting of two turntables, a mixer, amplifier, and speakers are affordable and easy to assemble and maintain. Finding hip-hop artists among undergraduate students to demonstrate turntable techniques may pose a challenge, although most major cities house a substantial hip-hop community that includes turntablists. Local recording studios can often provide the names of DJ turntablists in the area who may be willing to lead workshops or demonstrations. As with rock drumming and beatboxing, YouTube provides access to an extensive library of video performances and tutorials.

Like drumming, which is particularly suited to students with a strong bodily-kinesthetic learning style, the tactile aspects of turntablism provide an opportunity for a physical approach to rhythmic training within the traditional music theory classroom. Basic scratching techniques presented in Webber's book and record set include straight and syncopated rhythm exercises at the quarter-, eighth-, and sixteenth-note levels that can be practiced with or without written notation. Single- and double-handed fader techniques and maneuvers such as "cutting," "stabbing," and "crabbing" require a high degree of coordination and rhythmic dexterity.[10] Even at early stages of training, students can use scratching techniques to practice creating and performing rhythmic patterns from basic to complex levels of difficulty and for improvisation and composition activities. British music educator Mike Challis documents a successful foray into using DJ techniques in teaching composition to secondary students in the UK (Challis 2007), attesting to turntablism's potential for use in music education.[11] Additionally, *beat matching*—adjusting the pitch or tempo of a track to match precisely that of the track currently sounding—is an integral aspect of turntablism, made possible with the development of sensitive sliding pitch controls and fine tempo adjustments on the direct-drive motors of current DJ turntables. As anyone who has practiced beat matching between simultaneously sounding LPs will attest, turntable setups prove a powerful tool for developing a familiarity with varied nuances of pitch and tempo.

Tempo Studies and Beat Matching

Developing the ability to identify and create given tempi with a high degree of accuracy is an area of rhythm studies that rarely receives attention in undergraduate music theory education, yet this skill is an essential aspect of rhythmic musicianship. As DJs practicing sophisticated beat-matching techniques recognize, in Western popular music, beats-per-minute (BPM) often directly corresponds to genre, particularly within electronic dance music. The rock music tradition is associated with a wider range of tempi than electronic genres and is, therefore, harder to characterize by BPM. Tempo recognition exercises in various popular music styles are singularly effective as a means of developing a keen sense of tempo, and instructors can draw from numerous online sites and software programs for ideas and information. In "BPM and Genres: From Hip Hop to Break-Beat, Techno to Trip Hop," Rob Wegner offers the table reproduced in example 4.3 as a rough guide to the relationship between BPM and several popular music styles (Wegner 2004).

Music theory teachers working on tempo recognition can access several free online databases containing libraries of songs listed by BPM. BPM Database, which is used and updated frequently by DJs worldwide, currently contains 24,300 song titles, alphabetized by artist's name (www.bpmdatabase.com). Additionally, several downloadable "beat counters" (e.g., TapTempo, available at www.analogx.com/contents/download/audio/taptempo.htm) enable listeners to determine a song's precise BPM by keeping time using the computer keyboard space bar.

Asymmetrical Meter, Changing Meter, and Polyrhythm

Popular music lends itself to more advanced study of rhythms and meter. Examples that are both easily accessible and musically interesting abound, and seeking out music featuring noteworthy meters provides further opportunity for students to search their personal popular music libraries in search of material for a variety of aural and written exercises, whether for independent study or general classroom use. Also, in the case of teaching and

Genre	BPM Range
Hip Hop/Rap/Trip Hop	60–110 BPM
Acid Jazz	80–126 BPM
Tribal House	120–128 BPM
House/Garage/Euro-Dance/Disco-House	120–135 BPM
Trance/Hard House/Techno	130–155 BPM
Breakbeat	130–150 BPM
Jungle/Drum-n-Bass/Happy Hardcore	160–190 BPM
Hardcore Gabba	180+ BPM

Example 4.3. BPM range in selected popular genres

learning complex rhythms and meters, studying familiar songs can help to allay students' anxiety as they grapple with advanced rhythmic principles.

Asymmetrical meters, changing meters, and polyrhythms abound in many popular music styles, and numerous examples are provided in appendix B at the end of this study. For music theory educators and students wishing to expand further their aural knowledge of complex meters in popular music, the online radio site Odd Time Obsessed streams odd-metered popular music online in real time and maintains an extensive and frequently updated playlist of songs (www.oddtimeobsessed.com). It should also be noted that popular music that initially seems metrically or rhythmically simple on its surface sometimes reveals unexpected intricacies. For example, electronic dance music, which at first hearing may seem deceptively rhythmically straightforward, uses layering techniques to create a subtle and deep rhythmic complexity and metric dissonance that is revealed upon more careful listening. Mark J. Butler examines this phenomenon, exploring electronic dance music's extensive use of *displacement dissonance*, which occurs in the asymmetrical patterning of its multilayered rhythmic texture (Butler 2001).

The two examples below illustrate the use of asymmetric and changing meters in mainstream popular music and serve as a basis for some practical suggestions for possible classroom activities. The song "Mother" by Andy Summers, guitarist for the Police, is in 7/8 meter throughout; the opening of the song is shown in example 4.4. (In his post-Police solo career, Sting has produced numerous songs in uneven meters, several of which are mentioned in appendix A.)

Example 4.4. Andy Summers, "Mother," opening bars. The Police, *Synchronicity*, A&M Records, 1983. Words and music by Andy Summers. © 1983 Magnetic Publishing/ EMI Publishing. International copyright secured. All rights reserved. Used by permission of Andy Summers.

"Mother" might serve any number of pedagogical purposes around the study of rhythm. Beginning with aural training, students can work from the recording to memorize the drum, bass, and synth parts separately, eventually performing them on solo rhythm instruments or as an ensemble. After the rhythmic lines of the part are memorized and performed, students can practice transcribing them, either with or without time constraints. The opening rhythmic ostinato could serve as the basis for a group performance that includes extended rhythmic improvisation. Students can practice conducting in 7/8 meter to a recording or performance of the song, gesturing to mark the separate rhythmic lines within the asymmetrical beat pattern. Going beyond strictly rhythmic aspects, the passage obviously provides examples of melodic intervals, particularly of the perfect fourth and the diminished fifth, and contains noteworthy harmonic features, such as the use of the flatted ninth and the omission of the third. Students would benefit from learning the individual guitar, bass, and synth melodies by ear and performing them vocally or on instruments, with and without rhythmic accompaniment.

In addition to its usefulness as aural training material, "Mother" can serve as a starting point for composition and arranging assignments. For example, students could be asked to create a new solo instrumental or vocal melody above the existing accompaniment or to give the rhythms a completely new melodic or harmonic treatment, which can then be compared and contrasted with the original song. These common-sense suggestions mirror activities that are hopefully already frequently realized in the music theory classroom, illustrating how easily time-honored methods can be adapted to include popular music examples.

As with asymmetrical meters, countless examples of changing meters that are suitable for teaching rhythmic principles can be found in the popular music repertoire. In "Bastard," songwriter Ben Folds uses mixed meters throughout. Example 4.5 shows the beginning of the first verse, in which 6/4 and 4/4 combine to give the simple melody, comprised of a pair of five-measure phrases, a lopsided effect, perhaps meant to evoke the "old bastard" that the lyrics describe. Concerning melodic rhythm, the subdivisions of the beat exemplify a "swung" triplet feel that should be pointed out to students, along with the use of eighth-note pairs as a means of representing swung triplets in notation. The relationships between the song's changing meter, the harmonic rhythm, and the explicit naturalness of Folds' text setting are further topics for examination.

Certain styles of popular music, such as progressive metal, tech metal, and the more marginalized grindcore and noise rock, hold extreme rhythmic complexity as a primary feature, often with drum set dominating the overall texture in sheer volume, speed of execution, and astonishing technical feats of syncopation and rhythmic intricacies. Interestingly,

Example 4.5.   Ben Folds, "Bastard," mm. 5–9. *Songs for Silverman,* Epic Records, 2005. Words and music by Benjamin Scott Folds. © 2005 Warner-Tamerlane Publishing and Free From the Man Publishing. All rights administered by Warner-Tamerlane Publishing. All rights reserved. Used by permission of Alfred Publishing.

grindcore and noise rock sometimes feature "microsongs" only seconds in length, begging a comparison with atonal miniatures from the European art-music tradition, such as Webern's *Six Pieces,* op. 6. In the context of the theory classroom, popular music featuring extravagant levels of rhythmic complexity, whether in extended passages or seconds-long structures, has limited use as material for memorization, transcription, or performance. Nevertheless, it can serve as an excellent focal point for aural analysis and group discussion and, thus, bears mention here. Among current popular styles, guitar- and drum-dominated *math rock* stands out for its complex rhythmic usage. The aggressive, noise-rock feel of the style is characterized by rhythmic unpredictability, including sudden stops and starts, asymmetrical rhythms, and frequent use of polyrhythm. Bands such as Battles, Cinemechanica, and Slint represent an evolving and fascinating genre that shatters our traditional sense of metrical organization in a reinterpretation of rock's rhythmic foundation. Selected math rock bands and other groups featuring extreme rhythmic usage are included in appendix B, and YouTube is also an invaluable resource.

The ideas presented above represent only the tip of the iceberg in terms of how popular music might serve in the teaching of rhythmic principles within the context of the traditional undergraduate music theory course. With each new idea for utilizing popular music in rhythmic training giving rise to others, faculty and students may find themselves engaged in a lively dialogue regarding new means of integrating popular materials into classroom practice around the teaching of rhythm. Many of the practices described above apply equally to the study of pitch, intervals, and scales. The popular music repertoire can be mined for musical examples, which can be compiled and updated for classroom use as ear-training and sight-singing material.

CONCLUSION

The ideas put forth above reflect the strong belief that undergraduate music theory education greatly benefits from the inclusion of student-centered activities around the study of popular music. Granting students a more active role in determining their learning materials and processes is a methodology supported not only by numerous current educational philosophies but also by practical need, for the influx of music made available through the music industry and online dissemination renders student input a necessity. With greater student involvement, the traditional teacher-student paradigm necessarily shifts, testing the competence of music theory instructors in several ways. Those with authoritarian leanings require tempering their attitudes to accept and learn from the superior knowledge of popular music repertoire that undergraduates are likely to possess. As instructors face new and sometimes completely unfamiliar musical material, their expertise may be challenged as they are called upon to spontaneously analyze, interpret, and provide cogent musical guidance. Carefully prepared, perhaps long-utilized lesson plans may diminish in usefulness and impact as they become less central to the workings of the class.

Despite the difficulties inherent in effecting even minor changes in teaching practices, whether in course organization, classroom dynamic, materials, and/or methodology, relatively small adjustments can have significant positive learning outcomes. The simple request that students explore their personal listening repertoire can be an extremely effective means of reinforcing concepts learned in class. Small-group cooperative learning projects foster a sense of common purpose and camaraderie. Allotting class time for students to share their musical discoveries with instructors and peers bolsters enthusiasm for the subject and fosters a sense of community while positively impacting students' developing musicianship skills.

For rhythmic study, the use of traditional classroom materials can be expanded to include educational drum patterns and transcribed drum charts of individual popular songs. Examples of asymmetrical and changing meters further underline popular music's usefulness as rhythmic training material. Certain styles are useful fields of study for specific rhythmic aspects, for example, hip-hop for its repetitive looping, math rock for its use of uneven and changing meters, and polyrhythms. Activities that stress kinetic processes, such as beatboxing and turntablism, balance intellectual and motor processes with the development of rhythmic musicianship.

Additionally, tools relating to popular music practice, such as drum kits, iPods, and the Internet, are important supplements to traditional methods.

This chapter outlines some basic procedures for integrating popular music into teaching and learning music theory concepts related to aspects of rhythm and meter, and music theory educators can and must go much further. It should be noted that many of the above rhythmic activities might apply to other areas of music theory education, such as pitch, intervals, scales, harmony, and form. As with the study of rhythm, the popular music repertoire can be mined for musical examples for use as melodic sight-singing material, melodic and harmonic ear-training, and as the focus for aural and written analysis. This and other student-centered activities around popular music have the potential to greatly enrich and enliven current music theory education. It is hoped that this discussion generates new ideas for integrating popular music into music theory classroom practices, pointing the way toward much-needed future research into popular music theory pedagogy.

APPENDIX A: SELECTED RESOURCES FOR POPULAR MUSIC DRUM PATTERNS AND RHYTHM SOFTWARE

Drum Patterns in Basic Drum-Kit Notation

Books

Ron Savage, Casey Sheuerell, and the Berklee faculty, *Berklee Practice Method: Drumset* (Boston: Berklee Press, 2001).

Dave Black and Steve Houghton, *Alfred's Kids Drumset Course* (Van Nuys, CA: Alfred, 2005).

Pete Sweeney, *Drum Atlas Series: Salsa; Drum Atlas Series: Cuba; Drum Atlas Series: Brazil* (Van Nuys, CA: Alfred, 2009).

Donny Gruendler, *Creating and Performing Drum Loops* (New York: Carl Fischer, 2008).

Tommy Igoe, *Groove Essentials: The Play Along* (Milwaukee, WI: Hal Leonard, 2005).

Ed Roscetti, *Rock Drumming Workbook/CD* (Milwaukee, WI: Hal Leonard, 2001).

Mike Michalkow, *The Total Rock Drummer* (Van Nuys, CA: Alfred, 2008).

Online Resources

http://www.rockdrummingsystem.com/underground/drum-beats/the-money-beat .php.

This site, created by drummer Jared Falk, offers short lessons on basic drum beats in many styles, including rock, heavy metal, punk rock, Latin, and jazz. An e-book, *Rock Drumming* (Railroad Media, 2006), is available as a free download. The second of the book's three sections ("Drum Theory," "Rock Beats," and "Rock Fills") contains five simple and useful graded lessons.

http://drumsetfun.com.

Drum Set Fun contains an extensive section on "Drum Lessons," including "How to Read Drum Notation," "How to Start Learning Drums Even if You Don't Have a Set," and "The Essential Easy Drum Beats of Rock Drumming." The third lesson listed here includes sections with notated examples of classic rock patterns, including 8th-note, 16th-note, half-time, and shuffle feels.

http://www.virtualdrumming.com.

This site has a section on "Coordination Exercises for Rock Drumming" with numerous downloadable .pdf files containing notated drum patterns. Under "Rock" are downloadable examples of "Basic Drum Beats," "Shuffle," "Dance," "Latin Jazz," "Jazz," and so forth, as well as grooves depicting the drumming styles of individual artists.

http://uk.geocities.com/paulvwilliams@btopenworld.com/DrumCharts.htm.

Paul Williams' site, Dorset Percussion, contains links to notated drum charts of many contemporary rock tunes, with accompanying MP3 files enabling students to follow along as they listen. Among the many artists whose music is represented are Coldplay, Green Day, AC/DC, Queen, Radiohead, Metallica, and Stevie Wonder. The site also contains downloadable groove charts, organized by level of difficulty.

http://www.studiodrumcharts.com/downloads.html.

Studio Drum Charts Publishing offers a limited selection of free downloads of studio drum charts for songs by bands ranging from Weezer to the Red Hot Chili Peppers.

Rhythm Software

Rhythm Rascal (Randy Brown). Virtual drum machine that can be programmed to play in any style; users designate meter and tempo to create unlimited patterns; includes drum samples.

MusicGoals Rhythm (Singing Electron). Shareware for Windows Vista and XP only.

APPENDIX B: SELECTED EXAMPLES OF RHYTHMS AND METERS IN POPULAR MUSIC

Simple, Compound, and Uneven Meters

3/4

Aceyalone, "The Hurt," *A Book of Human Language* (Project Blowed Recordings, 1992).

The Beatles, "She's Leaving Home," *Sgt. Pepper's Lonely Hearts Club Band* (Parlophone, 1967).

Beck, "Sing It Again," *Mutations* (Geffen, 1998).

Ben Folds Five, "Smoke," *The Complete Sessions at West 54th* (Sony, 2001).

The Clash, "Rebel Waltz," *Sandinista!* (Legacy, 1980).

Elvis Costello, "Sunday's Best," *Armed Forces* (Hip-O Records, 1979).

Bob Dylan, "Fourth Time Around," *Blonde on Blonde* (Columbia 1966).
Jimi Hendrix, "Manic Depression," *Are You Experienced?* (MCA, 1967).
Indigo Girls, "Caramia," *Shaming of the Sun* (Epic, 1997).
The Pogues, "Fairy Tale of New York," *If I Should Fall from Grace with God* (Rhino, 1988).
Seal, "Kiss From a Rose," *Seal* (Sire, 1994).
Elliot Smith, "Miss Misery," *Good Will Hunting* (Capitol, 1997).
Elliot Smith, "Waltz #2 (XO)," *XO* (DreamWorks, 1998).
Tom Waits, "Diamonds and Gold," *Rain Dogs* (Island, 1985).
Tom Waits, "Little Rain (For Clyde)," *Bone Machine* (Island, 1992).
Tom Waits, "Shiver Me Timbers," *The Early Years, vol. 2* (Manifesto, 1993).
True Margrit, "Electricity," *Seaworthy* (Bobo Tunes, 2005).

5/8

GZR, "Cycle of Sixty," *Plastic Planet* (TVT, 1995).
Queens of the Stone Age, "Hangin' Tree," *Songs for the Deaf* (Interscope, 2002).

5/4

The Beatles (George Harrison), "Within You Without You" (partially in 5), *Sgt. Pepper's Lonely Hearts Club Band* (Parlophone, 1967).
Nick Drake, "River Man," *Five Leaves Left* (Island, 1969).
Jethro Tull, "Living in the Past," single (Island, 1969).
Primus, "Here Come the Bastards," *You Can't Party without Me!* (unauthorized live recording, 1993).
Radiohead, "Morning Bell," *Kid A* (Capitol, 2000); appears in 4/4 on *Amnesiac* (Capitol, 2001).
Radiohead, "15 Step," *In Rainbows* (XL Recordings, 2007).
Slint, "Nosferatu Man" (5/4 in first section alternates with 6/4 in *b* section), *Spiderland* (Touch and Go, 1991).
Stereolab, "The Flower Called Nowhere," *Dots and Loops* (Elektra, 1997).
Sting, "Seven Days," *Ten Summoner's Tales* (A&M, 1993).
Sufjan Stevens, "All Good Naysayers, Speak Up! Or Forever Hold Your Peace!" *Michigan* (Asthmatic Kitty, 2003).
Sufjan Stevens, "Detroit, Lift up Your Weary Head!" *Michigan* (Asthmatic Kitty, 2003).
Sufjan Stevens, "A Good Man Is Hard to Find," *Seven Swans* (Sounds Familyre, 2004).
Sufjan Stevens, "The Great Frontier, Pt. II: Come to Me Only With Playthings Now," *Illinois* (Asthmatic Kitty, 2005).
Sufjan Stevens, "The Tallest Man, the Broadest Shoulders, Pt. 1," *Illinois* (Asthmatic Kitty, 2005).
Tool, "The Grudge," *Lateralus* (Volcano, 2001).
Tool, "Vicarious," *10,000 Days* (Tool Dissectional, 2006).
Venetian Snares, "Hiszekeny" ("Gullible"), *Rossz csillag alatt szuletett* (Planet Mu, 2004).

6/16

Joni Mitchell, "Cherokee Louise," *Night Ride Home* (Geffen, 1991).

6/8

Battles, "Atlas," *Mirrored* (Warp Records, 2007).
The Beatles, "Norwegian Wood (This Bird Has Flown)" (3/4 in published transcription), *Rubber Soul* (EMI, 1965).
The Beatles, "This Boy," *Meet The Beatles!* (Capitol, 1964).
The Beatles, "You've Got to Hide Your Love Away," *Help!* (Capitol, 1965).
Eric Clapton, "River of Tears," *Pilgrim* (Reprise, 1997).
Coldplay, "Shiver," *Parachutes* (Parlophone, 2000).
Nick Drake, "Place to Be," *Pink Moon* (Island, 1971).
Jay-Z, "My First Song," *The Black Album* (Roc-A-Fella, 2003).
Alicia Keys, "Fallin'," *Songs in A Minor* (J, 2001).
Elliot Smith, "Angel in the Snow," *New Moon* (Kill Rock Stars, 2007).
The Stranglers, "Golden Brown" (alternating 6/8 and 7/8; 6/8 on the verse), *La Folie* (Liberty Records, 1981).
Tom Waits, "Gonna Take It with Me When I Go," *Mule Variations* (Epitaph, 1999).
Tom Waits, "The House Where Nobody Lives," *Mule Variations* (Epitaph, 1999).
Weezer, "Devotion" (slow 6/8), *El Scorcho* (DGC, 1996).
Weezer, "Holiday," *The Blue Album* (Geffen, 1994).

6/4

Alice in Chains, "Rain When I Die" (4+2), *Dirt* (Columbia, 1992).
Dave Matthews Band, "Satellite," *Under the Table and Dreaming* (Bama Rags Records, 1995).
The Ramones, "We're a Happy Family," *Rocket to Russia* (Sire, 1977).
Soundgarden, "Fell on Black Days," *Superunknown* (A&M, 1994).
Sufjan Stevens, "The Predatory Wasp of the Palisades Is Out to Get Us," *Illinois* (Asthmatic Kitty, 2005).
Weezer, "No Other One," *Pinkerton* (Geffen, 1996).

7/8

Alice in Chains, "Them Bones" (verse), *Dirt* (Columbia, 1992).
Genesis, "Dance on a Volcano," *A Trick of the Tail* (Virgin, 1976).
Traci Lords, "Good 'n Evil," *1000 Fires* (Radioactive Records, 1995).
Radiohead, "Paranoid Android" (mostly 4/4, 7/8 in middle section), *OK Computer* (Parlophone, 1997).
Radiohead, "2+2=5 (The Lukewarm)" (7/8 with 4/4), *Hail to the Thief* (Parlophone, 2003).
The Stranglers, "Golden Brown" (alternating 6/8 and 7/8; 6/8 on the verse), *La Folie* (Liberty Records, 1981).

Sting, "Love Is Stronger than Justice (The Munificent Seven)," *Ten Summoner's Tales* (A&M, 1993).
Sting, "Straight to the Heart," . . . *Nothing Like the Sun* (A&M, 1987).
Frank Zappa, "Don't Eat the Yellow Snow" (later sections in 6/8, 4/4), *Strictly Commercial* (Rykodisc, 1995).

7/4

The Beatles, "All You Need Is Love" (with 4/4), *Magical Mystery Tour* (Capitol, 1967).
David Bowie, "Soul Love," *The Rise and Fall of Ziggy Stardust and the Spiders from Mars* (RCA, 1972).
Broken Social Scene, "Ghetto Body Buddy," *The Chocolate Wheelchair Album* (Planet Mu, 2003).
Broken Social Scene, "7/4 Shoreline," *Broken Social Scene* (Arts & Crafts, 2005).
Peter Gabriel, "Solsbury Hill," *Peter Gabriel* (Atco Records, 1977).
Pink Floyd, "Money" (3+4, with middle section in 4/4), *Dark Side of the Moon* (Harvest, 1973).
The Police, "Mother," *Synchronicity* (A&M, 1983).
Porcupine Tree, "Dark Matter," *Signify* (Delerium, 1996).
Porcupine Tree, "So Called Friend," *Deadwing* (Atlantic, 2005).
Soundgarden, "Outshined" (with some 4/4), *Badmotorfinger* (A&M, 1991).
Soundgarden, "Spoonman," *Superunknown* (A&M, 1994).
Sting, "I Was Brought to My Senses," *Mercury Falling* (A&M, 1996).
Venetian Snares, "Szamar Madar," *Rossz csillag alatt szuletett* (Planet Mu, 2004).

9/8

Genesis, "Apocalypse in 9/8," section 6 of "Supper's Ready" (3+2+4), *Foxtrot* (Atlantic, 1972)
Lush, "De-Luxe," *Ciao! The Best of Lush* (4AD, 2001)
Sufjan Stevens, "Say Yes to Michigan!" (6+3), *Michigan* (Asthmatic Kitty, 2003)
Tool, "Jambi" (4+5), *10,000 Days* (Tool Dissectional, 2006)

12/8

Ben Folds, "Gone," *Rockin' the Suburbs* (Epic, 2001).
Death Cab for Cutie, "What Sarah Said," *Plans* (Atlantic, 2005).
OutKast, "The Whole World," *Big Boi and Dre Present . . . Outkast* (LaFace, 2001).
Queen, "Jesus," *Queen* (Elektra, 1973).
Queen, "Pain Is So Close to Pleasure," *A Kind of Magic* (EMI, 1986).

Complex Meters

10/4

Air, "Alpha Beta Gaga," *Talkie Walkie* (Astralwerks, 2004).
Grateful Dead, "Playing in the Band" (4+4+2), *Grateful Dead* (Warner Bros., 1971).

Radiohead, "Everything in Its Right Place," *Kid A* (Parlophone, 2000).
Radiohead, "Go to Sleep (Little Man Being Erased)," *Hail to the Thief* (Parlophone, 2003).

11/4

The Allman Brothers Band, "Whipping Post" (3+3+3+2), *The Allman Brothers Band* (Capricorn, 1971).
Primus, "Eleven" (3+3+3+2), *Sailing the Seas of Cheese* (Interscope, 1991).

15/4

The Pretenders, "The Wait" (7+8), *The Pretenders* (Sire, 1980).
Soundgarden, "The Day I Tried to Live" (7+8), *Superunknown* (A&M, 1994).

Changing Meters

The Beatles, "Blackbird" (opens 3+2+2+3+2+2), *The Beatles (The White Album)* (Apple, 1968).
The Beatles, "Good Morning" (3/4+3/4+4/4 // 3/4+3/4+2/4+4/4 // 3/4+2/4+4/4 // 3/4+3/4+4/4+4/4, etc.), *Sgt. Pepper's Lonely Hearts Club Band* (Parlophone, 1967).
The Beatles, "Happiness Is a Warm Gun" (uses 6/4, 4/4, 5/4, 9/8, 6/8, 10/8, 12/8; also see under "Polymeters"), *The Beatles (The White Album)* (Apple, 1968).
Ben Folds, "Bastard" (uses 4/4, 3/2, 7/4, 6/4, 3/4, and 5/4), *Songs for Silverman* (Epic, 2005).
The Fall, "Smile" (6/8+6/8+6/8+4/8+4/8+4/8), *Perverted by Language* (Rough Trade, 1983).
Incubus, "Make Yourself" (verse has 7/8+4/4), *Make Yourself* (Epic, 1999).
Led Zeppelin, "Four Sticks" (5/4+3/4 in verses), *Led Zeppelin IV* (Atlantic, 1971).
Metallica, "Master of Puppets" (4/4+4/4+4/4+5/8), *Master of Puppets* (Elektra, 1986).
Nine Inch Nails, "March of the Pigs" (5/8+7/8), *The Downward Spiral* (Nothing, 1994).
Sting "I Hung My Head" (8+1), *Ten Summoner's Tales* (A&M, 1993).
Tool, "Schism" (changes meter 47 times), *Lateralus* (Volcano, 2001); see Adam Perlmutter, *Guitar One Magazine*, August 2001, for song transcription and metrical analysis.
Frank Zappa, "Five Five Five" (5/8+5/8+5/4), *Shut Up 'n Play Yer Guitar* (Barking Pumpkin Records, 1981).

Polymeters

The Beatles, "Happiness Is a Warm Gun" (12/8 against 6/4 drums in Lennon's spoken section), *The Beatles (The White Album)* (Apple, 1968).
King Crimson, "Discipline" (17/16 against 4/4), *Discipline* (E.G. Records, 1981).
King Crimson, "Thela Hun Ginjeet" (7/8 against 4/4), *Discipline* (E.G. Records, 1981).

Mahavishnu Orchestra, "Birds of Fire" (guitar plays 5+5+5+3 while drums play 6+6+6, violin sometimes plays 3+3+2+3+3+2+2), *Birds of Fire* (Columbia, 1973).

Megadeth, "Sleepwalker" (2 against 3), *United Abominations* (Roadrunner, 2007).

Perfume, "Polyrhythm" (chorus has 5/8 against 6/8 and 4/4), *Game* (Tokuma Japan Communications, 2007).

Queen, "The March of the Black Queen" (8/8 against 12/8), *Queen II* (Elektra, 1974).

Trent Reznor, "La Mer" (piano plays 3/4 riff against drums and bass in 4/4), *The Fragile* (Nothing, 1999).

Selected Genres and Bands Using Complex Meters and Polyrhythms

Math Rock: Slint, Battles, Cinemechanica, Sweep the Leg Johnny, Don Caballero, Shellac

Metal: Meshuggah, Nothingface, Symphony X, Mudvayne

Progressive metal: Tool, Dream Theater

Tech metal: Ion Dissonance, the Dillinger Escape Plan, Candiria

Indie rock: Animal Collective, the Dodos, Liars, Ponytail, Sufjan Stevens

Noise rock: Melt-Banana

NOTES

1. For a definition of constructivism and a realistic examination of its principal claims, see Fox 2001.

2. John R. Savery defines and discusses problem- and inquiry-based learning in Savery 2006.

3. For a concise and useful discussion on the types and benefits of collaborative learning in postsecondary teaching, see Barbara Leigh Smith and Jean T. MacGregor, "What Is Collaborative Learning?" (learningcommons.evergreen.edu/pdf/collab.pdf), a summary of Smith and MacGregor 1992.

4. As of this writing, searching the phrase "learn to play rock drums" on YouTube yields 63,000 results.

5. Mike Michalkow, "Learn to Play Drums," http://www.youtube.com/watch?v=B63I1fFfFpY.

6. For a useful overview of music teaching methodologies, see "Teaching Methods" in Mark 1986, 107–202; for a comparison of the methodologies of Dalcroze, Kodaly, and Orff and of their respective applications to K–12 levels of music education, see Choksy and others 2000.

7. In 2006, Mark Splinter and Gavin Tyte developed a beatbox chart notation known as Standard Beatbox Notation or SBN, using lower-case letters from the English alphabet (http://www.humanbeatbox.com/tips/p2_articleid/231). Beatboxer and electronic engineer Dan Stowell has also developed a beatbox alphabet based on symbols from the International Phonetic Alphabet (http://www.mcld.co.uk/beatboxalphabet).

8. The documentary film *Scratch* (director Doug Pray, Palm Pictures, 2002) provides an excellent introduction to the art and history of DJ turntablism and features

many renowned DJs, including DJ Quest, Jurassic 5, Afrika Bambaataa, DJ Craze, Grandmaster Flash, and many others.

9. For a more detailed consideration of turntablism techniques and classes, see chapter 10 of this volume, Karen Snell, "Turntablism: A Vehicle for Connecting Music Making and Learning."

10. For a useful overview of scratching techniques, including illustrations, see "Scratching," at DJ Techniques, http://dj.wikia.com/wiki/Scratching#Cut.

11. Ethnomusicologist Joseph G. Schloss examines hip-hop sampling techniques from historical, aesthetic, ethical, and practical perspectives in Schloss 2004.

REFERENCES

Butler, Mark J. 2001. Turning the beat around: Reinterpretation, metrical dissonance, and asymmetry in electronic dance music. *Music Theory Online* 7, no. 6 (December). http://mto.societymusictheory.org/issues/mto.01.7.6/mto.01.7.6.butler.html.

Challis, Mike. 2007. The DJ factor: Teaching performance and composition from back to front. In *Music education with digital technology*, ed. John Finney and Pamela Burnard, 65–75. London: Continuum International.

Choksy, Lois, Robert M. Abramson, Avon E. Gillespie, David Woods, and Frank York. 2000. *Teaching music in the twenty-first century.* 2nd ed. Upper Saddle River, NJ: Prentice Hall.

Dalby, Bruce. 2005. Music learning theory methods in the undergraduate music theory and ear training curriculum. In *The development and practical application of music learning theory*, ed. Maria Runfola and Cynthia Crump Taggart, 359–72. Chicago: Gia.

Dmitri, Holiday. 2002. Welcome to spin class at UC Berkeley. Holiday Editorial Features. http://www.holidaydmitri.com/turntablism.html.

Fox, Richard. 2001. Constructivism examined. *Oxford Review of Education* 27, no. 1: 23–35.

GIML. 2009. Music learning theory. The Gordon Institute for Music Learning. http://www.giml.org/mlt_menu.php.

Green, Lucy. 2001. *How popular musicians learn: A way ahead for music education.* London: Ashgate.

———. 2008. *Music, informal learning and the school: A new classroom pedagogy.* London: Ashgate.

Hebert, David G. 2009. Rethinking the historiography of hybrid genres in music education. In *De-canonizing music history*, ed. Lauri Vakeva and Vesa Kurkela, 165–84. Newcastle, UK: Cambridge Scholars.

Karja, Antti-Ville. 2006. A prescribed alternative mainstream: Popular music and canon formation. *Popular Music* 25, no. 1: 3–19.

Lebler, Don. 2007. Student-as-master? Reflections on a learning innovation in popular music pedagogy. *International Journal of Music Education* 25, no. 3: 205–21.

Lilliestam, Lars. 1996. On playing by ear. *Popular Music* 15, no. 2: 195–216.

Mark, Michael L. 1986. *Contemporary music education.* 2nd ed. New York: Schirmer.

Savery, John R. 2006. Overview of problem-based learning: Definitions and distinctions. *Interdisciplinary Journal of Problem-based Learning* 1, no. 1: 9–20.

Schloss, Joseph G. 2004. *Making beats: The art of sample-based hip-hop.* Middleton, CT: Wesleyan University Press.

Smith, Barbara Leigh, and Jean T. MacGregor. 1992. What is collaborative learning? In *Collaborative learning: A sourcebook for higher education,* ed. Ann Goodsell and others, University Park: National Center on Postsecondary Teaching, Learning, and Assessment, Pennsylvania State University.

Taggart, Bruce. 2005. Music learning theory in the college music theory curriculum. In *The development and practical application of music learning theory,* ed. Maria Runfola and Cynthia Crump Taggart, 345–58. Chicago: Gia.

Webber, Stephen. 2003. *Turntable technique: The art of the DJ.* Boston: Berklee Press.

Wegner, Rob. 2004. BPM and genres: From hip hop to break-beat, techno to trip hop. Disc Jockey 101. http://www.discjockey101.com/oct2004.html.

White, John D. 2002. *Guidelines for college teaching of music theory.* Lanham, MD: Scarecrow.

5

Teaching Traditional Music Theory with Popular Songs: Pitch Structures

Heather MacLachlan

This chapter provides a guideline for teaching conventional, common-practice period music theory concepts using well-known English-language popular songs. I developed the lessons included here in the crucible of the university classroom while teaching music theory to undergraduate students at Cornell University in 2007. This approach to teaching theory, therefore, has the advantage of having been created in conjunction with recent students, who ultimately demonstrated mastery of the concepts presented and enjoyed doing so. While this tactic has not been tested with a large enough group of students to provide reliable data, it is clear that the students who participated in these lessons deeply appreciated the opportunity, and they said as much on their course evaluations, all of which were quite positive. Individuals made comments like, "It was incredible to hear what we were learning in pieces that we knew," and "The teacher should write her own textbook using examples from modern music!!!" This chapter represents a first attempt at presenting this approach to a larger audience.

BENEFITS OF INCORPORATING CONTEMPORARY POP SONGS INTO TRADITIONAL MUSIC-THEORY CLASSES

The story of how I came to use this approach to music theory demonstrates some important pedagogical principles. I was working as a teaching assistant for a professor of music theory who had developed a clear and consistent approach to the topic. Over the course of about 20 years, he honed his curriculum. He used it annually with non–music majors, who signed up for his music theory course in order to earn a humanities credit. He taught music theory historically, presenting theoretical concepts not only in order of complexity but also in order of their chronological appearance in compositional practice. Furthermore, he was committed to initially presenting each concept by showing the students how the concept was captured in real music. All of his musical examples came from the *Norton Scores* (Forney and Hickman 2007), a collection of Western art music arranged in chronological order. The professor began the course with the concept of the diatonic scale, using scores and recordings of Gregorian chant to illustrate his point. He then focused on intervals, beginning with the perfect fourths and perfect fifths of parallel organum. The course concluded with Neapolitan-sixth chords encapsulated in music of the Classical period.

As a doctoral candidate in the music department, I appreciated the professor's method. The course material seemed clear to me, and I reiterated it enthusiastically during the twice-weekly sections I led, taking the students through the scores and accompanying recordings. No doubt, I would have continued down this path, convinced of its merits, had we not arrived at a moment that seems to occur in every semester: one day, in the middle of the fourth week, the teaching assistants had no course material to present during the section. "What should we do for an hour?" I asked the professor. "Ask the students how they think the class is going," he replied.

It is to my students' credit that they answered openly and honestly when I posed this question. They said that they were glad to learn about scales, intervals, chords, and so on—after all, this was why they had signed up for the course. (Although they were not music majors, many of them had studied introductory music theory in high school, and virtually all of them played an instrument.) But, they said, they were having difficulty absorbing the concepts. One young man expressed it thus: "It's hard enough learning all the different intervals—why do we have to do it with Gregorian chant? We've never heard Gregorian chant before, so that's two new ideas at once. Isn't there some contemporary music we could use for the example?"

This student and all of his colleagues, who immediately voiced agreement, hit the pedagogical nail on the head. Learners acquire new knowledge most easily when they can relate that knowledge to an idea they have already mastered. Piaget first articulated this theory of knowledge construction, arguing that children's learning is always governed by their preexisting mental maps (Piaget 1954, 350–86). When children encounter a new concept, they either assimilate that concept into their mental map or are forced to alter their mental map to accommodate the new information (Singer and Revenson 1978, 13–14). Over time, according to this "spiderweb" theory of learning, a learner's mental map develops new connections, growing increasingly large and complex. Thus, when we teach music theory—or any other subject—we ought to present new concepts in familiar contexts so that the students can relate these new concepts to something they already understand.

For me and my students, following this approach meant changing the musical examples used to demonstrate each new concept. For the remainder of the semester, I demonstrated theoretical concepts with popular songs. My students recognized virtually all of the songs I used as examples, and in most cases, they were able to sing along with some or all of the melody. Therefore, when I isolated part of the song and said, for instance, "This is called a suspension," the students were easily able to identify and understand the new concept. Since the sound was already familiar, the learning was a matter of assigning a label to the sound.

Importantly, our switch from historical to contemporary musical examples did not undermine the professor's goal of exposing the students to many of the works in the *Norton Scores*. During sections, I structured the lessons so that the new idea, embedded in the contemporary pop song, always came first. As soon as the students were comfortable with the concept (usually after hearing the song and reading the score once or twice), we moved on to standard theory exercises on staff paper. We resolved V^7 chords, for example, and then discovered how composers historically used and resolved them, using the examples in the *Norton Scores*. The students were, therefore, able to become comfortable with a succession of music-theory concepts, to use them in assignments, and to understand the enduring importance of ideas first articulated many centuries earlier.

Popular songs are useful tools for introducing new theory concepts because of their very nature: these songs are short—usually around four minutes long—and repetitive, having a strophic or compound strophic verse-chorus form. Returning to the example above, when I wanted to teach about suspensions, using a pop tune made excellent sense. The students would be able to hear the suspension multiple times, as the verse in which it occurred repeated, and they would understand it in the context of the complete musical work. Listening to an entire pop song even multiple times takes up only a small portion of the class period and is always worthwhile since it gives students a chance to listen repeatedly for a new concept in a brief span of time.

Using pop music to teach music theory produced another benefit: students showed a more active interest in the course than they had in the early weeks. For example, one student contacted me to ask what would be taught during an upcoming class that he had to miss. When I told him that we would be focusing on "Gangsta's Paradise," he expressed genuine regret. He knew the song well, he said, and would have appreciated the chance to study it in detail. Another student came to class with an anthology of

Billy Joel songs and offered to lend it to me in the hopes that I would find material for the class in the book. These reactions make sense. Students are more likely to be invested in a class and to contribute to it when they believe that they have something to offer. Since most young adults know a tremendous amount about popular music, focusing on it as a starting point for a class gives students the opportunity to be experts at the very beginning. It is the pedagogical equivalent to laying out a welcome mat. Naturally, this increases students' confidence in themselves and increases the chance that they will articulate their own ideas during the course. Furthermore, this approach allows students to clearly link common-practice theoretical concepts to their own music making. If successful living artists use these structures and techniques in their songs, then it is easy to understand how relevant they are to contemporary practice.

CHALLENGES INHERENT IN THIS APPROACH

One major obstacle to using contemporary pop songs to teach music theory is the lack of available tools. Although many current theory textbooks do make use of a few pop tunes, none of the most popular texts used to teach traditional theory depends primarily on pop tunes for examples. This is most likely due to the fact that copyright privileges for many recent hit songs are prohibitively expensive (as turned out to be the case with some examples originally intended for this chapter). My solution to this problem is straightforward: I present contemporary recordings and scores in class, using them as preliminary examples of the concepts I am teaching. As described above, these songs are always initial examples of new ideas that serve as tools to introduce the next point in the music-theory curriculum. When I first developed these lesson plans, they served as a kind of bridge between the students' experiences and the still unfamiliar art-music repertoire. I needed only one copy of the recording (usually available on iTunes for $0.99 or on YouTube for free) and one copy of a transcription (also available online or in print form at your local music store).[1]

Another challenge inherent in this approach is that contemporary examples become obsolete rather quickly. Teachers committed to using easily recognized popular tunes must constantly update their examples (for more on this point, see Stephenson 2009). The examples included in this chapter all worked well with a class of undergraduates in 2007. I offer them here to readers in hopes that they and their students will find them useful for at least some time to come. Additional examples of popular songs that can be used to demonstrate these and other topics are provided in an appendix at the end of this chapter.

GENERAL PRINCIPLES: A HOW-TO GUIDE

When using popular songs as examples, I usually followed a four-step method:

1. I verbally introduced the recording ("This song was part of the soundtrack for a hit movie called *X*; have any of you seen it?") and then played the song through once.
2. I presented an onscreen projection of the relevant portion of the sheet-music transcription, showing the students exactly where the notes we were going to listen for occurred. I then presented the technical term for the concept demonstrated by this group of notes and explained how it functioned in the larger musical context. Essentially, this step constituted the core of my teaching for each topic.
3. I played the recording again with the transcription still on the screen so that the students could both hear and see how this theoretical concept worked in real music.
4. I distributed an exercise sheet, which allowed students to practice identifying and constructing examples of the concept for themselves. After some minutes of working through the exercises, I presented the same theoretical concept in an art-music example from the *Norton Scores*. By this time, students were usually able to recognize and make sense of the concept in a less familiar musical idiom.

Readers may want to expand or alter these four steps but, in doing so, should keep the following points in mind. First, a standard piano/guitar/vocal transcription of your chosen pop song will likely be useful. The separation of melody and harmony is a helpful feature when emphasizing melodic movement or isolating a chord progression. Note that this type of score includes chord names written above the staff. I usually erased these markings since often one of our goals was to determine how best to identify a given chord or progression. However, near the end of the semester, I left the chord names in the score. The students were, at that point, familiar with Roman-numeral chord notation and were able to compare this system with the chord symbols in the sheet music. They discovered that popular music often interprets and designates note groupings differently—an important first step to understanding other analytical approaches to music.

Secondly, teachers using this method should be careful to choose recordings that feature a relatively transparent texture so that students can easily hear the four layers usually present in pop instrumentations: melody, harmony, bass, and percussion. Recordings that feature a slow tempo or a slow rate of harmonic change are particularly accessible to students who are listening actively for a particular sequence of pitches. Most importantly, the particular theoretical concept being examined should be easily locatable in the song's form. In many of the examples below, the relevant melodic or harmonic structure occurs at the beginning or end of the chorus. Focusing on a musical moment that occurs at or near a point of structural demarcation allows students to recognize and isolate that moment more easily than in the middle of a phrase or section. Of course, if a good example is buried in the middle of a song, the lyrics can help the students locate it without too much trouble (which is yet another advantage to using English-language pop songs to demonstrate theoretical concepts to English-language students).

SAMPLE LESSONS

Diatonic Major Scale

The diatonic major scale is a more abstract theoretical construct than many of the other concepts outlined below. Students need to learn this scale, as well as other scales, but they may be hard-pressed to understand why. Providing examples of complete scales used in real music is often helpful. Many readers will, I imagine, recall that the Christmas carol "Joy to the World" begins with a descending diatonic major scale. The "Pas de Deux" from Tchaikovsky's *The Nutcracker* ballet is another well-known example from art music. An example of a descending major scale used in popular music is the bass line at the beginning of Procol Harum's "Whiter Shade of Pale." Another example, this time in the melody, is the verse of the Beach Boys' "Heroes and Villains," which begins on scale degree 4 and descends through more than an octave, ending first on scale degree 2 and then repeating to end on the tonic. The notes of the scale are not presented in immediate succession; many of the pitches are repeated, but the melody moves inexorably down from one note to the next.

As an example of the ascending form, I suggest presenting Leonard Cohen's well-known and oft-recorded song, "Hallelujah."[2] This song is in strophic form, with each strophe constructed in *ab* form. The *a* section features a repeated phrase in which the melody reiterates the dominant and the submediant, while the underlying harmony moves I–vi. During the *b* section, the melody outlines an ascending major scale, from mediant to mediant. As in the Beach Boys example, many of the notes are repeated before they move to the next degree. Here is where having a piano/guitar/vocal score is immensely helpful: students looking at the *b* section melody in isolation may be tempted to identify this as a Phrygian scale. However, seeing the notes in the context of the diatonic chords that accompany them will clarify the function of these notes.

Lesson extension: the class can revisit this example after learning how diatonic harmonies are built on the various degrees of the scale. The lyrics to the first verse are "Well it goes like this / the fourth, the fifth / the minor fall and the major lift / a baffled king composing hallelujah." Students can decipher an added layer of musical meaning to the lyrics: the notes of the melody are harmonized by the chords named. "The fourth" is part of the IV chord, "the fifth" is part of the V chord, "the minor fall" is part of the (minor) vi chord, and "the major lift" returns to the (major) IV chord. The teacher may wish to describe this as a very specific and musically sophisticated example of the technique of word painting and then trace this compositional technique back to madrigals written in the 16th century.

Intervals

When I developed these lessons, the professor in charge of the course had students learn intervals by identifying them in real melodies—plainchant melodies more than 1,000 years old. I followed the same principle but used the melody from a popular song instead. The melody of Sophie B. Hawkins's "As I Lay Me Down" features most of the diatonic intervals, including the unison and the octave, although this latter interval appears in outline form only at the end of the first phrase in the verse. The intervals in the first phrase of the chorus are: ↑ P5, ↓ m6, ↑ m6, ↓ m7, ↑ m6, ↓ m3, ↓ M2, ↓ m2, ↑ M3, ↓ M2. The beginning of this phrase is more disjunct than is typical of popular songs. Teachers will find it worthwhile to have students identify the intervals in both the verse and the chorus in their entirety. This exercise will also demonstrate that although all sizes of intervals are used in compositional practice, small intervals such as seconds and thirds generally predominate in vocal genres.

Lesson extension: this song modulates from the tonic key of B-flat major to bIII (D-flat major) at the bridge. Things become even more interesting with the subsequent key change to E major (enharmonically F-flat major). When studying enharmonic modulations, students can analyze and compare these two successive moves to the flat mediant.

Tonic, Subdominant, and Dominant Chords

A useful example to demonstrate the primary triads is "The Rose," which was most famously recorded by Bette Midler. (I used Bianca Ryan's version with my students.) "The Rose" is a strophic *aaba* song form, and the *a* section consists of a circular progression that begins and ends on the tonic. The chord pattern of the *a* section is: one bar of tonic (I), one bar of dominant (V), half a bar each of subdominant (IV) and dominant, and one bar of tonic. The tempo is slow; the accompaniment generally consists of block chords falling heavily on the beat, and chord changes almost always occur on strong beats, usually on the first beat of each bar. Therefore, the chord movement is easily perceived.

Conveniently, most published scores for this song are in C major, so students encountering these chords for the first time can analyze them without the added complication of a key signature. In the particular piano/guitar/vocal score that I use (McBroom 1977), the piano accompaniment features the roots of the chords in the left hand, played as whole notes, with the rest of the chord tones filled in by the right hand. This makes the chords easy for students to see as well as hear. It is worth noting, however, that most scores of this song show the subdominant and dominant chords in inverted form; teachers can explain the significance of this during the next lesson (see below).

The texture of "The Rose" is simple enough that students can perform this song. Pianists can easily play the accompaniment, and even non-pianists can manage it in teams of three: each student can be assigned to play one of the three chords when it appears in the progression—even beginners can play root-position triads easily enough, using two hands.

Students can compare this progression to the one used in "Kiss the Girl," an Academy-Award nominated song from the movie *The Little Mermaid*. This is another song that uses nothing but tonic, subdominant, and dominant chords in the harmony. The verses are based on the 12-bar blues chord pattern (see example 5.1), a harmonic progression that has provided the foundation for thousands of blues, rock, and pop songs for more than a century.

Other songs that follow this pattern, using dominant-seventh chords instead of triads, are Bill Haley's "Rock around the Clock," Chuck Berry's "Roll over Beethoven," and the Beatles' "Birthday." Little Texas's recording of "Kiss the Girl" is especially helpful as an introductory example because the bass line, which moves from one root-position chord to another, is easy to hear.

Lesson extension: the lesson built on "The Rose" (mentioned above) can be extended to include chords built on other degrees of the scale. The *b* section of the strophe continues in the same style but includes iii and vi[7] chords. Another very common pattern including the vi chord is the "Heart and Soul" progression I–vi–IV–V, which is especially common in doo-wop and 1950's pop. It is used for the Five Satins' "In the Still of the Night," Ben E. King's "Stand By Me," the chorus of the Beatles' "Happiness Is a Warm

Example 5.1. Basic 12-bar blues pattern

I	I	I	I
IV	IV	I	I
V	V[7]	I	I

Gun," the verses of the Beatles' "Octopus's Garden" and Led Zeppelin's "D'yer Mak'er," and many other songs.

Inverted Chords

Although root-position chords are far more common than any other chord inversions in popular music, inverted chords are not too difficult to find. One example comes from "Trust Me (This Is Love)," recorded by Amanda Marshall. This song begins with a guitar playing the chords that underlie the chorus. This series of chords includes the first inversions of the tonic, subdominant, and dominant chords. The bass line is given below in example 5.2. Note that students will hear this chord progression many times throughout the song, so they will have repeated chances to recognize inverted chords in context. Interestingly, when the chorus occurs after the bridge (at 3:16 on the recording), Marshall sings the first two lines without harmonic accompaniment. Students can fill in the texture at this point by playing the chord progression they have learned, thereby reinforcing their understanding of how these chords support the melody.

"'Till Kingdom Come" by Coldplay features a clearly audible $^6_4$ chord at an easily identified cadence at the end of the chorus. It is a good example to use with students who are learning to listen for chord relationships because the entire verse is based on the tonic chord, making the tonal center of the piece easy to hear and remember. The bass guitar enters after the first verse. The bass is easy to follow in the texture as it plays the root of each chord until it arrives at the I^6_4–V–I cadence, when it plays the fifth scale degree. At the same time, the rhythm guitar and voice state the notes of the tonic chord, followed by the dominant.

Lesson extension: because the verse of "'Till Kingdom Come" is built on the I chord, it is easy to identify the three melodic pitches that belong to the tonic triad and then identify and categorize all of those that do not. Therefore, this song is useful for learning or reviewing nonharmonic tones.

Nonharmonic Tones: Passing Tones, Neighbor Notes, Suspensions, Anticipations, and Pedals

Studying a piano/guitar/vocal score of "The Rose" (discussed above in the context of primary triads), students can perceive not only the chord

Example 5.2. Amanda Marshall, "Trust Me (This Is Love)," opening bass line cadential 6/4 chord

Example 5.3.   Amanda McBroom, "The Rose," first phrase

progression underlying the melody but also how the melody relates to those chords. Thus, students can see and hear how nonharmonic tones work in real music. The first phrase, given below in example 5.3, contains a passing tone (P), an upper neighbor tone (N), and a suspension (S).

There are many examples of anticipations in this song; some singers use them more liberally than others, so students will identify them in various places depending on the recording chosen. Virtually every recording, however, contains an anticipation at the very end of the strophe as the harmony moves from V back to I (see example 5.4). The melody anticipates the return to the tonic pitch, moving from *re* to *do* (scale degree 2 to 1) on the penultimate syllable of the verse.

A clear example of an incomplete neighbor (Inc N or IN) occurs in the verses of "Save the Best for Last," recorded by Vanessa Williams. In each statement of the verse, the third note in both the second phrase and the fourth phrase is an incomplete neighbor. Here the melody outlines the tonic triad, and as it leaps upward to the third of the chord, it first lands on the pitch above. The incomplete neighbor is particularly easy to spot when Williams sings the tagline of the song. This motivic pitch sequence recurs frequently throughout the song, so students have many opportunities to hear the incomplete neighbor tone, internalize it, and sing along with it.

Example 5.4.   Amanda McBroom, "The Rose," last cadence of strophe

Among the types of nonharmonic tones, students seem to find it most difficult to understand the suspension. Luckily, examples of these abound in songs that students will instantly recognize. One is "Because You Loved Me," originally part of the soundtrack for the movie *Up Close and Personal*, recorded by Celine Dion. The easiest to hear suspension occurs during the last line of the chorus, which states the song's title. The melody note for "you," which is the fifth of the V chord or the supertonic degree of the key, is reiterated on the word "loved" on the first beat of the final measure. The melody then falls a whole tone to the tonic, creating a 2–1 suspension.

Martina McBride's "Independence Day" contains a clear example of an upward-resolving suspension in the first phrase, which is repeated later in the verse. Here, the melody is almost completely static: it focuses on only two pitches, and the second is the resolution of the suspension. The melody begins on the fifth of the tonic chord, reiterates this as the harmony, changes to the subdominant, and finally resolves the dissonance by moving upward to the sixth degree of the scale (the third of the subdominant), creating a 2–3 suspension over the root of IV.

A pedal tone is featured in the introduction and through the verse of Lionel Richie's "Hello." The song is in the diatonic natural minor (or the Aeolian mode), and the pedal tone is the fifth degree of the scale (the dominant degree). It is played on the beat or sustained over a i–VII–VI–VII–VI–i progression that repeats four times through the verse. In the recording, we hear this tone in the middle register, but in the score I used (Richie 1984), the pedal point is the only note played on the piano by the right hand. It is, therefore, isolated on the page and easy for students to spot. A more unusual subtonic pedal is sustained through a very similar progression, i–VII–VI–VII, at the beginning of the verses in Blue Öyster Cult's "Don't Fear the Reaper."

Once students have learned to identify a pedal tone, they will be able to comprehend a pedal tone in the bass voice. In art music, pedal tones occur most frequently in the bass since they derive from the pedal keyboard on an organ. One example of a tonic pedal occurs at the beginning of Martha and the Vandellas' "Dancing in the Street." Another easily accessible pop music example is Dan Hill's "Sometimes When We Touch." During the introduction and the first four measures of the verse of this song, the tonic pitch is sustained in the bass while the melody and accompaniment move freely above it. A harmonic reduction of the first phrase is given below in example 5.5.

Seventh Chords

"How Deep Is Your Love," recorded by the Bee Gees, is replete with examples of seventh chords. Students can quickly spot them in the sheet

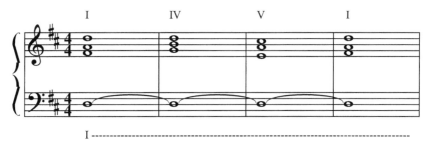

Example 5.5.   Dan Hill and Barry Mann, "Sometimes When We Touch," harmonies in first phrase. Words by Dan Hill; music by Barry Mann. © 1977 Sony/ATV Music Publishing and Mann and Weil Songs. All rights administered by Sony/ATV Music Publishing, 8 Music Square West, Nashville, TN 37203. International copyright secured. All rights reserved. Reprinted by permission of Hal Leonard Corporation.

music as they occur in almost every measure. The short introduction, for example, includes the I^{maj7} and the IV^{maj7} chords. The first phrase moves from tonic to iii^7 and then down a step to ii^7. Note that the melodic pitches on "morn-ing" and "sun" are the sevenths of those chords, so it is particularly easy for students to hear and sing the seventh above the root in the first phrase. The second phrase begins on a secondary dominant, V^7/ii, which resolves to a ii^7 that sets up the final chord of the phrase, V^{13}.

Two more contemporary examples come from the British band Coldplay. The group's song "The Scientist" features a chord progression that repeats four times through the verse; this progression begins with a minor seventh chord built on the submediant degree (vi^7). The chord progression is easily audible since the accompaniment to the melody (at least at the beginning) is dominated by block chords played on each beat.

For a chord progression that begins with a major seventh, listen to Coldplay's "Don't Panic." The most useful recording of this brief song comes from the soundtrack for the movie *Garden State*. On that recording—more clearly than on Coldplay's album version—the opening F^{maj7} chord is easily audible. This chord, which is VI^7 in the context of the home key of A minor, is also the concluding chord in the progression that shapes the verse.

Understanding seventh chords leads naturally to learning the form and function of the dominant seventh chord. "When I Get Where I'm Going," recorded by Brad Paisley and Dolly Parton, is useful in this regard because, like so many of the other songs mentioned, the recording features a transparent texture, making it easy to hear and identify what the voices and instruments are doing. The last line of the chorus—a spot that is easy to pinpoint—is harmonized by a V^7–I cadence. Importantly, at this point, the melody consists of the fourth scale degree (fa) falling to the third (*mi*), making it easy for students to hear the resolution of the dissonance.

Secondary Dominants

The song "I Dreamed a Dream" from *Les Misérables*, which never really faded into obscurity, vaulted to super-prominence not very long before this volume went to press when Susan Boyle performed it on the television show *Britain's Got Talent*. It is particularly useful for teaching secondary dominants. As Boyle performs it, "I Dreamed a Dream" begins in E-flat major. The first eight bars, which are diatonic to E-flat major, repeat and then the *b* section begins with "But the tigers come at night" (the chord pattern in shown in example 5.6). The first melody note in this section, which happens on the downbeat, is an E-natural. This note is the leading tone of ii (F minor), harmonized with the secondary dominant V/ii, which resolves to F minor in due course in the following measure. The placement of the non-diatonic E-natural in the melody, at the beginning of a new section and after so much emphasis on E-flat, makes for a very recognizable secondary dominant. Moreover, this section continues with a string of secondary dominants.

Lesson extension: another accessible example of secondary dominants is "Lady in Red," originally recorded by Chris de Burgh in the mid-1980s. Exactly halfway through the chorus, the harmony moves to the dominant of the subdominant (V^7/IV), which resolves to the expected IV and then to the dominant of the submediant (V^7/vi), resolving to vi.

Circle of Fifths

Like the diatonic major scale, the circle of fifths is a theoretical concept that students do not often hear operating in real music. It occurs more frequently in classical music and jazz than in popular music (for example, two well-known jazz standards that begin with this pattern are Harold Arlen's "Fly Me to the Moon" and Jerome Kern's "All the Things You Are"). However, Gloria Gaynor's well-known disco anthem "I Will Survive" consists of a repeating minor-key circle of fifths. The progression begins on the tonic; at each change of harmony, the root of the chord falls a fifth, finally landing on the dominant. The chords change precisely on the first beat of each measure, so the pattern is easy to follow.

Even students who are not adept on piano can play this bass line along with the recording. Using one finger from each hand, anyone can easily count up a fourth or down a fifth to find the next note in the pattern. Another example is The Beatles' "You Never Give Me Your Money," which uses

	V^7/ii		ii		V^7/ii		II = V/V	
	V		i		V		I	

Example 5.6. Alain Boublil, Jean-Marc Natel, and Claude-Michel Schönberg, "I Dreamed a Dream," chord pattern in *b* section

the same circle of fifths, but instead of ending on the dominant, it wraps back around to conclude on the tonic.

Modal Mixture

For millennial students, Elvis Costello's recording of "She," a beautiful *aaba* form song that was featured in the movie *Notting Hill*, is probably the best-known. Almost all of chords in the *a* section can be analyzed as belonging to the home key (diatonic major). One exception is shown in example 5.7. Midway through the *a* section, the dominant seventh of ii appears at the lyric "price I have to pay." This resolves to ii as the next phrase begins, but then the unexpected happens: at the text "song that summer sings," the melody note, which is the fourth scale degree, is harmonized with a minor chord. This is IV^{b3} or minor iv. The third of the chord, which is normally major in a major key, has been lowered by a half-step to create a minor chord. We can think of this chord as being borrowed from the parallel minor mode in an instance of modal mixture.

The Foo Fighters' recording of "Learn to Fly," which is also a good example of modal mixture, does not meet the criteria I outlined above. Heavily distorted guitars are integral to the sound in this song, so the texture is intentionally fuzzy rather than transparent. However, the chord changes are clear enough, particularly after students have had a chance to follow the sheet music or a chord chart. The song, which is firmly rooted in B major, uses modal mixture, incorporating several chords that are borrowed from the parallel minor key, B minor. The verse is built on a repeated I–Vm–IV progression. Students will be able to easily hear the flattened scale degree 7 that is part of the minor dominant (F-sharp minor) because it is part of the melody. The chorus continues in this vein and then cadences with bVI–bVII–I. The flat submediant and the subtonic are diatonic to B-natural minor or B Aeolian, but the concluding tonic reestablishes B major.

Example 5.7.   Charles Aznavour and Herbert Kretzmer, "She," excerpt from *a* section
As a material consideration for the rights granted herein Licensee agrees to accord the following credit: "SHE" (Theme From the BBC/TV Series *Seven Faces of Woman*) Lyric by Herbert Kretzmer; Music by Charles Aznavour © Copyright 1974 (renewed) Standard Music Ltd., London, England. TRO—Essex Music International, Inc., New York, controls all publication rights for the U.S.A. and Canada. International Copyright Secured. Made in U.S.A. All Rights Reserved Including Public Performance for Profit. Used by Permission.

Modulation

Many popular songs have sections in different but closely related keys. An example is "One Sweet Day," recorded by Mariah Carey and Boyz II Men. The song begins in A-flat major, and the music underlines this tonal center through two statements of the verse and chorus—for example, the melody begins with and frequently returns to a *ti-do* motive (leading-tone to tonic). The bridge, however, modulates to the relative minor (F minor), then back to the tonic key, and then again to F minor. This is easy to hear in the recording and to see in the score because of the presence of the new leading tone, E-natural. Note, however, that the notated melody in the standard sheet music does not come close to capturing the singers' work on the recording. Teachers can take advantage of this by initiating a discussion of the limitations of notation, which is probably a needed corrective in a class that focuses so often on the "right" and "wrong" ways of notating music.

"One Sweet Day" modulates to the relative minor, which is the key closest to the home key (sharing a key signature and pitch collection) and, therefore, effects a smooth tonal transition. Eric Clapton's "Tears in Heaven" also modulates at the bridge, but in this case, it moves to a more distant key, bVII. The verse and the chorus are in A major, but the bridge section stands out starkly in G major. The previous tonic, A major, is transformed into a minor ii chord in the bridge, and the new tonic, G, appears for the very first time here. The bridge ends with the home dominant, E, leading back into A major.

Lesson extension: "One Sweet Day" can also be used to demonstrate common-tone modulation to a remote key. Immediately after the bridge discussed above, the chorus returns ("And I know," etc.) but this time in the new key of B major, enharmonically C-flat, which is the flat mediant of the home key, A-flat major. The music pivots at this point, where both the melody and the bass are on E-flat, which has previously functioned as the dominant. This pitch can be written as a D-sharp, and indeed it is in the published sheet music, beginning at the next downbeat. This respelling of the pitch reflects that its function has changed, and it is now the third of the tonic chord. This is an enharmonic change, a more advanced concept to present to theory students.

Writing Four-Part Homophony

One of the best-selling hip-hop singles of all time, "Gangsta's Paradise" by Coolio, was featured in the movie *Dangerous Minds*. It is useful as a music-theory example because it features an SATB choir singing a four-measure ostinato in C minor. Students will be able to hear the chordal movement

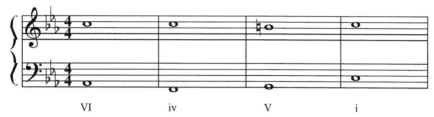

VI   iv   V   i

Example 5.8. Coolio, "Gangsta's Paradise," outer voices of backing vocals. From the motion picture *Dangerous Minds*. Words and music by Stevie Wonder, Doug Rasheed, Artis Ivey, and Larry Sanders. © 1985 Jobete Music, Black Bull Music, Universal—Songs of Polygram International, Madcastle Muzic, T-Boy Music Publishing, Boo-Daddy Music, 2 Fargone Music, and Large Variety Music. All rights reserved. International copyright secured. Used by permission. Reprinted by permission of Hal Leonard Corporation.

repeated over and over as the song progresses. I gave my students the two outer voices and asked them to fill in the inner voices, as shown below in example 5.8. Teachers can as easily give just the bass line or just the soprano line with the chord symbols and have students write the three remaining parts. As with many of the other examples included here, "Gangsta's Paradise" is intended as a bridge to the less-familiar work of J. S. Bach, whose chorales are so often used as the basis for part-writing exercises.

Motive

"You Needed Me," originally recorded by Anne Murray in 1978, is a clear and well-known example of a melody built on a recurring motive. Millennial students will likely be familiar with the more recent recording by Boyzone. This song begins with an upward-leaping motive of a repeated pitch followed by an ascending octave, from upbeat to downbeat, which is repeated eight times before the verse concludes.

This song is a useful example because the motivic statement is so simple and so clear and because the verse melody consists of almost nothing but this motive. If students track how many times they hear the opening motive and then look at the notation, they will discover that what they heard as a pattern is not, in fact, precisely the same each time. The song demonstrates two important principles: that motives are often made up of a combination of characteristic melodic and rhythmic elements and that motives retain their distinctive character if, in each iteration, the rhythm is the same and the general melodic contour is the same. Students can be encouraged to bring in other examples of repeated motives, which are not difficult to find in the popular-music repertoire.

Example 5.9. Terry Gilkyson, Richard Dehr, and Frank Miller, "Memories Are Made of This," sequence in verse. Words and music by Richard Dehr, Frank Miller, and Terry Gilkyson. © 1955 (renewed 1983) EMI Blackwood Music. All rights reserved. International copyright secured. Used by permission. Reprinted by permission of Hal Leonard Corporation.

Sequence

"Memories Are Made of This" may strike readers as inappropriate for this collection of current popular-music examples. Indeed, Dean Martin's original recording is too old to be considered contemporary, but the song itself remains current, having been recorded in the 1990s by Johnny Cash and still more recently by an Italian electronica band called Kirlian Camera. Martin's iconic recording is useful because, as in most of the above examples, he articulates the notes of the melody clearly, making it easy for students to hear the specific pitches. Once students have learned what a motive is, they are ready to learn how a motive, repeated at successive pitch levels, becomes a sequence. "Memories Are Made of This" contains a straightforward example. In the verse, just before the tagline, the melody consists of a simple motive that is repeated four times, each time beginning one tone lower, as shown in example 5.9.

The essential components of this motive are its even rhythm, its slightly syncopated position on the second and third beats of each bar, and the repeated pitch. The sequence is unified by the larger-scale repetition in the text of the words "one" and "some" on the first note of each motive.

CONCLUSION

Throughout this chapter, I have made the case for using pop and rock songs to teach traditional music theory concepts, to serve as a bridge of sorts to the art-music repertoire of the common-practice period. Following this approach, students will learn the now centuries-old concepts that are central to traditional music theory classes in the context of music that is immediately familiar. They will, therefore, be able to assimilate their new knowledge quickly, relate it to their own musical lives, and bridge the historical gap that exists between themselves and the music in which these concepts were first codified.

But is it appropriate, as one of my interlocutors commented, to use popular music as "bait on a hook to get students into the really 'important,' deeper music of the classics?"[3] This is a valid question. After all, pop and rock songs are part of a widely appreciated tradition that is fundamentally different from classical music, and the uniqueness of that tradition is apparent even at the structural level. Harmonies are organized differently in pop and rock, and responsible teachers should communicate this to students. Many do, of course, in rock and pop music theory courses offered at institutions around America. But what I have called "traditional" theory courses are much more widespread.

Teachers of such courses will need to address this issue with their students. They will need to explain that while contemporary popular music and historical art music have much in common and can, therefore, be usefully examined in the same theory class, analysis of pop music has given rise to an independent theory that merits study on its own terms. However, as Ken Stephenson, an important pop-music theorist, points out, "the interaction of melody and harmony in rock is best understood in relation to melody and harmony in Western music over the ages."[4] The approach I have outlined here—that is, using American pop songs to exemplify concepts first developed in the art music of Europe—can, therefore, serve as a beginning point for understanding the theories of both the common-practice period and our own times.

APPENDIX: POPULAR-MUSIC EXAMPLES
FOR UNDERGRADUATE THEORY TOPICS
compiled by Nicole Biamonte

Chord Types

Augmented Dominant

Gershwin, "Nice Work if You Can Get It," opening: $VI^{\#5}$–$bVI^{\#5}$–$V^{\#5}$
Chuck Berry, "School Days," opening chords
The Beatles, "Oh! Darling," opening chord
The Beatles, "I Want You," end of intro

Augmented Sixth

Ellington, "Sentimental Mood," end of chorus
The Beatles, "Mean Mr. Mustard," end of bridge

Common-Tone Diminished Seventh

Jobim, "Corcovado," end of *a* phrase
Queen, "Bohemian Rhapsody," intro and outro

Linear Bass Patterns

Descending Stepwise Bass—diatonic tetrachord in major

Eric Clapton, "Wonderful Tonight," verse: I–V^6–IV^6–V
The Who, "Pinball Wizard," verse: I$^{\text{sus4-3}}$–bVII$^{\text{sus4-3}}$–bVI$^{\text{sus4-3}}$–V$^{\text{sus4-3}}$

Descending Stepwise Bass—diatonic tetrachord in minor

Ray Charles, "Hit the Road, Jack": i–(P)–bVI–V^7
Joe McCoy, "Why Don't You Do Right?" verse: i–(P)–bVI–V^7
The Animals, "Don't Let Me Be Misunderstood," verse: i–bVII–bVI–V
The Beach Boys, "Good Vibrations," verse: i–bVII–bVI–V
Del Shannon, "Runaway," verse: i–bVII–bVI–V^7
Stray Cats, "Stray Cat Strut": i–bVII^7–bVI^7–V^7

Descending Stepwise Bass—diatonic octave

Procol Harum, "Whiter Shade of Pale": I–(P)–vi–(P)–IV–(P)–ii^7–(P) (= desc. third
     sequence)
James Taylor, "Your Smiling Face": I–V^6–vi–I$^6_4$–IV–I^6–ii^7
Billy Joel, "Piano Man," verse: I–(P)–IV^6–I$^6_4$–IV–I^6–V^7/V–V (seventh, not octave)

Descending Stepwise Bass—chromatic tetrachord

Elton John, "Sorry Seems to Be the Hardest Word," chorus: i–V^6–III$^6_4$–vi$^{\text{o}7}$–iv^6–V^7
The Beatles, "Being for the Benefit of Mr. Kite," verse: i–V$^6_{\#3}$–bVII–ii$^6_4$–V

Ascending Stepwise Bass

The Beatles, "Here, There, and Everywhere," verse: I–ii–iii–IV
The Beatles, "Getting Better," chorus: I–ii–iii–IV
Bob Dylan, "Like a Rolling Stone," verse: I–ii–iii–IV–V
Billy Joel, "Uptown Girl," verse: I–ii–I^6–IV–V^7

Sequences

Descending Fifth Sequence

Arlen, "Fly Me to the Moon," *a* section: i^7–iv^7–bVII$^{\Delta7}$–bIII$^{\Delta7}$–bVI$^{\Delta7}$–ii$^{\text{ø}7}$–V$^{7\flat9}$–i^7
The Beatles, "You Never Give Me Your Money," verse: i^7–iv^7–bVII^7–bIII–bVI$^{\Delta7}$–ii$^{\text{ø}7}$–
     V^7–i
Gloria Gaynor, "I Will Survive": i–iv–bVII–bIII$^{\Delta7}$–bVI$^{\Delta7}$–ii$^{\text{ø}7}$–V^7
Cat Stevens, "Wild World," verse: i–IV^7–bVII–bIII$^{\Delta7}$–bVI–iv–V
Simon and Garfunkel, "Mrs. Robinson," bridge: VI^7–II^7–V^7–I–IV
Blood, Sweat, and Tears, "Spinning Wheel," verse: VI^7–II^7–V^7–I

Ascending Fifth Sequence

Jimi Hendrix (the Leaves), "Hey Joe": bVI–bIII–bVII–IV–I^7
Rocky Horror Picture Show soundtrack, "Time Warp," refrain: bVI–bIII–bVII–IV–I
Deep Purple, "Hush," chorus: bVI–bIII–bVII–IV–I^5

Descending Third Sequence

Procol Harum, "Whiter Shade of Pale": I–(P)–vi–(P)–IV–(P)–ii^7–(P) (= desc. step-wise bass)

Ascending Third Sequence

The Animals, "House of the Rising Sun," antecedent phrase: i–bIII–IV–bVI–i–bIII–V

Paired-Fifth Sequences

The Eagles, "Hotel California," verse: i–V, bVII–IV, bVI–bIII, iv–V
Aerosmith, "Cryin'": I–V, vi–iii, IV–I, V (modified Pachelbel Canon progression)

Other Chord Progressions

Plagal Cadence

The Beatles, "Let It Be," end of verse and chorus
America, "Sister Golden Hair," end of verse and chorus
Elton John, "Rocket Man," refrain
Pink Floyd, "Nobody Home," end of verse

Deceptive Cadence

Paul Simon, "Still Crazy after All These Years," refrain: V–vi, then V–iv
The Beatles, "P.S. I Love You," end of verse: bVI, then I
The Beatles, "I Want to Hold Your Hand," penultimate phrase: III^7 (V^7/vi)

Cadential 6/4

Elvis Presley, "Can't Help Falling in Love," end of verse
Eric Clapton, "Tears in Heaven," end of first two phrases
The Doobie Brothers, "Long Train Running," refrain

Modulations

Diatonic Third

The Beatles, "When I'm 64," bridge: vi
Diana Ross, "Ain't No Mountain High Enough," bridge: III

Chromatic Third

The Beatles, "You're Going to Lose That Girl," bridge: bIII
The Beach Boys, "Wouldn't It Be Nice," bridge: bVI
Bonnie Tyler, "Total Eclipse of the Heart": i–bIII–bV–bVII

Modes

Dorian (i–IV)

Santana, "Evil Ways" (1969)
The Doors, "Riders on the Storm" (1971), main riff
Styx, "Renegade" (1978), verse
Pink Floyd, "Another Brick in the Wall" (1979), verse

Phrygian (1^5–$b2^5$)

Alice in Chains, "Would?" (1992), verse
Tool, "Sober" (1993), chorus

Mixolydian (I–bVII)

The Doors, "The End" (1967), *a* section
Steppenwolf, "Born to Be Wild" (1968), chorus
J. J. Cale, "Cocaine" (1976), verse
Grateful Dead, "Fire on the Mountain" (1978)

Aeolian (i–bVII)

The Doors, "Break on Through" (1967)
Deep Purple, "Child in Time" (1970)
Black Sabbath, "Paranoid" (1971), verse
R.E.M., "The One I Love" (1987) *a* section

Locrian (i^5–bV^5)

Black Sabbath, "Symptom of the Universe" (1975), intro and verse
Rush, "YYZ" (1981), intro

$\Delta7$ = major seventh
$ø7$ = half-diminished seventh (m7b5)
5 = power chord (open fifth)

NOTES

1. A number of the songs mentioned in this chapter are published in Evans and Lavender 1999, the anthology *Great Songs of the 20th Century: 1950–2000*.

2. I use Jeff Buckley's recording, and I also like k.d. lang's version. I avoid Cohen's own recordings because his distinctive parlando singing style sometimes obscures the pitches in his melodies. Buckley's version is the best for our purposes as he clearly enunciates each pitch of the ascending scale.

3. Martin Hatch, personal communication, September 2009.

4. Stephenson 2002, 74. See also Everett 2008, 192, for similar comments.

REFERENCES

Evans, Peter, and Peter Lavender, comps. 1999. *Great songs of the 20th century: 1950–2000*. Background notes by Michael Kennedy. London: Wise.

Everett, Walter. 2008. *The foundations of rock: From 'Blue Suede Shoes' to 'Suite: Judy Blue Eyes.'* Oxford: Oxford University Press.

Forney, Kristine, and Roger Hickman, eds. 2007. *The Norton scores*. 10th ed. New York: W. W. Norton.

McBroom, Amanda. 1977. The Rose. Warner-Tamerlane.

Piaget, Jean. 1954. *The construction of reality in the child*. Trans. Margaret Cook. New York: Basic Books.

Richie, Lionel. 1984. Hello. Brockman Music (ASCAP).

Singer, Dorothy G., and Tracey A. Revenson. 1978. *A Piaget primer: How a child thinks*. New York: New American Library.

Stephenson, Ken. 2002. *What to listen for in rock: A stylistic analysis*. New Haven: Yale University Press.

———. 2009. Popular music in the theory classroom. AP Central, College Board. http://apcentral.collegeboard.com/apc/members/homepage/36106.html.

6

Using Pop-Culture Tools to Reinforce Learning of Basic Music Theory as Transformations

James R. Hughes

INTRODUCTION

Pedagogical Philosophy

An idea often acknowledged but less often implemented in college class-rooms is that students learn better when presented with examples relevant to their everyday experiences. Examples that resonate with students' present and past experiences give them immediate opportunities to make active use of new concepts and ways of organizing and understanding information. In basic music-theory classes, much of the material presented (e.g., intervals, chords, tonality, modality, etc.) is readily demonstrated using examples from popular music familiar to students. Even somewhat more sophisticated concepts, such as musical transformations acting on musical spaces, can easily be illustrated with popular music.[1]

Students' sense of cultural identification with popular-music examples—and the concomitant learning value of such examples—is intensified when the students are challenged to find and share the examples themselves. Both the finding and sharing of such musical examples are facilitated by means of tools from contemporary popular culture—MP3s, iPods, Internet search engines, YouTube, video games, and so forth. Moreover, the use of pop-culture tools themselves (the medium) further contributes to the connections students make between the examples and their own everyday experiences (the message).

It is worth noting that the usefulness of pop-culture tools for finding and sharing examples is not confined to music classes. In mathematics classes on probability and statistics, for example, the relevance of course material can be demonstrated with examples drawn from online news sources (Hughes and Batakci 2006). Furthermore, students' engagement with the material in any course can be enhanced by assigning them to find and share their own "real world" examples of course material at work. Such assignments are now more feasible and immediately rewarding than ever before thanks to the speed and scope of online search engines.

Two serious issues that must be addressed at this point are copyright and reliability. With regard to copyright, it is an unfortunate (and, by now, well-known) fact that much of what is easily available on the Internet—particularly music and video content—has not been posted there legally.[2] Therefore, the convenience and spontaneity of using a search engine to obtain direct access to a musical example must be balanced with concern over whether such access is legitimate. Some ideas for handling copyright issues in a classroom setting are discussed below, but in general, the tension between convenience and legality is still far from being resolved in a satisfactory way.

The other serious issue, reliability of information, concerns the fact that not all information unearthed by search engines has been appropriately vetted for accuracy. Reliability of information is a concern to which students and instructors must be attuned under the rubric of "information literacy." But as long as one exercises due diligence, the presence of questionable information on the Internet also presents additional teaching opportunities. Often the "non-examples" students find are just as instructive as the examples, if not more so. A case in point is described below in the section on examples of particular chord types.

Importance of the Transformational Point of View

Basic music-theory courses have long included the study of such elements as rhythmic patterns, intervals, scales, chords, harmonic progression, tonality, modality, functional harmony, and voice leading. In these topics, the idea of mapping or measuring "musical space" is already present, albeit implicitly. On the other hand, a great deal of music-theoretical research in the past half century focuses more explicitly on musical spaces (usually pitch and, more recently, rhythm) and on the transformations that act on those spaces. Using methodologies inspired by contemporary mathematics, transformational theory in music focuses on the relationships between musical elements as functions or operations, rather than on the objects themselves. David Lewin, for example, was an early and prolific champion of the transformational perspective (Lewin 1987, 2007). Likewise, neo-Riemannian music theory represents a tonal branch of transformational theory, and recent geometrical approaches to harmony and voice leading explore mathematical spaces ("orbifolds") derived by collapsing or conflating all elements related by specific transformations (Callender, Quinn, and Tymoczko 2008). Although it is not reasonable to expect beginning students to understand transformational theory at the level of contemporary research, introducing the basic ideas of transformations on musical spaces in beginning-level courses—not in place of but in addition to traditional content—can help position students well for further study in music theory.

Pedagogical Context

In the spring semester of 2009, I taught an undergraduate honors course entitled "Mathematics in Music," which I designed under the auspices of an in-house grant program, Collaborative Interdisciplinary Scholarship Projects (CISP). The overall goal of the course, as stated in the course syllabus, was to deepen and enrich the creative experience of music by developing mathematical ways of understanding, analyzing, and synthesizing the elements of music (including but not limited to acoustics, tuning, theory, composition, and performance) on various levels. A secondary goal was to instill appreciation for the idea that the emotive and intellectual aspects of creative expression are intertwined parts of a related whole. I designed the course content to be primarily in music (in fact, it was approved to fulfill an institutional "creative expression" core curriculum requirement), with mathematical ideas introduced as appropriate means for solving problems or explaining structures. As such, the course is a natural venue for infusing traditional elements of basic music theory with the mathematical concepts of space and transformation.

All of the students in the class had at least some formal instruction on a musical instrument as well as ensemble experience; however, none of them was pursuing a major in music. On the other hand, all of the students were enrolled in the college-wide honors program and possessed appropriately well-developed study skills and academic maturity, which was a key factor in the success of a course relying on student-generated examples and discussion. I structured the course around a series of topics presented in collaborative worksheets, for which full and thoughtful class participation was an essential component.

BASICS OF MUSICAL SPACE AND TRANSFORMATIONS

Musical Space and Its Dimensions

In the first worksheet, in the context of reviewing notation for pitches and rhythms, I asked students to consider a standard musical staff as a two-dimensional space, with the vertical dimension corresponding to pitch and the horizontal axis corresponding to time (fig. 6.1).

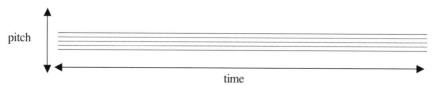

Figure 6.1. A two-dimensional musical space

Although this first consideration may seem somewhat obvious, several of the students noted its novelty to them, as demonstrated by the following online discussion board posting: "I had never thought of the staff as a sort of discrete coordinate plane with pitch and time as the axes. Looking at it from this perspective allows me to visualize it better as I am more familiar with mathematical coordinate systems and discrete functions."[3]

Further along in the worksheet, I invited the students to consider variations on the idea of the staff as musical space. One possible variation is a percussion line where the pitch axis is suppressed, yielding a one-dimensional number line representing time, in which only rhythm is encoded. In other percussion lines, such as drum-kit notation, the vertical axis might be present but only loosely correlated with pitch, representing primarily timbre. Another possible variation is guitar tablature (an especially pertinent example since three of the students in the class had studied guitar, and for one it was the primary instrument). The horizontal axis represents time, as in previous examples, but the design of the instrument requires two additional dimensions to establish pitch location, one to specify the string (shown vertically, like staff lines) and one to specify the fret (represented by numbers in place of note heads).

Consideration of guitar tablature leads nicely to the pop-culture example of the simplified tablature-derived notation used in Guitar Hero and similar electronic games, which are ubiquitous in college dormitories and lounges and form part of the everyday experience of many students. In the worksheet, I asked the students to consider the game from a spatial point of view: "If you have played the video game Guitar Hero, describe the dimensions of the space where the game is played, and what they represent. How are they similar to standard music? How are they different?" Somewhat surprisingly, only a small number of the students explicitly mentioned in their responses the fact that Guitar Hero uses depth to represent time; that is, time flows toward the player, rather than horizontally as in most standard music notation. Hence, the "game space" is actually three-dimensional, although only two of these are used: rhythm is represented on the scrolling fretboard from the front to the back of the game space, and the horizontal dimension represents relative pitch with note buttons roughly analogous to fret location. The availability of a third dimension suggests reconsideration of the guitar tablature example—why not make use of a third dimension to represent fret location in tablature? The underlying point of the exercise, of course, is to stimulate students to think about other possible models for musical spaces that they may have encountered or might construct.

More generally, the idea of "musical space" can be demonstrated and developed in numerous ways and in a variety of educational contexts using pop-culture tools. In a class populated by mathematically well-prepared students (e.g., those familiar with analytic geometry), one could have them translate from music written in traditional staff notation to the coordinate plane typically used in mathematics. In such a context, a single musical line (or voice) would correspond to a function $f(t)$, where t represents time and $f(t)$ represents pitch. One could then invoke mathematical ways of analyzing and understanding functions and their graphs—intersections, extrema, slope, concavity, inflection points, and so forth—to describe and explain musical phenomena found in popular music familiar to the students. One could also explore other possible uses of a third (or even fourth!) dimension, such as overtone pattern, dynamic level, or moving images, as in music video.

With students more inclined to abstract mathematics, one could make use of the mathematically rigorous definitions of "function," "domain," and "range" to model musical phenomena such as rests, multiple voices in unison, and *divisi* of a single voice. Some care would be needed, in such a context, to distinguish between "set theory" as it is understood by music theorists (to apply only to pitch sets) and the mathematical notion of "set theory," which is much more general and foundational. At the other end of the educational spectrum, for example, with students majoring in elementary education, one could discuss the use of Cuisenaire rods, which are traditionally used to teach mathematical concepts of grouping and subdivision in the primary grades, to model rhythm with manipulatives (tangible objects that can be handled by students to facilitate understanding particular ideas).

Basic Tonal Theory Background: Intervals, Chords, and Progressions

Following consideration of the basic idea of "musical space," I had the students learn or review the basic ideas of intervals and chord types. I solicited examples from familiar music of various melodic intervals, which, in terms of the two-dimensional space described above, can be understood as transformations operating on notes both vertically (moving the pitch up or down) and horizontally (sounding the transformed note earlier or later in time). The students shared their examples in class, and we put to use the immediate availability of pop-culture tools. In a classroom equipped with a computer projection system and speakers, a student-suggested example— such as the opening of John Williams's *Star Wars* theme for an ascending perfect fifth or the opening of the Beatles' "Hey Jude" for a descending minor third—could be played for the class for discussion and verification or rejection. We compared suggested excerpts with intervals played via an online keyboard application;[4] one student even had such an "app" loaded onto his iPhone. At this point, the tension between the spontaneity of Internet searches and copyright concerns became acute. I cautioned students that they should obtain a legal copy of any example of recorded music presented to the class. I explained that playing a few seconds of a legally obtained recording in a closed classroom setting for purposes of educational discussion would arguably qualify as "fair use."[5]

We then focused solely on the vertical dimension of pitch: chords. In a subsequent worksheet, I asked the students to collect examples of various chord types occurring in music familiar to them. While major and minor triads were easy for the students to find, diminished and augmented triads presented more of a challenge—not surprisingly, given their relative rarity (especially in popular music) and dissonance in a tonal context. Although the intention of the exercise was to have students listen for the characteristic sound of each triad in familiar music, one student resorted to a pop-culture reflexive shortcut, the Google search engine, to fulfill the more difficult request for an example of an augmented triad. The result led to an interesting "teachable moment," regarding both the pitfalls of Internet searching (i.e., information literacy) and the ambiguities inherent in labeling chords. The example of an "augmented chord" offered by the search engine was among a collection of chords used in heavy-metal music, for which guitar tablature was included. Analysis of the guitar tablature indicated that only two-note chords were involved. (These are called "power chords" among rock musicians for reasons having to do with acoustics and distortion; specifically, power chords are triads without thirds, that is, open fifths or fourths, sometimes doubled at the octave.) The "augmented chord" in question was part of a progression that proceeded from a two-note "B chord" consisting of B and F-sharp to a two-note "B augmented chord" consisting of B and G. Class discussion centered on whether a two-note chord could be considered "augmented" at all since the assigned task had been to find an example of an augmented *triad*, with its characteristically ambiguous sound. I pointed out that in the absence of a D-sharp or other contextual information, most theorists would consider the combination of B and G to be part of a first-inversion G major chord or a second-inversion E minor chord. Nevertheless, the class acknowledged that the combination *could*, with the appropriate enharmonic renaming of G as F-double-sharp, be considered part of an augmented triad, especially given the prior establishment of the key of B. In terms of the intersection of popular culture and pedagogy, what is interesting is that the Internet search for familiar examples led to issues and discussion that would never have arisen otherwise. Since the ambiguous nature (and potential for misnaming) of the augmented chord is readily encountered elsewhere in more esoteric contexts, the example described here illustrates the potential for significant and complex theoretical issues to arise in a natural way when one invokes the power of search engines in the realm of pop culture.

The example just described suggests a broader opportunity for including similarly ambiguous or problematic examples. One could, as an exercise in a tonal music-theory course, have the students use online search engines to search for the commonly accepted names of various chord types and then analyze and critique the resulting instances for accuracy of terminology and clarity and correctness of explanation. Such an exercise would not only promote higher-level student engagement with the material in the form of critical thinking but also would be inherently interesting to students because of the pop-culture medium (web search engines) and message (examples found in popular music).

In the next worksheet, we reintroduced the horizontal dimension as expressed through chord progressions. I asked students to find examples of some common harmonic progressions. In class, I played excerpts of the examples suggested by the students, and we analyzed them to determine if they indeed represented the requested progression. What was surprising to me was not only the students' speed and accuracy in thinking of possible examples but also the variety of musical styles they presented. Examples ranged from the Five Satins' "In the Still of the Night" (1956), demonstrating IV–I at the end of the verse, to Don McLean's "American Pie" (1971), demonstrating V–vi, the second and third chords in the first verse, to Pearl Jam's cover of "Last Kiss" (1998), demonstrating I–vi–IV–V throughout each verse. Once again, the accessibility of the pop-culture medium made real-time, spontaneous, in-class consideration of all these examples, spanning almost half a century, possible.

Any course that includes tonal chord progressions could make use of pop-culture tools to enrich the set of available examples. The examples could be chosen in advance by the instructor, suggested in advance by students as part of an exercise, or, more exhilaratingly, sought collaboratively and spontaneously in class. The use of contemporary technology and its associated media is helpful in at least three ways: the medium itself connects the material to students' everyday lives, the examples found are familiar to the students, and access to the examples is speedy enough to obtain them in real time, during class.

Elementary Transformations

To reinforce the concept of transformations, in a subsequent worksheet, I provided exercises for demonstrating transformational relationships. Just

Solution:

Solution to a variation on the exercise where "one beat" is replaced by "one half beat," which is

particularly relevant to popular music since it makes extensive use of syncopation:

Figure 6.2.   Rhythmic shift transformation exercise

as pitch transpositions shift the pitch up or down, rhythmic shifts can move
a selected passage either forward or backward in time. Here is an example
demonstrating a rhythmic shift transformation: "Shift the following passage in the 'time' dimension forward by one beat, using ties as needed. Note
that this is (mathematically) exactly analogous with 'shifting' or transposition, which occurs in the other (i.e., 'pitch') dimension!" (fig. 6.2).

Other exercises were designed to focus on transposition of scales,
intervals, chords, and short passages and also inversion. The following
example highlights the difference between mirror inversion, a reflection
of exact pitch distances, and diatonic inversion, which is constrained to a
particular scale and, thus, reflects only generic pitch distances: "Write the
'mirror' inversion and the 'diatonic' inversion of the following melodic
fragment. For the diatonic inversion, you may assume the underlying
scale is G major" (fig. 6.3).

The value of these and similar exercises became more significant when
the students embarked on their own transcription projects, as described
below.

TRANSCRIPTION EXERCISE

Rationale

Transcription or dictation exercises in music have pedagogical value on
multiple levels. At a very basic level, they force students to review and apply notational conventions for encoding music in symbols. As ear-training
exercises, they help reinforce interval identification and rhythmic decod-

"Mirror" solution:

"Diatonic" solution:

Figure 6.3. Pitch inversion exercise

ing skills. On a more analytical level, the process of attempting to encode heard music, with its temporal component, in written symbols naturally leads students towards pattern recognition—in particular, those resulting from transformations such as rhythmic shifts and pitch transpositions and inversions.

Assignment

At the end of the unit on basic music theory, I assigned each student in the course an individualized transcription project. In a deliberate attempt to increase the students' sense of identification with the assignment, I asked each student to choose his or her own passage to transcribe. In this section, I provide more detailed discussion of the intention, parameters, and learning outcomes of the assignment.

I first defined music transcription for the students as converting music that is heard into standard written musical notation (i.e., mapping from aural to visual domains). Since transcription of a lengthy, fully orchestrated piece of music is a very long and demanding task, we restricted ourselves to transcription of a single line of music. Furthermore, to keep the task manageable, I only asked for transcription of between 20 and 30 seconds of music (roughly 4 to 16 measures, depending on the tempo and meter). In practice, the students generally ended up transcribing the first verse or half-verse of a popular song. There were so many initial questions from students relating to the required transcription length that next time I plan to specify the length in terms of a formal section, such as a verse or chorus, rather than absolute time.

As noted above, in order to promote a sense of ownership, motivation, and interest on the part of the students, I had them choose their own passages to transcribe, stipulating only that it be a passage familiar and of interest to them—but not one for which they had seen a transcription—with a clear melody line. I also explicitly required them to obtain a legal copy of a recording of the piece.

As a warm-up and orienting activity, students determined the key, appropriate key signature, meter, and appropriate time signature of the passage and chose the most suitable clef for transcription (in all cases, students chose the treble clef). I also had them determine whether there were one or more pick-up notes, or upbeats, at the beginning of the passage. The purpose of specifying these activities at the outset was both to encourage an efficient and timely start on the task and to emphasize the rather mathematical step of setting up the space, akin to choosing a coordinate system.

I required the final copy of the transcription to be neat and legible. At the outset, the students wrote their transcriptions by hand, but I later introduced them to the Sibelius software package (for which my institution has a site license), and some of the students opted to use it for later drafts. Finale or other notation programs, such as Noteworthy Composer, could be introduced in a similar manner. I allowed students to use an instrument to identify the first pitch of their excerpts but then exhorted them to find the remaining pitches just by identifying intervals. As the assignment progressed, I relented somewhat and authorized them to use an instrument to check their pitch-identification work but asked them to document how often they used an instrument to find pitches. My intention was to have students put to use the understanding they had gained of both pitch and rhythmic intervals as transformations acting on spaces to facilitate the transcription process.

Examples

All of the passages selected by students for transcription were from popular-music genres. Some, such as Nirvana's grunge anthem "Smells Like Teen Spirit," would now be considered classic rock. Others, such as Taylor Swift's "The Best Day" and "Fifteen," would be considered contemporary country; still others were from less well-established, aspiring artists, such as Ben Kweller's "On My Way." Most of the recordings were obtained by the students via iTunes, except for Kweller's, which is available from his own website. In addition to iTunes, MP3s are easily purchased and downloaded from sites such as Amazon, Rhapsody, Napster, and many others. The portability of the MP3 recording technology helped facilitate one-on-one help sessions with me, of which all the students took advantage. Because the passages consisted of "real" music and were chosen according to the students' own interests rather than to suit a particular pedagogical rubric, the students found the assignment quite difficult, despite their high level of motivation and interest. Most spent many hours and multiple help sessions with me on the assignment.

In the help sessions, I encouraged students to make use of transformational ideas to understand better the overall structure of a passage and to avoid "reinventing the wheel." On a basic level, I advised students to listen for instances of melodic or rhythmic repetition. Such repetition can be understood as a large-scale time shift, where the size of the shift is counted in measures, rather than in beats, as in the worksheet exercises. Most of the passages chosen by the students exhibited time shifts on this level. For example, the pitches and rhythms of the first four measures of the verse of Nirvana's "Smells Like Teen Spirit" are immediately repeated. Such an observation may seem obvious, yet—perhaps in an instance of "failing to see the forest for the trees"—nearly all of the students needed to be coached to recognize the repetition. Indeed, some students would arrive at a help session stuck on the second phrase of a passage, having already successfully transcribed the first melodically identical phrase. This demonstrates not only the usefulness of the concept of large-scale time shifts but also the need to reinforce these concepts through practice.

One might argue that formal repetition and rhythmic transformation are two distinct phenomena, but in keeping with the spirit and intention of the course, it is well worth noting that mathematically, they are both instances of the same type of transformation, differing only in the size of the shift. One might explain more fully using music-notation software with a "copy and paste" feature. The same tool can be used to create solutions to the "beat shift" exercises above (as indeed it was!) and to streamline the process of composition that includes simple repetition (I use such an expedient frequently when composing psalm settings for use in church). In this case, the technology in practice exactly matches the theoretical transformation.

In general, transcription in the time dimension (i.e., the rhythm) of the selected passages posed a greater challenge to the students than transcription in the pitch dimension, in no small part because of the prevalence of accent displacement, beat displacement, and other types of syncopation in popular music. Invoking transformational ideas was again useful in helping students to unravel the various rhythmic puzzles. For example, here is a communication sent to a student transcribing Swift's "The Best Day:" "As is typical of the folk/rock genre, there is a lot of syncopation going on, which makes transcription more difficult. In fact, *every syllable* from 'five' to 'got' in the first line is syncopated (i.e., starts on an upbeat). It sounds complicated, but since your relative note lengths in that passage are correct, all you have to do is shift the whole thing leftwards by a half-beat. (Recall the earlier exercise where you were asked to shift an entire passage rhythmically.)"

Awareness of shifts in the time dimension is also a useful tool in helping students with transcription of pitches. The student transcribing

Swift's "Fifteen" had done a remarkable job transcribing the rhythms, but some of the pitches were incorrect. In a communication to the student, I pointed out that one pitch pattern (G–F-sharp–D) was a large-scale time shift of a previously occurring statement of the same pitches: "Measures 11–12: This is very similar to the previous line—in particular, the pitches of 'senior boys' match those of 'freshman year' earlier."

Some students noted and made use of transformations on a more sophisticated level and, in so doing, went beyond the problem of simple transcription into the realm of analyzing compositional technique. The student transcribing "Smells Like Teen Spirit" noticed that the latter half of the fourth measure ("to pretend") is a pitch-dimension shift (i.e., a transposition) of the latter half of the second measure ("bring your friends"), in this case, down by an interval of a perfect fourth. This type of nontrivial transformation is extremely common in art music, especially from the classical era (e.g., Mozart). What is interesting for present purposes is its appearance and unprompted recognition in a student-selected sample from popular music.

From the examples listed above, one can generalize beyond transcription exercises to the larger analytical topic of using transformational ideas as a framework for understanding what is going on in a musical passage or a whole movement or work. Beginning with identifying exact repetition of motives (i.e., shifting by some number of beats or measures), students can be guided toward recognition of increasingly sophisticated transformations: exact transpositions and rhythmic shifts, diatonic transpositions and approximate rhythmic shifts, and, ultimately, inversions, augmentations, and retrograde motion. Although the transcription exercise described above offers an excellent (if potentially time-consuming) opportunity for such recognition, other opportunities abound. With the instant access provided by pop-culture tools, one could design exercises challenging students to recognize transformations "on the fly" as they listen to popular music or any other type of music. For example, after learning about transposition and hearing some examples, students should be able to recognize the presence of an exact and abrupt transposition in one of the many instances of the "truck driver's modulation": modulation of the final chorus up a whole step (for examples and further discussion of this technique, see London 1990). My favorite instance of this modulation occurs in the Beatles' "Penny Lane," but there are dozens, if not hundreds, more examples.

I did not build the explicit identification of transformations into my framing of the transcription exercise but took advantage of the opportunities to point out their occurrences when they presented themselves. I found the instances so numerous and compelling, however, that I will make such identification one of the main goals of the exercise in the next incarnation of my course. I also plan to design quicker, more spontaneous exercises in which students select short passages to play for their peers using pop-culture media and ask their classmates to immediately identify the transformation(s) at work therein.

CONCLUSION

The process of learning basic music theory becomes more meaningful and memorable to students if it is reinforced by student-generated examples from familiar popular genres. Such examples can be found and shared quickly by means of contemporary pop-culture media. While concerns about copyright and accuracy abound in situations involving students and popular music, the potential gain in student engagement and learning is significant enough to warrant addressing the concerns rather than letting them act as a deterrent.

The students in the course described here found the basic music-theory exercises to be challenging but worthwhile. In post-course evaluation, one stated, "The interval training and transcribing was very, very difficult for the average person to do, but overall the course was very beneficial." They also found the collaborative model to be effective: "I really enjoyed how the class was a group effort of all the students. Working together made it easier to understand the material."

Other pop-culture tools are developing that could have classroom applications similar to those described in this essay. For example, commercially available music search systems, such as the Midomi app for the iPhone, which can quickly identify pieces based on a few sung measures, could also be used to generate examples. Moreover, the music information-retrieval technology behind such devices is interesting in its own right and could be productively incorporated into college music courses.

The pedagogical ideas presented here are readily transferrable to any undergraduate music-theory course. A worthwhile outcome of such a course would be to have students, on hearing a new song on the radio, Internet, or a friend's iPod, think spontaneous, analytical thoughts, such as, "It's interesting how that song uses a tritone in its introduction," or, "The tune for the last words of the refrain is the same as that of the first words, just transposed." Such an outcome is more likely if students have developed the habit of seeking examples of the music-theoretical concepts they have learned not only in popular music but also via the delivery mechanisms of popular culture.

NOTES

1. The Society for Music Theory's electronic discussion list (http://lists.society musictheory.org/listinfo.cgi/smt-talk-societymusictheory.org), for example, includes

many threads in which excerpts from popular music are presented as examples of phenomena of current theoretical interest.

2. See, for example, Messiah College, Internet Downloading, "Online Piracy Sets Sail on the Web: The Top 5 Myths About Downloading Internet Music" at http://www.messiah.edu/etc/downloading.html.

3. Michael Patrick, online discussion board posting. Used by permission.

4. One example can be found at Wolfram Demonstrations Project, "Keyboard and Composer," at http://demonstrations.wolfram.com/KeyboardAndComposer. Others are available.

5. See, for example, Stanford University Libraries, "Copyright and Fair Use" at http://fairuse.stanford.edu/Copyright_and_Fair_Use_Overview/index.html.

REFERENCES

Callender, Clifton, Ian Quinn, and Dmitri Tymoczko. 2008. Generalized voice leading spaces. *Science* 320:346.

Hughes, James, and Leyla Batakci. 2006. Upgrade efforts for an introductory statistics course. In *Proceedings of the 3rd International Conference on the Teaching of Mathematics at the Undergraduate Level*, ed. D. H. Hallett, et al. Istanbul: Wiley.

Lewin, David. 1987. *Generalized musical intervals and transformations*. Oxford University Press.

———. 2007. *Musical form and transformations: Four analytic essays*. New York: Oxford University Press.

London, Justin. 1990. One step up: A lesson from pop music. *Journal of Music Theory Pedagogy* 4 (1): 111–14.

7

On the Integration of Aural Skills and Formal Analysis through Popular Music

Keith Salley

A well-formed music theory curriculum balances lecture topics and aural-skills development in a way that allows mutual reinforcement of thinking and listening—an interrelationship Michael Rogers considers central to the purpose and goal of music theory (Rogers 2004, 3–14). Success in one activity involves applying knowledge from the other, and when students synthesize these disciplines successfully, they become better, more well-informed musicians. Lamentably, many music-theory curriculums stop encouraging this synthesis at the very point where it becomes relevant to mature musicianship. While formal analysis is often the capstone course or sequence in a music-theory curriculum, the kind of synthesis required for success in such a class often does not involve many elements from the listening domain.[1] Students do combine knowledge of harmony, counterpoint, rhythm, and melody to understand music holistically, but too often, they only develop the ability to respond to visual cues in a score and rarely call upon their listening skills to any significant degree.

Writers have argued that the ability to hear formal relationships is not essential or even necessary.[2] Levinson (1997, ix) challenges the idea that "large-scale structural relationships" are even relevant to "basic musical understanding." Cook (1987, 24–5) questions the extent to which listeners "hear music in terms of traditional formal categories" and concludes, from his own observations and those of others, that "listening for form . . . is not a normal mode of aesthetic enjoyment." What Karpinski (2000a, 136) draws from Cook (1987) is that "more often than not listeners' musical memories fail them in what many music theorists and pedagogues feel are fundamentally important ways and at musically crucial moments." The observations of Karpinski and Cook might lead some readers to conclude that most musicians are not capable of learning to hear formal relationships, but at least one other interpretation is possible. I propose that musical memories fail in formal analysis because music students do not acquire the appropriate listening skills. In other words, the concepts students typically learn about form are not necessarily appropriate for aural comprehension.[3]

Textbooks that broach the subject of hearing form through aural analysis usually do so within the context of an aural-skills course.[4] The practice of integrating formal analysis within the context of another domain may be related to why students do not learn formal concepts that are appropriate for aural comprehension. While the environment of the aural-skills class-room is appropriate for intense and rigorous listening activities, it cannot accommodate the preliminary analytical lectures and discussions that can inform active, critical listening at levels that account for large-scale formal relationships. Courses devoted to form and analysis already present such information in the visual realm, and they create an atmosphere that is conducive to aural perception. This raises the question of which aspects of aural skills are important to develop in a course devoted to form and analysis. Cone (1968, 21) compares active listening to "a kind of vicarious performance," and this comparison is useful in communicating the dif-ference between passive and active listening. While it may be an effective aural-skills technique to mentally transform the listening experience into one that recreates a performance, active listeners in a form and analysis class must recreate a composition. In other words, active listeners must hear music as a series of gestures that relate or fail to relate to each other in various ways. Active listeners must understand how gestures flow from one to the other and how different gestures can both unify a work and stand alone as discrete musical ideas. Active listening in a form and analysis class should encourage students to translate the technique of thinking-as-vicar-ious-composition used to illuminate formal relationships into a similar mode of listening.

Readers might argue that the idea of vicarious composition can only give rise to an analytical approach that continually invokes intentionality, but this is not necessarily true. When listeners interpret musical form from a compositional perspective, they understand percepts as the results of compositional decisions and can begin to consider the aural implications of those decisions. A compositional listener must be able to conceptualize musical structure by responding to musical attributes and effects rather than searching for visual cues (e.g., cadences, chromaticism, abrupt changes in texture) on a score and not necessarily correlating them with the way the music sounds. A vicarious composer contemplates whether and how it is aesthetically effective or ineffective when y follows x. An aural approach in the form and analysis classroom can help to develop these abilities, particu-larly if it incorporates scoreless musical analysis.

A small number of texts situate active listening within the context of a form and analysis class, although the majority of these deal solely with Western art music. Each chapter of Wittlich and Humphries (1974) deals in part with aural analysis of form. De Stwolinski (1977) emphasizes aural analysis, providing a number of excerpts from baroque, classical and modern Western art music and presenting material in a manner that encourages critical listening. Similarly, the purpose of Spencer and Temko (1988, vii–viii) "is to provide students of form with perceptual tools that allow them to proceed from the aural experience to an understanding of the arch-principles upon which music is organized." Their textbook attunes students to specific phenomena that accompany changes in structural divisions, as well as defines four basic formal functions, discussed below. Alegant (2007) offers a paradigm for aural analysis of sonata form. His method develops students' sensitivities to elements of sonata form (e.g., keys, motives, sections) by weaning them from their reliance on musical scores. The goal of Santa (2009) is to teach students how to aurally recognize cadences, harmonic sequence types, modulations, formal sections, and complete musical forms (xi). Santa also briefly addresses pop, rock, jazz, blues, and 32-bar song forms, observing general formal and harmonic characteristics such as sectional repeats and providing criteria for distinguishing verses, choruses, and bridges.

This chapter integrates current approaches to analyzing classical form through formal function, hypermeter, and phrase rhythm within two overlapping repertoires of popular music: standard jazz and musical theatre. Standard jazz repertoire refers to the corpus of tunes from roughly the 1920s to the 1960s, often written for radio, theatre, and film, but also written directly for the bandstand by jazz performers. The body of work known as jazz standards comprises those tunes found in fake books and that are likely to be called on stage.[5] The musical theatre repertory intersects with standard jazz repertoire to a considerable extent, although the former is not entirely subsumed within the latter. For example, one would expect a jazz pianist to be familiar with the more popular songs of Cole Porter but not with selections from *Cats* or *Miss Saigon*. In fact, most music-theatre songs that are classifiable as jazz standards were written before 1950.

The ability to hear and comprehend a song like the Gershwins' "How Long Has This Been Going On?" or Alan Jay Lerner and Frederick Loewe's "How to Handle a Woman" might seem far removed from the ability to track themes and modulations across the first movement of a sonata. However, aural comprehension of form in popular music is a valuable skill in and of itself for students who can expect to engage in such repertoires as professionals, particularly those majoring in music education, musical theatre, jazz studies, and commercial music. In addition, developing the ability to perceive formal relationships in pop music can provide a cognitive scaffolding that prepares listeners to understand the more complex formal relationships in Western art music. Jazz and musical theatre repertoires provide appropriate teaching materials at a crucial stage of this development. First, they have much in common with much earlier and current pop music. Such characteristics as generally consistent four- and eight-bar phrasing, recurrent sections, and cyclic forms make the act of tracking form by ear easy in comparison with much art music.[6] This connection is significant because the vast majority of high school and college music students are experienced, competent listeners of popular music. As such, they are already adept at identifying its forms by distinguishing verses, choruses, and bridges, as well as its processes, such as repetitions, variations, and modulations. Second, a great deal of jazz and musical theatre repertory behaves according to well-established tonal conventions. That is, harmonic movement in these repertoires is characterized by conventional functional progression toward and away from tonic harmonies, and its goal-oriented melodic motion describes tonally centered diatonic collections. For this reason, standard jazz (of the non-modal variety) and musical theatre repertory has more in common with the standard repertoire of Western art music than some recent rock music, which is often characterized by aspects of modality (as opposed to tonality), a melodic-harmonic divorce, and markedly different normative harmonic motion.[7] Comparable tonal hierarchies in the repertoires of standard jazz, musical theatre, and Western concert music enable students to transfer concepts and paradigms from contemporary popular music—which forms the basis of most students' musical experience—to traditional concert repertoire in an aural-analysis course.

This chapter demonstrates a number of ways to implement jazz and musical theatre repertoires in a formal analysis class, specifically for the purpose of teaching students how to hear formal relationships. All of these methods engage students in active critical listening, and instructors should be able to assess comprehension of them without the aid of musical scores. These concepts require more of student listeners than the ability to track traditional lecture topics, such as parallel and contrasting phrase relationships, cadential strength, and overall formal type, although the ability to perceive these is a prerequisite to understanding deeper formal relationships. The methods presented below address aural comprehension of relatively advanced aspects of formal analysis, such as formal function, phrase structure, and hypermeter.

FORMAL FUNCTIONS

The idea of formal units fulfilling functions is certainly not new. Writers such as Schoenberg (1967), Ratz (1973), and Caplin (1998) have taken formal analysis beyond mere structural description and observed relationships that are arguably more informative. The idea of function, however, can mean many things. When Huron (2007, 371–2) asserts that "one cannot decipher function through descriptive analysis alone," his conception of the term is considerably broad. Indeed, analysts must engage with the interrelationships of melody, harmony, rhythm, and other aspects of music, whether their purpose is to describe its structure or decipher its functions. Accounts of formal function in the following discussion describe the organization of thematic and harmonic materials over the course of a phrase, a section, and sometimes an entire song form, as well as the way such materials relate to each other. A thorough account of formal functions in a composition reveals how tonal stability and motivic unity fluctuate and how such changes affect the relationship between harmony and melody. While this chapter makes use of a somewhat limited conception of the idea of "formal function," sensitivity to this idea will begin to direct students' attentions to large-scale relationships between formal units and will prepare them to make more challenging distinctions in classical repertoire.

The working conception of formal function set forth in this chapter does resonate with previous scholarship. Berry (1986, 403–4) enumerates five "processes by which form, as an aspect of structure, is articulated" in tonal Western art music, and Berry (1987) expounds on these ideas. Four of these five, the expository, developmental, resolution, and transition processes, are relevant to this study. Similarly, Spencer and Temko (1988, 51ff.) present four structural functions, called expository, developmental, terminative, and transitional.[8] The authors define these processes and functions mainly in terms of harmonic stability and melodic characteristics, although they also observe aspects of rhythm, phrase-structural fragmentation, and changes in dynamics. The model described below applies a similar array of functional categories to phrases, sections, and entire song forms in jazz and musical theatre repertoires. In this model, expository, developmental, cadential, and connecting functions are determined primarily by harmonic activity, but melodic activity conveys characteristics of these functions as well.

The discussion below explains these functions and offers examples of phrases and sections from compositions that demonstrate them. For purposes of this study, phrases are formal units of at least four measures and are marked at their conclusion by points of harmonic and melodic arrival. The term "sub-phrase" refers to a unit of two to four measures. Sub-phrases often consist of II–V or II–V–I motion and are combined with at least one other sub-phrase.[9] Sections consist of one or more phrases. Throughout the chapter, measure numbering begins at the downbeat of the "head" of a jazz standard, and at the onset of the chorus or the "song proper" of a musical theatre song, unless otherwise noted.

Example 7.1. Wayne King, Victor Young, Egbert Van Alstyne, and Haven Gillespie, "Beautiful Love" (1931), mm. 1–4

Passages that fulfill the expository function establish a single key or, at the very least, an overriding sense of a single tonality. The latter criterion is especially relevant to multi-phrase sections with fleeting tonicizations that may misdirect the expectations of less experienced listeners. This function sounds most strongly within completely closed progressions or II–V–I motion and is characterized melodically by the presentation of a single theme. Example 7.1 shows a phrase that unambiguously fulfills the expository function.[10] Harmonic progression through the conventional II–V–I cycle establishes a single key, and the melody consists of a single statement of a four-measure theme.

A phrase or section that fulfills the developmental function is tonally unstable and does not spend a disproportionate amount of continuous time in a single key. Melodies that exhibit developmental characteristics involve restatements, sequences, or fragmentation of a motive or theme. Such characteristics sound most strongly when a recurring motive or theme has been previously established in an expository context. Middle sections of *aaba* song forms often fulfill this function. Example 7.2 shows the *b* section of Ray Noble's "Cherokee." Here, a descending arpeggio motive recurs within each eight-measure phrase, providing continuity across sudden changes of key. Variation of a single eight-measure melodic theme at different pitch levels occurs across this section as well. Thus, motivic recurrences unite the key centers in each phrase, and thematic recurrences unite the phrases in the section.

Passages may fulfill the developmental function without firmly establishing a key. In such cases, they may refer to key centers only obliquely. Example 7.3 shows mm. 1–8 of Victor Young's "Stella by Starlight," where a series of II–V motions gesture toward two keys (B minor and G major)

Example 7.2. Ray Noble, "Cherokee" (1938), mm. 33–48

Bm: II   V   G: II   V   C: II   V   I   IV(dom)

Example 7.3.   Victor Young, "Stella by Starlight" (1944), mm. 1–8

before a complete II–V–I progression establishes a local tonic (C major) across mm. 5–7.[11] Students may observe that the establishment of C major does provide a degree of tonal stability in the second half of the passage, but the major minor-seventh on F that follows at m. 8 carries the falling-fifth bass pattern through the phrase and destabilizes the key.

Example 7.3 raises the issue of just how long a key may sound within a modulatory passage before its continuous duration is sufficiently disproportionate with respect to other key centers. A good rule of thumb places this value above 50 percent of the passage, but the answer may vary from case to case, depending on the rate of harmonic change and other factors. For instance, a passage with local II–V–I motions in closely related keys may sound to some listeners like local tonicizations that prolong a single key. Students must determine from careful listening whether or not the questionable passage establishes an overriding sense of one tonality.

Although the developmental function is harmonically unstable, it is not necessarily confined to internal sections. Take, for instance, the *a* section of Dave Brubeck's "In Your Own Sweet Way," shown in example 7.4.[12] Students should have no problem identifying its function as developmental. This passage modulates three times over eight measures, but since the modulations occur at regular two-measure intervals, it spends no disproportionate amount of continuous time in any key. While the arrival on B-flat at m. 8 does provide a fair amount of harmonic closure, the consistent two-measure segmentation of harmony and melody makes the analogous arrival at m. 4 seem more like another fleeting tonicization than the close of a four-measure phrase. The change of harmony to a major seventh on E-flat at the second half of m. 4, which continues a well-established pattern of falling fifths in the bass, contributes to this effect. Furthermore, the melody encourages students to hear a collection of two-measure sub-phrases, rather

Gm: II   V   I   IV(dom) Bb: II   V   I   IV

Gb: II   bII(dom)   I   IV   Bb: II   V   I

Example 7.4.   Dave Brubeck, "In Your Own Sweet Way" (1955), mm. 1–8

than a pair of phrases, by varying a simple descending-step motive over mm. 1–2 (E-flat–D and C–B-flat) and mm. 6–8 (B-flat–A-flat and G-flat–F) and a larger melodic idea over mm. 3–6. Overall, student listeners will have experienced a number of gestures in different key centers over the course of the passage and should not attempt to understand the bulk of it in terms of a single tonality.

The foregoing examples present passages where melodic characteristics reinforce harmonically-determined formal functions. Quite often, however, expository and developmental melodic characteristics contrast with formal function. Such contrasts are not necessarily disruptive. In fact, they can mitigate the overall effect of a sounding function. Compositions in standard jazz and musical theatre repertoires often feature expository passages that exhibit typical developmental melodic characteristics, such as motivic variation or sequencing. Example 7.5, an excerpt from the beginning of the chorus of "I'm Glad There Is You," illustrates this juxta-position. Strictly speaking, this melody iterates a single theme, but that theme begins to exhibit developmental characteristics when the motive that sounds across mm. 2–3 undergoes variation across mm. 4–5. The temporary shift to the minor mode in the harmony contributes to the developmental character of the theme.

Expository sub-phrases with expository melodic characteristics often combine to create phrases where recurrent melodic themes or motives create developmental characteristics. The same relationship can occur between phrases and sections.[13] In fact, at the level of the multi-phrase section, one should expect to find motivic or thematic variation. For this reason, students should direct their attention to determining not if but how a composition exhibits developmental melodic characteristics. Students can make important distinctions between the structural levels at which motivic or thematic variations occur. Example 7.6 shows the expository function at the section level, where melodic variation occurs at the phrase level. This *a* section consists of two expository eight-bar phrases from "On the Street Where You Live." Within each phrase, varied repetitions of a two-measure opening motive invite comparison to a sentence form, with recurrences

Example 7.5. Jimmy Dorsey, Paul Madeira, and Paul Mertz, "I'm Glad There is You" (1941), mm. 1–8

Example 7.6. Alan Jay Lerner and Frederick Loewe, "On the Street Where You Live" (1956), mm. 1–16

of a basic idea across mm. 3–4 and 11–12 and continuations across mm. 5–8 and 13–16. These resemblances are particularly strong if one hears the reiterated notes across mm. 5–6 and the recurring three-note motive across mm. 13–15 as instances of liquidation.[14]

When students can perceive how melodies characterize the formal functions of passages, they can begin to make comparisons between works. This activity becomes increasingly relevant as students become more familiar with repertoire. When students have heard a sufficient number of works, they can make informed distinctions about historical style periods and the development of compositional practice over time, as well as composers' individual styles. In addition, directing students to recognize melodic correspondences encourages them to produce more informed performances and more motivically related improvisations. Example 7.7 presents the *a* section to the Gershwin brothers' "I Got Rhythm," published 26 years earlier than "On the Street Where You Live." Although the *a* section consists of a single expository phrase in this analysis, comparison to the initial phrase of example 7.6 reveals interesting correspondences. In both examples, an opening motive varies across the phrase in adjacent two-measure units that first ascend, then descend, creating four-measure units with arch-shaped contours. The second four-measure units begin with ascending forms of their motives that extend the range of each melody. Finally, each excerpt concludes with an embellished stepwise melodic descent of a third. While these are simple, descriptive observations, they point to an interesting process of motivic variation common to both compositions. A student

Example 7.7. George Gershwin and Ira Gershwin, "I Got Rhythm" (1930), mm. 1–8

well-versed in repertoire may notice similarities between these passages and those from other compositions, such as the *a* section of Noble's "Cherokee" (not shown), where a recurrent five-note theme sounds across an expository phrase, changing overall direction with every recurrence and gradually expanding in range.

Instances of developmentally functioning passages with expository characteristics are relatively rare. To qualify as such, a passage must involve more than one key while simultaneously presenting only one theme with no motivic variation. Example 7.8 shows mm. 1–4 of John Coltrane's "Countdown," where tonicizations of major-third related key centers sound beneath a single melodic idea. The relationship between function and character in this passage may be a reflection of the fact that "Countdown" is a reharmonization of Miles Davis's "Tune Up," a much simpler composition with harmonically expository phrases. However, the first two four-measure phrases of Coltrane's "Giant Steps" are also developmental with expository characteristics, and this composition is not based on any other work. Although students will probably require scores to make informed comparisons between "Tune Up," "Countdown," and "Giant Steps," doing so can reveal an interesting aspect of Coltrane's compositional style during the late 1950s and early 1960s.

Distinctions between expository and developmental harmony and melody are not too difficult to make by ear, and identifying melodic characteristics of functions enables instructors to sidestep the unfortunate pigeonholing that often accompanies analytical applications of formal terminology. Passages whose melodic characteristics are arguably expository or developmental create opportunities for discussion, where students may assess the various factors supporting one function or the other and make critically informed decisions for themselves. Students will be less inclined to dismiss a song as "just another 32-bar *aaba* form" if they can appreciate the relationships among its sections in terms of their harmonic stability and melodic characteristics. Furthermore, these concepts allow students to make useful distinctions between different songs with the same overall form. Consider, for example, the Gershwin brothers' "How Long Has This Been Going On?" and Duke Ellington's "Prelude to a Kiss" (not shown). Both songs are 32-bar *aaba* forms, but while the former features expository *a* sections and a developmental *b* section, the latter has developmental *a* sections and a *b* section that is chiefly expository.[15]

The cadential function is characterized by directed harmonic motion toward a goal that terminates a phrase or section. Conventional falling-fifth

Example 7.8.   John Coltrane, "Countdown" (1960), mm. 1–4

sequences that end on I or V and involve more than two or three chords typically fulfill this function.[16] No resolutions to local tonics normally occur within a cadential sequence, although tonicizations of dominants and pre-dominants are common. The cadential function differs from the developmental function in that the overriding harmonic goal of a cadential passage overrides the incidental chromaticism that might have the potential to imply different keys. The cadential function is typically characterized by a lack of expository melodic characteristics, but often occurs in conjunction with developmental melodic characteristics.

Phrases that fulfill the cadential function typically occur after expository or developmental phrases. Example 7.9 shows a phrase from Jerome Kern and Oscar Hammerstein's "The Song Is You," where a cadential passage prolongs the arrival on the dominant and sets up a varied repetition of the initial *a* section.[17] This passage consists of two approaches to the global dominant. The first sounds across mm. 5–6 and the second across m. 8. The melodic characteristics of this passage are developmental, as a single melodic idea undergoes varied repetition throughout the passage.

Chromatic sequences may also establish cadential contexts. For example, the *b* section of the Gershwins' "I Got Rhythm" (not shown) consists of a chain of regularly spaced secondary dominants (D^7–G^7–C^7–F^7) that ultimately prolongs the global dominant. Example 7.10 represents mm. 25–32 of Victor Young's "Stella by Starlight," where a stepwise descending sequence of II–V relationships brings the song's form to a conclusion and finally confirms the tonic. The relationship between this excerpt and the rest of the song creates an excellent opportunity for discussion about the perception and interplay of functions and characteristics, as well as the difference between local and global tonics. The cadential phrase is a variant of the opening phrase, with much the same melody but with a different harmonic structure. As all of the preceding phrases of this composition are developmental, the cadential phrase is the most tonally stable. On the other hand, every tone in the melody across mm. 1–24 falls squarely within

Example 7.9. Jerome Kern and Oscar Hammerstein, "The Song Is You" (1932), mm. 5–8

Example 7.10. Victor Young, "Stella by Starlight" (1944), mm. 25–32

the G-major scale, while the cadential phrase introduces chromaticism just before it confirms the G-major tonic.

The connecting function is most relevant to musical theatre, although listeners may find passages that fulfill an analogous function in specific arrangements of standard jazz tunes. This function is relatively easy to identify because connecting passages are transitional and sometimes wordless, linking structural elements such as the introduction of a song and the more easily identifiable song proper. The most important part of a connecting passage is its final cadence, which is often a half cadence. When connecting passages modulate, they frequently end on the dominant of the key of an approaching section. Example 7.11 presents an excerpt from Richard Rodgers and Lorenz Hart's "Where or When," in which a non-modulating passage fulfills the connecting function. The song's introduction concludes with a perfect authentic cadence on G. A short connecting passage follows where musicians may interpret the pulse more freely. The half cadence at the end of this passage sets up the tonic at the onset of the song proper.

The task of visually identifying functions is too easily done. Most students can tell at a glance whether a passage modulates, and they can identify thematic or motivic development just as easily. For this reason, assessment with lead sheets will not be of much educational benefit. This will most likely be as true for those lead sheets with chord symbols (e.g., D^7, Cm) as it will be for those with only a grand staff. The best way to assess comprehension of formal functions is to test students' abilities to hear them without the aid of a score. In devising a suitable assessment strategy for this type of perception, instructors must make sure that their students can identify the different formal functions and melodic characteristics of phrases and sections, and ask students to explain their answers and provide supporting evidence. Another reasonable goal is for students to create a diagram of a composition based only on listening, noting formal relationships, conventional harmonic passages, and even motivic correspondences along the way.

Example 7.12 is a sample assessment template and answer key for a scoreless aural analysis of Duke Ellington's "Prelude to a Kiss." Instructors may find it appropriate to provide less or even more information than what is given in this formal diagram. Upon hearing the composition a number of times, students demonstrate their aural comprehension by answering questions about motivic connections and overall form.[18] Most importantly,

Example 7.11. Richard Rodgers and Lorenz Hart, "Where or When" (1937), connection and introduction of song proper

1) Listen to Duke Ellington's "Prelude to a Kiss" and diagram the form of the composition, parsing it into four-measure phrases. Please account for all phrase and section relationships, and be sure to label all cadences at the ends of phrases. The initial melodic rhythm has been given to you.

A (Dev.)
a   b
|♩♩♩♩| | | | | | | |
A' (Dev.)
a   b'
| | | | | | | | |
B (Exp.)
c   c'
| | | | | | | | |
A''(Dev.)
a   b''
| | | | | | | | ||

2) Indicate on the diagram the function fulfilled by each section and explain your answers below, accounting for the functions fulfilled by each phrase.
A sections are developmental. Their first phrase of each A section seems to have two cadences at different pitch levels. The second phrase of each A section cadences on another tonic.
The B section is expository. The first phrase establishes a single key, and the second phrase only begins change key toward its end, in order to set up the key of the next section.

3) Indicate on the diagram the melodic characteristics of each phrase and explain your answers below.
All 'a' phrases are developmental. They each state a two-measure theme at different pitch levels.
All 'b' phrases are expository. While they consist of two melodic ideas, these ideas are not motivically related, and combine to make a single thematic presentation.
All 'c' phrases are developmental. They both develop a motive consisting of a step followed by a large leap in the opposite direction (a variation of the last three notes of the second ending). The second half of the first phrase also consists of varied repetition of a motive.

4) In terms of melodic and motivic structure, how do mm. 5-8 relate to mm. 1-4? What is different? Any similarities?

Measures 5-8 feature ascending semitones in the melody, while mm. 1-4 consist of descending semitones.

5) In terms of melodic and motivic structure, how do mm. 17-24 relate to mm. 1-16? What is different? Any similarities?
Both passages feature distinct two-measure sub-phrasing. Both sections make use of the step-and-leap motive in recognizable ways. Measures 17-24 consist primarily of leaps with few steps, while mm. 1-16 consists of a more even distribution of both.

Example 7.12.   Duke Ellington, "Prelude to a Kiss" (1938), assessment

they must distinguish between developmental and expositional functions and identify corresponding or non-corresponding melodic characteristics.

Example 7.13 is a sample assessment with answers for Lerner and Loewe's "The Simple Joys of Maidenhood." This rather involved song form features an introduction with a modulating passage that fulfills the connecting function. This connecting passage sets up the key of the following section with a half cadence. Again, students are asked to construct a graphic representation of the form and identify all formal functions.

Students should not have too much trouble identifying functions aurally, although mistakes will certainly occur. For instance, students may confuse developmental and cadential functions, particularly if the latter involves a chromatic sequence. Instructors must remind students that the difference involves the amount of the phrase that is directed toward a harmonic goal and that cadential passages typically only establish tonics at their conclusions. The ability to identify functions is a prerequisite to understanding forms and processes in classical music, such as those described in Caplin (1998). In addition to the fragmentation discussed above in reference to example 7.6, attention to developmental melodic characteristics in jazz and musical theatre repertoires will enable students to differentiate among different types of repetitions. The ability to recognize the directed motion exhibited by the cadential function will prepare students to identify where transitions of sonatas and rondos begin and end. Understanding the typicality of falling-fifth sequences in cadential passages in these repertoires facilitates comprehension of Caplin's concluding function, as well as his cadential idea, which comprises stylistically "conventional" traits and a removal of "characteristic" features (11). Students who are able to distinguish expositional, developmental, and cadential functions while recognizing their melodic characteristics will find it easier to recognize Caplin's tightly knit and loosely organized themes—and the degrees to which they meet all of Caplin's criteria—in classical music.

HYPERMETER

The regular four- and eight-measure phrases in standard jazz and musical theatre repertoires establish relatively rigid hypermetric structures. A hypermetric analysis of 32-measure *aaba* or *abab* forms (which are very common in these repertoires) will often reveal regular four-beat hypermeasures at the level of the four-measure phrase and duple or quadruple hypermeasures at the levels of eight-measure sections and sixteen-measure halves, as well as across entire forms.[19] Hypermetric perception is an important skill for jazz musicians. Berliner (1994, 372) observes that "while the soloist extends phrases over principal harmonic section boundaries or highlights them by

1) Consider the opening line *"Genevieve! St. Genevieve! It's Guenevere! Remember me?"* to constitute a single phrase, and please graph the phrase structure up to the monologue in the spaces below.

```
        *                    *
| a  | a'  | b  | c  | c  | c  | c  |con. v| a  | a' ||
 exp.  exp.  exp.  exp.  exp.  exp.  exp.         exp.  exp.
```

2) Use a star to mark where any modulations occur.

3) Mark any passages that fulfill the connecting function with "con." Include 'I' if the passage ends on tonic, and 'V' if the passage ends on dominant.

4) Please indicate the function of each phrase with "exp.," "dev.," or "cad."

5) What is the function of the *section* that spans phrases 4–7? **developmental**

After the monologue:

6) Consider the line "Where are the simple joys of maidenhood?" to constitute a single phrase, and graph the phrase structure in the spaces below.

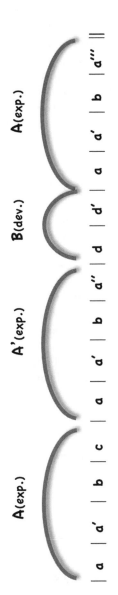

A(exp.)   A'(exp.)   B(dev.)   A(exp.)

| a | a' | b | c | a | a' | b | a'' | d | d' | d | a | a' | b | a''' ||

7) Please group the phrases into larger sections and label them.

8) Indicate the overall function of each section.

Example 7.13. Alan Jay Lerner and Frederick Loewe, "The Simple Joys of Maidenhood" (1960), assessment

resting, rhythm section players define structural cadences through various combined operations in the last two bars of sections." Over the course of performances, hypermetric levels can even extend beyond the level of the chorus to collections of choruses, and musicians in the rhythm section can articulate these larger-level beats. Gary Bartz recalls how Art Blakey builds large-scale background structure behind soloists at a level that subsumes a number of choruses (Berliner 1994, 372). Jazz musicians also typically count measures as beats when "trading," a practice wherein soloists—usually a drummer and at least one melodic player—take turns playing brief solos of equal length over a composition's form. Quite often, players only trade two- or four-measure units, but it is not unusual for them to trade larger units, such as sections, half-choruses, and even whole choruses. Hypermetric perception becomes increasingly important when soloists trade these larger formal units, especially when the harmonic accompaniment drops out of the texture for longer periods of time.

On the musical-theatre stage, choruses are not repeated nearly as much, and performers do not improvise. However, hypermetric perception is just as important in this repertoire. Singers who are already developing personal and intuitive processes for chunking large groups of pulses can sharpen their sensitivity by learning about hypermeter. Irregularities in hypermeter are more common in this repertoire than in standard jazz, and students can learn to identify, interpret, and respond to them in more informed ways. The normative four- and eight-measure phrases and predictable harmonic rhythm characteristic of this repertoire create a hypermetrically rigid background against which students can perceive irregularities clearly. Example 7.14 shows the opening section of Rodgers and Hart's "Where or When," where a 10-measure phrase is the result of an extended hyperbeat 3. The hypermeter can be regularized by recomposing the passage with mm. 5–6 omitted.

In contrast, example 7.15 shows a passage from the opening section of Claude-Michel Schönberg's "On My Own" where hyperbeats contract. This excerpt provides an instructive example for class discussion. After giving

Example 7.14.   Richard Rodgers and Lorenz Hart, "Where or When" (1937), mm. 1–10

Example 7.15. Claude-Michel Schönberg, "On My Own" (1980), mm. 1–8

students the opening meter and the basic quarter-note pulse, the instructor should play the example several times. The first four measures of this excerpt establish the duple hypermeter clearly, but changes of meter at mm. 7 and 8 interrupt the regular hypermetric flow. Students should try to determine what happens to the duple hypermeter in the second half of the section without the aid of a score. After opening the excerpt to discussion, the instructor can provide a solution by recomposing the excerpt in a more metrically regular fashion. Example 7.16 proposes one such solution. It interprets m. 6 as a hypermetric upbeat analogous to those of mm. 2 and 4. Similar melodic rhythms at the onsets of these measures, as well as in the beats that lead into these measures, support this analysis. Example 7.16 also asserts that m. 7, as a hypermetric downbeat, is metrically stronger than m. 8. By hearing the difference between examples 7.15 and 7.16, students can appreciate the perseverance of hypermetric relationships in the midst of this metrically unstable passage, and they can use this knowledge to develop a more rhythmically confident interpretation of it.

Examples of hypermetric expansion and contraction in popular songs are relevant to student listeners for a number of reasons. In a broad sense, they can facilitate students' understanding of the same processes when they occur in other repertoires, such as Western art music. In a more immediate sense, these examples help students to perceive how strong and weak

Example 7.16. Claude-Michel Schönberg, "On My Own" (1980), mm. 1–8 recomposed

beats, measures, and hypermeasures fluctuate regularly across the form of a composition. They also offer students a descriptive model for articulating what is rhythmically compelling about certain passages, as well as what larger-scale implications may arise due to changes in meter. Such sensitivities are especially important for students interested in composition—and particularly for those interested in songwriting.

PHRASE STRUCTURE

Rothstein (1989) accounts for phrase rhythm in music in terms of the relationship between phrase structure, which is determined primarily by harmonic and melodic factors, and hypermeter, which is created by the hierarchical nature of meter and determined primarily by long-range rhythmic factors. As explained in his book, many of Rothstein's ideas regarding phrase rhythm may be difficult for undergraduates to read, but to a large degree, they are easy to hear. Many pieces from standard jazz and musical theatre repertoires demonstrate interesting relationships between phrase structure and hypermeter, and for this reason, instructors can use them to acquaint students with concepts fundamental to understanding phrase rhythm.

Rothstein's discussion of Strauss's *The Blue Danube* explains how two 16-measure phrases combine to create a 33-measure period (20). The reason for this "curious arithmetic" is that the melody and harmony are one measure out of phase. While the harmonic aspect of the waltz's phrase structure aligns perfectly with the hypermeter, the melodic aspect consistently anticipates the hypermetric downbeats by a single measure. Misalignments between harmony and melody often occur in jazz standards and musical theatre songs. A common cause of this is the treatment of the turnaround, a chord or short chord progression at the end of a phrase or section—usually after tonal closure has already sounded there—that sets up the harmony on the hypermetric downbeat of the next phrase.[20] A turnaround typically consists of the dominant of the chord on the following hypermetric downbeat, and it is common practice in jazz performance to inflect that dominant with a supertonic pre-dominant.

In turnarounds, harmony functions as an anacrusis that precedes the hypermetric downbeat of a phrase or section, where the melody typically begins. The opposite arrangement seems to occur more often in Western art music, as Rothstein observes: "When only one of the two elements, melody or harmony, is out of phase with the metrical pattern, it is usually the melody" (22). Turnarounds are clearly subordinate to the harmonies they prepare, and in most cases, they do not play significant structural roles at deeper levels of harmonic reduction. Still, the difference between harmony-first and melody-first misalignments points to an intriguing distinction

Example 7.17.   Harry Warren and Mack Gordon, "There Will Never Be Another You" (1942), mm. 1–8

between popular music and Western art music. Because of this difference, instructors can provide examples of both types of misalignment, helping students develop a well-rounded sensitivity to phrase structure.

Turnarounds often occupy the final two to four beats of a four- or eight-measure phrase, but in some cases, they can be considerably longer. As turnarounds occupy more space, very perceptible misalignments occur between harmony and melody at the level of phrase structure. Example 7.17 presents an especially striking instance of harmony-first misalignment in the first eight measures of Harry Warren and Mack Gordon's "There Will Never Be Another You." Here, the melodic phrases are in general alignment with the hypermeter. They span four-measure segments, anticipated only slightly with quarter-note pickups. The harmonic spans are offset by two measures with respect to the melodic phrases, and this results in an overlapping of phrase-structural elements.[21] Example 7.18 provides an assessment template and answer key for "There Will Never Be Another You" that requires students to account for all misalignments over the course of the composition. This assignment assesses students' abilities to perceive II–V–(I) motion, which is an important skill for two reasons. First, the II–V–(I) progression is virtually ubiquitous in standard jazz and common in musical theatre. Second, all of the harmonic-melodic misalignments in this song are the direct result of II–V turnarounds.

CONCLUSION

The vast majority of people listen to music without the aid of a score. Even those who do read and study music spend most of their listening time without score in hand. To make analysis worthwhile—that is, to make analysis practical—instructors must transform scoreless listening into a critical endeavor. Engaging student listeners at the level where their cumulative knowledge of music and music theory synthesizes into a clear understanding of musical experience is no easy task. This chapter speaks to the value of meeting students halfway by allowing them to vicariously compose more accessible and familiar-sounding music than the complex structures and processes of sonata movements and other characteristic art-music forms. Standard jazz and musical theatre repertoires embody certain formal relationships that can

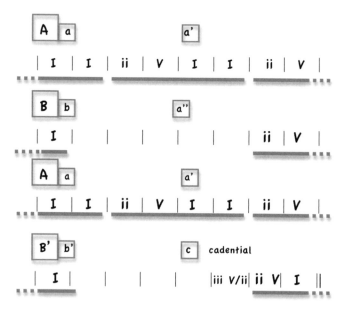

A	a						a'	

I	I	ii	V	I	I	ii	V

B	b						a''	

I						ii	V

A	a						a'	

I	I	ii	V	I	I	ii	V

B'	b'				c	cadential

I				iii	V/ii	ii	V	I ‖

1) Please label all four-bar phrases by placing appropriate lowercase letters in the smaller boxes.

2) Label all eight bar sections by placing appropriate uppercase letters in the larger boxes.

3) Indicate where each II-V-I occurs (in any key) by placing the appropriate chord symbols in the appropriate measures, and underline them. If a II-V-I crosses sections, use dashed lines to show continuity.

4) What can you observe about the relationship between harmonic grouping and phrase structure during (and immediately after) the A sections?

Harmonic grouping and melodic phrase structure are misaligned by two measures.

5a) What function does each phrase of the A section fulfill? *expository* Why?

Despite the misalignment, only one key is established in each phrase, only one theme sounds in each phrase.

5b) What function does the A section fulfill? *developmental* Why?

A theme occurs in two keys.

6) Label any phrases that fulfill the cadential function, and fill in the appropriate chord symbols.

Example 7.18. Harry Warren and Mack Gordon, "There Will Never Be Another You" (1941), assessment

develop students' aural sensitivity to relatively advanced analytical concepts. The virtue of these repertoires is that overall form and structure are more easily perceived. A teaching approach that integrates these styles of popular music will encourage students to apply aural analysis to repertoires where the same relationships are more latent.

This chapter allows us to reengage the question of whether or not it is essential or even important to hear and appreciate formal relationships. An honest but somewhat terse answer is that critical listening and long-range hearing are vital skills, just as perception, memory, and pattern recognition are vital skills not only in music but also in everyday life. Ultimately, this chapter addresses the question of what kinds and levels of relationships are pedagogically appropriate for aural comprehension of form. Demonstrating how attention to formal functions, hypermeter, and phrase rhythm can begin to reveal commonalities and differences between and within musical styles offers a concrete answer to the second question and an implied affirmative answer to the first question. Certainly, consideration of other facets of musical form and the application of other analytical tools will enable scholars to answer this second question equally well or even more appropriately. Nonetheless, any contributions that truly develop critical listening skills in formal analysis must address ways to direct the attention of student listeners to audible relationships among harmony, melody, and large-scale rhythm.

NOTES

1. White (2001, 127) advises instructors to "capture student interest" by beginning with aural analysis but offers no strategies for proceeding with more comprehensive approaches to aural analysis or assessment.

2. Karpinski (2000a, 135–7) provides a brief summary of this dispute.

3. Cook (1987, 24) states "it might be that the traditional formal categories are too rigid, or simply inappropriate."

4. See, for example, Phillips, Marvin, and Piper Clendinning 2004–5, Benward and Kolosick 2010, and Karpinski 2006.

5. Compositions in this repertoire that do not follow traditional tonal syntax, such as many works by Wayne Shorter and Joe Henderson, are outside the scope of this chapter, although readers are welcome to adopt strategies informed by this chapter to instruct students' perception and comprehension of formal relationships in these more recently developed compositional styles.

6. See Covach 2004 for an explanation of a number of formal archetypes in popular music, their cultural import, and significant variations of them.

7. See Biamonte 2010; Doll 2007; Moore 2001; Stephenson 2002, 102–4; and Temperley 2007.

8. The resemblance between the structuring of Berry's ideas and those of Spencer and Temko is uncanny, though Spencer and Temko make no claim in the text to have derived their terms from Berry (1986).

9. In this chapter, Roman numerals are always capital. They refer only to the scale degree on which a chord root sounds.

10. Examples in this chapter omit many embellishing harmonies present in recordings and published sheet music. As many of the compositions have been arranged and performed in numerous ways, I have adopted a level of harmonic reduction that should be relevant to all of them.

11. The harmonies in this example are based on common practice in jazz performance (although musicians often play the song in the key of B-flat). The accompaniment in Victor Young's original version of the composition is somewhat simpler. See Forte 1997–98.

12. As the melodic rhythm in the *a* sections of this composition varies across any single performance, this excerpt presents the first *a* section of Brubeck's first published recording.

13. At the sub-phrase to phrase level, consider the first 16 measures of Alan Jay Lerner and Frederick Loewe's "How to Handle a Woman" or the first phrase of Thelonious Monk's "Hackensack." At the phrase to section level, consider the first two phrases of Richard Rodgers and Lorenz Hart's "Falling in Love With Love," or Thelonious Monk's "Brilliant Corners."

14. See Schoenberg 1967, 20–24 and Caplin 1998, 40–43 for a discussion of the process of liquidation within the sentence form.

15. Over the last two measures of the bridge to "Prelude to a Kiss," the harmony modulates to the key of the next *a* section.

16. Certain substitutions and embellishments can change the harmonic structure and overall sound of the phrase without undermining its function. Consider, for example, the replacement of a dominant seventh with its tritone substitute or the insertion of a pre-dominant II before a composed or substituted dominant seventh. See Martin (1988) and Strunk (1979) for more on harmonic substitution in jazz.

17. The passage in the original score has fewer chords than what is shown here. However, the harmonic structure of example 7.9 is typical of what a jazz musician or arranger would prefer. See, for example, Hal Leonard 1998, 352 or Billy May's arrangement in Sinatra 1959. In these cases, a passage's latent but implicit formal function is made explicit through reharmonization.

18. Due to the chromatic nature of the melody and the relatively dense harmonic rhythm, instructors will find it useful to establish the key of the piece before playing it and to exaggerate the cadences by changing either the dynamics or tempo.

19. Examples are Rodgers and Hart's "Falling in Love with Love" and Harry Warren and Mack Gordon's "There Will Never Be Another You."

20. Benward and Kolosick (2005, 382) refer to this as a "tag."

21. For other occurrences of overlapping to this degree in standard jazz repertoire, see Morgan Lewis and Nancy Hamilton's "How High the Moon," mm. 4–8 or Miles Davis's "Solar," mm. 1–8.

REFERENCES

Alegant, Brian. 2007. Listen up! Thoughts on iPods, sonata form, and analysis without score. *Journal of Music Theory Pedagogy* 21:141–60.

Benward, Bruce, and J. Timothy Kolosick. 2010. *Ear training: A technique for listening.* 7th rev. ed. Boston: McGraw-Hill.

Berliner, Paul. 1994. *Thinking in jazz: The infinite art of improvisation.* Chicago: University of Chicago Press.

Berry, Wallace. 1986. *Form in music.* 2nd ed. Englewood Cliffs, NJ: Prentice-Hall.

———. 1987. *Structural functions in music.* New York: Dover.

Biamonte, Nicole. 2010. Triadic modal and pentatonic patterns in rock music. *Music Theory Spectrum* 32, 2: 95–110.

Caplin, William. 1998. *Classical form: A theory of formal functions for the instrumental music of Haydn, Mozart, and Beethoven.* New York: Oxford University Press.

Cone, Edward T. 1968. *Musical form and musical performance.* New York: W. W. Norton.

Cook, Nicholas. 1987. Musical form and the listener. *Journal of Aesthetics and Art Criticism* 46:23–29.

Covach, John. 2004. Form in rock music: A primer. In *Engaging music*, ed. Deborah Stein, 65–76. New York: Oxford University Press.

De Stwolinski, Gail. 1977. *Form and content in instrumental music.* Dubuque, IA: W. C. Brown.

Dodson, Alan. 2002. Performance and hypermetric transformation: An extension of the Lerdahl-Jackendoff theory. *Music Theory Online* 8, no. 1 (February).

Doll, Christopher. 2007. Listening to rock harmony. PhD diss., Columbia University.

Dubiel, Joseph. 2000. Analysis, description, and what really happens. *Music Theory Online* 6, no. 3 (August).

Forte, Allen. 1995. *The American popular ballad of the golden era: 1924–1950.* New Jersey: Princeton University Press.

———. 1997–98. The real "Stella" and the "Real" Stella: A response to "Alternate Takes." *Annual Review of Jazz Studies* 9:93–101.

Hal Leonard. 1998. *The ultimate jazz fakebook.* Winona, MN: Hal Leonard.

Huron, David. 2007. *Sweet anticipation.* Cambridge, MA: MIT Press.

Karpinski, Gary S. 1993. Reviews of *Introduction to sightsinging and ear training*, 2nd ed., by Bruce Benward, Maureen Carr, and J. Timothy Kolosick; *Basic ear training skills*, by Robert Ottman and Paul E. Dworak; *Aural awareness: Principles and practice*, by George Pratt. *Music Theory Spectrum* 15:241–56.

———. 2000a. *Aural skills acquisition: The development of listening, reading, and performing skills in college-level musicians.* New York: Oxford University Press.

———. 2000b. Lessons from the past: Music theory pedagogy and the future. *Music Theory Online* 6, no. 3 (August).

———. 2006. *Manual for ear training and sight singing.* New York: W. W. Norton.

Lerdahl, Fred, and Ray Jackendoff. 1983. *A generative theory of tonal music.* Cambridge, MA: MIT Press.

Levinson, Jerrold. 1997. *Music in the moment.* Ithaca, NY: Cornell University Press.

Martin, Henry. 1988. Jazz harmony: A syntactic background. *Annual Review of Jazz Studies* 6:9–30.

Meyer, Leonard. 1973. *Explaining music.* Berkeley: University of California Press.

Moore, Allan F. 2001. *Rock: The primary text.* Burlington, VT: Ashgate.

Phillips, Joel, Elizabeth West Marvin, and Jane Piper Clendinning. 2004–5. *The musician's guide to aural skills.* 2 vols. New York: W. W. Norton.

Pratt, George, Michael Henson, and Simon Cargill. 1998. *Aural awareness: Principles and practice*. New York: Oxford University Press.

Ratz, Erwin. 1973. *Einführung in die musikalische formenlehre: Über formprinzipien in den inventionen und fugen J. S. Bachs und ihre bedeutung für die kompositiontechnik Beethovens*. 3rd ed. Vienna: Universal.

Rogers, Michael R. 2004. *Teaching approaches in music theory*. 2nd ed. Carbondale: Southern Illinois University Press.

Rothstein, William. 1989. *Phrase rhythm in tonal music*. New York: Schirmer.

Santa, Matthew. 2009. *Hearing form: Musical analysis with and without the score*. New York: Routledge.

Schoenberg, Arnold. 1967. *Fundamentals of musical composition*. ed. Gerald Strang and Leonard Stein. London: Faber & Faber.

———. 1969. *Structural functions of harmony*. rev. ed., ed. Leonard Stein. New York: W. W. Norton.

Sinatra, Frank. 1959. *Come dance with me!* Capitol, 94754.

Spencer, Peter, and Peter M. Temko. 1988. *A practical approach to the study of form in music*. Englewood Cliffs, NJ: Prentice-Hall.

Stephenson, Ken. 2002. *What to listen for in rock*. New Haven, CT: Yale University Press.

Strunk, Steven. 1979. The harmony of early bop: A layered approach. *Journal of Jazz Studies* 6:4–53.

Temperley, David. 2007. The melodic-harmonic "divorce" in rock. *Popular Music* 26:323–42.

White, John. 2001. *Guidelines for college teaching of music theory*. 2nd ed. Lanham, MD: Scarecrow Press.

Wittlich, Gary E., and Lee Humphries. 1974. *Ear training: An approach through music literature*. New York: Harcourt Brace Jovanovich.

8

Musical Representation in the Video Games Guitar Hero and Rock Band

Nicole Biamonte

This chapter explores some pedagogical applications of the videogames Guitar Hero and Rock Band through their representations of music notation and form.[1] Guitar Hero and Rock Band are part of a uniquely performative genre of games that includes Dance Dance Revolution, Karaoke Revolution, SingStar, DJ Hero, and similar games, which create a new kind of performance space through kinesthetic interaction with musical recordings. In Guitar Hero and Rock Band, songs are "played" or reproduced through instrument-shaped controllers that mimic guitars, drums, and microphones. Accurate responses to onscreen notated cues trigger playback of a prerecorded song. The games have been described as sonic realizations of air guitar (or air drums), and their success is undoubtedly due in no small part to their performativity. There is as yet no keyboard instrument controller for the games, which is not only because of the difficulty of designing a simplified version but also because playing keyboards requires relatively minimal movement and is, thus, inherently less performative than guitar, vocals, or drums. Guitarists and vocalists can move around in ways limited only by their ability to simultaneously continue producing sound; the drummer is stationary but often very kinetic, with large, rapid, potentially showy gestures.[2]

In addition to their performative aspects, other reasons for the games' popularity are the social space created by the gameplay format, with multiplayer options and complex background scenes that are clearly designed for viewers rather than players, and, most germane to this study, the unprecedented level of musical interaction with the songs in the games. The success of these performance-based games has impacted not only the video-game industry but also the music industry, fostering new interest not only in the songs and bands included in the games but also in learning to play the real musical instruments, as demonstrated by increases in instrument sales and beginning lessons (Ahmed 2008) and the wide availability of tablature and sheet music for songs from the games, explicitly marketed as such.[3]

The potential pedagogical applications of games such as Guitar Hero and Rock Band in an individual lab format are extensive. The visual and aural separation of song tracks into lead, rhythm, and bass guitars, drums, and vocals (depending on the particular game version and song) trains listeners to parse layers of musical texture. Many players have commented that their gameplay experiences have led them to hear textures more completely, not only in the songs within the games but also in all of their music listening (Miller 2009a). The games are part of a genre known as "rhythm games," and while their focus on rhythmic elements at the expense of pitch and other musical domains has been a prime source of criticism, they can serve as excellent tools for demonstrating tempo, meter, and rhythm and for teaching basic beat-matching and rhythmic patterns.[4] Matching generalized pitch—or timbre in the drum parts—and rhythm cues during gameplay is a built-in exercise in error detection since if the correct response to a note cue is not provided within a certain adjustable window of time, audio playback of the note is omitted or muffled and replaced with a jarring noise. The games also train sight-reading skills: experienced players have described their development of essential techniques taught in aural-skills classes, such as scanning ahead and chunking (Miller 2009b). The kinesthetic response to notation that is cultivated through playing the games may very well provide cognitive scaffolding for development of the greater physical coordination required to play the real instruments. The social aspects of gameplay would doubtless provide excellent motivation for students to complete game-based assignments.

However, because of the extensive startup resources required for lab use—purchasing multiple copies of the games, controllers, and headphones, as well as access to monitors or televisions and lab space and a means of securing the equipment—this essay focuses on applications of the games in a classroom lecture or discussion format, with demonstrations through video clips or a single copy of a game. Considering the alternative notations used in the games and their unprecedented three-dimensionality provides a window into a broader exploration of notational conventions and their omissions. While not intended as such, the detailed breakdowns of songs into sections and subsections in the games' practice modes and score tallies comprise implicit formal analyses. These formal interpretations of the songs can be profitably examined within a broader consideration of the various musical parameters that typically combine to create structure. Similarly, while not originally interpretive in purpose, the relationships between note cues at different levels of difficulty in the games create large-scale hierarchies of melodic and rhythmic segmentation, which can be reimagined as implicit analyses.

NOTATION

The developers of Guitar Hero and Rock Band have created simplified forms of notation for the instrument controllers, which symbolize specific rhythmic attack points and durations but only relative pitches and pitch contours. These simplified notation systems ensure that the games are easy to learn (although not necessarily to master). The stripped-down notations work well in this context because complete representations of the music are unnecessary. The tracks are already recorded and are merely played back during the game, in an act of recreation rather than creation. What was needed as a basis for interaction with the music was something more than pressing "play" but something less than complete notated transcriptions of the vocal and instrumental parts.

Most guitar controllers for the games have between 18 and 20 frets, which approaches the usual number of 21 to 23 frets on a typical electric guitar. Only 5 of these frets, however, are supplied with playable buttons. On Rock Band guitar controllers, the main buttons are duplicated at the top of the neck for rapid tapping techniques, such as hammer-ons and pull-offs, which are played without strumming (and are also helpful for those with small hands), but otherwise, they function exactly like the main buttons. The reduction from over 20 frets to the equivalent of 5 may seem drastic, but as Dominic Arsenault has pointed out in an article comparing real-guitar technique to Guitar Hero guitar technique:

> The act of playing the guitar is a combination of two playing styles. The first can be described as moving the left hand up and down the neck (horizontally) . . . to reach different frets. The second, commonly called "position playing," consists in covering four frets with one's four fingers and playing across all six strings (vertically) without moving the hand up or down the neck, stretching the little finger to cover a fifth fret when needed. This method gives access to 29 different notes in a single position, and is necessary for one to successfully play fast passages. Thus, while the game controller only offers five buttons, there is a similarly sizable proportion of guitar playing that involves only five frets at a time. What is missing from the simulation is not the 20-or-so other frets found on a real guitar, but rather the quick transitions from one five-fret position to another on the fretboard. This feature reduces the apparent gap in complexity between the game hardware and an actual instrument. (2008, 3)

All guitar controllers have a single strum bar, which seemingly eliminates the harmonic dimension of the guitar's multiple strings. The strum bar reduces the inherent two-dimensional pitch range of the guitar's horizontal fretboard and vertical strings down to a single horizontal dimension that is more akin to the linear design of a single-keyboard instrument (or a single-string instrument, like the one-string guitars sometimes used in Delta blues). This reduction allows the pitch dimension of the guitar controller to be mapped along a single axis, as shown in example 8.1. The topmost line, examples 8.1a and 8.1b, shows the standard arrangement of strings, with the lowest on top and the highest on the bottom, which is normally the same for both right-handed and left-handed guitars. The left side of each diagram corresponds to the left side of the fretboard rather than the top of the guitar neck. The reversal of fretboard direction between right-handed and left-handed guitar playing reverses its pitch direction. Both Guitar Hero and Rock Band include a "lefty flip" option that reverses the order of fretboard buttons in the same way, as shown in examples 8.1c and 8.1d. In traditional guitar tablature (see example 8.1e), the strings are rotated 90 degrees counterclockwise from their arrangement on the fretboard, which is symbolized vertically, with the lowest frets at the top. It is worth noting that the vertical dimensions of guitar fretboards and traditional guitar tablature are cross-mapped in relation to traditional staff notation and Internet tablature (see example 8.1f), which symbolize low to high pitches from bottom to top, rather than top to bottom.

The guitar notation in the games is inspired by guitar tablature, an instrument-specific notation that provides a visual schematic of the player's hand position. The game notation for guitar and bass consists of glowing note heads on a scrolling fretboard that are both color-coded and spatially coded, showing players where to place their fingers (see example 8.2). When a note is played correctly, it explodes in a metaphorical depiction of the energy released when a sound is produced. Having exploded, the note then disappears, enhancing the player's sense of the temporality of music. Notes that are not played correctly remain visually intact but are replaced in the audio track with an unmusical clinking noise.

Unlike traditional staff notation, in which the horizontal or x axis represents time while the vertical or y axis represents pitch, the scrolling fretboard represents pitch on the x axis and time on the z axis. The horizontal onscreen pitches map onto the horizontal row of buttons on the guitar fretboard. This mapping, as well as left-right hand coordination, is kinesthetically reinforced through gameplay. The scrolling fretboard extends along the z axis into the screen so that the notes flow toward the player. This orientation allows for scanning ahead and also draws both players and viewers into the game, symbolizing the music as a physical space that is moved through and creating an unprecedented sense of being inside the song. A still more intensively three-dimensional experience of the music

(L = low, H = high)

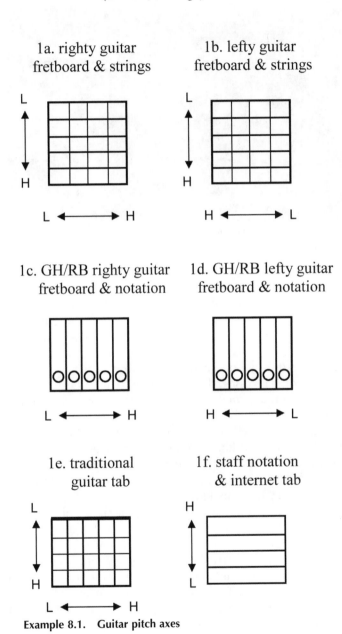

Example 8.1.   Guitar pitch axes

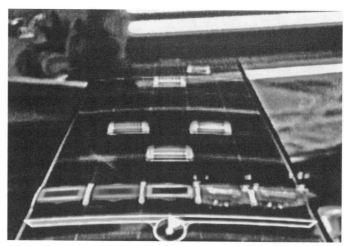

Example 8.2. Scrolling guitar notation

could be constructed with a transparent fretboard or tablature notation that maps pitch onto both the x and y axes and time onto the z axis.

The spatial arrangement of the onscreen fretboard, with the z axis representing time, is unusual for scrolling notation, which more typically flows along the x axis from left to right, as in Karaoke Revolution and many digital-audio editing software programs, such as GarageBand and Logic Pro. The z-axis orientation is quite common, however, in first-person shooter and driving videogames; indeed, the scrolling fretboard is referred to as the "note highway" in the games' online discussion forums.[5] A similar scrolling notation system is used in Synaesthetic Software's Virtual Drum Clinic. This visual paradigm bears some resemblance to the vertical staff of Dutch klavarskribo,[6] a simplified keyboard notation that offers a possible model for a keyboard-controller game notation. Klavar notation, like most vertical systems, such as Chinese, Korean, and many Japanese notations, is read from top to bottom. It seems likely that the top-down direction in vertical notation is privileged because most instruments are played at or above waist level most of the time. An exception is the bottom-to-top vertical scrolling of Dance Dance Revolution, which originates at the bottom of the screen because the game is performed with the legs and feet.

In Guitar Hero and Rock Band guitar notation, the five colors and positions of the note cues correlate with the five buttons on the guitar controllers. Since most songs use more than five notes, this notation symbolizes relative pitches and contours rather than specific pitches or scale degrees, and is, thus, more generalized than other simplified systems, such as shape-note notation. The onscreen note cues control groups of notes at lower skill levels of the game and smaller groups or individual notes at higher skill levels. The one-to-one note correspondences at higher levels of difficulty result in counterintuitive contour shapes on the fretboard when there are more than five notes in a single direction. For example, the chorus of Heart's "Crazy on You" has a six-note descending pattern. The game notation for this section, shown in example 8.3, preserves the relative contour of the first five notes (the descending scale E–D–C–B–A) and, separately, that of the last note in each phrase. Thus, in the game notation, F below A is notated as the same pitch and both G and the final A (the last note of the pattern) as one step above F. This disjunction between contour fragments creates a surprising change of direction in the third statement of the pattern, when the descending step A–G is notated onscreen as an ascending step. Such contour shifts are particularly common in arpeggiated or chordal textures, where the limited range necessitates many notational compromises.

Like the guitar notation, drum notation in the games is also shown along the *z* axis on the scrolling fretboard, and note cues are correlated to color-coded drum pads. Rock Band drums have four pads, which represent a snare, a crash cymbal, and either two additional cymbals or toms. Guitar Hero drums have three drum pads, which always represent a snare and two toms, and two cymbal pads, representing crash and high-hat cymbals. This is not only more consistent but also more rigid than Rock Band's setup, which can distinguish between open and closed high-hat or notate a third cymbal or tom. In the drum notation for both games, a different type of indicator, a glowing bar across the fretboard rather than a note head, represents the kick pedal for the bass drum. Because of the more constrained pitch and timbral resources of a drum kit in comparison with the guitar, the drum parts in the games are a much closer simulation of actually playing the drums than the guitar or bass parts. Rhythm in both the guitar and drum notation is symbolized by the relationship of onscreen notes to frets, which function like bar lines but delineate each beat. Slightly thicker frets serve as bar lines, and thinner, fainter frets mark the offbeats. This provides a clear visual representation of the relationship of each note to the beat, which, in contrast to much art music and some folk musics, is usually explicitly marked by the drum part in rock music and related genres.

The notation of vocal parts in the games, shown in example 8.4, is the most similar to traditional notation: the *x* axis represents time, and the *y* axis

Example 8.3.   Heart, "Crazy on You," chorus riff. Guitar notation from Guitar Hero II, rotated (top) and staff notation (bottom)

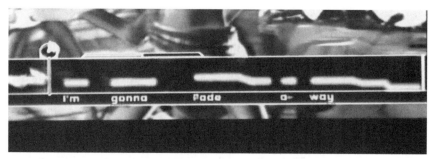

Example 8.4.   Scrolling vocal notation

represents pitch, with low to high mapped from bottom to top as in conventional staff notation. As with the guitar notation, pitch relationships are shown in the same spatial dimension as the player's performed response, although in the vocal notation, this relationship is inherently more embodied because the onscreen positions of high and low notes reflect the physical resonance of the sound in the singer's body.

As in karaoke and karaoke-based games, singers use their own voices, and thus, the vocal parts are more authentically performative than using the instrument controllers. Singers have a much greater personal responsibility for the sound than instrumental players and receive constructive feedback on pitch accuracy (although not on other aspects of vocal production). However, since the games have no text-recognition feature, subversive substitutions such as alternate texts, humming, or even using a kazoo will not affect the game score. During instrumental sections in some songs, the vocal part is transformed into a regular percussive beat symbolized by discrete dots, representing a tambourine or other handheld percussion instrument. These percussion notes are played by striking the microphone controller against one's hand.

The horizontal orientation of the scrolling vocal part allows the text to be aligned with the notes and read normally from left to right. In the vocal parts, relative pitch levels are shown over the text, like the heightened neumes of medieval chant. Unlike neumatic notation, the width of the notes is proportional to their duration, resembling piano-roll notation. Thus, the visual portrayal of rhythm in the vocal parts is less symbolic than that of other musical parameters in the game. Because the notation scrolls, there are no limits on the amount of space used by this proportional notation, which would be impractical for printed music. The horizontal orientation also allows the full-band notation, with three vertical scrolls and one horizontal, to fit easily on a television screen.

The reduction of note cues at easier difficulty levels creates a large-scale hierarchy of melodic and rhythmic structures. At lower levels, on-screen notes often cue the first pitch of sequences or other repeated patterns. For

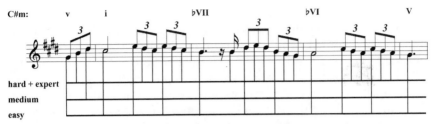

Example 8.5.   Kiss, "Detroit Rock City" (Rock Band), beginning of solo

example, in the guitar solo of Kiss's "Detroit Rock City" (see example 8.5), at the easy level, only the first note of each triplet is cued, creating a rhythmic reduction to the stable chord tones on beats one, three and four. The "hard" and "expert" levels include all of the notes of the guitar solo in a one-to-one correspondence.

In contrast, the syncopated verse riff of Boston's "More Than a Feeling" (see example 8.6) has no obvious repeats, although the registral shifts of the compound melody suggest groupings. The easy-level reduction reveals the hidden repetition of the 4–3–1 gesture in the upper register over the tonic in mm. 1–2 that occurs in the lower register over the subdominant in mm. 3–4.

In his essay "Music Theory in Music Games," Peter Shultz asserts that these relationships can train players to think analytically about the music: "[The game] makes connections between the musical reductions used at different difficulty levels, encouraging the player to hear and think about each level in terms of the ones they have already played. To the extent that this happens (and I believe it usually does), the game becomes an advocate for a hierarchical order of musical awareness: players conceive of difficult patterns as elaborated versions of simpler ones" (2008, 187). While I am reluctant to advance such claims without more direct supporting evidence, the pedagogical potential of this aspect of the games is certainly intriguing and worthy of further exploration.

Example 8.6.   Boston, "More Than a Feeling" (Guitar Hero), guitar verse riff

An examination of notation in these games could be incorporated into a fundamentals or beginning theory class as part of an introduction to notation that briefly surveys its history from heightened neumes, to the single-line staff, to the multiple-line staff, to the use of clefs to shift the pitch range of the staff. Tablature, chord charts, and graphic notation—especially an example where the *y* axis represents volume rather than pitch—could also be included in this unit. An exercise to reinforce this material is to have the students transcribe a familiar song (such as a children's song, Christmas carol, or "Happy Birthday") in heightened neumes, reflecting only relative pitch height, and then in piano-roll notation, reflecting proportional durations as well. Students who are already notation-literate could be asked to make a reduction of a melody appropriate to an easy-level guitar part, taking into consideration the various domains in creating note groupings: pitch, register, contour, durational or metric emphasis, and repeated or sequential patterns.

Examination of the games' forms of notation offers a basis for consideration and discussion of the indeterminacy of notation in both art and vernacular music. Traditional Western notation typically specifies pitch in great detail and proportional duration in lesser detail, with additional markings to indicate dynamics and articulation and minimal significations of timbre. Yet the range of possible sounds that can be generated by any performer or instrument are too variable, complex, and nuanced to be entirely represented by any abstract system. Staff and tablature notations are particularly inadequate representations of most popular musics, which originate from largely unwritten traditions. Difficulties with transcriptions are created by the extensive "participatory discrepancies" in pitch and rhythm characteristic of many vernacular styles: bending, sliding between, or falling off pitches, highly syncopated rhythms or notes that are placed just ahead of or behind the beat. Like the swung rhythms of jazz and blues shuffles, these performance practices are not well represented by existing systems of written notation.

FORM

The games' descriptors of formal song sections, while practical in purpose, nonetheless constitute de facto analyses of their structures. The formal designations used in the games provide an opportunity for critical consideration of these implicit interpretations and examination of the various musical parameters that typically combine to create structure. In all the versions of Guitar Hero after the first, a practice mode allows the opportunity to work on particular sections of songs, chosen from a detailed breakdown of the song structure into brief sections. In Rock Band, in contrast, only complete songs can be played in practice mode, and while the names of formal sections appear at the top of the screen, the structural divisions are far less detailed.

Many of the formal descriptors employed in Guitar Hero and Rock Band are familiar terms. Example 8.7 provides a glossary of formal terminology used to describe song sections in the games. Most of the sections listed under "Standard Terms" are usually two, four, or eight phrases long, with the exception of solos, which may be considerably longer. In Guitar Hero's formal charts, these units are frequently divided into multiple subsections: up to three sections for verses, choruses, and bridges, and up to eight sections for solos.

However, even these standard terms are not used with complete consistency. For example, in Cream's "Sunshine of Your Love" from Guitar Hero III, the same musical material is designated "intro," "intro riff," and "main riff" at different points in the song. The instrumental beginning of the Police's "Message in a Bottle," one of the songs in Guitar Hero II, is labeled as part of verse 1. The guitar and bass play the accompaniment to the verses, but the first two statements of the pattern are clearly introductory in nature, as there are no vocals yet. A more subtle signifier of the difference between the introduction and verse is the change in the drum pattern, which shifts to half as many bass and snare hits and more use of the open high-hat at the beginning of the verse. When this repeated instrumental pattern returns near the end of the song (at 3:17 on the audio track), it is labeled "outro" in the game, strongly suggesting that its initial presentation in the song should use the parallel terminology of "intro." Conversely, the opening a cappella chorus of Kansas's "Carry On Wayward Son" from Guitar Hero II is described as the "vocal intro" rather than the chorus. In both of these cases, practicing the section in question as an independent unit is superfluous, which is likely the reason why the introduction to "Message in a Bottle" is conflated with the opening verse, and the instrumental tacet chorus of "Carry On Wayward Son" is designated as introductory.

In other cases, the formal designations of songs in the games express motivic relationships that might not otherwise be clear to the casual listener or player. In Rush's multi-sectional instrumental "YYZ" from Guitar Hero II, the first two sections following the introduction are labeled "verse" and "chorus," not because they are especially verse-like or chorus-like but because they recur at the end of the song, after several other intervening sections. The formal breakdowns of Muse's "Knights of Cydonia" and Metallica's "One" from Guitar Hero III employ more fanciful terminology but, nonetheless, help to clarify the complex structures of these songs.

Most of the "Nonstandard Terms" are actually fairly common designations used in nonstandard ways; for example, the first four terms ("riff," "hook," "guitar break," and "melody") refer to sections constructed from

Standard Terms

Intro: initial section, usually instrumental and leading into the first verse; typically begins with a thinner texture than the main body of the song, which is either maintained or built up into a fuller texture over the course of the introduction

Verse: recurring strophe with changing lyrics; sometimes concludes with unchanging refrain

Chorus: recurring strophe with unchanging lyrics; usually stylistically and structurally more conservative and regular than verses and often has a thicker texture

Bridge: section generally stated only once or twice in a song that provides harmonic, melodic, and lyrical contrast; commonly has a re-transition function, ending on the dominant

Solo: instrumental display of virtuosity and improvisational skill; usually over the accompaniment to the verse or chorus but sometimes over an entirely new pattern

Outro: coda; often motivically related to intro or body of song

Nonstandard Terms

Riff: melodic, rhythmic, or harmonic pattern that repeats to form a structural framework

Hook: motivic gesture with a characteristic melody and rhythm (less commonly a harmonic pattern), repeated only intermittently

Guitar Break: alternate term for guitar hook

Melody: alternate term for slow-moving guitar hook (compared to rest of texture)

Breakdown: sudden thinning of the texture as an ensemble; often, the bass drum drops out

Jam: ostinato or vamp section with increasing variations (like a *montuno*)

Ending: alternate term for outro; most commonly a slowed-down final phrase or a non-motivic ending with repeated chords or a break in the texture

Nonserious Terms

Solo-ette: brief solo; used in Aerosmith's "Same Old Song and Dance" and DragonForce's "Operation Ground and Pound"

Feeling Sax-y: sax solo in Aerosmith's "Same Old Song and Dance"

Riff of Doom: riff in Black Sabbath's "Paranoid"

Riffus Maximus: riff; used in Living Colour's "Cult of Personality," Def Leppard's "Rock of Ages," and DragonForce's "Revolution Deathsquad"

Outro Madness: long, rapidly strummed chord concluding Cream's "Sunshine of Your Love"

End Wankery: excessive display of virtuosity at the end of a song, either over-repeating choruses to a fade-out or between the last functional harmony and the final chord; used in Van Halen's cover of the Kinks' "You Really Got Me" and Lynyrd Skynyrd's "Free Bird"

Example 8.7. Formal terminology used in Guitar Hero and Rock Band

the repeated shorter units they normally signify. The terms "riff" and "hook" are used interchangeably both in Guitar Hero and in popular-music scholarship. However, a useful distinction can be made between them: both consist of single phrases or sub-phrases, but "riff" typically refers to a melodic, rhythmic, or harmonic pattern that repeats to form a structural framework, while "hook" more often refers to a motivic gesture with a characteristic melody and rhythm—usually not a chord pattern—that is repeated only intermittently. "Hook" has also been used more generically to refer to any particularly memorable element of a song (see, for example, Burns 1987). The game also uses "guitar break" as a label for some riffs and "melody" for slow-moving guitar hooks. What all of these units have in common is their brevity, regular rhythm, and regular phrase structure, in contrast to the extended length, differentiated rhythm, and irregular phrasing of most solos. The term "solo" is reserved only for those sections characterized by distinctly improvisatory qualities.

"Breakdown," like guitar break, refers to a sudden thinning of the texture as an ensemble, with no particular instrument standing out. This usage is different from its normal meaning in bluegrass music (as in "Foggy Mountain Breakdown") of a series of contrasting instrumental solos. Another nonstandard usage in Guitar Hero is of the term "jam," which in the Allman Brothers Band's "Jessica" is applied to a constant repeated pattern (from 1:40 to 2:28 on the audio track) that would be called an ostinato in art music, a *montuno* in Latin jazz, and a vamp in Broadway music. A jam more typically means an extended section of collective improvisation without a consistent surface pattern, such as those that characterize the music of "jam bands," such as the Grateful Dead and Phish. Guitar Hero uses both "outro" and "ending" to label the final sections of some songs. The distinction between the usage of these terms is not entirely clear, and both in succession are used for "Misirlou" in Guitar Hero II. "Outros" are more often motivically related to the song and tend to be longer, while "ending" refers either to a slowed-down final phrase or a non-motivic ending with repeated chords or a break in the texture.

Admittedly, the aim of the game designers was practical rather than pedagogical, as is demonstrated by the third section of nonserious terminology, which I will not explore further here—except to say that in regard to excessive displays of virtuosity at the end of a song, either over repeating choruses to a fade-out or between the last functional harmony of a song and its final chord, "end wankery" is an excellent and evocative term, and I hope it will catch on.

Some types of class assignments relating to form could be: to write a brief paper analyzing and critiquing the sections of a song as represented in one of the games, to construct and explain a similar formal parsing of a song not officially included in any of the games, to collect and discuss multiple musical examples of one of the games' nonstandard terms, or to compare the rhetorical functions of formal sections, such as expository, contrasting, or transitional, in the games' terminology and in common-practice art-music terminology or, more broadly, as demonstrated by examples from both vernacular and art song.

CONCLUSION

I have described here only two topics that could be addressed in the context of Guitar Hero and Rock Band: notation and form. Many other traditional music-theoretical topics would lend themselves equally well to similar treatment, including musicianship skills, such as ear-training, sight-reading, and rhythm-training. Aspects of the games could also be investigated in light of musicological or cultural-studies methodologies. For example, the rock-music canon established by radio and video programming is both re-flected and transformed by the games' selection of songs, bands, and down-loadable content. Examination of the selection and reception of these songs and bands and the implicit commentary on these choices provided by the numerous playable tracks of user-generated songs not officially included in the games offer a basis for inquiry into issues of canon formation and rei-fication in rock music and its related subgenres. Similarly, the stereotyped musician avatars in the games can be critically assessed as constructed iden-tities, reflecting the designers' underlying conceptions of celebrity, gender, and rock subcultures and their associated styles.

These performance-based games are pedagogically useful because they offer a new kind of musical experience that resonates with our perception of embodied performance as well as with students' recreational listening and videogame entertainment outside of the classroom. Such games have valuable potential as tools for musical learning in a variety of domains. Their visual and kinesthetic representations of popular songs open new windows for reexamining our older hearings and understandings of music.

NOTES

1. Versions of the games included in this study are: *Guitar Hero, Guitar Hero II, Guitar Hero III: Legends of Rock, Guitar Hero Encore: Rocks the 80s, Rock Band,* and *Rock Band 2.*

2. Some well-known parodies of the energetic physicality of rock drummers are the character Animal, who is the drummer for Dr. Teeth and the Electric Mayhem from *The Muppet Show,* and the spontaneously combusting drummers of Spinal Tap.

3. *Guitar Hero Songbook: The Official Songbook of Guitar Hero I and II* (Milwaukee, WI: Hal Leonard, 2007); *Guitar Hero III: Legends of Rock Songbook* (Milwaukee, WI:

Hal Leonard, 2008); *Rock Band* and *Rock Band 2 Songbooks* (Milwaukee, WI: Hal Leonard, both 2009); /guitarherotab.com/, and others.

4. For a more detailed discussion of potential techniques, see chapter 9 of this volume, Auerbach, Aarden, and Bostock's "*DDR* at the Crossroads: A Report on a Pilot Study to Integrate Music Video Game Technology into the Aural-Skills Classroom," on using *Dance Dance Revolution* for rhythm training.

5. See, for example, the *Guitar Hero* discussion forum at hub.guitarhero.com/community and the *Rock Band* discussion forum at www.rockband.com/forums.

6. For examples, see Klavar Music Foundation, "The Klavar Method" at http://www.klavarmusic.org/Explanation.pdf or the Wikipedia entry for "Klavarskribo" at http://en.wikipedia.org/wiki/Klavarskribo.

REFERENCES

Ahmed, Murad. 2008. Guitar Hero leads children to pick up real instruments. *Times*, December 1. http://technology.timesonline.co.uk/tol/news/tech_and_web/gadgets_and_gaming/article5266959.ece.

Arsenault, Dominic. 2008. Guitar Hero: "Not like playing guitar at all"? *Loading . . .* 2, no. 2. http://journals.sfu.ca/loading/index.php/loading/article/view/32.

Burns, Gary. 1987. A typology of "hooks" in popular records. *Popular Music* 6:1–20.

Miller, Kiri. 2009a. Interview tidbits: On musicality in Guitar Hero and Rock Band. Guitar Hero: A Research Blog, January 12. http://guitarheroresearch.blogspot.com/2009/01/interview-tidbits-on-musicality-in.html.

———. 2009b. Schizophonic performance: Guitar Hero, Rock Band, and virtual virtuosity. *Journal of the Society for American Music* 3, no. 4: 395–429.

Musgrove, Mike. 2008. Some heroes want to get real. *Washington Post*, May 11.

Radosh, Daniel. 2009. While my guitar gently beeps. *New York Times*, August 16.

Shultz, Peter. 2008. Music theory in music games. In *From Pac-Man to pop music: Interactive audio in games and new media*, ed. Karen Collins, 177–88. Aldershot, Hampshire, UK: Ashgate.

Smith, Jacob. 2004. I can see tomorrow in your dance: A study of *Dance Dance Revolution* and music video games. *Journal of Popular Music Studies* 16, no. 1: 58–84.

Terdiman, Daniel. 2007. "Is Tomorrow's Clapton Playing 'Guitar Hero'?" *CNET News*, November 28, 2007. http://news.cnet.com/Is-tomorrows-Clapton-playing-Guitar-Hero/2100-1043_3-6220398.html.

9

DDR at the Crossroads: A Report on a Pilot Study to Integrate Music Video-Game Technology into the Aural-Skills Classroom

Brent Auerbach, Bret Aarden, and Mathonwy Bostock

The history of mainstream electronic music-games is a fairly recent one. There was a flurry of interest in the melody-based memory game Simon in the 1970s; however, the first music game to explode onto the world stage was the 1998 Dance Dance Revolution (DDR), a rhythm and dance video-game that dramatically expanded in popularity with its release for the PlayStation in 2001.[1] In 2006, we at the University of Massachusetts, Amherst became interested in exploring the applicability of Dance Dance Revolution to aural-skills instruction.[2] Though intended primarily as a form of entertainment, DDR has many qualities that make it ideal as a computer-aided instruction (CAI) device. It provides real-time, automated feedback on rhythmic attacks through objective scoring. It is, moreover, a highly flexible program that includes special modes for programming rhythms, sharing them, and practicing them at varied tempos, with and without a metronome. Further secondary advantages of DDR include students' general familiarity with the game from popular culture and the documented health benefits reaped from long-term exposure to it (Auerbach 2010; Barker 2005).

There are some significant downsides of the game with regard to rhythm-skills instruction. One is that the vast majority of the preprogrammed songs in DDR are in 4/4 time, making the drilling of other time signatures problematic. Another is that the step arrow motions are in the wrong orientation for trained musicians familiar with traditional staff notation: they scroll from bottom to top instead of from right to left. Neither of these complications detracts from the primary value of Dance Dance Revolution as a game that is concerned almost exclusively with rhythmic performance.[3]

DDR's focus on this particular domain of music makes it potentially a very useful tool for improving musicianship. Repeated studies have established that students' baseline rhythmic skills are the best predictor of their success in sight-reading and overall performance (Thomson 1953; Elliott 1982; McPherson 1994). Our decision to inquire into the pedagogical potential of DDR led to a successful bid for a $4,000 internal grant, the purchase of video game equipment and accessories, the design and execution of a classroom curriculum, and the development of a research agenda. The UMass Amherst DDR lab officially opened in the fall of 2006. Over the next two years, students attended the lab as required by their class syllabi, and a set of paid volunteers took part in a cognition experiment that measured the impact of DDR practice on sight-reading ability.

In the basic sense that we were carrying out groundbreaking work, this venture into technology succeeded. As research, however, its value is not measured in terms of activity but by results. We at UMass are currently formulating responses to the most pressing questions concerning DDR: What, precisely, did the students enrolled in aural skills get out of their practice regimen with the game? Does exposure to DDR measurably improve musicians' rhythmic accuracy? What about their sight-reading skills and their internal beat-clocks? We do have preliminary answers to some of these questions and will relate them below. Although most of our results remain, at this stage, incomplete and anecdotal, we hope our account of the rewards and challenges that we encountered during implementation of the DDR technology will help others who are interested in pursuing work in this area.

This essay is, thus, intended as a report "from the trenches" on our experiences with DDR. The report is organized in two parts in accordance with the two main venues chosen for DDR activity, the classroom and the cognition laboratory.[4] The first section, "Classroom Outcomes," summarizes how DDR was incorporated for one semester into an aural-skills class with an enrollment of 40 students. We then consider the viability of our approach in light of the real-world constraints of game design as well as students' abilities, schedules, and morale. Our assessment of the value of DDR as a teaching tool results from collating information obtained both through formal survey and observation. The section entitled "Lab Outcomes" describes a pilot experiment conducted in the spring of 2008 to measure the benefits of long-term rhythmic practice with DDR. Unfortunately, problems with the experiment design produced ambiguous results. Full consideration of the causes of that outcome lead to a more careful framing of DDR research in general, as we ponder not only improvements in experimental design, but deeper questions, such as whether DDR exposure will benefit all segments of the musical population equally.

CLASSROOM OUTCOMES

Context

Undergraduates enrolled in Aural Skills III at UMass Amherst are usually required to attend two 50-minute group lectures per week and one 50-minute section led by a teaching assistant. In the fall of 2006, an extra requirement was added in the form of ten 35-minute DDR practice sessions, also scheduled once per week. Students were free to drop in at their convenience to the DDR lab, which contained eight practice stations and was open for 9.5 hours every week. Under supervision of the instructors and lab managers, the students pursued the curriculum illustrated in figure 9.1.[5]

The curriculum design took a number of factors into account, primarily among them the difficulty level of the songs as determined by DDR's designers (in figure 9.1, the numerals in parentheses are difficulty rankings on a scale from 1 to 10). All songs chosen for the first two weeks are extremely easy.[6] They are rated as 1s and 2s, meaning that attacks are widely spaced, typically occurring on beats 1 and 3 of a measure. In the third and fourth weeks, students practiced songs characterized by increased attack densities and occasional "jumps," or two-note attacks. The remaining weeks feature faster songs and the gradual introduction of syncopation. Two strategies help compensate for the gradual increase in difficulty. First, songs requiring similar skills are generally grouped together (see the descriptors on the list). Second, the list takes advantage of spiral learning, as earlier songs periodically reappear at higher difficulty levels with more complicated dance routines.[7] The familiarity with the music from earlier weeks dramatically lessens any shock of newness, particularly since the new steps often reflect surface rhythms of the song.

It was originally planned that students' progress with the game would be measured in two ways. Half of their DDR grade, or 5% of the final course grade, was to be awarded for regular attendance and for recorded improvements on assigned songs. Students were required to keep a detailed log of all songs attempted and each grade given by the program. The other half of their DDR grade would be awarded on the basis of a live DDR skills test given at the close of the semester. In the end, this two-pronged arrangement could only be partially implemented due to considerations of time and fairness to class members. These and other complicating issues will be discussed more fully in subsequent sections of the chapter.

Observations

Dance Dance Revolution was deployed in the classroom three semesters in advance of the pilot cognition experiment. This means that DDR's

Week1:   "Remember You" (1)
              "Baby Baby Gimme Your Love" (1)
              "Ordinary World" (1: half/whole notes)
              "Peace Out" (2)
Week 2:   "Secret Rendezvous" (2)
              "Spin the Disc" (2: half notes and holds)
              "Let's Talk It Over" (2)
              "Sana Morette" (2)
Week 3:   "Overblast" (3)
              "Look to the Sky" (3: long stretches of quarters)
              "You Leave Me Alone" (3)
              "Share My Love" (3: first sixteenth-note push)
Week 4:   "Let the Beat Hit 'Em" IN YELLOW (3: offbeats)
              "I Was the One" (3: stretch of quarters and some jumps)
              "My Summer Love" (3)
              "Let the Beat Hit 'Em" IN GREEN (3: eighth notes)
Week 5:   "True (Trance Sunrise Mix)" (3)
              "Jam and Marmalade" (4)
              "Logical Dash" Light mode (3)
              "Love Again Tonight" (4: faster, first syncopations)
Week 6:   "Groove 2001" (4: faster, patterned, some eighths)
              "The Cube" (4: bare syncopated patterns)
              "Spin the Disc" MEDIUM (5: fun, some syncs)
Week 7:   "Celebrate" (4)
              "Love Again Tonight (for Melissa Mix)" (4)
              "Holic" (4)
Week 8:   "Let's Talk It Over" STANDARD (5)
              "Gambol 5.1.1" STANDARD (5)
              "Let the Beat Hit 'Em" STANDARD (5)
Week 9:   "Stomp to My Beat" (5)
              "Deep in You" (5)
              "Drop the Bomb" STANDARD (5)
              "Max 300" (6)
Week 10:   "Let the Beat Hit 'Em" IN GREEN—STANDARD (5)
              "Sana Morette" STANDARD (5)
              "Stomp to My Beat" STANDARD (6)

Figure 9.1. Ten-week introductory curriculum for Dance Dance Revolution, drilling rhythm and sight reading

effectiveness as a teaching tool for that particular set of students can be gauged only in terms of student feedback and instructor observations. Formal student feedback was gathered midway through the semester by means of a survey given in class. Of the 40 enrolled students, 33 took part. They rated their experiences by responding to the four statements printed below on a scale from 1 (strongly disagree) to 5 (strongly agree). The results of the survey are shown in figure 9.2.

1. "The DDR lab is an enjoyable part of this course."
2. "The pacing of tasks from week to week in the DDR curriculum feels appropriate."
3. "Practicing with DDR feels like it helps with rhythmic/sight-reading accuracy."
4. "I would like the DDR component to return in later semesters of study."

On the whole, students reacted largely positively to the DDR requirement, as determined by comparing the number of positive (4–5), negative (1–2), and neutral responses (3). For statement 1, 22 reported enjoying the DDR component, which translates to an overall favorability rating of 66.67 percent. Within the remaining third of students, more reacted neutrally to DDR (18 percent) than negatively to it (15 percent). Exactly two-thirds of the population agreed that the pacing of songs from week to week was very appropriate or appropriate, with about a quarter of total students (26.67 percent) feeling more neutral in this regard. As a testament to the success of the curriculum design, only two students in the group (6.67 percent) felt that the pacing was inappropriate. Unfortunately, we cannot know whether they felt rushed and unprepared by the succession of tasks or if, as experienced players, they were bored by it.

Critically, responses to statement 3 indicate that students did not feel strongly that practice with DDR helped them improve their skill levels. Only 46 percent agreed that DDR felt as if it were helping them, while nearly the same number of students, or 39 percent, *disagreed* in this regard. Comparatively few felt neutrally about this issue: only 14 percent responded with a 3. As measured by statement 4, students responded favorably to the idea of DDR study returning in subsequent semesters of aural skills. The overall 59 percent positive reaction closely corresponds to the 66.67 percent rating from statement 1. Here, however, the number of

	Statement 1 (Enjoyable)	Statement 2 (Pacing)	Statement 3 (Helps)	Statement 4 (Return)
Average value:	3.91	3.77	2.90	3.41
Total # of responses	33	30	28	32
disagree (1–2)	5	2	11	12
neutral (3)	6	8	4	1
agree (4–5)	22	20	13	19

Figure 9.2.   Complete response data to the in-class survey on DDR

neutral responses dropped from six to one, meaning that this question was far more polarizing than the first one.

Several notable correlations emerge from further inspection of the responses. We hypothesized that if students enjoyed their studies with DDR, then they should want this class component to return in subsequent semesters. This trend did emerge from a comparison of statements 1 and 4, although seven students (22 percent) reported fair to high levels of enjoyment but did not want the game to return. Further, we assumed that if students found their studies with DDR helpful, then that would influence their level of enjoyment. We found this to hold as well, with similar-value responses between statements 3 and 1 (equal or one point away) occurring 59 percent of the time. Tellingly, of the 12 students who gave sharply diverging answers, 11 of them gave a much higher rating to the enjoyment category than to the help category. The last correlation between statements 3 and 4 was the strongest: fully 79 percent (or 22 out of 28) felt that if DDR helped, then it should return and that if it did not, then it should not return. Of course, this result must be taken in the larger context of the finding that only 46 percent of students felt that practice with DDR helped at all.

All of the trends emerging from the survey were corroborated by instructor observation. Class members' engagement with DDR was evidenced first by their consistent strong attendance: at semester's end, a great majority of the students had fulfilled their once-a-week requirement on schedule, with only about five needing to cram the final three or four sessions. The class's enjoyment came across even more clearly in the attitudes displayed in lab, where good spirits abounded. Students of all abilities approached each set task as a challenge to be relished and overcome. We frequently heard students boast both inside and outside of the lab that they had "beaten" a difficult routine with a high score. We also heard many frustrated outbursts from students making errors in execution or becoming stuck on a particular routine, but they were always tinged with a healthy dose of mock exasperation. In addition, it was clear that a degree of camaraderie developed in connection with DDR, with students frequently soliciting classmates to accompany them to practice sessions.

In line with students' sentiments concerning the pacing of the curriculum, instructors witnessed steady improvement in their DDR skills from week to week. Most students appeared tentative and awkward in weeks one and two, even if they had past experience with the game. By the end of the semester, however, everyone's bearing on the footpad appeared more relaxed, as they were better able to keep balance and to use alternate feet to depress arrows (novices generally use a single foot as much as possible). Students' growing expertise manifested also in higher rates of routine completion, as they increasingly learned to recover from mistakes and rejoin the flow of a dance rather than bailing out under an onslaught of falling arrows.

With regard to the question, "Does DDR help students develop rhythmic and sight-reading accuracy?" two types of instructor observations must be recorded. First, there is the matter of what students said directly to the professors and teaching assistants or in their presence. Several class members remarked that practicing with DDR did make them more aware of tempo and beat; many others agreed that the "reading" aspect of the game was analogous to following a score.[8] The great majority, however, expressed doubts about the utility of DDR. Many did so directly: "This makes us better at playing video games, sure, but I don't see how it's making us any better at aural skills." Often, they voiced their suspicions about potential crossover benefits of the game in terms of sarcasm: "At least if DDR is included in my orchestral audition, I'll have an edge over the others. That's about all it's good for." Other students saw no benefit to the course of study but voiced no specific objections to it: "Well, this is useless, but it's fun anyway and counts for credit, so why not?" All these species of doubt converged to form a common complaint that time spent in the DDR lab encroached on time needed elsewhere. Some class members—generally, those concerned about receiving an overall poor grade in the class—expressed worry about the perceived lost opportunities to drill conventional tasks, such as sight-singing and dictation. Many of their classmates who did not share that concern worried more about losing time that had been earmarked for practice or rest.

Beyond recalling what students said in conjunction with DDR's value, there is the far more important matter of what we saw students achieve. First, we must admit we saw no evidence that time spent in the DDR lab accelerated these students' musical development measurably beyond that of previous classes. When called upon in class to sing prepared melodies or sight-sing new ones, students persisted in making the same types of rhythmic errors for the entire semester.[9] More disappointing was that students did not translate their newfound intra-exercise recovery skills attained in the DDR lab to their singing, despite frequent encouragement that they do so. Instead, hesitations and catastrophic failures in the midst of sung melodies were common as ever.[10]

We did, however, observe a trend that suggests practice with DDR might help students hone their performance skills. We described above how weekly exposure to DDR helped students gain confidence on the foot pad and complete more routines. As they grew comfortable with the interface, a pronounced change in their demeanor was also detected and a more relaxed playing style emerged. To say that this result was caused by entrainment of the routines would be accurate but would gloss over an important detail.

By virtue of the entrainment, students were able to read the screen differently, scanning for familiar "chunked" patterns of steps rather than reading from note to note.[11] It has long been known that different eye movement patterns correlate closely with differing levels of sight-reading ability. In 1994, Thomas Goolsby carried out experiments using an infrared device to track musicians' progressive and regressive eye movements during reading and performance tasks (the forward and backward glances made between present location in the music and upcoming information in the score). The results conclusively showed that "skilled sight-readers had more but shorter progressive as well as regressive fixations than less-skilled sight-readers. This suggests that skilled readers direct fixations well ahead of the performance to see what happens later in the melody and then go back to the point of performance. The use of regressive fixations is different in comparison with the skilled reading of text, in which regressive fixations are minimized" (Gabrielsson 1999, 511). Karpinski (2000) situates Goolsby's findings within an overview of the topic of "Visual Tracking." This discussion is especially helpful for highlighting techniques instructors can use to "foster the habit of looking ahead while reading music," such as pattern-recognition tasks, "mumbling" during preperformance scanning, and hiding the active portion of a score with note cards during performance (Karpinski 2000, 175). To this list of techniques we would add one more. Prolonged exposure to DDR and, in particular, to its scroll-reading mechanism will help students develop the core, interrelated elements of successful sight-reading: chunking, scanning ahead, and relaxed mindset.

General Assessment and Recommendations for Future Implementation

Based on the observations and feedback, we feel that the initial attempt to incorporate DDR into the aural-skills curriculum was successful. Numerous factors indicate that it would be worthwhile to re-implement the program: high levels of student enjoyment and participation, the benefits of exposure to novel technologies and musics, the fostering of good sight-reading habits, and a very reasonable cost of lab upkeep.[12] Just as importantly, the levels of time commitment required of the primary instructor and concomitant stress, while substantial, are eminently manageable and diminish quickly with experience. These stresses will be minimized if care is taken to make the students as comfortable as possible with the DDR program. To that end, we strongly recommend that instructors keep the following considerations in mind.

1. A proper introduction to DDR is essential

In advance of being sent off to their weekly practice sessions, students must be properly introduced to the course's DDR component. An orientation session should cover: first, the basics of game play and, second, the proper procedure for accessing and utilizing lab equipment. All aspects of the game should be demonstrated, including how to navigate menus with the dance pad for the purposes of selecting songs and setting difficulty levels. The presentation should be highly interactive, with students having ample opportunity to stand on the dance pads and attempt songs. They should be encouraged to voice thoughts and concerns about the game, class policies, and grading.

Although the orientation session should be designed in part to convey information, it is more important that it be used to set the proper tone for the course of study. Students need to be convinced that practice with DDR is fun, worthwhile, and will not cause any anxiety or humiliation. The latter goal may be realized in part by establishing the proper, supportive environment in class meetings, where aural-skills students are more accustomed to performing before their peers. Whenever possible, it is best to have the class professor demonstrate the technology. We were fortunate in our experience in that, ultimately, none of our 40 students was too timid to play DDR in front of classmates. For the few that exhibited some initial wariness, the group's laughter at seeing the instructor performing—and occasionally faltering on—several routines quickly dissolved their fears of any impending embarrassment.

2. The students must be convinced of the value of DDR practice

Most academic music instructors in universities infuse their teaching with at least a modicum of salesmanship. To sustain an experimental curriculum such as DDR over 10 or more weeks, a higher than normal level of enthusiasm will be required to combat student reticence. In this regard, instructors should consistently express their commitment to DDR, citing the expected benefits and sharing their observations of positive outcomes as they occur. They may supply reading materials to the class in the form of short articles or excerpts concerned with rhythmic pedagogy, the documented success of computer-assisted instruction, and/or the mechanics of sight-reading and rhythm training. Brief classroom discussions of the readings will help students sense the relationship between the lab exercises and their general musicianship. Such discussions may also prompt students to suggest new modes of practice as well as "crossover" strategies for translating the rhythmic patterns from DDR routines into separate, classroom drills.

Instructors should bring skills learned through DDR practice into the classroom as often as possible. One way to do this is to add a DDR component to the course's final exam. Having the students prepare a difficult routine or task and then succeed in that task will reward their semester-long efforts and confirm that they "counted." We note further that these tested skills need not be limited to conventional DDR performances. Students can be asked to stand off of the dance mat while conducting and counting out rhythms that appear on the screen. A set of rhythms prominent within a given song can be performed in the skills portion of the aural-skills final and then reappear in the dictation portion of the test.

Students' morale may be further boosted by making them aware that the skills learned through playing DDR will impact their general music-making abilities. To this end, we recommend that aural-skills teachers explicitly strive to build a classroom "culture of fluency," wherein mistakes in singing, tapping, and conducting are tolerated but pauses and stops are not. To facilitate this shift in priorities, instructors in class settings may use metronomes, fellow students, or even elements of the DDR program (displays, sounds, and dance pads) to create a steady tempo that is as "unforgiving" of deviations as the game is. As a result of such persistent conditioning, students will come to class more prepared. They will not merely be familiar with the strings of notes and rhythms in their assignments but will have practiced specifically how to get through every exercise; this is a key, professional skill that will carry over to the practice room, the coaching studio, and the recital hall.

3. Lab conditions must be favorable

Whatever level of motivation a student might have had in advance of attending a DDR practice session, it will be noticeably depressed if technical difficulties are expected or experienced. It is essential that the class have access to functional equipment. All of the televisions, game consoles, DDR software, dance pads, radio transmitters, and headphone receivers should be adequately powered and regularly calibrated. In addition, care must be taken that the DDR equipment is operated in a suitable location. A large room will minimize the danger of crowding or interference between stations: the footprint of each practice station, including one AV cart and two dance pads, is approximately 42 square feet (see figure 9.3). A carpeted surface is best to keep the rubberized dance mats from slipping during dance routines. If only a wooden or tiled floor is available, then the mats can be secured to the floor with packing tape, duct tape, or nonslip carpet pads.

It is important to remember that DDR is a physical activity, although a low-impact one. To counteract the additive effects of body heat, the lab room should be kept cool and dry through proper ventilation. Yet even if care is taken in this regard, a good number of students will perspire within minutes of starting their dance session. The syllabus is a good place to make students aware of this possibility and remind them to hydrate properly before and after they practice. If a student needs to dress well on a particular day for a recital, he or she should be encouraged to change clothes or to attend the lab on an alternate day.

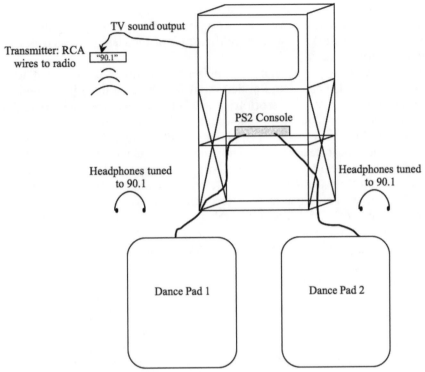

Figure 9.3. Schematic of a DDR lab station, indicating proper placement of AV cart, television, dance pads, and wireless sound equipment

4. *The instructor should remain flexible*

The initial installment of a DDR curriculum will create a number of new stresses for instructors and class members. As long as the equipment is maintained, the requirements are fair, and everyone is willing to work together, however, there is no reason for any of these stresses to become unmanageable. Students, for their part, must be open to trying something new. Most will begin the semester in this frame of mind, quite willing at first to sacrifice more time and dignity to the pursuit of aural skills than they originally anticipated. To help preserve this delicate condition, instructors must do all they can to make clear their good faith and intentions regarding this new class requirement.

Previous discussion touched on some in-class ideas for convincing students of the value of DDR practice. Equally important is that the students feel that the demands concerning this course element are fair. To maintain this perception, it may be necessary for instructors to employ greater flexibility than they customarily would. As a result of unexpected lab closures, students should be allowed to make up missed work. Students should be granted at least one or two chances to make up lab absences. By the end of the semester, more than half of the class will need it, and all will appreciate it.

The above four considerations represent a mixture of policies that actually were implemented and policies that we wish had been implemented in our one-semester classroom trial of DDR. We have repeatedly reported a positive response to the program; this, we feel, had much to do with our ability to anticipate many of the issues listed above. Where student resistance and dissatisfaction were encountered, it resulted more often from philosophical shortcomings—specifically, the students' lack of faith in the pedagogy—than from glitches in delivery. In making plans to reinstate DDR as an element of aural skills, we intend to follow all of our own advice printed above. Special care will be taken to follow the recommendations of heading 2, as that is the area that originally proved least successful.

At the same time, it is important that we not overlook some further ramifications brought up by consideration 4, concerning flexibility. Simply invoking this topic offers a most fitting way to conclude the first part of this essay. Instructors who remain wary of this new technology should remember that, as a true supplement to conventional aural skills, DDR can be tailored to any classroom. It can appear regularly or infrequently to supply warm-up activities, to drill rhythm and pulse, or to provide material for examinations. Alternatively, DDR can be assigned purely as an extracurricular activity or can be brought to class once or several times to spark the students' imaginations. Future music instructors will be particularly well served by exposure to this and other music video-games. As an increasing number of primary and secondary school youths play these games in their spare time and as school districts continue investing in this software, the opportunities for—and necessities of—piggybacking music instruction onto leisure and physical education activities will expand drastically.[13]

A teacher who uses DDR on at least a semi-regular basis must apply the tenets of flexibility to many aspects of class structure. A lab requirement means an extra time commitment, and thus, other assignments must be scaled back.[14] The schedule of activities in class may need to be adjusted to accommodate demonstrations, discussions, and activities involving DDR. In light of this possibility, we wish to head off concerns that DDR tasks will necessarily steal time from traditional class pursuits. On the contrary, the new technology may inspire some to reconsider the standard class model.

Rather than practicing every skill en masse—or in small subsets of students observed by the entire group—students could be divided into teams so as to migrate among skill stations in the manner of circuit training.[15] This would dramatically raise the total practice output for most classes, as each student attempts many tasks and observes few (rather than attempting few and observing many). Some stations would involve live interaction with instructors or teaching assistants. Others, featuring one or more CAI programs such as DDR, would drill skills and automatically evaluate performance. All of these activities can be seamlessly integrated, as most home versions of DDR feature a programmable "edit mode." With a bit of planning and preparation, all CAI activities can be customized to match the target singing and dictation material established for each class meeting.

If we are to put the effort into expanding the use of DDR in the aural-skills classroom, it would be helpful to have concrete evidence of its utility. The following section describes the design and execution of a pilot experiment to measure the impact of DDR practice on students' ability to sight-read and execute rhythms accurately. Although the experiment proved inconclusive, a discussion of the method and results may yet prove useful to the musical community as progress is made toward determining the potential of this rhythm-based video game.

LAB OUTCOMES

Context

There is a scattered history of research into the advantages of rhythm-training techniques for sight-reading. In one study, error-detection exercises were shown to improve students' aural awareness of rhythmic patterns and, consequently, their sight-reading abilities (Kostka 2000). Separate investigations conducted by Boyle (1970) and McCabe (2006) show that middle school and high school instrumentalists who learned new rhythms while marking the beat with tapping or clapping had significantly better outcomes in sight-reading accuracy than those who were restricted from bodily movement. In general, there are many studies that investigate the correlates of good sight-singing; however, research into the efficacy of specific pedagogies is generally absent. This may be in part a consequence of unreported studies with null results.

To begin the inquiry into whether DDR training actually results in stronger rhythm skills, we conducted a pilot study of rhythmic sight-reading performance. Our experiment consisted of a pre-test of rhythmic sight-reading ability, several sessions of DDR training similar to that in the class lab, and a nearly identical post-test. The goal was to measure meaningful improvements in performance on the post-test as compared to the pre-test. A control group was included in the study that took the pre-test and post-test at similar intervals, but with no DDR training between them.

Methods

Because the pilot study was conducted outside of normal lab sessions, we relied on a small number of participants. The study included three control-group subjects (including two graduate students) and ten experimental subjects (including four graduate students). Except for one volunteer in each group, students were paid for their participation. The experimental group had an average of 10 years of musical training and 4.1 years of aural-skills experience; the control group reported an average of 11 years of musical training and 7.5 years of aural-skills experience. Two members of the experimental group reported that they had intermediate skills in DDR, one reported being an expert, and the others considered themselves beginners; all of the control group ranked themselves as beginners. The implications of the differing levels of expertise in this study population will be discussed below.

During the experiment, students were seated at a Linux machine running a low-latency kernel, using software written in Perl/Tk that played sounds through a dedicated MIDI sound card to minimize audio latency.[16] A notated rhythm appeared on the screen, and a two-measure metronome count-off began. All of the rhythms were four-measure phrases in common time presented at 100 BPM (beats per minute). The computer measured the timing of each tap. Students were instructed to begin tapping the rhythm on the downbeat of the third measure, using a key on the computer keyboard. They were asked to tap only once per note and not to correct mistakes. The metronome sound continued for the entirety of the rhythm except in select cases where it was removed as a variable (see the entry "Asynchrony," below).

Before the experiment began, each student was asked to practice the task. Practice continued until the student could perform three rhythms in a row without mistakes. The practice examples were basic four-bar phrases without dotting, syncopation, or other complications. The experiment consisted of 30 distinct rhythms presented in random order. The rhythms were assembled from the 22 rhythmic cells shown in figure 9.4. Each one was classified as exhibiting one or more of the following characteristics: meter reinforcing (not annotated), pauses (P), metrical or sub-metrical syncopation (S/s), dotted values (D), or cross rhythms (C). The same rhythms were used on the pre-test and post-test but with different randomized orderings.

Definitions

One challenge in designing an experimental study is to clarify exactly what the intent is (the hypothesis), how to define its terms (the independent measures), and what exactly is being studied (the dependent mea-

Figure 9.4. The 22 rhythmic cells used to construct all of the 4-measure rhythmic stimuli

sure). In identifying our goals, it was critical to determine how to measure rhythm performance on the task. The most common measure of rhythm performance in prior studies was simply "correct" or "incorrect" as heard by the investigator (e.g., Allen 1987; K. Smith 2002). Another, more systematic approach using MIDI data categorized a note as an error if it was displaced by more than a given proportion of its duration (Drake and Palmer 2000; Palmer and van de Sande 1995). For our timing assessment, we created two measures of performance analysis: gross accuracy and micro-timing accuracy. Each participant's tap was assigned to the nearest expected note onset, either before or after the tap. Any note onset without an assigned tap was considered to be a gross accuracy error. Micro-timing accuracy was measured as the absolute difference in milliseconds between the expected note onset and its nearest assigned tap.

Aspects of rhythmic performance are much more subtle than simply correct or incorrect, of course. To understand the characteristic strengths and weaknesses of a DDR approach to rhythm, we defined six categories of rhythm difficulty that might benefit from training. The first four of these are exemplified in the individual rhythmic cells, the last two by the design of the experiment.

1. *Pauses.* Prior research has shown that long notes are the greatest cause of timing variance in rhythm performance (Vos and Ellermann 1989). Whether this is because accurate performance of long notes requires mental counting, flexible subdivision, or greater attention, the inclusion of long pauses in a rhythm should result in decreased timing accuracy.

2. *Syncopation.* One of the most common sources of rhythm errors is syncopation, and the stimuli included two distinct types: rhythmic displacements of an entire quarter-note beat (metrical) and displacements at the eighth-note level (sub-metrical). We hypothesized that sub-metrical rhythmic syncopations would be more difficult because faster subdivisions require more attention and sometimes faster reflexes.

3. *Dotted rhythms.* Although they are not as difficult to perform as syncopations, dotted rhythms, nonetheless, require the performer to subdivide accurately and to pause for longer between notes than in even rhythms.

4. *Cross-rhythms.* Although not categorically distinct from syncopations, we included a separate category for cross-rhythms, which we defined as having multiple adjacent metric displacements that can imply a different meter (for instance, two dotted quarters, implying a temporary 3/8 or 6/8 grouping, followed by a quarter that reestablishes 4/4).

5. *Heterogeneity.* Even a complicated rhythm will become easier if it occurs homogeneously (i.e., if it is repeated several times). Complicated rhythms presented without immediate repetition are more difficult. The 30 stimuli were constructed such that it was equally likely that participants would be presented with the same cell four times in succession ("homogeneity"), two of one type and two of another ("partial heterogeneity"), or four contrasting cells ("total heterogeneity").

6. *Asynchrony.* We hypothesized that entrainment to a beat could be strengthened by DDR training. Although the standard practice in the

experiment was to have the metronome continue to play the beat throughout each exercise, there were four rhythms in each test in which the participant was warned that the metronome would drop out on the first beat of the rhythm. These four rhythms were not novel but rather duplicates of rhythms that did have a metronome accompaniment.

Results and Conclusions

To determine the significance of the result in each category, the results were subjected to ANOVA and *t*-tests.[17] As mentioned earlier, the results of the pilot study were not entirely clear-cut. Between the pre-test and the post-test we found a modest decrease in gross errors for the experimental group (dropping by 25 percent from a 4 percent error rate to 3 percent). This was close to a significant result but within the standard definition of chance. We also observed a modest increase in micro-timing accuracy of 6 percent. Again, this result hinted at the possibility of significance but was not sufficient to attain it. Means from the analysis are reported in figures 9.5 and 9.6.

There were significantly more micro-timing and gross rhythmic errors in rhythms with maximal heterogeneity and for the asynchronous rhythms; there was also significantly less gross accuracy in the dotted rhythms. But these are a straight measure of difficulty, not of improvement due to training.

| | Pre-Test (%) | | Post-Test (%) | | |
Factor	Mean	SD	Mean	SD	N
Experimental group					
Overall	95.99	5.04	96.69	4.43	442
Syncopations					
Beat-level	97.34	2.22	96.56	3.95	64
Subbeat-level	93.42	7.72	95.77	6.64	149
None	97.21	2.52	97.73	1.21	229
Control group					
Overall	97.92	1.76	97.26	1.43	442
Syncopation					
Beat-level	98.96	1.80	96.88	1.56	64
Subbeat-level	95.97	0.67	96.64	0.67	149
None	98.84	0.25	98.25	1.75	229

Figure 9.5. Factor means, standard deviations, and number of observations (N) from the gross accuracy analysis

	Pre-Test (ms)		Post-Test (ms)		
Factor	Mean	SD	Mean	SD	Na
Experimental group	43.8	20.0	41.2	18.7	420
Control group	29.0	6.6	28.5	12.0	425

aMissing values resulted in varying N values, so minimum values are reported.

Figure 9.6. Factor means, standard deviations, and number of observations (N) from the micro-timing accuracy analysis

The one interesting result we did find was a significant effect of training on the gross accuracy of different levels of syncopation ($p < 0.05$).[18] This is a consequence of improved performance of sub-metrical syncopation, resulting in a one-third drop in the error rate.[19] (This result was not found for the control group, but neither was there a significant difference between groups.) In summary, only one of the expected interactions among rhythm type and training was significant. Both the accuracy and timing measures showed modest but not significant effects of training.

There are a number of possible reasons for the lack of meaningful results in this pilot study. First there was the matter of education level and experience. All of the volunteers in the study were either upper-level undergraduates or graduate students. Although there may have been reason to hope that participation in DDR would have a salutary effect on these students, if it did, it was generally not a strong effect. It may also be that the stimuli were insufficiently difficult, resulting in a ceiling effect where everyone performed strongly on most stimuli. Again, this may be relative to the experience level of the participants.

More important to any interpretation of the results is a comparison to the control group. This was a particular problem because the proportion of graduate students was higher in the control group than in the experimental group, and the control group out-performed the experimental group on both the post-test and pre-test. Without a matched control group, we were ultimately unable to clarify whether any post-test improvements were due to ongoing musical studies or something specific to DDR exposure. This is perhaps too much to ask from a pilot study; however, at least any effects that were present in the data point to at least some improvement in rhythm skills.

More troublingly, it must be conceded that the small effect sizes may have been due to a lack of transfer between DDR activities and sight-reading skills. There is a long history of belief that kinesthetic activities translate into musical skills (à la the Dalcroze and Montessori methods), but this may not be directly true. Recent educational research has shown that even a popular mainstream educational theory, such as the belief in distinct visual, auditory, and kinesthetic learning styles, can be misguided or incorrect (Kavale and Forness 1987).

The fact of this negative result highlights both the importance and the challenge of empirically testing pedagogical theories. Music-theory pedagogy as a field is replete with creative strategies for improving student learning, but controlled studies showing clear benefits are harder to come by. The pilot study we conducted establishes a framework for continued study of alternative methods for rhythm pedagogy, and we are continuing to pursue this line of research. Neither of our two measures—gross timing or micro-timing—came out as a clear winner, though either might be a good measure under better testing conditions.

CONCLUSION: DDR AT THE CROSSROADS

As indicated by the title of this essay, the future role of Dance Dance Revolution in college-level music instruction is uncertain. Though it holds much promise as a CAI device, DDR remains largely untested on a significant scale. Some sizable obstacles must be overcome for this to change. First, stronger empirical data must be gathered in support of using this program to teach and drill rhythm and sight-reading. Next, standardized approaches and multiyear curricula must be set. Finally, instructors need to obtain hardware and software to support their student populations and to become adept at managing that equipment. Should it come to that, it seems likely that more "musician-friendly" versions of the game could be developed, featuring options for advanced rhythmic and metric training and a more traditionally horizontal orientation of the scrolling arrows.

Being among the first to explore the potential value of musical instruction via DDR, we felt obligated to make this account of our experiences as honest and forthright as possible. The ambivalent tone of the discussion reflects, to a large extent, the mixed results obtained in the classroom and lab, yet it also reflects our sentiments concerning the DDR enterprise as a whole. We remain hopeful that this music- and skill-based game can be profitably adapted to rhythm and sight-reading instruction. We plan to institute it in upcoming semesters of aural-skills instruction and to continue investigating its efficacy in the cognition lab. It may very well be that some or all of these efforts may come to but little. If we choose not to press forward, however, the result will not be that an unconventional pedagogical idea was proven unfounded but rather that it was not given a chance.

In looking ahead, encouragement may be found beyond the foreground of the results reported above in the form of other important, though intangible, gains. The pilot lab experiment was inconclusive but illuminated a key issue that will require consideration in all subsequent experiments: the ceiling effect. Is there a global ceiling effect that prevents DDR from teaching musicians *anything* once they have achieved certain levels of proficiency? There is evidence that the feedback from CAI can help with basic skill acquisition in singing, for instance, but that this effect is usually strongest for early training (Ewars 2004; Rossiter, Howard, and DeCosta 1996). Perhaps only beginners with very limited experience in rhythm and sight-reading would be measurably influenced by prolonged exposure to DDR, whereas musicians at the college level and beyond possess deeply entrenched behaviors to handle pulse sensation, rhythm counting, and score scanning.

On the classroom side, the present account of incorporating Dance Dance Revolution into aural skills began by focusing on pragmatic concerns of managing equipment, curricula, and student morale. Gradually, however, the discussion evolved into a meditation on ways to redesign the classroom in terms of environment and activity flow. Our arrival at a somewhat fanciful endpoint—the circuit-training model—should not be regarded as gratuitous but rather a reminder of the real power of how technology impacts pedagogy. New equipment and new ideas challenge instructors to re-envision what and how they teach and to find ways to deliver material more effectively to students. Perhaps that is why it is easy to remain so deeply enthused about a game that, in arcade years, has technically passed its prime.

NOTES

1. The origins of music video-games from precursors to Dance Dance Revolution and beyond are summarized by J. Smith 2004 and Chan 2004.

2. In DDR, players listening to electronic dance music respond to arrows scrolling upward on the display screen (oriented as up, down, left, and right) by stepping on buttons on a dance pad with corresponding arrow markings. The precise moment for pressing a button is signaled when an arrow on the screen intersects the "step zone" at the top. All the attacks are perfectly coordinated with the pulses and rhythms of the electronic dance tunes. A more detailed overview of Dance Dance Revolution, including graphic and video examples, is provided in Auerbach 2010.

3. Since it is played with the feet, DDR's on-screen instructions encode a minimum of "pitch" information in the form of the four arrow types; this is in stark contrast to other music video-games, such as Guitar Hero and Rock Band, which use mock instruments (basses, guitars, drums) as the interface and demand that players negotiate fast and highly technical musical lines. With regard to the inherent differences between video game play and music performance, Auerbach 2010 provides a number of detailed pedagogical techniques to help students associate DDR screen content with conventional music notation.

4. In recent years, increasing academic attention has focused on all types of music video-games, in which control-pad actions are synchronized with musical events (notable examples include DDR, Karaoke Revolution, Guitar Hero, and Rock Band). Nearly all of the discourse has analyzed these games in terms that are occasionally music-theoretical (Shultz 2008) but far more often sociological (Demers 2006; Miller 2009; J. Smith 2004). As far as can be determined, the present project at UMass represents the first practical examination of music video-games' utility for classroom training.

5. This curriculum was based on the specific software and hardware chosen for the lab: DDRMax (Konami of America) in the version developed for the PlayStation 2 console (Sony Corporation). See figure 9.3 for a diagram of a lab station; further details concerning lab setup are provided by Auerbach 2010.

6. Entering students reported all levels of prior DDR experience, ranging from "no previous exposure" to "expert user." With the great majority of students describing themselves as minimally familiar with the game, this curriculum was an ideal fit for most of them. Students with advanced DDR training were not excused from the lab requirement but rather were instructed to improve their scores on these same songs starting from higher initial settings.

7. Spiral learning occurs as a "core set of concepts"—in this case, the basic rhythmic patterns of songs—are "constructively recycled again and again at increasingly sophisticated levels" (Rogers 1984, 145).

8. Records were not kept on the number and type of comments made and overheard over the course of the semester. It is not at all difficult to recall the overall proportion of positive to negative comments, which were, lamentably, few to many. Unfortunately, it is impossible to remember how many of the positive comments were offered freely (there were some) as opposed to those that were solicited by an instructor. (Positives in the latter category are far more likely to be false positives.)

9. Bear in mind that there are multiple ways to document group improvement in sight-singing. Very frequently, a class establishes baseline levels of speed and accuracy that remain consistent all semester, while the task difficulty level steadily increases.

10. To some extent, lack of improvement in this regard may have resulted from a strict requirement that all students conduct while singing. Combining these tasks frequently trips up aural-skills students of all levels, possibly to the extent that some of this interference might have masked more subtle improvements in timing and execution.

11. A practical measure of chunking ability is eye-hand span (EHS), which refers to the amount of output a musician can generate at an instrument starting from the moment that the visual stimulus is removed. Sloboda found that "the levels of EHS corresponded closely with people who made many mistakes in a large set of sight reading tasks versus those who made few" (2005, 37).

12. The total cost of replacing worn hardware (dance pads, headphones, batteries) and the salaries for lab managers would not exceed $600 per semester. This amount may be halved if instructors, teaching assistants, or trustworthy student volunteers share five hours per week of unpaid lab monitoring responsibilities.

13. In 2007–8, the state of West Virginia committed to installing Dance Dance Revolution in all 765 of its public schools for use in physical education classes

(Schiesel 2007). In January 2009, the electronic news service Business Wire reported that Nintendo of America and the National Association for Music Education (MENC) collaborated to "help teachers in 51 cities across the nation integrate Wii Music into their K–6 curricula, making use of the game's 60-plus instruments and fun array of tutorial exercises in rhythm, tempo and song structure."

14. By failing to do this, we unfairly added a substantial time commitment to a two-credit class that was already overloaded. As a concession to a class that had been highly cooperative, the DDR performance portion of the final exam was officially discarded.

15. Developed in 1953 by R. E. Morgan and G. T. Anderson, circuit training is a "resistance training method in which single sets of several different exercises . . . are completed in succession with little or no rest between exercises" (Brown 2007, 143). This "full-body" approach, proven in effectiveness and still widely in use, combines the virtues of efficient muscular training with cardiovascular training: according to Brown, "heart rates during circuit training are typically higher than during most other weight training programs" (143). Given the frequency with which training in music is analogized with training in athletics, it is surprising that we have found no reports of circuit training being brought into music classrooms.

16. Better timing accuracy results in higher quality data in a reaction-time study. Low audio latency means the sound card plays a note almost exactly when the computer asks it to, and a low-latency kernel means the computer can record responses almost exactly when they were entered on the keyboard.

17. ANOVAs test whether there are significant differences among the subcategories of a variable and can be used with multiple variables at the same time. When comparing differences between only two groups, a simple t-test was used.

18. The probability of this result occurring purely by chance is less than 5 percent. This is the usual standard adopted in the social sciences to indicate a significant result.

19. Note that we might want to be concerned about multiple tests: we tested six separate categories, so the likelihood that one of the six would produce an apparently significant result is actually higher than 5 percent. If we compensate for this, a family-wise correction of the significance threshold means this result could have happened by chance.

REFERENCES

Allen, Debra H. 1987. The effect of mastery of selected music theory and ear training skills presented in a computer-assisted format on the sight playing performance of second-year band students. MA thesis, University of Missouri, Kansas City.

Auerbach, Brent. 2010. Pedagogical applications of the video game *Dance Dance Revolution* to the aural skills classroom. *Music Theory Online* 15, no. 5 (January).

Barker, Allison. 2005. Study uses video games to fight obesity. Technology, *USA Today*, April 2.

Boyle, John D. 1970. The effects of prescribed rhythmical movements on the ability to read music at sight. *Journal of Research in Music Education* 18:307–18.

Brown, Lee, ed. 2007. *Strength training*. Champaign, IL: Human Kinetics/National Strength & Conditioning Association.

Chan, Alexander. 2004. CPR for the arcade culture: A case history on the development of the Dance Dance Revolution community. Unpublished paper, Stanford University.

Demers, Joanna. 2006. Dancing machines: "Dance Dance Revolution," cybernetic dance, and musical taste. *Popular Music* 25, no. 3: 401–14.

Drake, Carolyn, and Caroline Palmer. 2000. Skill acquisition in music performance: Relations between planning and temporal control. *Cognition* 74:1–32.

Elliott, Charles A. 1982. The relationships among instrumental sight-reading ability and seven selected predictor variables. *Journal of Research in Music Education* 30, no. 1: 5–14.

Ewers, Marla S. 2004. Computer-assisted music instruction as supplemental sight-singing instruction in the high school choir. PhD diss., University of Illinois at Urbana-Champaign.

Gabrielsson, Alf. 1999. The performance of music. In *The psychology of music*, ed. Diana Deutsch, 501–602. New York: Academic.

Goolsby, Thomas. 1994a. Eye movement in music reading: Effects of reading ability, notational complexity, and encounters. *Music Perception* 12, no. 1: 77–96.

———. 1994b. Profiles of processing: Eye movements during sightreading. *Music Perception* 12, no. 1: 97–123.

Karpinski, Gary. 2000. *Aural skills acquisition: The development of listening, reading, and performance skills in college-level musicians*. New York: Oxford University Press.

Kavale, Kenneth A., and Steven R. Forness. 1987. Substance over style: Assessing the efficacy of modality testing and teaching. *Exceptional Children* 54, no. 3: 228–39.

Kostka, Marilyn J. 2000. The effects of error-detection practice on keyboard sight-reading achievement of undergraduate music majors. *Journal of Research in Music Education* 48, no. 2: 114–22.

McCabe, Melissa. 2006. The effect of movement-based instruction on the beginning instrumentalist's ability to sight-read rhythm patterns. *Missouri Journal of Research in Music Education* 43:24.

McPherson, Gary E. 1994. Factors and abilities influencing sightreading skill in music. *Journal of Research in Music Education* 42, no. 3: 217–31.

Miller, Kiri. 2009. Schizophonic performance: *Guitar Hero, Rock Band,* and virtual virtuosity. *Journal of the Society for American Music* 3, no. 4: 395–429.

Palmer, Caroline, and Carla van de Sande. 1995. Range of planning in skilled music performance. *Journal of Experimental Psychology: Human Perception and Performance* 21:947–62.

Rogers, Michael. 1984. Teaching approaches in music theory: An overview of pedagogical philosophies. 2nd ed. Carbondale: Southern Illinois University Press.

Rossiter, David, David M. Howard, and Mike DeCosta. 1996. Voice development under training with and without the influence of real-time visually presented biofeedback. *Journal of the Acoustical Society of America* 99, no. 5: 3253–56.

Schiesel, Seth. 2007. P.E. classes turn to video game that works legs. Health, *New York Times*, April 30.

Shultz, Peter. 2008. Music theory in music games. In *From Pac-Man to pop music: Interactive audio in games and new media*, ed. Karen Collins, 177–88. Aldershot, Hampshire, UK: Ashgate.

Sloboda, John. 2005. *Exploring the musical mind: Cognition, emotion, ability, function.* New York: Oxford University Press.

Smith, Jacob. 2004. I can see tomorrow in your dance: A study of Dance Dance Revolution and music video games. *Journal of Popular Music Studies* 16, no. 1 (March): 58–84.

Smith, Kenneth H. 2002. The effectiveness of computer-assisted instruction on the development of rhythm reading skills among middle school instrumental students. PhD diss., University of Illinois at Urbana-Champaign.

Thomson, Albert G. 1953. An analysis of difficulties in sight reading music for violin and clarinet. PhD diss., University of Cincinnati, Ohio.

Vos, Piet G., and Henk H. Ellermann. 1989. Precision and accuracy in the reproduction of simple tone sequences. *Journal of Experimental Psychology: Human Perception and Performance* 15, no. 1: 179–87.

Watkins, John G., and Stephen E. Farnum.1962. *The Watkins-Farnum performance scale.* Winona, MN: Hal Leonard Music.

10

Turntablism: A Vehicle for Connecting Community and School Music Making and Learning

Karen Snell

Over the past several years in particular, scholars in music education have been calling for clearer connections between the ways people make, learn, and appreciate music in the community and the approaches to teaching and learning music in schools (for example, see Jones 2005 and Veblen 2005). Furthermore, in light of the pioneering work of Lucy Green (2006 and 2002), music educators are beginning to recognize the potential value of informal learning processes in settings outside of institutional contexts. However, music educators continue to struggle with finding successful ways to bring outside music making and learning processes inside the school walls. In response to this gap, this chapter looks at turntablism (i.e., using multiple phonograph turntables for making music by actively spinning, scratching, beat matching, etc.) as a relatively new and unexplored area for teaching and learning music in schools at both the public school and college or university levels, as one way of making effective connections to music making in society. Teaching turntablism can help to develop students' rhythmic skills, pitch discernment, improvisation skills, and broad awareness of musical subgenres and styles.

Although turntablism has been the subject of research over the last several years, the bulk of this scholarship has been in popular-music studies,[1] musicology, ethnomusicology, and sociology.[2] There are two notable dissertations about the use of turntablism within educational settings; however, none of these considers the possible benefits of teaching turntablism either in younger grades or at the post-secondary level. Gustavson's 2004 study is oriented toward the cross-curricular implications of hip-hop culture, including written language and graffiti art as well as turntablism. Pasagiannis's 2007 research highlights the therapeutic and psychological benefits of teaching turntablism to "at-risk" youth, rather than musical or educational benefits, which are the concern of the current chapter.

This chapter contributes to filling the research void by looking at the potential musical and educational value of including turntablism in both secondary and post-secondary school music programs. Because turntablism is, at present, rarely an integral part of music programs at any level, a large part of the research for this chapter consisted of seeking out and investigating formal educational settings where turntablism is employed successfully. The learning processes of practicing turntablists in the community at large were not explored directly; however, detailed observations about these processes in several U.S. cities can be found in Schloss's informative ethnography (2004), which has informed the ideas in this chapter.

Through my observations of and participation in turntablism in two different educational settings, a number of common themes emerged about the ways turntablism can be successfully taught, the kinds of musical knowledge and skills it typically elicits, and the benefits for the student participants. Turntablism is an excellent way to improve students' overall musicianship through beat matching, pitch awareness, the development of sensitivity to a variety of musical styles, and improvisation. Perhaps most importantly, turntablism is especially appealing to students because it allows them to make music in ways they find interesting, challenging, and relevant to their lives outside the music classroom. Turntablism has real potential not only to serve as an effective vehicle for teaching aspects of music but also to connect the music students listen to outside of school with the music they make and learn about in school.

ROYAL CONSERVATORY OF MUSIC

The first educational setting I explored was the Urban Music Department at the Royal Conservatory of Music (RCM) in Toronto, Ontario, Canada, which has historically been oriented toward traditional lessons, classes, and examinations in Western art music. The department offers only three courses; one is in turntablism, and the other two are Beats from Scratch ("the next step for DJs who want to create tracks") and Rock the Mic: Hip-Hop Workshop ("the program for developing as a hip-hop songwriter and MC").[3] In contrast, the RCM offers well over 100 classes that are focused, for the most part, on Western art music.[4]

I attended a one-week intensive series of five three-hour evening classes in March 2008, directly engaging with turntablism for the first time. The course, DJ Fundamentals: Scratch from Scratch, was designed for beginners with no prior experience and explored the basics of turntablism through the techniques of mixing, scratching, beat matching, and so forth. Typically, most of the participants in RCM's turntable classes are of high school age, although younger and older students do sometimes also take part. In general, the class tends to have more male than female students.

The course was taught by a currently practicing and successful Toronto DJ, Omar Barclay—DJ T.R.A.C.K.S., Juno Award, and Urban Music Awards of Canada nominee and one of three founding DJs in Toronto-based Trilogy Sound Crew—who has collaborated with well-known artists, including Kardinal Offishall, Choclair, Jully Black, Saukrates, and Agile from Brass-Munk (Steryannis 2006). Barclay taught using his own handouts and crates of records rather than any published textbook or method book for teaching this course.

The five sessions for this course took place in a classroom similar to a typical high school band or choral room, with five levels of risers, a blackboard and table at the front of the room, and cupboards and shelves along the sides. There were five or six student workstations on each riser and a teacher station at the front of the room. Each student station had two turntables, a mixer, and headphones. The teacher station was similar but had a larger mixing board that was connected to the classroom sound system, allowing him to play demonstrations for the whole class, tune in to hear individual students practicing, and even broadcast individual students' sounds for the whole class. Since the classroom was set up quite similarly to many traditional band, orchestra, or choral rooms, incorporating turntablism classes would likely require only the purchase of equipment, rather than any large-scale physical restructuring of classrooms.

BERKLEE COLLEGE OF MUSIC

The second educational setting investigated was the Berklee College of Music in Boston. The course observed was called Turntable Techniques, which is described on the school's website as follows: "Students will develop basic skills using the turntable both as a means of live expression and performance and as a production tool. Weekly hands-on exercises will be emphasized. The course traces the historical development of the turntable from its origins in Jamaican music through its importance as a major expression of hip-hop culture, and to the turntable's prominence in contemporary music. Artistic, ethical, and legal issues surrounding the use of the turntable will be examined. For students with little or no prior experience."[5] I observed two different sections of the same course, taught by different instructors, but did not actively participate. The first class, observed in fall 2008, was taught by the course developer and turntable specialist at Berklee, Stephen Webber. In 2000, Webber began advocating for turntable courses to be taught at Berklee, which is known as a progressive school, especially in regard to teaching jazz and popular music. Nonetheless, it took several years to convince his colleagues that it was a viable course that would be both popular with students and a valuable addition to their musical training (Endelman 2003). It was, however, the first institution of higher learning in North America to offer courses in turntablism, and since its inception, the course has become increasingly popular, running two or three full sections each semester, with 40 or 50 students on a waiting list. Berklee hopes to expand the course capacity by establishing a dedicated lab.[6]

The second class I observed at Berklee was in April 2009, taught by Brian (aka Raydar) Ellis, Webber's talented protégé. The basic structure of the course, including the textbooks and method books used, which were both written by Webber (2008 and 2003), was the same in both classes. The classes were held in a smaller room than those at RCM, perhaps half the size of a typical high-school music room, which was more cramped but still had enough space for one teacher and ten student workstations. The equipment for these classes was stored in a back area and wheeled out on a large cart and connected to the classroom wiring system just before the start of each class. Each student station had two turntables, a mixer, and headphones and faced into the center of the classroom. The teacher's station was at the front of the class and was similar to the students' stations, although it also included a large mixing board, allowing the teacher to tune in and out of individual student stations and broadcast teacher or student demonstrations over the classroom sound system; the teacher station also had some additional equipment, such as specialized CD turntables. These portable workstations would allow turntable classes to be held anywhere in the school. Furthermore, equipment that can be securely stored will likely last longer and be more easily and better maintained.

TURNTABLISM'S CONTRIBUTIONS TO STUDENTS' MUSICIANSHIP

Four themes emerged, common to all three classes, as to how turntablism relates to more traditional aspects of music study: beat matching, pitch awareness, improvisation, and sensitivity to musical styles. The following discussion of these themes examines the kinds of musical knowledge turntablism can help to develop, successful teaching methods and strategies employed by the three teachers, and the benefits to the students in each setting. In outlining these themes, I demonstrate the potential benefits of teaching and learning music through the art of turntablism to current and future music educators and students in both public and post-secondary schools, and suggest possible directions for engaging with this kind of music instruction in their own particular school settings.

Beat Matching

One of the first things students learned in each of the three classes was beat matching, a fundamental skill in turntablism that is required of students before they can move on to more complex techniques. The steps and processes involved in beat matching are noted as essential starting points for all turntablists by such researchers as Schloss, Souvignier, and Webber, and also in interviews with practicing turntablists. Furthermore, in Webber's textbook and method book, used in both Berklee classes, beat matching is outlined as an essential, basic skill in learning the art of turntabling.[7] This skill involves matching the beats per minute (BPM) of a track on one record precisely with that of a different track by adjusting its speed. This can be done using the students' own two turntables or with a recording played over the classroom sound system. Students located the downbeat of the second track using their headphones and then held the record in this location, moving it back and forth manually before releasing it in time on the downbeat of the track already playing.

In order to execute this technique, an understanding of basic rhythm and meter, as well as tempo, is essential. It is often impossible to match the BPMs of two tracks in different meters. Being able to aurally identify the downbeats in each track is essential in order to line them up properly. Experienced musicians have already developed these skills, but for students with little or no formal musical training, mastering beat matching provides an opportunity to learn the basics of meter and rhythm, including the concepts of time signatures and note values. More importantly, beat matching provides an opportunity to concretely reinforce these concepts through active music making, as students practice aurally identifying and relating tempos, meters, and rhythmic patterns. Such concrete and active reinforcement is all too often lacking in traditional theory curricula.

No matter what their musical background, the students I observed benefitted from the aural acuity gained from practicing fine adjustments in turntable speed. This required students to be fully involved in actively listening to the music at hand, which Green calls "purposive listening" (Green 2002, 23–24). Matching downbeats also developed ear-eye coordination, as students visually pinpointed the location of the selected downbeat on the record groove, and a more general kinesthetic involvement of their bodies, in terms of feeling the rhythm and moving the record back and forth in time.

Executing the physical release of the record to line up the two recordings was a fun and exciting task for all students in each of the three classes. Releasing the record too quickly or with too much force caused it to skip ahead or speed up, throwing off the carefully matched tempos. Likewise, releasing too slowly without enough forward motion of the hand caused a lag in the tempo of the second recording. Releasing the record at exactly the right time, with the proper force and with perfectly matched speeds with no deviations, is a skill that takes significant practice. In sum, learning and perfecting the steps for beat matching is an excellent way to internalize the concepts of meter and rhythm as well as develop a finely calibrated sense of timing, through active, embodied music making.

Pitch Awareness

Learning to beat match can also develop pitch awareness. This was particularly evident in the RCM class when a student with no formal training in music came to realize that slower speeds lowered the pitch of the music and faster speeds raised the pitch. He expressed this on his own with no prompting from the teacher, who mentioned that such realizations were a common occurrence. Perhaps this is at least partly because students in this course typically work primarily with music they regularly enjoy listening to outside of class. The recordings used in this class were primarily from hip-hop, the most common genre used in turntablism, and students interested in turntablism are likely to be very familiar with this music and, thus, more aware of slight changes in pitch for these songs than they might be for unfamiliar music.

Even students with extensive musical experience can improve their perception of pitch through practicing beat matching. As an experienced musician myself, I found that learning to control the speed and pitch of each recording with the fine tuning knobs on my turntables increased my sensitivity to fine tuning when playing my main instrument (trumpet) in other settings. I suspect that similar experiences were likely the case for many of the Berklee students as well.

As this sensitivity to fine gradations of pitch increased, so too did a more general sense of melodic contour, tonality, and register. For instance, pairs of songs with similar and often prominent bass lines were popular choices for beat matching, especially when the songs were in the same key or in closely related keys. Likewise, students often took into account the vocal range and style of singers in order to pick songs with either similar or sometimes contrasting vocal registers and styling. Thus, an aural awareness of pitch clearly developed alongside knowledge of meter, rhythm, and tempo as students progressed through the early stages of developing turntablism skills.

Improvisation

Another theme that emerged among the classes researched for this chapter is that turntablism provides an excellent opportunity to teach music with a focus on improvisation. All three classes regularly used improvisation, both as a group and individually, as a way to reinforce new skills as well as experiment with longer musical statements. For instance, both of the Berklee classes were organized as progressions from demonstration of a new skill, to individual practice of the skill, to group practice, to full-class improvisations.

To begin, the instructor demonstrated a new scratch technique, often combining the cross-fader with manipulation of the vinyl record in different ways. Students gathered around to see the demonstration, then practiced at their own stations with headphones on. During this time, the teacher could tune in to students through his headphones to listen to their progress and guide them through any difficulties, in addition to walking around the class to physically observe what students were doing and offer hands-on guidance.

Next, the whole class worked on the new skill together with a backing track played over the classroom sound system. The teacher played a one- or two-bar pattern employing the new technique, and then the students echoed what they had heard. This exercise was repeated a number of times with a variety of different rhythmic patterns in order to give students ample time to become comfortable using the new skill.

Finally, the class practiced improvisation using the new skill. The teacher again played a backing track over the classroom sound system and improvised a two-bar scratch sequence, employing the new skill in combination with techniques taught earlier as he saw fit. Each student then took a turn creating a unique two-bar scratch sequence as the role of soloist moved clockwise around the room in time, much like the tradition of "trading twos" in jazz improvisation. This exercise could be repeated with solos of different lengths, pairs of students "trading ones," or a focus on multiple skills. It could also be used with smaller groups or individuals. As part of their final exam, the Berklee students were required to record improvisations of a certain length, highlighting their ability with specific skills.

These types of improvisation exercises were not only excellent ways of reinforcing the new skills learned in each class period, but also they served to strengthen students' grasp of meter, phrase structure, and rhythm; to reinforce their listening skills, as they were required to come in on time directly after the previous soloist, as well as to link their improvised ideas in some way to those before them; and, of course, to provide a creative outlet for new sounds and patterns.

Other research on the informal learning practices of DJs and turntablists outside these formal educational settings clearly shows that improvisation forms the basis of their music making. These artists never use sheet music and rarely, if ever, use written instructions of any kind when performing, although some do plan out or practice their set in advance. However, because the actual mixing, scratching, and other techniques are performed live, variations in the ways albums are layered and mixed together and in the effects used and the way they are executed are all part of the performance of any given DJ set. Thus, improvisation is fundamental to turntablism for practicing DJs in the community and has been successfully included in more formal settings, such as turntablism classes, as well.

Sensitivity to Musical Styles

The students' active music listening in these classes also helped to develop their knowledge and recognition of a variety of musical styles and sub-genres. From the inception of hip-hop culture, DJs have sought out rare and exciting recordings. Because hip-hop music is, by definition, a genre that incorporates sounds from preexisting recordings through sampling and mixing techniques, seeking out new and interesting sounds from a variety of musical styles is a natural part of learning the art of turntablism. As Schloss points out by quoting the well-respected DJ Mr. Supreme, "If you really are truly into hip-hop, how can you not listen to anything else? Because it comes from everything else . . . you *are* listening to everything else" (Mr. Supreme 1998). The influential DJ Afrika Bambaataa, one of the founders of the genre, was known as "Master of Records" because of his familiarity with little-known musicians and recordings in "funk, rock, and Latin, but also reggae, calypso, new wave, and European electronic sounds. His large, diverse record collection was accompanied by a vast, authoritative musical knowledge" (Souvignier 2003, 132). It is no accident that Jamaicans call DJs "selectors," as a large part of this culture revolves around seeking out and selecting recordings from among the myriad popular-music genres and styles and then selecting samples from within these recordings to use and combine in active music-making. These selection techniques can hone students' decision-making skills as well as their musicianship skills as they choose styles of music and songs to mix together and experiment with different combinations of musical parameters.

Students strive to emulate the broad-based musical knowledge as well as the technical skills of artists such as Afrika Bambaataa, Mr. Supreme, and others when learning to turntable. This offers an opportunity for teachers to broaden students' musical horizons by presenting a wide variety of popular and other musics, both within and outside of turntablism courses. Such eclectic listening will not only deepen and expand the kinds of music students can make through turntabling, but also it will encourage them to seek out new and interesting musics on their own, as they develop into more discriminating and well-informed music listeners as well as amateur—or even professional—DJs.

CONCLUSION

This research provides only an initial glance into turntablism's potential as a vehicle for teaching music in formal educational settings. Further investigation, particularly into the use of turntablism in public school settings, is warranted. Nonetheless, several generalizations can be made about its potential benefits for teaching music in secondary and post-secondary music programs.

Turntablism clearly has the potential to teach or reinforce music fundamentals such as meter, rhythm, and tempo through active, hands-on music making. This is true not only for beginning musicians with little or no formal musical training, such as most of the students who enroll in the RCM classes, but also for students with more extensive musical backgrounds, such as the author and the students in the Berklee classes. Turntablism holds great potential for helping students of any level, even musically advanced students, to improve their overall musicianship through increased aural acuity, including a greater sensitivity to gradations of pitch as well as meter, rhythm, and tempo. These skills are transferable to other instruments, styles, and genres.

Through its extensive use of improvisation, turntablism is a form of creative, active music-making that requires the understanding and synthesis of a number of other musical skills in the domains of rhythm and meter, pitch, and style. Practicing turntable improvisation can improve students' overall musicianship in this and other performance situations. The greater ease of and comfort with improvisation developed through turntablism study could quite likely lead to more experimentation and risk taking in all kinds of music making.

Turntablism is also an ideal vehicle for teaching young people about the myriad styles and genres of popular music, and their social, cultural, and historical connections. With its rich history in the urban United States during the 1970s and 1980s, the study of the origins and development of hip-hop and its relationship to other musical genres would be interesting and exciting to include as part of teaching turntablism, as well as situating the active, embodied music-making in a meaningful context. A broad awareness of vernacular styles and genres would likely encourage students to be more discerning, critical, and well-informed music listeners, appreciators, and consumers, and would be useful for students to use or emulate as turntablists.

Cross-curricular connections, although not highlighted in the current study, could certainly be made when teaching turntablism. Turntablism's focus on technology and computer skills through the related use of sampling and mixing software could transfer into information technology, audio engineering, sound design, or electronic music. The close relationship between the work of DJs and MCs opens avenues to poetry and creative writing through the lyrical wordplay of rapping and to the study of percussion through beatboxing (vocal percussion) techniques. Hip-hop culture also encompasses graffiti art, which has an obvious connection with the visual arts, and break dancing. Hip-hop's association with dance, more generally, can broaden how music is taught through the incorporation of dance and movement into the music classroom or with links to dance or physical education departments. As mentioned earlier, teaching the historical roots of hip-hop can be related to history and sociology, as well as black studies courses.

Perhaps most importantly, the potential of turntablism for teaching music to students who might not connect with more traditional band, orchestral, or choral music programs in public schools seems great. Given the importance of hip-hop culture among African American, urban youth in particular, student populations that are representative of this demographic seem like particularly fruitful places to engage in this kind of music making. Furthermore, as Pasagiannis's 2007 study showed, turntablism can engage students in music learning who might be considered "at-risk" due to learning difficulties or social, behavioral, or psychological problems. It seems clear, based on Pasagiannis's positive findings as well as the enthusiasm I witnessed in the three classes researched for this chapter, that this kind of music making might very well resonate with and reach more students in these and other populations than would more traditional music education programs. Youth from a broad range of demographic groups, not just African American, urban, or "at-risk" students, could benefit from turntablism's connections to their musical tastes and experiences outside the school walls.

For all of these reasons, turntablism seems to be a valuable kind of music making for music educators to learn and to teach in turn. As a student in one of the Berklee classes noted to me after one of the classes I observed: "Turntablism would be amazing to include in middle or high school music. Not only is it a challenging and fantastic way to learn music, I've found that it really boosts my self-esteem. I think this is because I'm learning to make music that my friends and I enjoy listening to and dancing to outside of school. I can relate to what I'm doing in such a clear way that it makes me excited to learn more and motivates me to practice so that I can keep getting better."[8] Turntablism can serve as a clear link between the ways musicians learn and perform in the community and the ways music is taught in schools.

NOTES

1. See, for example, Fairchild 2008, Shiu 2007, Schloss 2004, and Souvignier 2003.

2. For example, see Neill 2002, Waxer 2001, and Riddell 2001.

3. Royal Conservatory of Music, Departments, http://www.rcmusic.ca/Content Page.aspx?name=Urban_Music_Department.

4. Royal Conservatory of Music, Course Listings, http://register.rcmusic.ca/rcms/ capricorn?para=calendarWelcome.

5. Berklee College of Music, Course Listings, http://www.berklee.edu/courses/ details.php.

6. Stephen Webber, e-mail message to author, June 18, 2009.

7. See, for example, Webber's explanation of the fundamental need for all DJs to learn beat matching before moving on to extending breaks and beat juggling (Webber 2008, 224).

8. Student conversation with the author, April 8, 2009.

REFERENCES

Berklee College of Music. Course Listings. http://www.berklee.edu/courses/details .php.

Endelman, Michael. 2003. Turntable U? In D.J.'s hands professor sees an instrument. *New York Times*, February 11.

Fairchild, Charles. 2008. The medium and materials of popular music: "Hound Dog," turntablism and muzak as situated musical practices. *Popular Music* 27, no. 1: 99–116.

Green, Lucy. 2002. *How popular musicians learn*. Aldershot, Hampshire, UK: Ashgate.

———. 2006. Popular music education in and for itself, and for "other" music: Current research in the classroom. *International Journal of Music Education* 24, no. 2: 101–18.

Gustavson, Leif. 2004. Zine writing, graffiti, and turntablism: The creative practices of three youth. PhD diss., University of Pensylvania.

Jones, Patrick M. 2005. Music education and the knowledge economy: Developing creativity, strengthening communities. *Arts Education Policy Review* 106, no. 4: 5–12.

Mr. Supreme. 1998. Interview by Joseph G. Schloss. Tape recording. July 16. Seattle, WA. Quoted in Schloss 2004, 19.

Neill, Ben. 2002. Pleasure beats: Rhythm and the aesthetics of current electronic music. *Leonardo Music Journal* 12:3–6.

Pasagiannis, John P. 2007. Hip-hop music treatment with at-risk adolescent populations. PhD diss., Gordon F. Derner Institute of Advanced Psychological Studies, Adelphi University, NY, 2007.

Riddell, Alistair. 2001. Data culture generation: After content, process as aesthetic. *Leonardo* 34, no. 4: 337–43.

Schloss, Joseph G. 2004. *Making beats: The art of sample-based hip-hop*. Middletown, CT: Wesleyan University Press.

Shiu, Anthony Sze-Fai. 2007. Styl(us): Asian North America, turntablism, relation. *CR: The New Centennial Review* 7, no. 1: 81–106.

Souvignier, Todd. 2003. *The world of DJs and the turntable culture*. Milwaukee, WI: Hal Leonard.

Steryannis, Theo. 2006. Big Black Lincoln. *Klublife Magazine*. http://www.klublife. com/features/main/big-black-lincoln.

Veblen, Kari. 2005. Community music and praxialism. In *Praxial music education: reflections and dialogues*, ed. David J. Elliott, 308–28. New York: Oxford University Press.

Waxer, Lise. 2001. Record grooves and salsa dance moves: The viejoteca phenomenon in Cali, Colombia. *Popular Music* 20, no. 1: 61–81.

Webber, Stephen. 2003. *Turntable technique: The art of the DJ*. Boston, MA: Berklee Press.

———. 2008. *DJ skills: The essential guide to mixing and scratching*. Oxford, UK: Focal.

III

TEACHING MUSIC ANALYSIS AND CRITICISM

11

Using *American Idol* to Introduce Music Criticism

James A. Grymes

The ability to listen critically to all types of music is without a doubt one of the most important skills we can teach our students. Whether we are preparing a music major for a career as a professional musician or a general student for what we hope will be a life enriched through the enjoyment of music, it is crucial that we help that student develop the techniques of careful and thoughtful listening that combine practical knowledge and historical perspective with interpretive analysis. The former two skill sets are at the heart of most music appreciation textbooks: a unit on the elements of music presents the basic vocabulary necessary for musical understanding and a series of units on the major style periods of the Western musical tradition (with perhaps some world and popular music either sprinkled throughout or tacked onto the end) provide a conceptual framework for contextualizing significant developments in music history. The problem with this approach is that students are taught to become passive consumers of music. When both repertoire and recordings are prescreened by the textbook author and the classroom teacher, the students are not compelled to develop the skills necessary to delineate between compositions or specific performances that are of high artistic quality and those that are not.

To infuse some sense of critical interpretation, students in music appreciation classes are commonly asked to attend a concert and submit a critique of that performance. To prepare the students for this assignment, textbooks and instructors often propose suggestions for how to choose concerts, tickets, and seats; how to plan ahead by researching both the repertoire on the program and the appropriate attire for that venue; and how to observe standard conventions of concert etiquette.[1] Armed with these instructions, the students are prepared to turn in a sociological field report on what the concert hall looked like, how the other patrons were dressed, and the rituals of concert decorum. They are also able to paraphrase key facts about the composers and the repertoire that they have gleaned from their preparation and from the concert program. While they may even provide a personal reflection of their experience, they are ill-equipped to produce a true critique of either the music or the performance itself, assessing the interpretive decisions and technical idiosyncrasies that separate a specific concert performance from any other live or recorded rendition of the same work.

If we are to teach our students to become critical listeners—a skill that is surely at the heart of "music appreciation"—we must expose them to experiences beyond those typically required for concert reports. Performances by professional symphonies, opera companies, and chamber ensembles certainly provide outstanding models of finely developed musicianship skills, but they tend to be so polished that there is little constructive criticism to be offered. On the other hand, while student performances may present a few concrete examples of deficiencies, asking inexperienced evaluators to be critical of their schoolmates—even if they have the requisite skills to do so—can often be inappropriate.

A set of case studies that are ideal for introducing the methods of music criticism can be found in the post-audition "performance shows" of the televised *American Idol* competition, in which amateur musicians prepare popular songs for evaluation by the show's judges and millions of viewers. In the spring of 2005, I taught an elective course at the University of North Carolina at Charlotte that used these performances to illustrate a number of issues related to music criticism, treating *American Idol*'s fourth season, which was being broadcast that spring, as a common text. I found that the performances on *American Idol* offered excellent opportunities to explore a wide variety of issues related to performance criticism, including vocal technique, stage presence, interpretation, and the psychology of performance—concepts that can be transferred to any type of performance of any type of music. This chapter will describe the materials and techniques that I developed for this course, in the hopes of providing a model for course design for those who wish to incorporate *American Idol* or similar shows into their own classes. While the examples below are obviously drawn from my personal experience during the show's fourth season, the pedagogical techniques they represent can be easily applied to any season, as well as to other televised singing competitions.

COURSE STRUCTURE

Because a sophisticated understanding of technical vocabulary is indispensable to critical discourse, I dedicated the first third of the 15-week semester to establishing the basic terminologies of music and music theory. Following the model typically used in music appreciation classes, I introduced elements of music, such as pitch, melody, harmony, dynamics, timbre, rhythm, and form, being careful to draw examples from popular culture as often as possible. For example, to illustrate tessitura and range, I played the "Diva Dance" from *The Fifth Element*, in which a soprano voice is digitally manipulated to create a superhuman vocal range. To demonstrate aspects of meter and rhythm, Bob Marley's "One Love"—complemented by the syncopated saxophone solo from James Brown's "I Got You (I Feel Good)"—served as an ideal example of off beats, while Dave Brubeck's "Take Five" and Pink Floyd's "Money" typified complex meters. At the end of the unit, the class analyzed musical form in Traci Chapman's "Give Me One Reason" (12-bar blues); Gordon Lightfoot's "The Wreck of the Edmund Fitzgerald" (strophic form); Queen's "Bohemian Rhapsody" (multi-sectional); and the Beatles's "She Loves You," "Something," and "The Ballad of John and Yoko" (verse-chorus form). Students were then asked to apply the theoretical concepts from the first unit by analyzing popular songs from their personal collections. By scrutinizing repertoire that reflected their own experiences and preferences and discussing the analyses of those songs in class, the students were able to begin the process of developing critical techniques.

In the sixth week of the semester, the class turned its attention to the history of performance and performance criticism, using as our textbook John Rink's *Musical Performance: A Guide to Understanding*. This unit began with a chapter on "Performing through History" that establishes some of the "idols" from the history of Western classical music, including legendary performers such as J. S. Bach, W. A. Mozart, Niccolò Paganini, and Franz Liszt (Lawson 2002). This was followed by a chapter on "Listening to Performance," which provides a survey of listening from the centuries-old "social embeddedness" of music in churches, courts, secular celebrations, domestic entertainment, and the military, to the concert culture that arose in the 19th century, and finally to the advent of recorded and broadcast music that has irrevocably separated the audience from the performers (Clarke 2002a).[2] Finally, a chapter on "The Criticism of Musical Performance" offers a history of music criticism that includes influential periodicals such as the *Allgemeine musikalische Zeitung* and individual critics like Eduard Hanslick and Bernard Shaw (Monelle 2002).

To accommodate the unique subject matter of the class, a number of supplemental readings were selected from a variety of sources. For example, the class began its examination of the techniques of criticism with a chapter on "Common Sense and the Language of Criticism" from Simon Frith's *Performing Rites: On the Value of Popular Music*, which describes the distinctly different types of musical judgments made by musicians, producers, consumers, and critics (Frith 1996). To determine the procedures that the students—as both consumers and critics—would use to judge the contestants on *American Idol*, the class studied research from the *British Journal of Music Education* and *Research Studies in Music Education* that focuses on the issues related to establishing and implementing reliable criteria for critiquing musical performances. An article on "Assessing Musical Performance" (Elliot 1987) introduces some tools for evaluating performances that proved to be relatively reliable, but one on "Performance as Experience: The Problem of Assessment Criteria" argues that regardless of the established criteria, music criticism will always be somewhat subjective (Johnson 1997). Some of the reasons for this subjectivity were demonstrated in another article, "Assessing Music Performance: Issues and Influences" (McPherson and Thompson 1998), which shows how a judge's appraisal of a performance can be biased by both musical factors (including the choice of repertoire, the form and structure of the music, the skill of accompanists, and the performer's expressivity) and nonmusical factors (the order of appearance, interaction with others, and distractions, such as equipment malfunctions), as well as the characteristics of both the performer (technical and musical skill, level of preparation and experience, and such thought processes as performance anxiety) and the evaluator (personality, mood, and attitude; experience and musical ability; training in adjudication; familiarity with the performer; and familiarity with the repertoire).

Having surveyed the histories and theories of both music and music criticism, the students now possessed the tools to begin examining the performances on *American Idol*. Although the spring semester had started at almost the same time as *American Idol*'s season, I had not brought the early rounds of auditions into many class discussions because I wanted the students to first establish a critical perspective that went well beyond the show. I did, however, end up playing a handful of carefully selected examples during the first unit to demonstrate vocal techniques, such as diction and vibrato.

Before evaluating the performances, it was necessary to confront some of the factors mentioned in "Assessing Music Performance: Issues and Influences," to establish whether these factors could indeed bias the students' opinions of the performances on *American Idol*. An article that appeared in *Time* at the end of *American Idol*'s previous season highlights how the show itself influences both musical and nonmusical factors for each contestant:

> Their week is grueling, filled with song-selection sessions, rehearsals, run-throughs, commercial and promo shoots, performances, and interviews . . . But in ways subtle and more blatant, the singers are also getting persona coaching. While they ultimately make their own decisions, they get advice on their song choices and performance to counter the judges' feedback, which often amounts to personal critiques: that [Diana] DeGarmo is too girlish or [LaToya] London too staid. On one shopping trip for show-night clothes—the Idols get $450 a

week for duds—stylist Miles Siggins encouraged London to "funk up" her look, saying that she sometimes mistook boring for classy. Conversely the coaches discouraged [Jasmine] Trias from selecting edgier music. (Poniewozik 2004, 72)

Moreover, an article from *Newsweek* confirms that at least one judge deliberately attempts to influence not only the singers themselves but also the audience's perceptions of their performances: "'You are going to be slightly tactical,' [Simon] Cowell admits. 'What you're trying to do, if you can, is to tell the audience who you want to be in the final. You're not getting accurate judging. You're not.'" (Peyser and Smith 2003, 54). Of particular interest to the students was whether age and sexuality should be taken into consideration when assessing contestants. A 50-year-old community college instructor has claimed that the show's producers discriminated against his age when they prohibited him from auditioning (*American Idol* requires contestants to be between 16 and 28 years old),[3] and the *Advocate* has questioned whether the show was biased against homosexuals (Glitz 2004).

After researching other ways of assessing performances and debating the traits necessary to be an "American Idol," the class established its own criteria for appraising the performances on the show. The evaluation system that the students devised was divided into three categories: vocal ability (which included as subcategories mechanics/technique, pitch accuracy, rhythmic accuracy, range, diction, and vocal quality), musical expression (including dynamics, interpretation, and style), and stage presence (including appearance, charisma, marketability, and confidence). The students also voted to create a summative category that used a five-point Likert scale to rate whether each contestant "has what it takes to be an American Idol." Later in the semester, the class decided to recognize the importance of repertoire choice as a musical factor by adding song selection as a fourth category. This system of assessment made for an interesting comparison with an "official scorecard" for contestants that a member of the class found in *American Idol: the Magazine*, which gave equal weight to five categories: vocal ability, appearance, song choice, personality, and stage presence.[4] The students noted that three of the four major categories evaluated in their criteria assessed musical factors, while three of the five categories in the "official scorecard" appraised nonmusical ones.

By the time *American Idol* had narrowed the field of contestants to 24 semifinalists (12 male and 12 female contestants), the semester had progressed into its seventh week, and I began to structure our weeks around the broadcasts. The class met on Mondays, Wednesdays, and Fridays, and Monday classes were dedicated to the historical survey of American popular music, using Jean Ferris's *America's Musical Landscape* and its accompanying recordings as our textbook.[5] Every Monday featured one chapter in the history of popular music, from the colonial period through such 20th-century genres as Broadway, Motown, disco, and film music, which are all prevalent themes for *American Idol* performance shows.

The performance shows were originally on Monday and Tuesday nights, and were later consolidated to Tuesdays only as the number of contestants was whittled down to 12 finalists. The syllabus required students to watch the shows prior to Wednesday's class and log into a course website to fill out surveys that rated each contestant according to the guidelines established by the class. The students were also asked to supply general comments about each performance and to rank the contestants. I projected the data from the online surveys during Wednesday classes, pointing out statistical anomalies and probing students for more specific feedback when necessary. To provide critical models to which all students could aspire, I also shared comments from the free-response sections of the surveys that I felt were particularly insightful.

Wednesday night *American Idol* broadcasts announced which contestants were being eliminated from the competition that week based on the votes cast by the show's viewers. On Fridays, the class would examine these results, especially if they varied greatly from the students' responses. In general, the outcomes of the elimination shows resembled the data from the student surveys. Throughout the three weeks of semifinals, which eliminated two males and two females every week until only twelve contestants remained, both of the females dismissed each week had been ranked among the bottom four females by the students. Similarly, the male contestant whom the class had ranked last was always one of the two males removed from the competition. It was, however, the discrepancies between the eliminations and the class's rankings that yielded the most interesting discussions. In the first round of the semifinals, for example, Judd Harris was eliminated by the viewers after being ranked fourth by the class.[6] The students concluded that Harris's failure on the show probably had less to do with the musical factors favored in their evaluation criteria than with the nonmusical ones that often influence the general public. Harris might have progressed further in the competition, they hypothesized, had the show's producers allowed him to establish a wider fan base through more appearances on camera earlier in the season.

One of the more interesting contestants at this stage of the competition was 17-year-old Janay Castine. The class ranked Castine at the bottom of the female contestants after her performance in the first round of the semifinals,[7] but she received enough votes from the show's viewers to avoid elimination. In the following week, the class ranked her last among the remaining 10 females,[8] while the show's voters eliminated the female contestants whom the students had ranked eighth and ninth. In their assessments and written comments from both weeks, the students took issue not so much with Castine's voice as with her song selection and stage presence, specifically what appeared to be a lack of confidence. "She looks so much more grown up than last week," wrote one student after the second round of the competition. "She also looks more comfortable on the stage. The song she sang didn't really display her vocal range very well, but I think all she needs is some time. She can grow and mature if she's given the chance." Castine was eliminated the next week, in the last round of the semifinals.

Because *American Idol* only announces which contestants receive the fewest votes and are, therefore, subject to elimination, there was no way of knowing whether the contestants whom the students ranked highest also received the most votes. Nevertheless, in their surveys of the 12 male semifinalists, the students' clear preferences were Mario Vasquez—an early fan favorite who withdrew from the competition at the end of the semifinals—and Bo Bice, who would become the season's runner-up. Carrie Underwood, who would ultimately win the competition, consistently scored among the highest ranked women in the online surveys.

As class discussions unfolded, I often polled the students using a classroom response system. Classroom response systems are instructional tools that elicit student interaction in real time by collecting and displaying student responses to questions posed by the instructor, either verbally or projected on a screen. Each student responds by pressing a button on a handheld radio-frequency transmitter (often called a "clicker"), and receivers transmit that data to a computer. The classroom response system software tallies the responses, and the students and instructor receive instant feedback in the form of histograms and detailed reports. Because each student transmitter has a unique signature that has been registered to its owner, response data can also be tabulated to assess attendance, participation, and long-term answer trends. This is a technology that I use daily in my music appreciation classes but found to be especially helpful in the *American Idol* class, where student responses to planned and impromptu questions often spurred further discussion.

In addition to reviewing *American Idol*'s weekly results, I designed Friday classes to introduce a variety of topics related to the business of music and performance studies. On the seventh Friday of the semester, the class delved into the role of the music industry in American society by studying a chapter from David Willoughby's *The World of Music*.[9] A survey of the music industry by popular-music expert Roy Shuker uses the tour profits, marketing agreements, and album deals of artists, such as Alanis Morissette, the Rolling Stones, and REM, to typify how large the market is for music and describes the dominance that a handful of major recording companies, such as Universal and Sony, hold over that market.[10] A firm understanding of the traditional music business provided a prologue to considering the ways in which *American Idol* has changed that industry. An article by media columnist Simon Dumenco argues that the show has rendered the record industry's star-making machinery irrelevant:

> Talent has seemingly come out of nowhere before, but "nowhere" has almost always been the record industry's farm system. Eminem, for instance, was hand-picked by an L.A. radio D.J. and carefully nurtured in the studio by rap impresario Dr. Dre before emerging, seemingly overnight, as a fully formed icon. Christina Aguilera spent years as a diva-in-training, putting in time as a Mouseketeer on *The Mickey Mouse Club* and recording a laboratory-tested song for a Disney movie soundtrack before breaking out with "Genie in a Bottle." Justin Timberlake was famously cast by a boy-band impresario in 'N Sync—a band whose seemingly overnight success in the U.S. was actually the culmination of a phased rollout in Europe during the mid-nineties. The bottom line is that most A-list artists require years, and millions of dollars, of investment. (Dumenco 2003)

American Idol contestants are, conversely, plucked from obscurity and made into best-selling recording artists over a period of weeks. *Advertising Age* confirms that the presale orders for season two finalists Clay Aiken's and Ruben Studdard's debut singles were numbers 1 and 4 on Amazon.com one week before they were released, noting that "both were ahead of Norah Jones, who won this year's best new artist Grammy" (Friedman 2003). Another article from *Time* sheds light on the disdain felt by many members of the staff at RCA Records—the Sony label that owns the contractual rights to record all *American Idol* finalists—at the prospect of dealing with the show's contestants rather than musicians who have taken more traditional routes to success:

> One RCA executive, who insisted on anonymity, cited *Idol* as proof that "Americans have no taste" and described Aiken as "Barry Manilow, but with less talent." [Executive Vice President and General Manager Richard] Sanders says he understands that some of his employees are "skeptical about the selection process and skeptical about selling a pop artist with no credibility." But, he adds, "I've told everyone they need to look at it this way: Americans buy more vanilla ice cream than any other flavor. Yes, they like their Rocky Road and Cherry Garcia, but ultimately America wants to consume vanilla. So we're going to sell the best vanilla. Given the problems we're facing as an industry, we cannot afford to be judgmental." (Tyangiel 2003)

For better or worse, *American Idol* has clearly revolutionized the way in which stars are discovered, marketed, and recorded, and an awareness of its function as a star-maker helps to explain the aforementioned steps the show takes to cultivate both the performers and their fans.

On the eighth and ninth Fridays of the semester, the class returned to readings from Rink's *Musical Performance*. The first session was based on an essay titled "Understanding the Psychology of Performance," which examines three major topics that often arise during critiques of the contestants on *American Idol*: performance skills, expression, and movement (Clarke 2002b). For valuable insight into how performers perceive the interpretive process, the students read a chapter on "Performers on Performance" (Dunsby 2002). The second class provided a historical survey of performance pedagogy, from the 18th-century treatises by Johann Joachim Quantz and C. P. E. Bach through the modern conservatory system (Ritterman 2002). A particularly informative source was Jane Davidson's chapter on "Developing the Ability to Perform," which discusses musical potentiality. In her investigation of the impact of both "nature" and "nurture" in the development of musical skills, Davidson lists three genetic factors that suggest potentiality: the development of motor skills, physical advantages (such as hand span), and mental advantages (such as problem-solving skills). Using Louis Armstrong as an example, Davidson continues by listing the environmental factors that can stimulate musical success: casual but frequent exposure to music, ample opportunities to develop performance skills, early opportunities for musical engagement, abundant opportunities to practice, and such external motivators as teachers and mentors. The five areas of study that Davidson found to form the basis of musical instruction (structure, notation, and reading skills; aural skills; technical and motor skills; expressive skills; and presentation skills) yielded obvious comparisons to typical collegiate music curricula (2002b).

Having attained a general understanding of the fundamentals of music pedagogy, the students were able to concentrate specifically on vocal pedagogy by the 12th week of the semester. For an overview of the mechanics of singing, the students relied on several passages from John Glenn Paton and Van Christy's vocal textbook *Foundations in Singing*. A chapter on "Breath and the Body" examines proper posture as well as the fundamentals of breathing, from the anatomy of the breathing mechanism to the physical processes of inhalation, turnaround, exhalation, and recovery.[11] A chapter on "Free Tone" was especially effective in giving the students commonly accepted terms for describing vocal quality (agile vs. stiff, breathy vs. clear, brassy vs. velvety, etc.), while also explaining proper and improper techniques for attacks and releases (2002, 18–26). Lastly, a chapter on "Vowels and Vocal Color" provides an introduction to good diction (41–49).

In the following week, the students combined readings from *Musical Performance* and *Foundations in Singing* to explore how musicians practice. A chapter on "Preparing for Performance" from *Musical Performance* illustrates how much practice is required to achieve musical excellence ("the 'best' and 'good' violinists practised for an average of 24.3 hours per week, whereas the likely music teachers averaged 9.8 hours per week") and describes how musicians develop technical expertise and formulate interpretations (Reid

2002). As always, the chapter from *Musical Performance* focuses on classical music, while the chapter from *Foundations in Singing* ("Preparing a Song") offers more practical advice, providing tips such as "Choose words that you can believe in" (Paton and Christy 2002, 34–40).

Finally, the students were ready to discuss interpretation. The readings for this class included a chapter on "Performing a Song" from *Foundations in Singing* (Paton and Christy 2002, 60–67), as well as chapters from Laura Browning Henderson's *How to Train Singers* and Roy Shuker's *Understanding Popular Music*.[12] During the lecture, I focused on how a singer might interpret Franz Schubert's early 19th-century Lied "Erlkönig." Obviously, an understanding of the German text is crucial to any interpretation, as is a firm grasp of the narrative structure of the poem, which requires the singer to provide different vocal colors for each of the four characters: the narrator, the father, the son, and the Erlkönig. Moreover, an accurate interpretation is not possible without a recognition of the underlying chromatic structure, in which the Erlkönig's three entrances in the successively ascending keys of B-flat Major, C Major, and E-flat Major (although ending in D minor) alternate with the son's tonally ascending pleas to his father and the father's increasingly angry tonal ascending responses. Lastly, a performance of "Erlkönig" requires not only a familiarity with the 19th-century Lieder tradition but also with opera, to reach the full dramatic potential of the brief concluding recitative. The ensuing class discussion represented an interesting turning point in the semester; while I had been relying on popular music to introduce tools of critique that can subsequently be transferred to classical music, this particular class used a masterwork of the classical repertoire to demonstrate how a singer can combine vocal technique, analysis, and stylistic awareness to interpret any song, including those from the popular repertoire.

On the final Friday of the semester, the students returned to two chapters from *Musical Performance* that introduced issues related to performance anxiety—something with which many of the students had struggled themselves. A chapter on "Communicating with the Body in Performance" stresses the importance of preparing for performances in a way that anticipates and overcomes the physiological and psychological over-arousal that can tarnish a performance (Davidson 2002b). Elizabeth Valentine's chapter on "The Fear of Performance" goes into stage fright in much more detail, including the physiological, behavioral, and mental symptoms. After surveying the causes of performance anxiety, Valentine proposes cures that are both physical, such as beta-blockers and the Alexander technique, and psychological, such as systematic desensitization and cognitive behavior therapy (Valentine 2002).

In addition to watching *American Idol*, responding to each performance through the online surveys, reading the course materials, and participating in class discussions, the students were required to submit critiques of other types of performances: two concerts sponsored by our department of music, one professional classical concert, and two performances of the student's choice. There were also three examinations on the materials from the lectures. At the end of the semester, each student was required to submit a 10-page paper that began with a survey of the most important factors a music critic must consider when judging performances, using materials from the course readings, class discussions, and their independent research. The students were then asked to give their assessments regarding which of the remaining contestants should win the contest (there were still five singers remaining when the semester ended). Using the responses they had entered into the online surveys throughout the semester, the students defended their selections with critiques of all of the performances given by that contestant since the beginning of the performance shows, comparing each to performances by other contestants. Finally, each paper concluded with a summary of that contestant's strengths and weaknesses, applying the autonomous criteria the student had established in the first part of the paper.

EXAMPLES FROM *AMERICAN IDOL*

The most challenging—and rewarding—aspects of teaching the *American Idol* class involved selecting the performances that would serve as the focus of the Wednesday classes. In reviewing the 12 finalists' performances of songs from the 1960s, for example, I concentrated on Anwar Robinson, a 25-year-old music teacher with a degree from Westminster Choir College, whom the students had ranked highest among the males in the previous week but whom they now ranked eighth. The students had praised Robinson when he sang standards such as Johnny Mercer and Henry Mancini's "Moon River," Marvin Gaye's "What's Going On," and "What a Wonderful World" (made famous by Louis Armstrong)[13] but described Robinson's rendition of "A House Is Not a Home" (recorded by Dionne Warwick) as "drabby," "boring," and "predictable."[14] During the class discussion of the performance, it became clear that much of the students' criticisms stemmed from the fact that none of them had ever heard "A House Is Not a Home" before. The students were consequently forced to acknowledge that their unfamiliarity with the repertoire had indeed influenced their assessment, just as the article "Assessing Music Performance: Issues and Influences" had predicted it could. This also reinforced awareness of the students' need to have knowledge of and appreciation for a large number of genres and styles.

Another particularly stimulating class focused on interpretive choices. Successful musicians (and victorious contestants on *American Idol*) do more than offer a karaoke-worthy copy of the original; they find a way to put their own personality into each performance. During the top nine contestants' performances of songs from Broadway musicals, Nikko Smith's soulful rendition of "One Hand, One Heart" presented the opportunity to familiarize students with the version from the *West Side Story* original cast recording, which the class then compared to a very different rendition by contemporary jazz duo Tuck & Patti. Although the students felt that Smith's performance was one of his best,[15] he was eliminated from the competition that week.

The most interesting interpretive decision of "Broadway Night"—and perhaps the entire season—was by Bo Bice, who confessed that musicals were "not my strong point" in the taped interview segment that preceded his live performance. Bice opted to sing "Corner of the Sky" from *Pippin* but admitted "the way I came up with it was just closing my eyes, pointed to the page, and fingers crossed."[16] I began the discussion of "Corner of the Sky" by playing a faithful rendering by musical-theatre specialist Jackie Trent. The class then observed the differences between Trent's interpretation and the Motown version recorded by the Jackson Five, before contrasting both with Bice's *American Idol* performance. The Jackson Five eliminated the six-measure prelude that typically initiates autonomous performances of "Corner of the Sky" (including Trent's) and began directly with a modified version of the syncopated riff that introduces each verse (see example 11.1). Bice, a die-hard fan of classic rock, also omitted the prelude, but he put an even more significant stamp on his interpretation by cleverly replacing Stephen Schwartz's intro riff with the syncopated chorus tag from Stephen Stills's "Love the One You're With" (see example 11.2).

There were, of course, times when the episodes of *American Idol* offered examples of both good and bad performing decisions. When the top eight contestants performed songs from their respective birth years, Anwar Robinson transposed "I'll Never Love This Way Again" (another song made famous by Dionne Warwick) from its original key of D Major to B Major, which allowed him to be in full voice during the chorus, especially after

Example 11.1.   Stephen Schwartz, "Corner of the Sky," *Pippin*, intro riff

Example 11.2.   Bo Bice, "Corner of the Sky," intro riff (a modified version of Stephen Stills, "Love the One You're With," chorus tag)

a modulation to C Major.[17] Vonzell Solomon also took full advantage of her range by transposing "Let's Hear It for the Boy."[18] Although I generally ignored the critiques provided by the show's three judges, preferring to instead encourage the students to generate their own assessments, I could not help but react to pop icon Paula Abdul's comment that the song was "right in the right register of your voice, and I think you even sang it an octave higher than Deniece Williams, I think. Did you? Did you sing it higher?" The answer was yes; Solomon had wisely transposed the song upwards, but it certainly was not an octave; it was a whole step, from C Major to D Major (putting the chorus in E Major). I then went over to the piano, and, leading the class in singing with my very best falsetto, performed the first few bars of the first verse in C, D, E, F, G, A, and B before we all failed miserably at singing it in C Major, an octave higher than Deniece Williams. To demonstrate what happens when a vocalist selects a song and/or a key that does not suit his or her voice, I compared the performances by Robinson and Solomon with one by Scott Savol, who opted to sing Hall and Oates's "She's Gone." When Savol performed the song in its original key of E Major, the pitches that began each verse proved to be too low for his voice.[19] While some students criticized Savol for not transposing the song to a higher tessitura, others argued that the modulation to F Major near the end of the performance had already pushed him to the top of his comfortable range, rendering transposition unviable. The class ultimately agreed that Savol's difficulties stemmed not from neglecting to transpose "She's Gone" but a failure to realize that its tessitura—in any key—exceeded his range.

CONCLUSION

Despite—or perhaps because of—its popular success, *American Idol* is often derided in the scholarly community as the antithesis of "serious" music. Once, during a board meeting of a professional music society, I sat across the table from a colleague who—upon learning of my *American Idol* class—disdainfully reminded me that many of the contestants could not read music and that the winner of the previous season, Fantasia Barrino, was functionally illiterate. The implication was that the contestants were not "real" musicians and were, therefore, unworthy of scholarly attention. Others, however, have acknowledged that "popular shows such as 'American Idol' could become the jumping off point for non-major class discussions in performance value, different cultures valuing music in different ways, and different periods valuing music in diverse ways" (Johns 2006).

My experience with teaching a course that used *American Idol* as a baseline for the introduction of critical-listening skills convinced me that the show can indeed be a springboard for serious discourse about music and music criticism. The performances on *American Idol* provide excellent catalysts for the exploration of such complex issues as vocal technique, stage presence, interpretation, and expressivity. When combined with the practical knowledge required for musical analysis and the historical perspective that results in stylistic awareness, *American Idol* can be an extraordinarily effective learning tool in the music classroom. These lessons, of course, transcend the television show and even transcend popular culture; over the course of the semester, my students developed into discriminating critics with the tools to think, speak, and write intelligently about all types of music.

NOTES

1. See, for example, Forney and Machlis 2007, 4–11. See also the "Concert Goer's Guide" that accompanies Kamien 2008b at http://highered.mcgraw-hill .com/sites/007340134x/student_view0/concert_goer_s_guide.html.
2. An exceptional survey of early concert culture can be found in Morrow 1989.
3. "Florida Instructor Files Discrimination Charge against TV Show," *Community College Week* 15, no. 14 (February 17, 2003): 16; Jamilah Evelyn, "Simon Says, Puhleeze," *Chronicle of Higher Education* 49, no. 22 (February 7, 2003): A7.
4. "Official Scorecards," *American Idol the Magazine*, February 2005, 1.
5. Jean Ferris, *America's Musical Landscape*, 4th ed. (Boston: McGraw-Hill, 2002). This textbook is now in its 5th edition.
6. Judd Harris, "Travelin' Band," February 21, 2005, http://www.youtube.com/ watch?v=JsBs5bxCMzY.
7. Janay Castine, "I Wanna Love You Forever," February 22, 2005, http://www .youtube.com/watch?v=8fRljMnzl9s.
8. Janay Castine, "Hit 'em Up Style" March 1, 2005, http://www.youtube.com/ watch?v=BvQfLffzLmQ.
9. David Willoughby, "Music in American Society," in *The World of Music*, 5th ed. (Boston: McGraw-Hill, 2003), 346–59. This textbook is now in its 7th edition.
10. Roy Shuker, "'Every I's a Winner:' The Music Industry," in Shuker 2001, 27–49.
11. John Glenn Paton and Van Christy, *Foundations in Singing*, 7th ed. (Boston: McGraw-Hill, 2002), 7–17. *Foundations in Singing* is now in its 8th edition. For more on the physiology of singing, see the chapter on "Understanding Your Vocal Instrument," 75–82.
12. Laura Browning Henderson, "Tested and Effective Performance Techniques," in *How to Train Singers*, 2nd ed. (West Nyack, NY: Parker, 1991), 159–70; Roy Shuker "'I'm Just a Singer (In a Rock 'N' Roll Band)': Making Music," in Shuker 2001, 99–114.
13. Anwar Robinson, "Moon River," February 21, 2005, http://www.youtube .com/watch?v=QdljjO35ISQ; "What's Going On," February 28, 2005, http://www. youtube.com/watch?v=LBloyTv5E7k; and "What a Wonderful World," March 7, 2005, http://www.youtube.com/watch?v=mVD7Wvu72n0.

14. Anwar Robinson, "A House Is Not a Home," March 15, 2005, http://www.youtube.com/watch?v=yYGgUOIT8Dw.

15. Nikko Smith, "One Hand, One Heart," April 5, 2005, http://www.youtube.com/watch?v=6Tyl2I-usHM.

16. Bo Bice, "Corner of the Sky," April 5, 2005, http://www.youtube.com/watch?v=YccQG-fcx7U.

17. Anwar Robinson, "I'll Never Love This Way Again," April 12, 2005, http://www.youtube.com/watch?v=icFUS73udgY.

18. Vonzell Solomon, "Let's Hear It for the Boy," April 12, 2005, http://www.youtube.com/watch?v=3TluCejPmoI.

19. Scott Savol, "She's Gone," April 12, 2005, http://www.youtube.com/watch?v=CLUl0Q7llTk.

REFERENCES

American Idol: The Magazine. Official scorecards. February 2005, 1.

Clarke, Eric. 2002a. Listening to performance. In *Musical performance: A guide to understanding*, ed. John Rink, 185–96. Cambridge: Cambridge University Press.

———. 2002b. Understanding the psychology of performance. In *Musical performance: A guide to understanding*, ed. John Rink, 59–72. Cambridge: Cambridge University Press.

Davidson, Jane. 2002a. Communicating with the body in performance. In *Musical performance: A guide to understanding*, ed. John Rink, 144–52. Cambridge: Cambridge University Press.

———. 2002b. Developing the ability to perform. In *Musical performance: A guide to understanding*, ed. John Rink, 89–101. Cambridge: Cambridge University Press.

Dumenco, Simon. 2003. The un-star system. *New York Magazine*, September 8: 43.

Dunsby, Jonathan. 2002. Performers on performance. In *Musical performance: A guide to understanding*, ed. John Rink, 225–36. Cambridge: Cambridge University Press.

Elliot, David. 1987. Assessing musical performance. *British Journal of Music Education* 4, no. 2: 157–83.

Evelyn, Jamilah. Simon says, puh-leeze. *Chronicle of Higher Education* 49, no. 22 (February 7, 2003): A7.

Ferris, Jean. 2002. *America's musical landscape*. 4th ed. Boston: McGraw-Hill.

Florida instructor files discrimination charge against TV show. *Community College Week* 15, no. 14 (February 17, 2003): 16.

Forney, Kristine, and Joseph Machlis. 2007. *The enjoyment of music: An introduction to perceptive listening*. 10th shorter ed. New York: W.W. Norton.

Friedman, Wayne. 2003. Fox's "Idol" makes mark on music marketing. *Advertising Age*, June 9: 4.

Frith, Simon. 1996. *Performing rites: On the value of popular music*. Cambridge, MA: Harvard University Press.

Glitz, Michael. 2004. Why can't the idol be gay? *Advocate*, May 11: 78–79.

Henderson, Laura Browning. 1991. *How to train singers*. 2nd ed. West Nyack, NY: Parker.

Johns, Lana K. 2006. Reflection on the participatory plenary session on "Redefining the Universe: Music and Musicians in the 21st Century." *College Music Society Newsletter*, January: 22.

Johnson, Peter. 1997. Performance as experience: The problem of assessment criteria. *British Journal of Music Education* 14, no. 3: 271–82.

Kamien, Roger. 2008a. Concert goer's guide. In *Music: An appreciation*. 6th brief ed. Boston: McGraw-Hill. http://highered.mcgraw-hill.com/sites/007340134x/student_view0/concert_goer_s_guide.html.

———. 2008b. *Music: An appreciation*. 6th brief ed. Boston: McGraw-Hill.

Lawson, Colin. 2002. Performing through history. In *Musical performance: A guide to understanding*, ed. John Rink, 3–16. Cambridge: Cambridge University Press.

McPherson, Gary E., and William F. Thompson. 1998. Assessing music performances: Issues and influences. *Research Studies in Music Education* 10:12–24.

Monelle, Raymond. 2002. The criticism of musical performance. In *Musical performance: A guide to understanding*, ed. John Rink, 213–24. Cambridge: Cambridge University Press.

Morrow, Mary Sue. 1989. *Concert life in Haydn's Vienna: Aspects of a developing musical and social institution*. Stuyvesant, NY: Pendragon.

Paton, John Glenn, and Van Christy. 2002. *Foundations in singing*. 7th ed. Boston: McGraw-Hill.

Peyser, Marc, and Sean M. Smith. 2003. 'Idol' worship. *Newsweek*, May 26: 54.

Poniewozik, James. The making of an idol. *Time*, May 24: 72.

Reid, Stefan. 2002. Preparing for performance. In *Musical performance: A guide to understanding*, ed. John Rink, 102–12. Cambridge: Cambridge University Press.

Rink, John, ed. 2002. *Musical performance: A guide to understanding*. Cambridge: Cambridge University Press.

Ritterman, Janet. 2002. On teaching performance. In *Musical performance: A guide to understanding*, ed. John Rink, 75–88. Cambridge: Cambridge University Press.

Shuker, Roy. 2001. *Understanding popular music*. 2nd ed. London: Routledge.

Tyangiel, Josh. 2003. Building a better pop star. *Time*, October 13: 73.

Valentine, Elizabeth. 2002. The fear of performance. In *Musical performance: A guide to understanding*, ed. John Rink, 168–82. Cambridge: Cambridge University Press.

Willoughby, David. 2003. *The world of music*. 5th ed. Boston: McGraw-Hill.

12

An Analytic Model for Examining Cover Songs and Their Sources

Victoria Malawey

Cover songs—songs that have been previously written or recorded by one artist, performed again by another—have become ubiquitous in Western popular culture. Because of this, cover songs can serve as a useful pedagogical tool in a variety of music classes.[1] In music theory, music appreciation, and music fundamentals classes, comparisons of cover songs and their sources can demonstrate simple and audible differences in style, tempo, texture, instrumentation, timbre, as well as chord function, melody, and rhythmic structure. In courses on structure and analysis, students can examine different versions of a single song to find subtleties of difference in musical form. In interdisciplinary courses on gender and music, students may investigate cross-gender covers in attempt to understand how gender and sexuality are constructed by musical artists and received by audiences.

In his dissertation on blues cover songs, Thomas Schneider argues for the development of an analytic model that would systematically compare cover versions and their sources.[2] How can we adequately account for, describe, and measure the subtle (and not-so-subtle) dissimilarities between different versions of a song? How can we better understand differences in style and genre? How might musical analysis or transcription, as a mode of analysis, elucidate the differences in meaning[3] and value listeners intuit in cover songs, particularly cross-gender covers? In what ways can we systematically observe differences in elements that are harder to convey through transcription, such as vocal articulation, inflection, and timbre? This study seeks to answer these questions and develop a systematic approach for articulating musical difference. The model will be applied to analyses of three different pairs of cover songs to show its effectiveness. The first application of the analytic model examines two very similar versions of "Somewhere Only We Know," originally recorded by Keane in 2004 and covered by Lifehouse in 2006. The second application of the model examines a striking cross-genre cover song, Obadiah Parker's 2007 folk-inspired pop cover of OutKast's 2003 hip-hop hit "Hey Ya." The third application focuses on a cross-gender cover song, New-York singer-songwriter Swati's 2007 version of Bruce Springsteen's 1984 pop hit "I'm on Fire." It is my hope that this model will have pedagogical value for other studies of cover songs as appropriate for different music classes.

A basic outline of the analytic model appears in figure 12.1. This model directs observations into four different broad categories: (1) voice and words, (2) sound, (3) pitch, and (4) time.[4] The first two categories are appropriate for student analysts at any level, from beginners to more advanced students, since little knowledge of musical notation is involved. The first broad category (voice and words) invites analysts to compare the cover song with its source in terms of vocal timbre, articulation, and quality; emotional affects; implied personas; and differences in the lyrics. This category contains the most immediate musical observations; often the voice and lyrics are central to the most obvious changes in perceived meaning. The second broad category (sound) consists of information on instrumentation, texture, dynamics, and studio-produced effects. The third and fourth categories (pitch and time, respectively) are more useful for students with a greater knowledge of music theory because an understanding of notation, transcription, and tonal function may be necessary in fleshing out thoughtful comparisons in these areas. Depending on the students' skill level, modifications can be made. Not all students possess the skills necessary to create an accurate transcription, for example, but still general observations about melody, harmony, and rhythm can be made in a less formal way.

An approach based upon considering various parameters in turn to understand relationships between cover songs and originals is not new. In an analysis of Dolly Parton's 1984 cover of Petula Clark's "Downtown" with the original version, John Wallace White compares components of each version of the song: "the message," form, text, instrumentation and overall sound ("mix"), tempo and rhythm, harmonic scheme, and "dynamic profile" (1997). Similarly, Rob Bowman analyzes differences among four versions of "Try a Little Tenderness" by comparing the following elements: form, melody, harmony, timbre, dynamics, "playful voicedness," and instrumentation.[5] What sets the model proposed in this study apart from previous approaches to cover songs is that it offers a systematic methodology that can be applied to any set of songs, regardless of degree of similarity, change in genre, or change in meaning. Furthermore, by completing comparative worksheets side-by-side, the analyst can at once see differences that might otherwise be more difficult to trace in prose.

The primary function of this model is to assist in the process of making observations and collecting data by relating a cover version to its source. The model should be used in a directly comparative manner—as observations are made within one category for the cover song, the student should consider how those observations relate to those made for the source or vice versa. The model as it appears in figure 12.1 can be printed onto two handouts, which can be placed side-by-side and filled with observations as students listen for specific musical characteristics. The model is focused on what Kevin Holm-Hudson, following Nattiez, refers to as "the neutral level" of analysis, which he defines as the "quantifiable elements independent of both creation and reception."[6]

Once observations are made in all of the appropriate categories, students can then begin to ponder how the musical observations intersect with one another, and shape the meanings they may intuit after casual listening, as well as suggest new meanings they may not have considered. From this process, students may draw conclusions for an essay, presentation, or simple preparation for class discussion. In a broader context, students can relate musical elements to extramusical social and cultural meanings—for example: how changes in vocal delivery can have a profound impact on subject position.[7] In other cases, extramusical meaning may not be central to the objectives of the lesson—for example, in a music-theory class where the goal is to hear the difference between progressions using only chords on primary scale degrees (1, 4, and 5) and those that use both primary and secondary diatonic triads.[8] Still, students may find this analytic activity most rewarding when they are able to show the technical musical differences between a cover song and its source and then relate them to an extramusical idea that may resonate with their own life experiences.

Kurt Mosser presents a typology for understanding cover songs, which range along a continuum from "reduplication covers," marked by extreme similarity, to "parody covers" that use humor and difference to mark themselves apart from their sources (Mosser 2008). Another type included in Mosser's model is "interpretive covers," which divides into two different subcategories, "minor interpretations—the homage" and "major interpretations." "Send-up covers" go beyond the degree of difference found in interpretive covers and transform the original significantly for ironic effect. The analytical model proposed in this study is designed to be flexible enough to accommodate all different kinds of cover songs, including the wide range of types described by Mosser; however, its function is not to place a cover song into one of Mosser's categories, although observations gathered through applying the model might lead to such categorization.

```
COVER
Song:                                    Artist:

I.   Voice and Words
     A.   Voice (timbre, quality, manner of delivery, persona)

     B.   Lyrics (changes/additions/omissions, manipulations in delivery)

II.  Sound
     A.   Instrumentation and effects

     B.   Texture

     C.   Dynamics

III. Pitch
     A.   Melody (changes, embellishment)

     B.   Harmony (chord substitution, other changes)

IV.  Time
     A.   Rhythm

     B.   Meter

     C.   Tempo

     D.   Form

     E.   Pacing of events
```

Figure 12.1.   Model for analyzing cover songs

SOURCE:

Song: Artist:

I.   Voice and Words
     A.   Voice (timbre, quality, manner of delivery, persona)

     B.   Lyrics (content, characteristics, changes from verse to verse)

II. Sound
     A.   Instrumentation and effects

     B.   Texture

     C.   Dynamics

III. Pitch
     A.   Melody (content, characteristic turns of phrase)

     B.   Harmony (content, chord structure, voice leading)

IV. Time
     A.   Rhythm

     B.   Meter

     C.   Tempo

     D.   Form

     E.   Pacing of events

Figure 12.1.   (*continued*)

A CASE OF EMULATION: LIFEHOUSE'S COVER
OF KEANE'S "SOMEWHERE ONLY WE KNOW"

A skeptic might argue that there is little to be learned from a study of a cover song produced in homage to a source version, asking why one should bother when the correspondences are so close. Yet we shall see that by using the model proposed in this study, subtleties of difference may emerge over the course of analysis—differences that may not be readily perceived on a casual listening of the song pair. Perceiving these types of differences can show students the value of close listening and analysis.[9]

Lifehouse prefaced their performance of "Somewhere Only We Know" with the following statement: "We picked this song because this is one of our favorite bands and one of our favorite records that came out last year."[10] Given this statement and the tight correspondence between their version and the source, we can safely assume that this cover qualifies as a case of emulation, one in which the band covering the song (Lifehouse) closely copies the original in homage to the source (Keane). Using Mosser's system of classification for cover songs, Lifehouse's cover of "Somewhere Only We Know" would best fit within the category of "minor interpretation—the homage" because it shows respect for its source and maintains its basic musical characteristics.

To apply the analytic model for cover songs, students should begin by listening and jotting down some notes beneath each category in figure 12.1. Ideally, students should focus on a single aspect of the music at a time. For instance, during the first hearing, students may remark only on the quality of vocal delivery; then during the next hearing, they may shift their focus to the lyrics and so forth. Some categories will require multiple hearings in order for the students to make worthwhile observations. A sample model completed for "Somewhere Only We Know" appears in figure 12.2. This detailed comparison confirms our intuition that the cover has many aspects in common with the source: the lyrics are not significantly changed; the standard pop-rock texture, dynamics, and instrumental structure are maintained; the lead vocal of the cover faithfully reproduces the melody and rhythm of the source, including embellishments and other nuances; the overall harmonic functions are kept intact—although there are some significant chord substitutions; the composite rhythm and standard rock pattern in the drums are similar; and the metric and hypermetric structure, pacing of events, and form are identical. The only aspect that differs between the two versions in the fourth broad category (time) is tempo—the cover version is slightly faster than the source.

Through this comparison process, we also identify some of the more striking differences between the two versions. Although Jason Wade, lead singer of Lifehouse, carefully imitates Tom Chaplin's vocal melody in the source recording, the timbre of Wade's voice is rougher and less even than Chaplin's. Whereas Chaplin maintains a clear and even tenor over the course of the song, Wade breaks into falsetto at times, drawing attention to the phrases "oh, simple thing" and "so tell me when" in the pre-chorus sections. Also, Wade's pitch is slightly out of tune in a few passages, whereas Chaplin sings in tune consistently throughout. The difference in intonation is most striking on Wade's articulation of the word "everything" in the chorus sections.

Perhaps the most immediate difference between the two performances has to do with instrumentation. The Keane version relies heavily on piano, which articulates continuous eighth notes throughout the song. The Lifehouse cover does not use piano, and the guitar takes on the rhythmic and harmonic role the piano has in the Keane version. The Keane version also uses tambourine, which comes to the fore in the first pre-chorus, but Lifehouse does not use tambourine. In the Keane version, the tambourine smoothly bridges the pared-down instrumentation of the first verse (which features only piano and voice) to the fuller instrumentation of the second verse (which features the entire band). No such textural bridge smoothes the respective instrumentation change in the Lifehouse version, and thus, the section changes are more abrupt in their version.

The Keane version features the voice of Chaplin only; whereas in the Lifehouse cover, there are a few passages that feature backing vocals. These occur in the second and third pre-chorus sections on the lines "I'm getting older and I need something to rely on" and "I'm getting tired and I need somewhere to begin," as well as in the vocalization that takes place before the final chorus. The use of backing vocals sets the Keane and Lifehouse versions apart from one another stylistically and aesthetically. Chaplin singing the lead vocal part alone in Keane's version highlights the individual message and personal nature of the song, positioning his performance within a larger tradition of singer-songwriters performing their own songs. Authenticity, personal subjectivity, and honesty are values that are closely associated with this genre and, more specifically, with the type of performance that Chaplin conveys through his direct vocal delivery, unencumbered by backing vocals. The Lifehouse version, on the other hand, projects less individuality and more of a collective delivery through the use of backing vocals, and the individual and highly personal nature of the lyrics become somewhat diffused. In this version, the backing vocals become an extension of Wade's projected persona as lead singer. This collective sound, coupled with the use of multiple guitars in lieu of piano, positions Lifehouse's version within the tradition of rock, whose success as a genre relies on "authentic" performance as conveyed through a collaborative, group effort.

In terms of tonal difference, the Lifehouse version is transposed down a semitone from A major to A-flat major as a result of tuning down a half

COVER

Song: "Somewhere Only We Know"   **Artist: Lifehouse**

I. **Voice and Words**
   A. **Voice (timbre, quality, manner of delivery, persona)**
      - Good imitation of vocal quality of the source by Jason Wade, lead singer; voice does break into falsetto in a few marked places, placing emphasis on those phrases: "oh simple thing," "so tell me when"
   B. **Lyrics (changes/additions/omissions, manipulations in delivery)**
      - Follows lyrics of the original very closely.

II. **Sound**
   A. **Instrumentation and effects**
      - Also uses standard pop-rock ensemble (voice [lead and backing vocals], drum kits, bass, guitar) but has several striking difference to the Keane version: no keyboards, no tambourine
      - Use of backing vocals
   B. **Texture**
      - Accompanied melody, but interaction of instruments a little different (no keyboards)—in places where in the Keane version, there is just voice and keyboards, whereas the Lifehouse version uses just guitar with voice
   C. **Dynamics**
      - Follows similar dynamic structure, but with less contrast between louds and softs.

III. **Pitch**
   A. **Melody (changes, embellishment)**
      - Lead vocal very similar to source, down to the minor embellishments made in later pre-chorus
      - Pitch in lead vocal is a little out of tune in places where Chaplin's delivery is spot on
   B. **Harmony (chord substitution, other changes)**
      - Half-step lower than Keane version; in A-flat major
      - Ends with a tonic triad in guitar
      - Simplification of harmony, perhaps due in part to lack of keyboard in this version

IV. **Time**
   A. **Rhythm**
      - Maintains standard rock pattern in drums (compared to Keane)
      - Maintains rhythm of lead vocal (compared to Keane)
      - Composite rhythm—pulsing eighth notes (articulated in the bass, but not piano)
   B. **Meter**
      - Standard 4/4 meter; also four-bar hypermeter. Follows source.
   C. **Tempo**
      - A bit faster than Keane version, approximately a little slower than quarter = 92
   D. **Form**

Time	# of bars	Section
0:00	N/a	spoken introduction
0:17	8	introduction
0:38	8	verse 1
1:00	8	pre-chorus
1:22	8	verse 2
1:43	8	pre-chorus
2:04	12 (8+4)	chorus + interlude
2:36	8	pre-chorus
2:57	12 (8+4)	chorus +interlude
3:29	8	chorus

   E. **Pacing of events**
      - Same as Keane's version

Figure 12.2.   **Sample model for "Somewhere Only We Know"**

SOURCE
Song: "Somewhere Only We Know"   Artist: Lifehouse

I.   **Voice and Words**
    A. **Voice (timbre, quality, manner of delivery, persona)**
        • Clear, pop tenor voice of Tom Chaplin; fairly even type of delivery
    B. **Lyrics (content, characteristics, changes from verse to verse)**
II. **Sound**
    A. **Instrumentation and effects**
        • Standard pop-rock ensemble: voice, piano/keyboards, drum kit with tambourine, bass, guitar
        • No backing vocals
    B. **Texture**
        • Accompanied melody; Builds to a fairly dense texture using entire ensemble
    C. **Dynamics (and orchestration)**
        Fairly consistent throughout. Starts at a solid *mf*, pulls back a bit (more to do with orchestration than dynamics) to piano and voice at beginning of verse 1. By first pre-chorus, builds a bit, add tambourine, bass, synth. By second verse, back to dynamic level of introduction with all instruments (piano, voice, guitar, bass, drums). Dynamics and orchestration pull back again in the four measures following the first chorus (considered an interlude) and resume with the following pre-chorus. Dynamics and orchestration pair down again near the end at around 3:34.
III. **Pitch**
    A. **Melody (content, characteristic turns of phrase)**
        • Lead vocal very consistent; a few minor embellishments in later pre-chorus
    B. **Harmony (content, chord structure, voice leading)**
        • In A Major
        • Ends with a tonic add9 chord in piano
        • More nuanced harmony
IV. **Time**
    A. **Rhythm**
        • Standard rock pattern in drums
        • Pulsing eighth notes as composite rhythm (articulated in the piano and the bass)
    B. **Meter**
        • Standard 4/4 meter; also four-bar hypermeter
    C. **Tempo**
        • Approximately a little faster than quarter = 84
    D. **Form**

Time	# of bars	Section
0:00	8	introduction
0:24	8	verse 1
0:47	8	pre-chorus
1:09	8	verse 2
1:32	8	pre-chorus
1:54	12 (8+4)	chorus + interlude
2:27	8	pre-chorus
2:49	12 (8+4)	chorus +interlude
3:24	8	chorus

    E. **Pacing of events**
        • Standard sort of pacing for pop-rock songs. Eight- and twelve-bar sections, nothing unusual
        • Chorus comes in with melodic apex and climax of song almost half way through the song

Figure 12.2. (*continued*)

step, perhaps to accommodate Wade's lower vocal tessitura. Although the basic harmonic functions remain consistent, there are subtle differences between the versions. Close listening, perhaps aided with some transcription, can be useful in pinning down these specific chord differences. In the pre-chorus sections, the pre-dominant harmony in the fourth and eighth measures is a IV chord in the Lifehouse version instead of ii$^6_5$ in the Keane version. Example 12.1 provides a transcription of the first pre-chorus from the Keane version, and example 12.2 shows the parallel passage from the Lifehouse cover. Measures 20 and 24 feature the pre-dominant substitution. A similar pre-dominant substitution takes place in the chorus sections on the text "so why don't we go."

The interlude material demonstrates the clearest chord substitution because the texture is somewhat thinner in these passages. In the Keane ver-

Example 12.1.   Keane, "Somewhere Only We Know," pre-chorus. "Somewhere Only We Know" words and music by Tim Rice-Oxley, Richard Hughes, and Tom Chaplin. © 2004 by Universal Music. This arrangement © 2010 by Universal Music. All rights in the United States Administered by Universal Music—Careers. International copyright secured. All rights reserved. Reprinted by permission of Hal Leonard Corporation.

Example 12.3.   Keane, "Somewhere Only We Know," interlude

Example 12.5.   Keane, "Somewhere Only We Know," ending

sion, we clearly hear a succession of first-inversion chords in the piano—an oscillation between ii⁶ and iii⁶₅ (Bm/D and Cm⁷/E). This passage is transcribed in example 12.3. In the Lifehouse cover, the oscillating chords are reduced to root-position triads—IV and V (Db and Eb; see transcription in example 12.4). Despite the chord substitutions, the bass part in this passage remains the same in both versions.

Similarly, there is a clear case of chord substitution at the end of the song. The Lifehouse version has less variety and fewer chord changes compared to the Keane version. Compare the Keane ending notated in example 12.5 to the Lifehouse version in example 12.6. In mm. 77–80, the Keane version uses an embellished oscillation between the supertonic and submediant chords, whereas the Lifehouse version uses an unembellished alternation of subdominant and dominant. The harmonic rhythm in the penultimate

Example 12.2.   Lifehouse, "Somewhere Only We Know," pre-chorus

Example 12.4.   Lifehouse, "Somewhere Only We Know," interlude

Example 12.6.   Lifehouse, "Somewhere Only We Know," ending

measure is different as well. The use of IV and V in the Lifehouse version leads smoothly into the plagal cadence that ends the song, without any feeling of disruption or harmonic change. The use of ii, iii$^{(7)}$, and the chromatic inflection on $^{\flat}$iii bridging the restatement of the oscillation gesture ii–iii in Keane's version provide a less tonally directed but more colorful approach to the cadence at the end of the song.

We have an opportunity here to show how different categories intersect with one another. The most likely reason for the harmonic changes discussed above is the difference in instrumentation. Although both bands create a convincing standard pop-rock sound, the use of guitar in lieu of piano in the Lifehouse version lends itself to simpler harmonies. Added-note chords and embellishing tones, such as the ones found in the Keane version, are easily performed at the keyboard but are less idiomatic on guitar. Thus, even small changes in instrumentation can affect chord choice.

Filling out the worksheets and drawing initial conclusions are crucial steps for students who have a difficult time getting started or producing concrete results. These steps also ensure that students will consider many aspects of the music equally instead of focusing on only one or two. After the worksheets are completed, students may begin to evaluate further the differences between the songs in order to better understand the meaning(s) they perceive when listening casually. They may also find that new, previously unconsidered meanings emerge.

Having gathered all of these observations, we should look for overarching trends that might support new meanings or other conclusions regarding the cover band's treatment of the song. In Lifehouse's performance of "Somewhere Only We Know," several elements contribute to a more urgent and rawer effect than the source. The Lifehouse version features less consistency in the vocal delivery and vocal intonation, giving the song a rougher edge, and it has a slightly faster tempo, suggesting greater urgency. These qualities— particularly the rawer, rougher effect—are reinforced through the changes in instrumentation. The use of the piano in the Keane version lends a more polished, pop quality to the song in contrast to the simpler, visceral rock sound of the guitar, which takes on the piano's role in the Lifehouse cover. These changes create a slightly different feel and make the cover version identifiable as a song performed by Lifehouse and not Keane. Furthermore, completing the analytical model for the song pair compels us to articulate the precise reasons why we associate particular values with a cover and its source. In this case, we can attribute specific aspects of instrumentation and vocal quality as the markers of difference, which support the broader claims that the Lifehouse version is more rock-oriented with a more rugged, less polished sound compared to the Keane version, which is more pop-oriented with a more polished and smoother overall sound.

A CASE OF DISPARATE GENRES:
OBADIAH PARKER'S COVER OF OUTKAST'S "HEY YA"

Stylistically, Obadiah Parker's cover version of OutKast's "Hey Ya" could not be more different from the original. Their cover is a folk-inspired pop version of the hip-hop hit and was made famous by a YouTube video recording of the song performed by Obadiah Parker's lead singer Mat Weddle.[11] Journalist Scott Craven describes the unlikely cover as a transformation of "one of the most danceable songs recorded into a ballad" (Craven 2006). Completing the comparative model helps to articulate the specific differences that create the overall stylistic contrast listeners perceive between these two songs. A completed model for this song pair appears in figure 12.3.

There are many differences between the two versions, but let us begin with what the songs have in common. The Obadiah Parker version retains most of the melodic, rhythmic, and metric structures, as well as the tempo, of the OutKast recording. This is significant because the uniquely irregular metric structure is preserved throughout both versions. A basic transcription of the first line appears in example 12.7. This metric pattern consists of three bars of 4/4 followed by one bar of 2/4 and two bars of 4/4. Every line of the verse and chorus is structured metrically in this way. Considered in either 4/4 or 2/4, the structure is asymmetrical. In 4/4, the pattern is either a 5-bar grouping with an extra half bar or a 6-bar grouping missing half a bar. In 2/4, each line is 11 bars. This alternate interpretation is reflected in the transcription in example 12.8. The "bump" which causes the asymmetry in this passage occurs in mm. 7–8, where the previously established duple hypermeter receives an arrival on m. 8, when it is not expected until the downbeat of m. 9.

Although there are many more changes in the Obadiah Parker cover version, the most significant of these involve manner of delivery, lyrics, and pacing of events. First, Weddle's vocal delivery in the Obadiah Parker version could not be more different from André 3000's delivery in the OutKast version. Weddle sings in a folk style throughout the song, departing from André 3000's sometimes spoken and half-sung hip-hop delivery. The categories of vocal delivery, texture, and instrumentation combine to create considerable stylistic difference. Not only do the respective lead singers have striking performance differences, the use of multiple layers of text (particularly in lines 13–16 and 27–28), layers of voices, and resultant denser texture in the OutKast version contrasts starkly with the simpler folk-inspired textures that draw attention to a single vocal line in the Obadiah Parker version.

Some of the differences in texture relate to differences in how the lyrics are used. Referring back to figure 12.3, all changes in the lyrics are shown

COVER
Song: "Hey Ya"   Artist: Obadiah Parker

I   Voice and Words
  A. Voice (timbre, quality, manner of delivery, persona)
    • Greater focus on voice (related to folk texture); more intimate manner of delivery
  B. Lyrics (changes/additions/omissions, manipulations in delivery)
    • There are a number of significant changes to the lyrics (differences appear in boldface below)
    • Fewer spoken/half-sung, guttural injections in this version compared to the source
    • Lyrics lend themselves to a single voice—monologue as opposed to dialogue
    • Has fewer lines that are dance oriented

1   My baby don't mess around because she loves me so and this I know for sure
2   But does she really wanna but can't stand to see me walk out the door
3   **Can't stand** to fight the feelin' 'cause the thought alone is killing me right now
4   Thank god for mom and dad for sticking two together 'cause we don't know how

5   *Hey Ya, Hey Ya*
6   *Hey Ya, Hey Ya*

9   You think you've got it, oh, you think you've got it but got it just don't get it 'til there's nothing at all
10 We get together, oh, we get together but separate's always better when there's feelings involved
11 If what they say is "nothing is forever" **then what makes, then what makes, then what makes** love the exception?
12 So why are, why are, why are, why are, why are, are we so in denial when we know we're not happy here?

13 *Hey Ya, Hey Ya*
14 *Hey Ya, Hey Ya*
15 *Hey Ya, Hey Ya*
16 *Hey Ya, Hey Ya*

17 Hey, alright now fellas,
18 Now what's cooler than bein' cool?
19 I can't hear ya, **oh no,** I say what's cooler than bein' cool?
20 Alright, alright, alright, alright, alright, alright, alright, alright, alright, alright, alright, alright, alright, **alright, now ladies,**
21 **We gonna break it down** in just a few seconds here
22 Now don't have me **break it down** for nothin'
23 Now I wanna see y'all on **y'all's** baddest behavior
24 **I say** lend me some sugar, I am your neighbor
25 Shake it, shake, shake, shake it, shake, shake, shake it, shake, shake, shake it, shake it, shake, shake, shake it like a Polaroid,
26 Shake it, shake, shake, shake it, shake , shake, shake it, shake, shake, shake it, shake it, shake it, shake, shake, shake it like a Polaroid picture now
27 shake it, oh no, shake it, shake, shake, shake it, shake it, shake it, shake, shake, shake it like a Polaroid picture now
28 Shake it, I say shake it, shake, shake, shake it, shake it, **oh no, shake it up and shake it up and**

29 *Hey Ya, Hey Ya*
30 *Hey Ya, Hey Ya* (oh no)

Figure 12.3.   Sample model for "Hey Ya"

31 *Hey Ya, Hey Ya* (oh no)
32 *Hey Ya, Hey Ya*
33 *Hey Ya, Hey Ya*

II. **Sound**
   A. **Instrumentation and effects**
     • Folk instrumentation and texture—opens with voice and guitar, later adds bass and piano, backing vocals
   B. **Texture**
     • Accompanied melody; no use of call and response as in the OutKast version
   C. **Dynamics**
     • Greater variation in dynamics

III. **Pitch**
   A. **Melody (changes, embellishment)**
     • More melodic delivery (no spoken or half-spoken portions), but uses basic melodic structure of source
   B. **Harmony (chord substitution, other changes)**
     • Transposed down a minor third (in EM)
     • The end of each harmonic progression in the verses concludes with minor vi chord (never VI)

IV. **Time**
   A. **Rhythm**
     • Follows, roughly, similar rhythmic structure (rhythmic articulations in the bridge section a little different)
   B. **Meter**
     • Uses the same unique metric structure
   C. **Tempo**
     • Slower tempo than the source in youtube video; tempo roughly equivalent in CD recording
   D. **Form**
     • Differences: addition of vamp for introduction (no introduction in OutKast version)

Time	Section	Lines	Total Time
0:00	introduction		0:17
0:17	verse 1	1–4	0:33
0:50	chorus	5–6	0:17
1:07	verse 2	9–12	0:35
1:42	chorus	13–16	0:33
2:15	verse 3	17–24	0:51
3:06	bridge	25–28	0:34
3:40	chorus	29–32	0:45

   E. **Pacing of events**
     • Slightly different pacing—greater variation in section lengths; postponement of first verse through addition of introduction
     • First chorus cut in half (only four statements of "Hey Ya" instead of eight); creates a parallel pacing to the first two section—compare introduction + verse 1 to chorus + verse 2.
     • The third verse is the longest section, lasting 52 seconds instead of 33 as in the source.
     • An extra repetition of "Hey Ya" and slowing of tempo at end creates a longer final chorus section (at 45 second instead of 35).

Figure 12.3. (*continued*)

SOURCE
Song: "Hey Ya"   Artist: OutKast

I. **Voice and Words**
    A. **Voice (timbre, quality, manner of delivery, persona)**
        • Combination of singing and speech; less intimate manner of delivery (more
          geared for a dance club interacting with a group); call and response
    B. **Lyrics (changes/additions/omissions, manipulations in delivery)**
        • Contains a number of guttural spoken or half-sung interjections ("oh, oh";
          "uh"; "ah, here we go"; etc.)
        • Lyrics lend themselves to multiple layers, dialogue, and call & response
        • Features many lines that are physical and/or dance oriented

0   **One, two, three, (uh!)**

1   My baby don't mess around because she loves me so and this I know for sure **(uh!)**
2   But does she really wanna but can't stand to see me walk out the door
3   **Don't try** to fight the feelin' 'cause the thought alone is killing me right now **(uh!)**
4   Thank god for mom and dad for sticking two together 'cause we don't know how **(uh!)**

5   *Hey Ya, Hey Ya*
6   *Hey Ya, Hey Ya*
7   *Hey Ya, Hey Ya*
8   *Hey Ya, Hey Ya*

9   You think you've got it, oh, you think you've got it but got it just don't get it 'til
    there's nothing at all
10 We get together, oh, we get together but separate's always better when there's feelings
    involved
11 If what they say is "nothing is forever" **then what makes, then what makes, then what
    makes, then what makes, then what makes** love the exception?
12 So why are, why are, why are, why are, why are, are we so in denial when we know
    we're not happy here?

13 **Y'all don't want me here, you just wanna dance**, *Hey Ya* (oh, oh), *Hey Ya* (oh, oh)
14 **Don't want to meet your daddy**, *Hey Ya* (oh, oh), **Just want you in my caddy** (oh,
    oh), *Hey Ya* (oh, oh)
15 **Don't want to meet yo' mama**, *Hey Ya* (oh, oh), **Just want to make you cumma** (oh,
    oh), *Hey Ya* (oh, oh)
16 **I'm** (oh, oh), **I'm** (oh, oh), *Hey Ya*, **I'm just being honest** (oh, oh), **I'm just being
    honest**, *Hey Ya*

17 Hey, alright now, alright now fellas, **(Yeah?)**
18 Now what's cooler than bein' cool? **(Ice cold!)**
19 I can't hear ya, I say what's cooler than bein' cool? **(Ice cold!)**
20 Alright, alright, alright, alright, alright, alright, alright, alright, alright, alright, alright,
    alright, alright, alright, **okay now ladies, (Yeah?)**
21 **And we gon' break this thing down** in just a few seconds
22 Now don't have me **break this thang down** for nothin'
23 Now I wanna see y'all on **y'all** baddest behavior
24 Lend me some sugar, I am your neighbor, **(ah!) here we go**

Figure 12.3. (*continued*)

25 Shake it, shake, shake it, shake it (**oh, oh**), shake it, shake it, shake, shake it, shake it, shake it (**oh, oh**), shake it, shake it like a Polaroid picture

26 Shake it, shh, shake it, shake it, shh, shake it, shake it, shake it, (**shake it sugar**), shake it like a Polaroid picture

27 **Now while Beyonce's and Lucy Lui's (shake it, shake it . . .) and baby dolls, get on the floor, get on the floor (shake it like a Polaroid Picture . . .)**

28 **You know what to do, you know what to do, you know what to do**

29 *Hey Ya (oh, oh), Hey Ya (oh, oh)*
30 *Hey Ya (oh, oh), Hey Ya (oh)*
31 *Hey Ya (oh, oh), Hey Ya (oh, oh)*
32 *Hey Ya (oh, oh), Hey Ya (oh, oh)* [fade out . . .]

II. **Sound**
   A. Instrumentation and effects
     • Electronic beats, voice (lead and backing), guitar, bass, hand claps, synthesized countermelodies—percussive instrumentation overall
   B. Texture
     • Dance texture—emphasis on rhythmic patterns, dance beat—focus on beats; a lot going on
     • Uses some call and response textures
   C. Dynamics
     • Maintains a constant dynamic level—*mf*—for the most part

III. **Pitch**
   A. Melody (changes, embellishment)
     • Third verse departs from melodic structure in previous verses
   B. Harmony (chord substitution, other changes)
     • In GM
     • Uses repetition of chord progression: I, IV, V, VI (or vi)

IV. **Time**
   A. Rhythm
     • Uses syncopation typical of the style, creates interesting rhythm especially when coupled with irregular metric structure
   B. Meter
     • This song has an irregular metric structure (see transcription).
   C. Tempo
     • A little slower than quarter = 160
   D. Form

Time	Section	Lines	Total Time
0:00	verse 1	0–4	0:34
0:34	chorus	5–8	0:33
1:07	verse 2	9–12	0:33
1:40	chorus	13–16	0:34
2:14	verse 3	17–24	0:33
2:47	bridge	25–28	0:33
3:20	chorus	29–32	0:35

   E. Pacing of events
     • Even pacing of sections, all approximately 33 or 34 seconds

Figure 12.3. (*continued*)

in boldface, and each line is numbered for reference on the left side. There are three primary types of difference regarding lyrics when examining this song pair. First, there are fewer spoken, guttural interjections in the Obadiah Parker version. The OutKast version features many interjections: "uh!" (lines 1, 3, and 4), "ah, here we go" (line 24), "oh, oh" (lines 13–16, 25, and 29–32), and "shake it, sugar" (line 26), which are not found in the cover version. Second, the OutKast version relies on call-and-response textures in lines 17–20, but the Obadiah Parker version leaves unanswered the questions that are answered so readily in the OutKast version. Although the ostensible sincerity of Weddle's singing might give rise to a parodic interpretation of these lyrics, listeners might also be able to treat these questions now as rhetorical—questions posed by a single man telling a story, as opposed to someone eliciting active responses in a dance setting. Third, Weddle omits the lyrics found in lines 13–16 and 27–28 in OutKast's version. These lines are cruder, more physical, and dance-oriented. Although the Obadiah Parker version certainly retains its share of other dance-related lyrics (such as the "shake it" passage in lines 25 and 26), the quality of the singing (Weddle's lyrical sincerity) creates a more dramatic, emotional story, particularly with the focus on the voice in the earlier verses and the lack of additional physically oriented lyrics used in the second chorus (lines 13–16). Unlike other appropriations of hip-hip or rap songs by white artists, Obadiah Parker's cover version seems to resist a parodic interpretation because of these changes.[12]

The bassist from Obadiah Parker, Daniel Zehring, describes his reaction to the lyrics when he first heard Mat Weddle play his acoustic version of "Hey Ya": "Honestly, I'd never listened to the verses before" (Craven 2006, E2). I had a similar reaction when listening to the Obadiah Parker recording for the first time. The lyrics, particularly in the first two verses, are quite sad, describing a relationship that is not working out. The meaning of the lyrics is obscured a bit by the catchy dance groove in the OutKast version. The Obadiah Parker version, on the other hand, brings these poignant lyrics to the fore through its more transparent folk instrumentation and dynamic shape.

Finally, there are some significant changes in the pacing of events. The OutKast version maintains regular, consistent section lengths of about 33 or 34 seconds, whereas the Obadiah Parker cover features greater variation in section lengths. After cutting half of the repetitions of "Hey Ya" in the first chorus, the section is reduced to 17 seconds. In addition, the length of the third verse is expanded to 51 seconds. Furthermore, Obadiah Parker begins with a 17-second introduction that establishes the metric and harmonic pattern before beginning the first verse, which is a style trait associated with both pop and folk traditions. The changes in section length fit improvisatory practices common in many folk traditions and further

Example 12.7.   OutKast, "Hey Ya," line 1. "Hey Ya!" words and music by Andre Benjamin. © 2003 by Chrysalis Music and Gnat Booty Music. This arrangement © 2010 by Chrysalis Music and Gnat Booty Music. All rights administered by Chrysalis Music. All rights reserved. Used by permission. Reprinted by permission of Hal Leonard Corporation.

Example 12.8.   Alternate transcription of OutKast, "Hey Ya," line 1

contribute to the song's asymmetrical character on a large-scale level. In addition, the more expansive length of the third verse allows the verse to build gradually into the bridge, which increases in energy level to a rousing and lively final chorus.

Some other changes may be useful in different pedagogical situations. For example, a simple harmonic difference in the verses—ending on major VI in the OutKast version, compared to ending on the minor diatonic vi in the Obadiah Parker version—would make a nice contextual listening example for hearing difference in chord quality. Comparing cover songs to their sources by applying this model allows for the discovery of these brief pedagogical examples, as well as setting students up for larger-scale analytical work.

A CASE OF CROSSING GENDERS: SWATI'S COVER OF BRUCE SPRINGSTEEN'S "I'M ON FIRE"

In the third and final song pair of this study, the cover artist is a different gender from the source artist: singer-songwriter Swati's version of Bruce Springsteen's famous hit "I'm on Fire." In comparing these songs, many immediate differences come to the fore—in terms of voice, phrasing, instrumentation, texture, dynamics, melody, harmony, rhythm, tempo, form, and pacing. The specific differences in each category are enumerated in figure 12.4.

One category in which we find little difference between the two versions is lyrics. Swati makes few changes in the lyrics, and she keeps all pronouns and other gender markers intact. When the gendered lyrics are coupled with her female voice, the opportunity for a queer reading of the song emerges.[13] The interaction between her vocal delivery and the lyrics suggests several different possible subjects: a lesbian ex-lover, a current lover, or an unrequited love. Her singing of the question, "Can he do to you the things that I can do?" implies that the persona projected through Swati's performance suspects that the subject she is addressing is gay and, as a lesbian, knows that a man cannot satisfy her sexually.

It is clear that in both Swati and Springsteen's versions, the song is about unrequited love or lust for someone who is in another relationship. Understanding Swati's version as projecting a lesbian protagonist, at least three reasons why the protagonist cannot act upon her desire seem plausible: the subject is (1) gay or bisexual but closeted and in a relationship with a man, (2) gay or bisexual, closeted, in another relationship, and not interested, or (3) not gay or bisexual and, therefore, not interested in the protagonist.

These images are very different from the ones conjured in Springsteen's version of "I'm on Fire." From the lyrics alone, listeners might imagine an older man lusting after a young woman (referred to only as a "little girl" or "baby") who is either involved with another man (referred to as her "daddy") or too young to be in a relationship (if "daddy" is taken literally). Musical elements noted in figure 12.4 also help to shape the persona that emerges through Springsteen's performance. His rapid, syllabic delivery of the lyrics, phrase elisions, and the continual motoric 16th notes in the drum pattern create an urgent and perhaps aggressive masculine persona. Ian Biddle (2007) describes imagery associated with masculinity in Springsteen's "Born in the U.S.A.," including the idea of machinery, automobiles, and gendered vocal delivery, among other things. The driving, continuous drum pattern in "I'm on Fire" may musically depict the notion of mechanized motion, conjuring masculine images of action and machinery. These masculine images map onto the content of the lyrics, which show a man lusting after a woman, to suggest a heterosexual male persona, which Springsteen embodies in his performance of the song. These elements are situated in contrast to the more relaxed delivery, pauses between phrases, and lack of drums altogether in Swati's version. Vocal delivery, especially, seems to establish the distinctly different gendered identity portrayed in both songs.[14] In both versions, however, the lyrics clearly paint the protagonist's desire as "bad." The lyric, "I'm on fire," has an important double meaning: "fire" implies hell—doing something wrong and getting caught—and it also conjures notions of sexual excitement (meaning "I'm hot"). Here desire equates both metaphorically and literally with heat and fire.

COVER

Song: "I'm on Fire"   Artist: Swati

I. **Voice and Words**
  A. **Voice (timbre, quality, manner of delivery, persona)**
      • Female voice, low range
      • Pauses between phrases in Swati's delivery
      • In relation to Springsteen's version: cross-gender, queer reading?
      • Some changes in the vocalizing, kind of like an extended moaning, longing
        occurs during interlude between bridge/verse 3 and the repetition of those
        sections (as opposed to vocalizing in the coda in Springsteen's version)
  B. **Lyrics (changes/additions/omissions, manipulations in delivery)**
      • Doesn't change many of the words (pronouns kept intact)
      • Omits Springsteen's characteristic "oh, oh, oh" in first refrain
      • Both songs share several features: both are about unrequited love or lust/desire
        for someone who is in another relationship
II. **Sound**
  A. **Instrumentation and effects**
      • More subdued sound
      • No drums; guitars and voice only
  B. **Texture**
      • Sparser than Springsteen's version
      • Echo-like patterns in the guitar; some new patterns introduced in the guitar (cf.
        Springsteen's version)
      • More static, less aggressive?
  C. **Dynamics**
      • More dynamic growth in Swati's version, especially in the last verse "like
        somebody took a knife . . ."
III. **Pitch**
  A. **Melody (changes, embellishment)**
      • Song transposed to Ab major
      • Greater variation in refrains, other subtle melodic changes
      • More syncopation in the melody
  B. **Harmony (chord substitution, other changes)**
      • Ends on IV7
      • Harmonic rhythm slows down near the end
      • Much longer time elapses before we hear tonic function:
        • Tonic (Ab) not heard until 0:56 (m. 17) at the beginning of verse 2 [not used
          in the first verse and refrain, nor the introduction]
        • Submediant (Fm) not heard until 1:07 (m. 20) right before the second refrain
          [not used in the introduction or the previous sections]
        • First SDT progression heard at 1:14 (mm. 22–23) with the second refrain
IV. **Time**
  A. **Rhythm**
      • More syncopation in Swati's version
      • Use of augmentation and rhythmic variation/extension in the final refrain
      • Greater variation
  B. **Meter**
      • Simple quadruple
      • Does not preserve metric reinterpretation
  C. **Tempo**
      • Slower tempo, quarter = 67

Figure 12.4.   Sample model for "I'm on Fire"

Form
- Swati repeats the bridge and last verse. This is when the music really builds up—increased sound, more activity, and louder dynamics. The interlude prior to these repeated sections resemble in some ways the coda of Springsteen's version (vocalizing, oscillation between I and vi)

Time	# of bars	Section
0:00	8	introduction
0:27	8	5-bar verse 1
0:49		3-bar refrain
0:56	7	5-bar verse 2
1:14		2-bar refrain
[NO INTERLUDE HERE]		
1:23	5	bridge
1:39	7	5-bar verse 3
1:57		2-bar refrain
2:04	10	interlude
2:43	5	bridge (repetition)
2:58	14	5-bar verse 3 (repetition)
3:17		9-bar refrain (repetition, extension)
3:50	9	coda

E. **Pacing of events**
- Overall duration = 4'27" (almost two minutes longer than Springsteen's version, due to slower tempo and extra breaks in vocal delivery—whereas Springsteen continues verses + refrain with no break, Swati adds an extra measure in between)
- More time with refrains at end and changes vocalizing. The refrain at the end is extended to nine bars as opposed to two or three (as in previous statement of the refrain) through the use of augmentation, a slower harmonic rhythm, repetition, embellishment, and variation.
- Instead of repeating the refrain three times in succession at the end like Springsteen does, Swati slows down the harmonic rhythm, vocalizes on the neutral syllable "oh" and extends a single refrain over the course of nine measures.
- Harmonic rhythm slows down near the end
- Change in proportion and section lengths: the interlude occurs after the bridge, third verse, and third refrain in Swati's recording, whereas the interlude precedes the bridge in Springsteen's version. However, Swati repeats the bridge, third verse, and refrain after the interlude.
- Swati changes the number of bars in the sections, using 5 bars for verses as opposed to 4.

Figure 12.4. (*continued*)

COVER
Song: "I'm on Fire"   **Artist: Bruce Springsteen**

I. Voice and Words
    A. Voice (timbre, quality, manner of delivery, persona)
        • Male voice, middle range
        • Syllabic, rapid delivery
        • Elisions in Springsteen's delivery
        • Vocalizations in the coda (cf Swati's version)
    B. Lyrics (content, characteristics, changes from verse to verse)
        • "I'm on fire" implies hell, doing something wrong, getting caught, also sexual
          excitement ("I'm hot")
        • "a bad desire" = what he can't have
        • Both songs share several features: both are about unrequited love or lust/desire
          for someone who is in another relationship

II. Sound
    A. Instrumentation and effects
        • Male voice / Drums / Guitar (arpeggiated chords) / Synthesizer
        • Constantly driving rim shots, drum pattern (implying motion)
        • Repetition also in guitar
    B. Texture
        • Steady, continuous texture: arpeggiated chords in guitar filling out texture;
          synthesizer playing longer, sustained melody and/or countermelodies when
          Springsteen is singing; continuous drum pattern (hi hat attacked on sixteenth
          notes, rim shots on the off beats)—driving pattern
    C. Dynamics
        • Not much dynamic variation (compare to growth in the repetition of the
          bridge and last verse in Swati's version

III. Pitch
    A. Melody (content, characteristic turns of phrase)
        • Song in E major
        • Consistent melodic and rhythmic structures in all sections
    B. Harmony (content, chord structure, voice leading)
        • Ends with fade out alternating vi-I-vi-I. This oscillation occurs in several
          passages in this song (less variation than Swati's version); however, the
          harmonic pattern EM-C#m is inverted C#m-EM in INTERLUDE section (m.
          21ff) compared to introduction. Same melody; opposite chord succession

IV. Time
    A. Rhythm
        • Continual rhythm pattern of sixteenth notes articulated in drum pattern; off
          beats articulated by rim shots
    B. Meter
        • Simple quadruple
        • Metric reinterpretation: bridge section at 1:15 begins highly out-of-phase with
          meter and harmonic rhythm, like a pick-up. Halfway through this passage,
          beat 3 becomes metrically re-interpreted as a downbeat (or this could be
          heard as a measure with two extra beats, a measure in ¼)
    C. Tempo

Figure 12.4. (*continued*)

- Faster tempo, quarter = 88

D. Form

Time	# of bars	Section
0:00	8	introduction
0:20	6	4-bar verse 1
0:32		2-bar refrain
0:37	6	4-bar verse 2
0:48		2-bar refrain
0:53	8	interlude
1:15	3.5	bridge
1:25	10	4-bar verse 3
1:36		2-bar refrain
1:42		2-bar refrain
1:47		2-bar refrain
1:53	16	coda (fade out)

E. Pacing of events
  - Overall duration = 2'34" (almost two minutes shorter than Swati's cover)

Figure 12.4. (*continued*)

Differences in the treatment of the refrains reflect the different personae each singer portrays. Springsteen performs each refrain in the same manner—the harmonic progression, the melody, and the pacing remain constant. The pitch, rhythm, and chords for his refrain appear in example 12.9. In contrast, the refrains in Swati's recording, transcribed in example 12.10, feature variation. The two middle refrains (which begin at 1:14 and 1:57 respectively) are the closest to Springsteen's, using the same harmonic functions (IV–V–I) and melodic scale degrees but still featuring rhythmic contrast (syncopation on the last syllable). The first refrain (at 0:49) is remarkably different from both Springsteen's and the others in Swati's version, in terms of harmonic progression and the omission of the lyrics "oh, oh, oh," which precede all of the other versions of the refrain. Springsteen's refrain uses the normative IV–V–I (A–B–E) progression in E major, whereas Swati's first refrain uses IV^{maj7}–vi^9 (Db^{M7}–Bbm^9) in A-flat major. Swati's refrains at 1:14 and 1:57, however, use the IV–V–I pattern established in Springsteen's version. The last refrain that appears in Swati's version is lengthened from two bars to nine, featuring an extended oscillation of the IV and V chords and concludes not with a tonic triad but with IV^{maj7}. This pre-dominant deflection and nondirected harmony creates a sense of open-endedness that is not present in Springsteen's version. Swati's non-tonic conclusion suggests a question, perhaps the protagonist questioning the nature of her desire. No such questioning is suggested in Springsteen's version, which ends on tonic. The consistency found in his version might add to the perception of the protagonist having greater confidence, pride, and assurance in himself and his feelings—perhaps acknowledging the questionable nature of his desire but never questioning it.

Oh . . .

Example 12.9.   Springsteen, "I'm on Fire," refrain

Example 12.10.   Swati, "I'm on Fire," refrains

Other aspects of Swati's performance lend a sense of hesitation to the character she portrays. The extended length of each song section serves as a musical equivalent of "hemming and hawing," as if the protagonist is putting off what she has to say, perhaps because she is ashamed or afraid to admit the nature of her desire. In fact, what seems to be a minor change in the lyrics in Swati's version—omitting the "I" from "I got a bad desire" in the first verse—suggests that the protagonist wants to avoid identifying as the agent of the "bad desire," initially at least. However, as the song progresses, the hesitation implied in these earlier passages gradually decreases. By the repetition of the bridge, third verse, and final refrain, the protagonist finally expresses her feelings, louder and with greater conviction. The dynamic and textural build-up that occurs in these final sections highlights the repetition of previous musical material. In contrast, Springsteen's version has no formal repetition, perhaps because his persona was never tentative to begin with and does not need to restate anything. The repetition of the bridge and third verse and long extension of the final refrain suggest that Swati's persona is finally letting her emotion out, feeling relieved to release it, and perhaps not wanting the release to end.

The interpretations set forth in this comparison are, of course, subjective, but they are grounded in the observation of musical characteristics gathered through the analytic model. One productive use of the model is to derive as many different interpretations as possible from the same musical observations, examining how different musical aspects interact with one another and especially with the portrayal of the lyrics even when few changes are made, as in Swati's cover of "I'm on Fire." This process of comparing multiple interpretations is most productive in the classroom. Students become more motivated to participate when they feel they have a stake in a debate, and through discussion of opposing viewpoints, they learn to value different ways of approaching an issue. Often multiple, valid interpretations attest to the richness of the music that is being analyzed, and learning to listen in different ways and for different musical elements is a practical aural skill. Furthermore, this activity shows that the meanings listeners garner when listening to any song are contingent upon the musical elements one attends to, as well as one's cultural background, values, and experiences.[15]

CONCLUSION

Oftentimes, students will want to begin an analytical project but do not know how or where to start. At its most rudimentary level, the model offered in this study can function as a basic checklist of items to compare, which can help students get started in analytical and critical work. Cover versions are a great resource for opening students' minds to analysis because many such songs transform the meanings of the originals and present striking musical differences that students can easily perceive and discuss. At more advanced levels, through transcription and close listening, students can compare pitch and rhythmic information, as outlined on the model.

In addition to functioning as a springboard to analysis and encouraging students to support their claims regarding extramusical meaning with specific musical observations, this model has further pedagogical advantages. It encourages the close listening required for expressing subtle differences between faithful cover versions and their sources, as we have seen in the examples of "Somewhere Only We Know." The model is also useful for articulating specific qualitative differences in genre analysis, as in the comparative analysis of OutKast's and Obadiah Parker's versions of "Hey Ya." Other examples of cover songs in disparate genres ripe for this type of analysis include: Dolly Parton's cover of Led Zeppelin's "Stairway to Heaven," Ben Folds's ironic pop rendition of Dr. Dre's "Bitches Ain't Shit," and the Gourd's country cover of Snoop Dogg's "Gin and Juice," just to name a few.[16] In addition to its application to cross-gender covers, the model can be similarly applied to other cross-cultural types of cover songs, including those that cross boundaries of race, class, and nationality.[17] In examining issues of authenticity and authorship, the model allows students to consider critically and problematically musical characteristics typically associated with "authentic" and "inauthentic" performances.[18] An interesting song pair for such a study would be the Counting Crows' cover of Joni Mitchell's "Big Yellow Taxi." One might also use the model to measure and describe musical differences that correlate to different degrees of success in terms of record sales or other measures of commercial success.[19]

The model described in this study provides a systematic approach for analytic comparison of a cover song and its source, regardless of the closeness of relationship between the song pair (ranging from highly contrasting to very similar and including every degree in between). Although four broad categories are at its core, other categories may be added or omitted depending on the nature and goals of an analytic project. It is my hope that its application to other songs can assist students in organizing their observations, ultimately to enhance their analytic skills.

NOTES

1. Characterizing 1980–2005 as the Cover Age, George Plasketes (2005) describes the increasing pervasiveness of cover songs since the 1980s, citing numerous examples of cover songs and their uses in popular culture.

2. Schneider 2001, 404–5. Because Schneider focuses more on quantitative information (such as counting the number of times songs by a set of artists are covered) than qualitative comparisons (dealing with analysis of style, melody, harmony, rhythm, etc.), proposing such an analytical model lies outside the scope of his dissertation.

3. Lori Burns (1999–2000) shows how similar musical structures can be recontextualized in cover versions to subvert original meanings entirely. In her analysis, Burns argues that k.d. lang resists positioning herself as a submissive object of the patriarchal gaze and instead "liberates herself from the submissive role of the torch singer and creates a performative opportunity for personal expression in which she is the subject" (319). Although the basic musical structures of the original version of "So in Love" as performed in Cole Porter's musical *Kiss Me, Kate* are kept intact in lang's performance, the actions portrayed in her music video, her style of delivery, and changes in the melodic "apex scheme" suggest a dramatically different interpretation.

4. A modified version of this model can also be applied to instrumental cover versions if the first category of voice and words is omitted.

5. Bowman 2003. Bowman's ultimate argument is that a performance should have an equal role to that of the songwriter in asserting ownership of a given song, particularly when the performer makes striking interpretive changes that transcend the confines of the sheet music, as in Otis Redding's recording of "Try a Little Tenderness." Cusic 2005 echoes this sentiment, arguing for greater recognition and legitimacy of singers who record cover songs.

6. Holm-Hudson 2002, par. 10. In his study of the Carpenters' and Sonic Youth's respective versions of "Superstar," Holm-Hudson draws upon concepts devised by Jean Jacques Nattiez in *Music and Discourse: Toward a Semiology of Music* (Nattiez 1990), including two other levels of analysis in addition to the neutral level: (1) the

"poietic," which deals with the music's creation and (2) the "esthesic," which deals with the music's reception.

7. A detailed analysis of this sort can be found Burns and Woods 2004. In an analysis of Tori Amos's cover of Eminem's "'97 Bonnie and Clyde," Amos is shown to embody the multiple voices, including that of the murdered mother, and in an analysis of a cover of Billie Holiday's "Strange Fruit," the authors argue that Amos presents an authentic voice, evoking "cultural memories and traumas authentic to her own experience" (par. 28).

8. An example of this type can be found in two different recordings of the folk song "Peggy-O," by Bob Dylan and Simon and Garfunkel. The Dylan version features only I, IV, and V7, whereas the Simon and Garfunkel version uses iii and vi in addition to the chords found in the Dylan version.

9. In some cases, near-exact replication can also be useful and interesting to study. For example, Bailey 2003 uses Todd Rundgren's 1976 album, *Faithful*, which reproduces well-regarded and technically virtuosic popular songs, to make the artistic argument that "not only is art reproducible, it no longer requires an original" (153–4).

10. Lifehouse, "Somewhere Only We Know," Yahoo! Cover Art Project Video, http://new.music.yahoo.com/videos/Lifehouse/Somewhere-Only-We-Know-(Live)--30161084.

11. As of this writing, the video, at http://www.youtube.com/watch?v=8-8nk-kOA_AM, has been viewed over five million times.

12. In an interesting study of Dynamite Hack's 2000 cover of N.W.A.'s famous 1988 rap song "Boyz-n-the-Hood," Hess 2005 argues that because Dynamite Hack's style is so far removed from hip-hop culture, their cover does not parody N.W.A. or hip hop, but rather they "parody their own whiteness [and] its distance from hip hop credibility" (179). Obadiah Parker's version of "Hey Ya" seems to go in an entirely different direction, bringing out the sadness of OutKast's lyrics in a genuine and direct fashion.

13. King 2000 examines the use of gendered lyrics and sexuality in cover songs by Luther Vandross.

14. Although she is not examining cross-gender cover songs, Burns 1997 does examine the ways masculinity and femininity are musically constructed in her analysis of k.d. lang's cover of Joanie Sommers's "Johnny Get Angry." Burns argues that at times, lang assumes the male role of "Johnny" instead of the female role of Johnny's submissive girlfriend, through changes in physical gesture and vocal delivery. Similarly, we can see different constructions of femininity and masculinity, as they intersect with sexuality, in Swati's and Springsteen's contrasting styles of vocal delivery in their respective versions of "I'm on Fire."

15. For example, in his study of cover songs recorded by the Pet Shop Boys, Mark Butler examines the tensions between two opposing views regarding authenticity in their music, as they relate to the cultural position of different audiences. He writes, "Some authors characterize their music as self-consciously inauthentic, an ironic celebration of artifice, while others position it as authentic within the context of contemporary gay culture" (2003, 13). These types of tensions come to the fore when conflicting interpretations present themselves, and the classroom is an ideal place to work out these tensions and potentially to open minds to different cultural perspectives through discussion.

16. The model can also articulate musical parameters that are key in genre transformation. Headlam 1997 addresses this topic and argues that through processes of

repeating a single signature riff taking on a harmonic role, as opposed to a melodic one, and regularizing irregular phrase groupings and metric structures, Cream transforms blues songs by Robert Johnson, Muddy Waters, Howlin' Wolf, and others into rock songs.

17. A number of additional cross-gender and cross-cultural cover songs are examined in Griffiths 2002.

18. Headlam 1995 uses musical analysis to understand issues of authorship in Led Zeppelin's music and explores the specific musical elements that become identifiable markers of the style of Led Zeppelin. Even though the band uses preexisting material as the basis for some of the songs that are considered hallmarks of their output, Headlam argues that because Led Zeppelin successfully uses their own unique set of distinctive style traits, they can rightfully claim authorship of songs that use preexisting musical material that they did not author.

19. Although the descriptions of how the music business operates are now a bit dated, White 1997 uses a similar approach to correlate differences between Dolly Parton's 1984 cover of Petula Clark's "Downtown" and the original version with their success or lack thereof in the pop charts.

DISCOGRAPHY

Counting Crows. "Big Yellow Taxi." *Hard Candy*. Geffen Records, 2002.

Dr. Dre. "Bitches Ain't Shit." *The Chronic*. Interscope Records, 1992.

Dylan, Bob. "Pretty Peggy-O." *Bob Dylan*. Columbia Records, 1962.

Folds, Ben. "Bitches Ain't Shit." Epic, 2005.

The Gourds. "Gin and Juice." *Shinebox*. Sugar Hill, 1998.

Keane. "Somewhere Only We Know." *Hopes and Fears*. Interscope Records, 2004.

Led Zeppelin. "Stairway to Heaven." *Led Zeppelin*. Atlantic, 1971.

Lifehouse. "Somewhere Only We Know." Yahoo! Cover Art Project Video. 2006. http://new.music.yahoo.com/videos/Lifehouse/Somewhere-Only-We-Know-(Live)--30161084.

Mitchell, Joni. "Big Yellow Taxi." *Ladies of the Canyon*. Reprise, 1970.

Obadiah Parker. "Hey Ya." *Obadiah Parker Live*. Obadiah Parker Music, 2007.

OutKast. "Hey Ya!" *Speakerboxxx/The Love Below*. Arista, 2003.

Parton, Dolly. "Stairway to Heaven." *Halos and Horns*. Sugar Hill/Blue Eye, 2002.

Simon and Garfunkel. "Peggy-O." *Wednesday Morning, 3 A.M.* Columbia Records, 1964.

Snoop Dogg. "Gin and Juice." *Doggystyle*. Death Row/Interscope, 1993.

Springsteen, Bruce. "I'm on Fire." *Born in the U.S.A.* Columbia CK 38653. CD, 1984.

Swati. "I'm on Fire." *Small Gods*. Bluhammock Music, 2007.

Weddle, Mat. "Hey Ya." http://www.youtube.com/watch?v=8-8nkkOA_AM.

REFERENCES

Bailey, Steve. 2003. Faithful or foolish: The emergence of the "ironic cover album" and rock culture. *Popular Music and Society* 26, no. 2: 141–59.

Biddle, Ian. 2007. The singsong of undead labor. In *Oh boy! Masculinities and popular music*, ed. Freya Jarman-Ivens, 125–44. New York: Routledge.

Bowman, Rob. 2003. The determining role of performance in the articulation of meaning: The case of "Try a Little Tenderness." In *Analyzing Popular Music,* ed. Allan F. Moore, 103–30. Cambridge: Cambridge University Press.

Burns, Lori. 1997. "Joanie" get angry: k.d. lang's feminist revision. In *Understanding rock: Essays in musical analysis,* ed. John Rudolph Covach and Graeme M. Boone, 93–112. New York: Oxford University Press.

———. 1999–2000. Genre, gender, and convention revisited: k.d. lang's cover of cole porter's "So in Love." *Repercussions* 7–8:299–325.

Burns, Lori, and Alyssa Woods. 2004. Authenticity, appropriation, signification: Tori Amos on gender, race, and violence in covers of Billie Holiday and Eminem. *Music Theory Online* 10, no. 2 (June). http://mto.societymusictheory.org/issues/mto.04.10.2/mto.04.10.2.burns_woods.html.

Butler, Mark. 2003. Taking it seriously: Intertextuality and authenticity in two covers by the Pet Shop Boys. *Popular Music* 22, no. 1: 1–19.

Craven, Scott. 2006. Acoustic "Hey"day: Mesa musician's folksy take on OutKast's anthem creates online stir. *Arizona Republic,* October 2, E1–E2. http://www.azcentral.com/arizonarepublic/arizonaliving/articles/1002heyya1002.html.

Cusic, Don. 2005. In defense of cover songs. *Popular Music and Society* 28, no. 2: 171–77.

Griffiths, Dai. 2002. Cover versions and the sound of identity in motion. In *Popular music studies,* ed. David Hesmondhalgh and Keith Negus, 51–64. London: Oxford University Press.

Headlam, David. 1995. Does the song remain the same? Questions of authorship and identification in the music of Led Zeppelin. In *Concert music, rock, and jazz since 1945,* ed. Elizabeth West Marvin and Richard Hermann, 313–63. Rochester, New York: University of Rochester Press.

———. 1997. Blues transformations in the music of Cream. In *Understanding rock: Essays in musical analysis,* ed. John Rudolph Covach and Graeme M. Boone, 59–92. New York: Oxford University Press.

Hess, Mickey. 2005. "Don't Quote Me, Boy": Dynamite Hack covers NWA's "Boyz-n-the-Hood." *Popular Music and Society* 28, no. 2: 179–91.

Holm-Hudson, Kevin J. 2002. Your guitar, it sounds so sweet and clear: Semiosis in two version of "Superstar." *Music Theory Online* 8, no. 4 (December). http://mto.societymusictheory.org/issues/mto.02.8.4/mto.02.8.4.holm-hudson.html.

King, Jason. 2000. Any love: Silence, theft, and rumor in the work of Luther Vandross. *Callaloo* 23, no. 1: 422–47.

Mosser, Kurt. 2008. "Cover songs": Ambiguity, multivalence, polysemy. *Popular Musicology Online* 2. http://www.popular-musicology-online.com/issues/02/mosser.html.

Nattiez, Jean Jacques. 1990. *Music and discourse: Toward a semiology of music.* Princeton, NJ: Princeton University Press.

Plasketes, George. 2005. Reflections on the cover age: A collage of continuous coverage in popular music. *Popular Music and Society* 28, no. 2: 137–61.

Schneider, Thomas A. 2001. Blues cover songs: The intersection of blues and rock on the popular music charts. PhD diss., University of Memphis.

White, John Wallace. 1997. Radio formats and the transformation of musical style: Codes and cultural values in the remaking of tunes. *College Music Symposium* 37:1–12.

13

Cotextuality in Music Video: Covering and Sampling in the *Cover Art* Video of "Umbrella"

Lori Burns, Tamar Dubuc, and Marc Lafrance

The processes of covering and sampling previously recorded popular songs and videos have become significant strategies in popular music culture. These processes result in the circulation of multiple versions and manipulations of a given popular song or video. Through the medium of the Internet, music consumers are exposed to a seemingly endless stream of song and video versions. For instance, a song title search in YouTube may yield a long list of results. A single search might lead to a series of links to the original sound recording or video, concert versions by the original artists, studio or concert versions by other artists, versions by fans performing the song, or versions by fans who have created new videos using stills or other film images. Adding to the variety of possible versions that exist, there are also videos that "borrow" from other videos. There is great potential for version comparison and interpretation. In this paper, we explore some of the theoretical and interpretive tools that are pertinent for an analysis of a video that prominently features covering and sampling. While the ideas we present are specific to a particular video, the analysis is meant to serve as a model for the application of these tools.

Our analysis of covering and sampling processes brings forward the interpretive potential of the relationship between an original video, which we will refer to as the *sourcetext*, and a version of that video, which we will refer to as the *adaptation*. We will qualify the relationship between the sourcetext and the adaptation as *cotextual*. The elements specific to our analytic method—covering, sampling, sourcetext, adaptation, cotextuality—receive further exploration below.

The video production of "Umbrella" created for the *Cover Art* segment of Pepsi Music, an exclusive of Yahoo! Music,[1] features Mandy Moore

performing a version of the hit song "Umbrella" as first performed, recorded, and released by Rihanna. The *Cover Art* video presents Moore and
her band in a traditional live-stage format performing in front of four background screens arranged in a pattern of two by two (stage left and right) on
which a manipulated version of the "Umbrella" video featuring Rihanna
is broadcast (see figures 13.1 through 13.11, below). The highly inflected
vocals performed by Moore, accompanied by gentle guitar, keyboard, and
drum kit, are in stark musical contrast to the synthesized pop/hip-hop style
of the song as performed by Rihanna, just as the staged live-band performance video is in stark visual contrast to the highly stylized original video.

Our analysis focuses on the manipulation of the sourcetext—the "Umbrella" video featuring Rihanna—in the *Cover Art* adaptation of "Umbrella" featuring Moore, since it raises many interpretive questions about
the processes that underlie its conception. We will refer to these processes
as *covering* and *sampling*. We understand the term *covering* as a process
through which previously recorded material, accredited to and identified
with a given performer, is re-performed, rerecorded, and rereleased by
another artist.[2]

The process of covering aptly describes the musical treatment of "Umbrella" by Moore, as this version offers a complete musical rendering of the
song first accredited to, identified with, and released by Rihanna. We do
not use the term *covering* to describe the visual materials of the adaptation,
as neither the foreground nor the background materials that constitute the
visual field approximate a covering. That is, the foreground visual material—the performer and her band in the traditional live-stage format—does
not derive from the visual materials of the sourcetext and, as such, is not
an instance of covering. Nor is the background broadcasting of the edited
video featuring Rihanna an instance of covering, as it constitutes a manipulated version of the sourcetext, a cut and spliced version of the original
"Umbrella" video. Instead, we adopt the term *sampling* to describe the
visual treatment of this sourcetext within the adaptation. Simply defined,
sampling "is a process in which a sound is taken directly from a recorded
medium and transposed onto a new recording."[3] The treatment of the images in the *Cover Art* video is analogous to the treatment of sound in sampling. In our chosen example, the images of the original "Umbrella" video
are reshaped, reinvented, and reintroduced to create an integral component
of the artistic presentation by Moore. Through an analysis of the musical
and visual materials, we demonstrate that the *Cover Art* video constitutes a
type of musical exchange or dialogue that leads the viewer to consider the
manufactured relationship between the adaptation and the sourcetext.

The term *adaptation* is applied in literary theory as a valuable rubric for
the consideration of texts that acquire new forms. The theory of adaptation aims to build a vocabulary and interpretive method for examining the

ways in which one text is transposed or translated to another—for instance, how a Shakespeare play is adapted for the screen. We draw on the term adaptation to theorize the relationship between the *Cover Art* video of "Umbrella" and its sourcetext. Adaptations are understood by Linda Hutcheon as double-natured, involving both a product and a process. As a product, "an adaptation is an announced and extensive transposition of a particular work or works" (Hutcheon 2006, 7). As a process, it is "a creative and an interpretive act of appropriation/salvaging [entailing] an extended intertextual engagement with the adapted work" (8).

Following Hutcheon's definition, the case under consideration here can be read as an adaptation. As a product, the *Cover Art* video of "Umbrella" definitively establishes its relationship to the identified sourcetext, rendering simultaneously a covered and sampled version of the song as first performed, recorded, and released by Rihanna. This relationship is further underscored by Moore's prefatory statement: "[W]e are performing "Umbrella," originally performed by Rihanna." As a process, the adaptation lays bare a discernable act of visual appropriation, which we will identify as an instance of sampling. This secures the intertextual reading of the "adaptation *as adaptation* . . . an interpretive doubling, a conceptual flipping back and forth between the work we know and the work we are experiencing" (Hutcheon 2006, 139). In other words, the process of visual appropriation, in conjunction with the introductory statement, defines the *Cover Art* video as an adaptation and calls upon the viewer to contend with the relationship between the adaptation and sourcetext.

Our analysis considers the musical and visual materials of the adaptation, its observable properties as captured in the *Cover Art* video, and the strategies at play in the adaptation. Our analysis will not address an intertextual reading of the adaptation, which would explore the multiple references that circulate in musical culture, not only through the many versions of the song but also through the full range of cultural references that emerge in connection with the musical artists, genres, and styles. An intertextual study goes beyond our objective, which is to consider the material relationship that exists between an adaptation and its sourcetext.

To that end, we coin a new term, *cotextuality*, to qualify and denote the relationship between the adaptation and its sourcetext, a relationship delimited by and subsistent in the musical and visual materials of the adaptation. We use the prefix *co-* since it signifies a joint, mutual, and reciprocal relationship between pairs, that is, a dynamic relationship. In the instance of this *Cover Art* video, cotextual shall pertain to the multidimensional relationship between the adaptation and its sourcetext as achieved through the processes of covering and sampling. By means of a cotextual analysis, we aim to demonstrate that the *Cover Art* video emerges not only as an adaptation but also as a commentary on the sourcetext. The manipulation of the sourcetext as explored through the processes of covering and sampling is key to establishing the adaptation as commentary.

In order to identify the elements that are covered and sampled, the adaptation will be scrutinized for its material content, as examined through the analytic categories of visual settings and musical settings. A cotextual analysis of the adaptation and its sourcetext will then be developed from the study of these materials.

VISUAL SETTINGS

The adaptation features two separate visual settings presented simultaneously within one visual field: one is the performance context of Moore and her band; the other is that of the sourcetext, which is a stylized dance performance of the song. We will address the following parameters of the visual setting: staging, figure movement, and camera technique. Given that the adaptation and its sourcetext are directly juxtaposed, it is meaningful to interpret each of these setting parameters according to a pair of contrasting modalities: for staging, the contrast of constant versus varying; for movement, the contrast of static versus dynamic; and for camera technique, the contrast of simple versus complex. These contrasting modalities emerge from the direct comparison of the visual settings at play in the adaptation; in other words, these analytic values were developed after a consideration of the *Cover Art* video materials and were not established as a priori assumptions.

The first visual setting parameter (staging, lighting, costumes, and makeup) reveals a contrast between the adaptation and sourcetext that can be interpreted as constant versus varying. The live-band setting featuring Moore remains constant throughout the video and is not subject to any variation. Rihanna, by contrast, is featured in a variety of settings, lighting effects, and costumes, which contributes to the highly stylized visual form. As we will demonstrate in the analysis below, the contrast between the two visual settings creates a number of noticeably dissimilar effects. For instance, the special effect lighting and theatrical stage setting of the sourcetext stand out as a dramatic contrast to the "naturalized" staging of Moore and her band.

The second visual setting parameter (figure movement) focuses on the body gestures and movements of the featured artists. Moore adopts a very static and still stance, whereas Rihanna is featured in choreographed dance sequences, creating a dynamic flow of gestures. This point of comparison—static versus dynamic—will once again prove fruitful in the analysis below. For instance, against the foreground image of a still Moore, Rihanna turns and bends at a fast pace of physical movement in the background.

Table 13.1. Visual setting parameters in adaptation and sourcetext

Parameters	Adaptation (Moore)	Sourcetext (Rihanna)
	Constant	*Varying*
Staging	1 setting "live band" format, Moore rarely alone in shot 4 background screens	8 settings use of props Rihanna alone dynamic background (sparks) virtual foreground (water)
Lighting	Backlighting from panels, cross-lighting	Variety of lighting: harsh, soft, direct, special effects
Costumes and makeup	1 "look": casual, contemporary, accessible, identifiable	8 different "looks" from wide spectrum; character development
	Static	*Dynamic*
Figure movement	Minimal physical movement	Movement-based performance, highly styled and choreographed
	Limited to singing/playing instruments and expressive gestures	Singing, posing, dancing in numerous styles
	Simple	*Complex*
Camera technique	Series of cuts; rotation of 11 shots	Numerous techniques (cuts, pans, etc.) and compositions

The third visual setting parameter (camera techniques) reveals yet another mode of contrast between sourcetext and adaptation. The adaptation features simple camera techniques; a total of 11 different shots are offered in rotation through a series of cuts. These shots include long shots of the band, medium shots of Moore and of certain band members, and close-up shots.[4] The camera techniques of the sourcetext, however, are complex and numerous, including quick cuts, panning, zooming, blurring, sequential action shots, and so forth. Once again, the interpreter has much to discover in considering the contrast between adaptation and sourcetext.

The three visual setting parameters are distinguished here in order to demonstrate the multilayered and multifaceted form of the visual field. Within each parameter—staging/lighting/costumes, figure movement, and camera techniques—the analyst can identify many elements that contribute to the cotextual relationship between the adaptation and sourcetext. From an interpretive standpoint, the juxtaposition of the visual settings points to the suggestive potential of the visual materials in the adaptation. It follows that the visual sampling of the sourcetext will be a key factor in establishing the adaptation as *commentary*.

MUSICAL SETTINGS

Our consideration of the musical materials of the adaptation and its sourcetext must also respond to the specific content of our chosen example and the analytic constraints imposed by that content. Whereas the visual content of the sourcetext is developed in the adaptation, this is not true of the musical content. We do not *hear* the musical track of the sourcetext. Our contact with Rihanna's musical performance is made only through the visual content, which leads to the following analytic question: how do we make contact with the medium of music through the medium of images?

We find that the answer here lies in the materials that are evident in the temporal domain of the music. As the sourcetext is presented within the adaptation, we see Rihanna move and deliver the lyrics, her physical gestures providing the viewer with cues to the timing of the musical track of the sourcetext. Our interaction with those timing cues is reinforced if the listener is familiar with the song. A viewer might know the song quite well and remember many of its characteristics. This musical memory could be activated in viewing the adaptation. But whether or not the viewer is familiar with the song, the timing is nevertheless evident and worthy of our consideration here.

In order to contextualize the temporal features of Rihanna's performance, it is important first to identify the general musical qualities of the track,[5] which can be organized according to the following parameters, as shown in table 13.2: recording values, sonic space, vocal delivery, and instrumental arrangement.

Table 13.2.   Musical setting parameters in Rihanna's "Umbrella" (92 BPM; B-flat minor)

Recording values	production piece: sample-based with many remix effects; rhythms are locked and synchronized
Sonic space	stereophonic field is panoramic, with a large reverb effect; the vocal has a lot of space to fill
Vocal delivery	the vocal is mechanically doubled to create an edgy, robotic sound; it has a percussive effect in its rhythmic delivery of the lyrics
Instrumental arrangement	instruments are synthesized and sampled, centered, and set to fit on the bottom of the mix as support for the voice; samples are edgy, compressed, gritty; the synthesizer has a grainy sound; bass synthesizer is locked with bass drum; the drum kit is central; dynamic range of cymbals and kick drum is highly compressed

Recording values: "Production piece," remix, lock and sync
Sonic space: "Panoramic," large reverb
Vocal delivery: "Robotic," mechanical, percussive
Instrumental arrangement: "Synthesized hip-hop," edgy samples, compressed

The song opens with an introductory rap section, featuring Jay-Z. The beat pattern is set by the bass drum, with the dry snare in a backbeat clap effect, and a steady high-hat. Jay-Z's rap prepares us for the arrival of Rihanna, and as she begins to appear in brief video shots, the song's hook also emerges. We hear Rihanna's vocal entry "eh, eh" with its fully wet reverb effect as a sudden spatial and sonic contrast to Jay-Z's dryer sound.[6]

The next step in our consideration of the temporal parameters is to map more precisely the musical events in relation to the image events. In order to do so, we used the audio software Peak (Bias), which yields a graphic linear representation of the dynamic (amplitude) levels of the right and left channels of the track. The timing indications below the amplitude graph allow for precise identification of the musical events, and it is also possible to identify the precise timing of the video frames. The format of the music-event timings and the image-event time codes are explained in the endnote below.[7] We will examine the interpretive potential of the music-image timing in a later section of the analysis. First, we will show how the amplitude diagram can be used for musical analysis.

Example 13.1 graphs the first two lines of the verse: "you had my heart, and we'll never be worlds apart." At the top of the example, we have

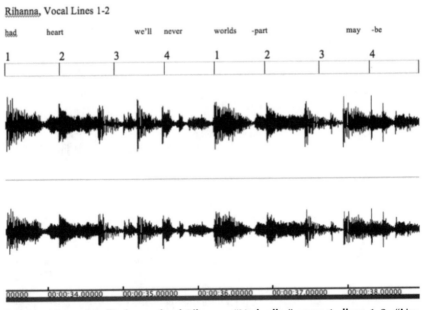

Example 13.1. Amplitude graph of Rihanna, "Umbrella," verse 1, lines 1–2. "Umbrella." Words and Music by Shawn Carter, Thaddis L. Harrell, Christopher Stewart and Terius Nash. © 2007 Carter Boys Publishing, SONY/ATV Music Publishing UK Ltd., Songs of Peer, Ltd., March Ninth Publishing, WB Music Corp., and 2082 Music Publishing. All rights reserved. International copyright secured. Used by permission. Reprinted by permission of Hal Leonard Corporation.

indicated arrival points in the lyrics. The first word of line 1 ("you") occurs on the anacrusis to the first bar, with the word "had" arriving on the downbeat. The word placement is difficult to represent, but the general principle is that the first letter of the word is placed above the attack point in the graph where it occurs. Underneath the partial lyrics, the four beats of each bar are shown, with the amplitude graph and timings aligned below.

The visual graph allows the analyst to examine the musical events and their attack points and relative dynamic emphasis as well as to compare one phrase with another. Here we see that the amplitude graph for line 1 (the first half of the graph) is remarkably similar to that of line 2 (the second half). The largest amplitude shapes in the graph are linked to the attacks in the drum kit, although Rihanna's vocal presentation is also very strong and rhythmic. The reader is encouraged to listen to the first verse while following this graph. Rihanna's voice is tightly synchronized with the kit and synthesizer, and each vocal phrase is delivered in a consistent rhythmic pattern. Each vocal line in the verse begins with an anacrustic gesture at the end of beat 3 or within beat 4, leading to an emphasis on the following downbeat (beat 1). Each lyric line is completed with a word or syllable that lands on the fourth 16th of beat 1, anticipating beat 2 in a syncopated pattern, but leaving the articulation of beat 2 to the snare. The vocal line thus attacks its final syllable at the end of beat 1 and sustains into beat 2, leaving space until the second half of beat 3. That vocal space is filled in by heavy reverb and delays, creating the effect of a vocal tag or extension at the end of each line.

Table 13.3.   Musical setting parameters in Moore's "Umbrella" (76 BPM; A minor)

Recording values	"live"-recording effect: balanced and "natural" instrumental blend, featuring Moore's voice centered in the mix; the physical arrangement of the players on stage is reflected in the stereophonic field
Sonic space	an intimate acoustic space is created by a small-hall reverb
Vocal delivery	the vocal is not highly treated but has a natural-sounding reverb, giving the voice a warm, lush, velvety sound; Moore's rhythmic delivery is gentle and smooth
Instrumental arrangement	standard rock-band arrangement with acoustic and electric guitars, keyboard, bass, and drum kit; the song opens with a sparse texture and low dynamic but gradually increases in activity, texture, and intensity. The rhythmic profile of the song is smoothed out—the guitar arpeggiation pattern places emphasis on beats 1 and 3 through repetition of the lowest pitch in the pattern but also on beats 2 and 4 with the highest pitch and with a harmonic interval

Recording values: "Live," stereo reflects stage arrangement
Sonic space: "Intimate," small hall reverb
Vocal delivery: "Lush," gentle, warm sound, relaxed delivery
Instrumental arrangement: "Rock-band," cumulative texture, increases in intensity

Let us turn our attention to the musical settings on the *Cover Art* track, with the same analytic parameters in mind. First, it should be noted that the tempo of the adaptation is much slower, at 76 beats per minute (BPM) compared with the sourcetext at 92 BPM. Moore's vocals are also lower in pitch, as she sings in A minor, compared with Rihanna's vocals in B-flat minor.

Example 13.2 presents an amplitude diagram of verse 1, lines 1–2, in the same format as example 13.1. The arrangement features a gentle and rhythmically even arpeggiated pattern in the guitar, the phrasing devoid of strong rhythmic accents. If we compare the amplitude graphs of examples 13.1 and 13.2, we notice a striking contrast between the two rhythmic profiles. In the sourcetext version (see example 13.1), the amplitude diagram reveals regular and marked rhythmic accents, but in the adaptation (see example 13.2), there is an obvious lack of regular rhythmic and accented patterning, especially at beat 3.

There is much more to be gained from an interpretation of the amplitude graphs. In particular, we will now demonstrate how these graphs can be coordinated with an analysis of the images in the video.

COTEXTUALITY: COVERING AND SAMPLING THE SOURCETEXT

In examining the materials of the adaptation and its sourcetext, we can consider the parameters of the visual and musical settings of the adaptation as they are juxtaposed with the visual and musical settings of the source-text. This juxtaposition is the basis of the cotextual relationship. As we

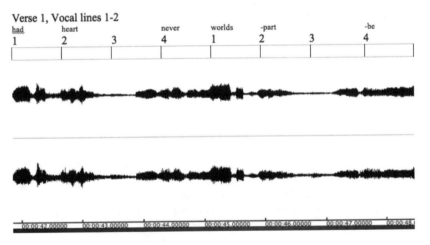

Example 13.2.   Amplitude graph of Moore, "Umbrella," verse 1, lines 1–2

have already mentioned, the visual field of the adaptation is our material contact with the musical track of the sourcetext. That is, we perceive certain temporal aspects of the music through the projected images of Rihanna's performance. Our consideration of musical cotextuality is thereby limited to the temporal domain. We can identify several key concepts through the visually delimited temporal domain that are valuable for the cotextual analysis: tempo, music and image event timing, and synchronization.

Tempo

The tempo of the adaptation is significantly slower than that of the sourcetext. The sourcetext runs at 92 BPM and the adaptation at 76 BPM. This difference has a significant impact upon the relationship between the sourcetext and the adaptation, to be explored below.

Music and Image Event Timing

As we view the *Cover Art* video, we perceive multiple relationships between and among the music and images of the adaptation and sourcetext. As the temporal narrative unfolds, the image events create a complex counterpoint to the musical events in Moore's performance. In the adaptation, there is a consistent formal relationship between the image edits and the musical structure—the shot changes in the video occur at the beginning of each of Moore's vocal phrases, creating a strong formal link between the video and the musical form. Through the cotextual relationship, correspondences also emerge between Moore's musical performance and the timing of the edited shots in the sourcetext video. For instance, as we perceive the visual rhythm of the *Cover Art* video, the sourcetext images change at a faster rate than the visual rhythm of the adaptation. While a single shot is sustained for Moore's vocal phrase, her consistent image is counterpointed by frequent edits and shot changes in the sourcetext. To add yet another layer in this relationship of music to images, the sourcetext has its own music-to-image event scheme, which is suggested by Rihanna's movements in time with the music as well as by means of the video editing. In the sourcetext, the shot edits frequently correspond to the beat structure of the music, articulating a visual change at a rate that aligns with the four musical beats per bar. In other words, the visual rhythm of the sourcetext changes with the beat of the music, whereas the visual rhythm of the adaptation changes with the articulation of the vocal phrase. The longer duration of each adaptation shot is thereby subdivided by the faster-changing sourcetext images. With this in mind, it is interesting to examine the music and image event timing in Rihanna's performance before we turn to the music and image relationships that emerge in the *Cover Art* video.

Example 13.3 reproduces the amplitude graph of the sourcetext track for verses 1 and 2, aligned with the image edits. As before, the vertical lines above the chart mark the beats within the bars, and the vertical lines that run through the table below the amplitude graph indicate the corresponding image edits (shot changes are shown in time-code notation). The content of each shot is briefly described within the table cell. From this chart, we see that every vocal line has an image edit at beat 3, most vocal lines correspond to image editing around beat 1, and a few lines feature image edits that align with beats 2 and 4 to create emphasis on the backbeat structure (this occurs in vocal line 2 of verses 1 and 2 and vocal line 4 of verse 2). A variable counterpoint emerges between the visual rhythm of the image edits and the rhythmic structure of the music, as the visual shot changes may occur rapidly (as in verse 1, lines 1–2) or at a slower rate with shots of longer duration (as in verse 1, lines 3–4). The visual rhythm is achieved not only by these shot edits but also by Rihanna's gestures. For instance, in line 4 of verse 1, there is no edit on or around beat 1; however, in that shot, Rihanna turns and bends in a way that is rhythmically synchronized with beat 1 of the bar. The reader is encouraged to watch the video of Rihanna's "Umbrella" and to focus on the musical phrasing in relation to the image editing in verses 1 and 2 as it is graphed in example 13.3.

Turning now to a similar graph of music and image event timing in the *Cover Art* video, example 13.4 reproduces the amplitude diagram for verses 1 and 2 of Moore's musical track, with the image edits marked below the graph, tracking both the image edits of the adaptation (the first line below the amplitude graph) and of the sourcetext (the last line). With this material arranged in chart format, we can easily consider the timing of musical events in relation to the lyrics, the rhythmic structure of the song, and the timing of the image events in relation to the music.[8]

Note that the sourcetext is not used in a strict timing sequence from beginning to end of the adaptation: some frames are cut, and others are repeated. In example 13.4, a jagged line in the image edits indicates moments when the sourcetext video is "rewound" to start again at the beginning of a running shot. For example, in verse 1, lines 3–4 (see example 13.4), the lengthy medium shot of Rihanna turning and bending, mentioned earlier, is of an even longer duration in the *Cover Art* video, as it is rewound to begin again. The jagged line shows where the repeat begins as the full shot of Moore changes to a close-up shot.

Synchronization

The process of synchronization is a significant aspect of the cotextual relationship. The rhythm of Rihanna's physical movement is aligned with the musical arrangement of the *Cover Art* video at key moments to amplify

Rihanna, Verse 1, Vocal Lines 1-2

had   heart   we'll never   worlds -part   may -be

| 1 | 2 | 3 | 4 | 1 | 2 | 3 | 4 |

| 00000 | 00:00:34.00000 | 00:00:35.00000 | 00:00:36.00000 | 00:00:37.00000 | 00:00:38.00000 |

:33 (11) | :34 (26) | :35 (28) | :36 (28) | :37 (18) | :38 (08) | :38 (23)

| Medium, front | Head | Medium (raises arms) | Head | Medium (arms above) | Arms | M e d |

Rihanna, Verse 1, Vocal Lines 3-4

mag-   zines   but   you'll   be   star   ba   -by

| 1 | 2 | 3 | 4 | 1 | 2 | 3 | 4 |

| 00:00:39.00000 | 00:00:40.00000 | 00:00:41.00000 | 00:00:42.00000 | 00:00:43.00000 | 00:00:44.0 |

:39 (20) | :40 (15) | :43 (01) | :44 (10)

| | Side, head over R shoulder | Medium Rear turn and bend | | | Rear, head over L shoulder | |

Example 13.3.   Amplitude graph of Rihanna, "Umbrella," verses 1 and 2, with image edits

<u>Rihanna</u>, Verse 2, Vocal Lines 1-2

| in | dark | | you | can | shiny | cars | | that's | when |

| 1 | 2 | 3 | 4 | 1 | 2 | 3 | 4 |

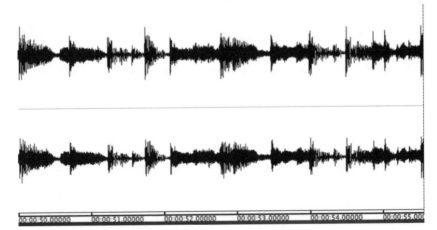

00000   00:00:45.00000   00:00:46.00000   00:00:47.00000   00:00:48.00000   00:00:49.00000

	:45 (19)		:47 (03)	:47 (23)	:48 (15)	:49 (15)
Rear, head over R shoulder	Medium, front		Side, head over R shoulder	Medium, front	Long, front forward bend	Rear, head turn to R

<u>Rihanna</u>, Verse 2, Vocal Lines 3-4

| need | there | | with | you | always | share | | be | -cause |

| 1 | 2 | 3 | 4 | 1 | 2 | 3 | 4 |

00:00:50.00000   00:00:51.00000   00:00:52.00000   00:00:53.00000   00:00:54.00000   00:00:55.00

	:51 (10)	:52 (21)	:53 (10)	:54 (12)	:55(02)
	Medium, front, raises arm straight ahead	Head and shoulders, hand over head	Head, right side profile	Medium, Left side, leg moving up, head back	Long, Right side, leg up, head forward

Moore, Verse 1, Vocal lines 1-2

had	heart		never	worlds	-part		-be
1	2	3	4	1	2	3	4

00:00:42.00000 00:00:43.00000 00:00:44.00000 00:00:45.00000 00:00:46.00000 00:00:47.00000 00:00:48.

:41 (22)	:43 (16)	:46 (22)
Long *exposition*	Medium (cropped image next to Moore and drummer) *blocking*	Long *exposition*

:33 (11)	:34 (26)	:35 (28)	:36 (28)	:37 (18)	:38 (08)	:38 (23)
Medium (front)	Head	Medium (front, raises arms)	Head	Medium (arms above, extends hip)	Head (arms over head)	Med. (rear turn)

Moore, Verse 1, Vocal lines 3-4

Mag- a- zines			you'll	be	star		ba -by
1	2	3	4	1	2	3	4

8.00000 00:00:49.00000 00:00:50.00000 00:00:51.00000 00:00:52.00000 00:00:53.00000 00:00:54.00000

Full	:50 (17) Close-up Moore *fragmentation*	:54(20)

:39 (20)	:40 (15)	:43 (01)	:44 (10)	
Head	Medium (turn from R to L and bend	Head and shoulders (look back L)	R	****

Example 13.4. Amplitude graph of Moore, "Umbrella," verses 1 and 2, with image edits of the adaptation and the sourcetext

Moore Verse 2, Vocal lines 1-2

In	dark		you	shiny	cars		when
1	2	3	4	1	2	3	4

	:56 (24)		1:01 (03)
Guitar	Medium (Moore and guitarist)		Close-up
interruption	*blocking*		*frag.*

	:45 (19)	:47 (03)	:47 (23)	:48 (15)	:49 (15)	
	Medium (front)	Head	Medium (front)	Long, front [head cut off, also blocked]	Head profile	....

Moore Verse 2, Vocal Lines 3-4

need	there		with	you	always	share		Be- cause
1	2	3	4	1	2	3	4	

	1:03 (04)		1:06 (06)	1:07 (14)
Long	Close-up Moore		Guitarist	Long
	fragmentation		*interruption*	*exposition*

⊞	:51 (10)	:52 (21)	:53 (10)	:54 (12)	:55 (02)	
	Medium (Front, raises arms)	Head and sh. (front)	Head (R profile)	......	Medium (blurry)	

Figure 13.4. (*continued*)

rhythmic effects. At other points, Rihanna's delivery of a lyric is synchro-nized with Moore's musical presentation. The synchronization of lyrics is most evident in the bridge section of the song, where Rihanna delivers the words in direct address to the camera; the *Cover Art* video maximizes this effect by bringing Rihanna's delivery into sync with Moore's lyrical articula-tion. The gap between tempi is narrowed here, as the tempo of the adapta-tion increases to 79 BPM and that of the sourcetext slows to 90 BPM, which, along with careful visual editing, enables the synchronized effect.

To understand the cotextual relationship of adaptation and sourcetext, it is also important to analyze the treatment of the image within its delimited visual field. In the analysis of a video presentation, many stylistic and ex-pressive features could be studied. In the context of the *Cover Art* video un-der consideration, the concept of visual sampling is especially meaningful, given the ways in which the sourcetext is processed in the adaptation. The sourcetext video is subjected to a number of manipulations as it appears as the backdrop to the adaptation. Several effects are evident in the image treatment: divided wide screen, screen duplication, exposition, interrup-tion, cropping, blocking, and repetition.

Divided Wide Screen

The sourcetext image is projected across two screens rather than one. To achieve the panoramic dimensions, the sourcetext image is cropped at the top and bottom. When the image is centered on a pair of screens, the cen-tral section of the image is lost in the split between the screens. For instance, as shown in figure 13.1, the centered image of Rihanna's face is cut out at the split in the screen. Rihanna, thus, becomes a faceless figure, with arms positioned around her head.

Screen Duplication

The divided screen is also duplicated in a two by two backdrop arrange-ment. In a long shot of the live band, the paired screens frame Moore, who is centered on the stage. In the instance of figure 13.1, Rihanna's faceless image is juxtaposed against the centered image of Moore's full body, hold-ing the microphone to her face and singing. In another instance of dupli-cation, instead of the panoramic stretching of the image across the screen pairs, the image is repeated on each screen. This only happens once (see figure 13.2), in the bridge, where the sourcetext features Rihanna's face in a close-up direct address shot.

Exposition

The establishing shot of Moore and the band on stage allows for a fully exposed screen presentation. During the instrumental introduction, the long shot allows us to see the full-screen panning of Rihanna's body.

Figure 13.1. Divided wide screen, frame 00:31 (21)

Figure 13.2. Screen duplication, frame 3:19 (16)

Interruption

The sequence of events in the sourcetext is sometimes interrupted, and we lose its flow. During the introduction, the hands of the pianist are featured (see figure 13.3), cutting off the shot of Rihanna, and when she reappears, we have lost several frames of that sourcetext shot sequence.

Cropping

The full screen image of the sourcetext is cropped so that we only see part of the image. For example, at the end of verse 1, the sides, top, and bottom of the image are cropped to zoom in on Rihanna's body (see figure 13.4). This contributes to the fragmentation of the sourcetext, as the field of vision that was developed for the sourcetext video is manipulated and cut to fit the adaptation.

Blocking

Sometimes a background image is not only cropped but also blocked by the figures of Moore and/or her band. In this scene from the second verse (see figure 13.5), the image of Rihanna is blocked by Moore and the guitarist, and we have to "peek" around their bodies to see her.

Figure 13.3.   Interruption, frame 00:47 (13)

Figure 13.4. Cropping, frame 00:51 (15)

Figure 13.5. Blocking, frame 00:58 (08)

Repetition

The adaptation incorporates frequent repetitions of the sourcetext as a method of temporal expansion. Figure 13.6 shows a series of frames from the final sequence of the video: Rihanna, in a cropped screen presentation, is posed with her back to the camera (see figure 13.6a), then gradually turns to expose her side (see figure 13.6b). Before this shot is finished, the shot of Moore changes; as a medium shot of Moore begins, the shot of Rihanna is rewound (see figure 13.6c) to repeat her turning movement, visible behind Moore and the guitarist. While the medium shot of Moore and the guitarist is maintained, the sourcetext runs into its final scene, but Moore's musical performance is not yet finished. For the final instrumental phrase of Moore's performance, the sourcetext is rewound to start again at a frame cue several seconds back. The repetition of frames leads to the repetition of the shot sequence of Rihanna's turning body, this time in full exposition, with Moore notably turning around to look at the screen as the turn takes place (see figure 13.7).

Figure 13.6a.   Frame 4:40 (06)

Figure 13.6b.　4:40 (29)

Figure 13.6c.　4:41 (22)

Figure 13.7.   Frame 4:59 (19)

SAMPLE COTEXTUAL ANALYSIS

An analysis of the first verse illustrates in greater detail how the processes of covering and sampling establish the cotextual relationship in a brief passage of the song. Our goal with this analytic account is to illustrate the many facets of the sourcetext and the adaptation, as their material contents exist in relation to one another within the adaptation. As we established in our introduction, we will not enter into an intertextual study of the adaptation nor will we draw interpretive conclusions. Rather, in our exploration of the adaptation and sourcetext, we aim to reveal the suggestive interpretive potential of the *Cover Art* video as that potential emerges from the material content. This approach brings forward the material elements in such a way that the reader can develop a concretely grounded interpretation. We base our analytic commentary on the theoretical parameters defined above. The analysis will be presented in a descriptive format, and the reader is encouraged to consider both the image stills from the video and the chart of image edits in example 13.4.

In the opening verse, Moore explores a low dynamic, smooth rhythms, and is accompanied by a gentle setting in the guitar and keyboard. Against this musical setting, the visual presentation establishes the stage configuration of Moore and the band and exposes the sourcetext in a series of shots from verse 1, lines 1–4. A detailed description of the material content of each of the four vocal lines is below.

Line 1: "You had my heart" [00:41 (22) – 00:43 (06)]

The first verse begins with an establishing long shot of Moore's band (see figure 13.8), allowing for the exposition of the sourcetext on the four-panel display; the medium shot of Rihanna is exposed in double-screen form. Moore is centered in the screen, with the duplicated image of Rihanna to her left and right. The image of Rihanna moves, and the camera blurs in and out of focus while Moore and the band remain very still. The dimensions of Moore's body in relation to Rihanna's appear comparable because of Moore's forward positioning on the stage. Next to the guitarist, however, Rihanna appears to be larger than life.

Rihanna's delivery of the lyrics "had my heart" is synchronized with Moore's musical presentation; however, Moore's rhythmic delivery of the line avoids the anticipation of beat 2 that distinguished Rihanna's lyric delivery and instead smooths out the line so that "heart" arrives on beat 2. The third beat in Moore's presentation is articulated by the rocking pattern of the guitar, creating a space between the lyric lines. In the sourcetext recording, this space is filled with intense rhythmic activity in the high-hat,

Figure 13.8. Frame 00:41 (22)

snare, and synthesized bass, and this strong rhythmic articulation is complemented visually by a blurring of the shot in time with the beat.

The filling of the space between lyric lines is an important strategy in the sourcetext verse structure, as it opens up the space for Rihanna's physical movement in the video. After each line closes in anticipation of beat 2, the space before the next lyric line begins at beat 4 is filled with Rihanna's physical gestures and edited camera-shot techniques that complement the rhythmic activity in the kit. In the *Cover Art* video, however, Moore is very still as she delivers the first line and waits for the next line to begin. There is a clear contrast between the level of activity in Moore's performance and that of Rihanna's gestures in the background. Behind Moore, in the visual field that is occupied by Rihanna, there is a lot of movement, and the editing rate and tempo are evidently faster. The contrasting modalities that we defined for the visual settings are very much in evidence here: the constant staging and lighting of the adaptation versus the varying staging and lighting of the sourcetext, the static figure movement of Moore versus the dynamic figure movement of Rihanna, and the simple camera techniques of the adaptation versus the complex camera techniques of the sourcetext.

Line 2: "And we'll never be worlds apart" [00:43 (07) – 00:46 (08)]

In line 2, the image of Rihanna changes to a close-up head shot, glancing back over her shoulder, while the long shot of Moore and the band is maintained. The dimensions of Rihanna's body are now clearly out of scale with the band musicians. In anticipation of Moore's lyric delivery of line 2, the shot changes to a medium shot of Moore, with a cropped screen in view to her left. As this edit occurs, a close-up shot of Rihanna is rewound to begin again, now in the newly cropped format. The size of Rihanna's body within the image is closer to the scale of Moore's body, and Rihanna's delivery of the lyric ("and we'll never be") is in sync with Moore's. Three more shot changes occur in the sourcetext while the medium shot of Moore is sustained. The first is a medium shot of Rihanna, posed with arms above her head and hip extended. The next is a close-up of her face as we see her sing the word "apart," which is again brought into sync with Moore's delivery of that word. The next shot of Rihanna is from her vocal delivery of line 3, but it begins before Moore's delivery of line 2 is finished. This shot features Rihanna as before in the medium shot with her arms raised and her hip extended (see figure 13.9).

Line 3: "Maybe in magazines" [00:46 (09) – 00:49 (18)]

As Moore delivers line 3, the foreground scene returns to a full exposition shot. Simultaneously with this edit of the foreground, the medium

Figure 13.9. Frame 00:46 (12)

shot of Rihanna begins again in the background so that we see this same shot in its entirety in the full-screen panorama. The image of Rihanna next changes to a close-up of her arms bent above her head and then to a movement sequence in which she lowers her arms and begins to turn her back to the camera, placing one hand behind her head and one on her hip, as the lyric "magazines" is delivered by Moore. Another shot change featuring Rihanna brings us back to her close-up, and we see her delivery of the syllable "-zines" in sync with Moore. Line 3 closes with a full exposition on the word "magazines," with Rihanna in a rear shot (see figure 13.10), turning back to the camera.

Line 4: "But you'll still be my star" [00:49 (19) – 00:53 (04)]

As Moore's delivery of line 3 comes to a close, a climactic movement sequence begins in the sourcetext. It is one of the longest shots in the sourcetext video (76 frames), featuring Rihanna in a rear pose (see figure 13.11a), turning her torso from her right side to a full back exposure and then bending down to her left. We will refer to this movement sequence as the "booty bend." About one-third of the way (28 frames) into the booty-bend shot, the shot of Moore changes (see figure 13.11b) with the beginning of line 4, "but you'll still be my star." The image of Moore is a close-up

Figure 13.10.   Frame 00:48 (21)

with the cropped screen on the left, zooming in on Rihanna's "booty bend" repeated from the beginning, thus lengthening an already lengthy shot. The treatment of this scene not only extends the shot but also brings the image of Rihanna into the context of the close-up of Moore. In other words, the cotextual relationship here emphasizes the booty bend of Rihanna by juxtaposing it with the close-up presentation of Moore. As Moore quietly delivers the cadential melodic line "be my star," she closes her eyes and remains still, which contrasts directly with Rihanna's movement (see figure 13.11c).

This brief account of the verse 1 material content exposes the ways in which the sourcetext and the adaptation are juxtaposed within the *Cover Art* video. In watching this video, multiple parameters are available for consideration: Moore's delivery of the lyric and the ways in which her delivery compares with Rihanna's; the staging and musical arrangement of the adaptation; Moore's disposition, singing at a microphone, compared with Rihanna's choreographed dance performance of the song; and the style and content of the sourcetext video in relation to the adaptation.

We summarize the outcome of the material analysis of the *Cover Art* video as follows: The process of covering pairs a panoramic and effect-laden pop vocal synchronized with a sampled beat pattern alongside a sonically balanced singer-songwriter vocal supported by a conventional live-band arrangement. The process of sampling pairs a varied presentation of staging,

Figure 13.11a. Frame 00:50 (07)

Figure 13.11b. Frame 00:50 (18)

Figure 13.11c.   Frame 00:52 (07)

lighting, and costumes, a dynamic treatment of figure movement, and a complex range of camera techniques alongside a constant presentation of staging, lighting, and costumes, a static treatment of figure movement, and a simple series of camera techniques.

Based on such concrete material analysis, we understand this *Cover Art* video to be an instance of the adaptation as commentary. Commentaries can take many forms, including homage, parody, expository critique, and so forth. Although an interpreter may develop a specific reading which favors one form of commentary over another, it is always necessary to base a reading upon the concrete materials that are in evidence in the artistic expression. In this *Cover Art* video, the commentary resides in the deliberate appropriation of the sourcetext materials through treatments such as cropping, repetition, and synchronization.

In the domain of the Internet, where viewers are bombarded with images, it is important to develop critical skills for the analysis of what we see, especially in relation to what we hear. The techniques of analysis presented here are intended to raise an awareness of the strategies that can underlie musical covering and video sampling, preparing the viewer to contend with the video and to draw conclusions that do justice to the sourcetext. In the "rush to interpretation" that is often tempting in the reception of contemporary popular forms, it is all too easy to bypass concrete material analysis. Our objective has been to illustrate the value of such analysis, as a foundational consideration in the multiple readings of cultural forms. As we take account of the numerous details in the visual and musical settings of "Umbrella" by Rihanna and by Moore, we acknowledge the complexity of the *Cover Art* video form, and we recognize its potential for cultural commentary.

NOTES

1. In 2005, Pepsi and Yahoo! Music partnered to launch Pepsi Smash on Yahoo! Music, a web initiative conceived as a new Internet-based performance and promotional forum for chart-topping popular music artists. Adapted from the Pepsi Smash summer concert TV program, Pepsi Smash on Yahoo! Music, later designated Pepsi Music, is an exclusive of Yahoo! Music, featuring original video programming. *Cover Art*, http://search.music.yahoo.com/search/?m=video&p=cover+art, a segment of Pepsi Music, features contemporary artists performing exclusive covers of current-day pop song hits. On occasion, the covering artist chooses to interpret older songs, for instance Matisyahu's cover of the Police's "Message in a Bottle" (1979), Daughtry's cover of U2's "Sunday Bloody Sunday" (1983), and Flyleaf's cover of Nirvana's "Smells Like Teen Spirit" (1991), arguably all anthems in their day. Notably, the Internet release of an artist's *Cover Art* video often coincides with an album release, thereby establishing the promotional function and value of the *Cover Art* Internet segment.

2. Readers interested in the subject of cover songs are encouraged to read the following articles: Burns and Woods 2004, Butler 2003, Mosser 2008, Middleton 2000, and Weinstein 1998.

3. Will Fulford-Jones, "Sampling," *Grove Music Online, Oxford Music Online,* http://www.oxfordmusiconline.com/subscriber/article/grove/music/47228.

4. We borrow basic terms from film theory to describe the visual field. For instance, the reader will repeatedly come across the following terms: *shot, cut, long shot, medium shot,* and *close-up shot.* A shot is a continuous section of film made with a single camera. A cut is an immediate transition to a new shot. A long shot, as defined in Bordwell and Thompson 2008, entails a "framing in which the scale of the object shown is small; a standing human figure would appear nearly the height of the screen" (479; see also 191). It follows that a medium shot corresponds to a framing wherein the human figure from the waist up would appear nearly the height of the screen and a close-up shot to a framing wherein the human figure from the neck up would appear nearly the height of the screen. Readers wishing to explore further the terms of film theory are invited to consult the glossary in Bordwell and Thompson 2008.

5. "Umbrella" by Rihanna was released on the album *Good Girl Gone Bad* (Def Jam, 2007) as the lead single in March of 2007. The video was released for sale on iTunes in May of 2007.

6. "Wet" and "dry" refer to the presence and absence, respectively, of reverb effects.

7. In order to import the video into the music software Peak, we captured the video using the media program Snapz ProX (Ambrosia). Because the iTunes format locks the file from further software importing, we captured the video on the AOL.com website. The captured recording was then imported into the media programs iMovie and Peak, both of which allow each frame of the video (at 30 frames per second) to be tracked individually. The timing of the musical events is indicated to the hundredth of a second; for example, 01:25.500 is the audio event timing at 1 minute and 25.5 seconds. The timing of the image events is indicated as a "time code"; for example, 01:25 (15) is the frame of the video that corresponds to the musical event at 1 minute and 25.5 seconds. We can refer to both sets of timings simultaneously by using the following format: 1:25.5 (15). In any captured recording, the timing of the first frame and musical sound must be identified as an important point of departure for all time references. In the recording of "Umbrella" by Rihanna that we captured, the first musical attack and frame occur at the time code 00:00.3 (09). All of our timings for the sourcetext will relate to that starting point. These timings will be used in our illustrations of the music and images. For instance, in example 13.1 and 13.2, the Peak diagram features the music timings at the bottom of the graph, and in example 13.3, the chart beneath the Peak diagram indicates image time codes for the beginning of each shot.

8. It is important to describe the source of the *Cover Art* video capture and the time codes embedded in that capture. Moore's video begins with an ad for the Pepsi Smash videos, and then an image of Moore appears in an overexposed shot, which fades to a clear presentation of Moore speaking about the video. Our timings and time codes are based on a Snapz capture from the Yahoo! site that presents the first image of Moore at 00:06 (12). At 00:28 (07), a flash signals that the introduction is over and the video proper is about to begin. The first image of the video fades for several frames from that flash of light.

REFERENCES

Bordwell, David, and Kristin Thompson. 2008. *Film art: An introduction.* New York: McGraw-Hill.

Burns, Lori, and Alyssa Woods. 2004. Authenticity, appropriation, signification: Tori Amos on gender, race, and violence in covers of Billie Holiday and Eminem. *Music Theory Online* 10, no. 2 (June). http://mto.societymusictheory.org/issues/mto.04.10.2/mto.04.10.2.burns_woods.html.

Butler, Mark. 2003. Taking it seriously: Intertextuality and authenticity in two covers by the Pet Shop Boys. *Popular Music* 22, no. 1: 1–19

Fulford-Jones, Will. Sampling. *Grove Music Online. Oxford Music Online.* http://www.oxfordmusiconline.com/subscriber/article/grove/music/47228.

Hutcheon, Linda. 2006. *A theory of adaptation.* New York: Routledge.

Mosser, Kurt. 2008. "Cover Songs": Ambiguity, multivalence, polysemy. *Popular Musicology Online* 2. http://www.popular-musicology-online.com/issues/02/mosser.html.

Middleton, Richard. 2000. Work-in(g)-practice: Configurations of the popular music intertext. In *The musical work: Reality or invention*, ed. Michael Talbot, 59–87. Liverpool, UK: Liverpool University Press.

Weinstein, Deena. 1998. The history of rock's pasts through rock covers. In *Mapping the beat: Popular music and contemporary theory*, ed. Thomas Swiss, John Sloop, and Andrew Herman, 137–51. Malden, MA: Blackwell.

14

Vocal Practices and Constructions of Identity in Rap: A Case Study of Young Jeezy's "Soul Survivor"

Alyssa Woods

Masculinity plays a large role in how rap music is defined in North America. As rap scholar Imani Perry has observed, hip-hop "constitutes a powerful location for asserting the particularity of black male identity" (2004, 118). Throughout rap's development, masculine posturing and male identity formation have dominated many aspects of this art form. This includes lyrical themes, visual images such as music videos and album art, and even the music and vocal presentation of rappers. Masculinity has been such an obvious and exaggerated facet of rap performance and marketing that some scholars have identified rap as "hypermasculine."[1] Rap's hypermasculinity has resulted in a sense of male exclusivity. Although female MCs have been active participants in rap since its inception, they have been strongly outnumbered by men. The continuing gender imbalance in many popular styles, such as jazz, blues, and rock, is heightened in rap music.[2] This has resulted in gendered norms that promote male dominance, control, confidence, aggressiveness, and even misogyny and homophobia.

One aspect of rap's exaggerated masculinity that has not been sufficiently explored is vocality. The vocal techniques used by rappers in their lyric delivery play an important role in the construction of meaning. MCs' vocal production and performances are not only primary carriers of the lyrics, but also convey musical meanings through vocal nuance, declamation, and rhythmic delivery. An examination of MCs' vocality in relation to other aspects of rap production and reception provides insight into the expression of gender roles and racial identities in rap, which can illuminate constructions of gender and race in larger social contexts.

This paper fuses music-theoretic perspectives with aspects of gender studies, cultural studies, and critical race theory in order to explore some of the ways in which masculinity is represented in rap vocality. I begin by discussing some of the lyrical and visual components of masculinity that are present in rap, as already observed and discussed by scholars in the field. After establishing some of the commonly held views on rap masculinity, I explore how these aspects of masculinity carry over into the musical realm. The final section of this paper illustrates how these musical elements participate in the construction of identity in the rap sphere through a case study of Young Jeezy's song "Soul Survivor." A reading of this song that combines interpretation of the lyrics and vocal delivery with a consideration of how the artist works within rap's conventions helps us to better understand the meanings and constructions of identity conveyed in the song. This case study also provides broader insight into the ways in which masculine identities are performed through rap vocality, which in turn can help us better understand rap's sociocultural dynamics. The concepts and methodologies demonstrated in this chapter are more generally applicable to studies of other performers in rap and related genres.

MASCULINITY: DEFINITIONS AND CONTEXT

In order to interrogate the ways in which masculinity is performed vocally in rap, I will first explore how masculinity is represented and performed in the rap sphere more generally. Although rap encompasses a variety of representations of masculinity, this study focuses on the ways in which masculinity is portrayed by the majority of mainstream American rap artists.[3] Many of the aspects of masculine representation discussed here contain stereotypical constructions of black masculinity, which are performed, reinforced, and manipulated by many popular rappers and are, therefore, an important area to explore.

Representations of masculinity in rap are closely related to the intersection of blackness and masculinity. Due to its origins in black culture and the continued dominance of black performers in mainstream rap, rap is at least partly defined in relation to blackness. As such, representations of masculinity are very often tied to the ways in which blackness has been understood in popular culture. Perry has discussed these intersections at length in her chapter "B-Boys, Players, and Preachers: Reading Masculinity" (Perry 2004, 119–122). According to Perry, masculinity in hip-hop is a version of black, urban masculinity, which "is complicated by the American exploitation of black male identity and fraught with sexist troping" (118). Referencing the work of bell hooks, Perry explores how the patriarchal objectification of black masculinity through the white male gaze has contributed to the hypermasculinity of black male rappers (Perry 2004, 121; hooks 1994). Perry and hooks have both argued that the objectification of black men has caused them to become feminized and that black men have fought back by embracing hypermasculinity (hooks 1994, 127).

Hypermasculinity in rap is achieved in a variety of ways. In many cases, images, lyrics, and music are violent and misogynist, presenting what Sut Jhally (2007) calls "a threatening and out of control black masculinity." These representations of masculinity are tied not only to race but also to a particular socioeconomic status. Constructs of black masculinity in the rap sphere are often linked to the hood or ghetto.[4] Even the more recent trend of rappers openly displaying wealth is underlaid by an understanding that they had to work their way from poverty to wealth, often through illegitimate activities.[5]

Masculinity in rap is a version of urban, black masculinity, but as Jhally has observed, it is important to remember that "these images do not reflect the reality of African-American masculinity, but how someone has chosen to represent it at this point in history" (Jhally 2007).[6] Although rap's representations may not directly reflect the reality of black male experience, they can serve as an important location in which to assert black male identity (Perry 2004, 118). The masculine stereotypes that are performed by many mainstream rap artists comprise a system of images and sounds that pervade media and promotional material, lyrics, music, and videos.[7] Although there are alternative representations of black masculinity in rap, these images are the most prominent.

MASCULINE IDENTITY IN RAP

Masculine identity in rap can be defined in part as a collection of specific attributes that are stereotypes of black manhood portrayed by the majority of mainstream rap artists. As Byron Hurt explains in his documentary film *Beyond Beats and Rhymes*, in hip-hop you have to fit into a metaphorical box (i.e., conform to a particular profile) to be considered masculine: "in order to be in that box you have to be strong, tough, have a lot of girls, you have to have money, be a playa or pimp, be in control, dominate other men, other people" (Hurt 2006). These behaviors are considered masculine norms in mainstream rap, and those who deviate from these norms lack credibility—more specifically, "street cred," which is an important measure of authenticity in the hip-hop community. According to Hurt, if you do not display the qualities described above, "people call you soft or weak, pussy, chump, faggot. Nobody wants to be any of these things, so everybody stays on this side of the box." Weakness is associated with both femaleness (as indicated by the use of the term "pussy") and homosexuality (indicated by the term "faggot"), thus further reinforcing the sense of male exclusivity present in hip-hop. Many of these attributes have become standard and even expected in rap performances. These norms are: male, black, hetero-sexual, tough, street-smart, business-smart, and powerful (having power over your women, crew, and adversaries).[8]

Although not every mainstream American male rapper exemplifies all of these traits all of the time, they rarely go against these norms—particularly not by showing weakness or affiliating with homosexuals. An example of-fered in *Beyond Beats and Rhymes* is that of rapper 50 Cent commenting on a video of fellow MC Ja Rule crying: "This is what a bitch nigga looks like." Calling someone a "bitch nigga" is equivalent to calling them a "pussy" or a "fag." The term implies weakness and calls the subject's manhood into question.[9] These attributes are not exclusive to black male rappers, but they have become associated with both blackness and maleness through the process of stereotyping, and in a vicious cycle, their normalization contrib-utes to the continued perpetuation of those stereotypes. Although female rappers may display some of these attributes as well, they are not always necessary to obtain credibility.[10]

Many male rappers embody archetypal roles within these stereotypes, including the gangsta (based on urban gang activity), the hustler (based on criminal activity for the purposes of upward mobility), the player or pimp (based on sexual prowess and control over women's sexuality), and the intellectual (based on sophisticated rhymes and social and political critiques).[11] In many cases, these roles only exacerbate the negative repre-sentations of black men in popular culture and society; however, within the hip-hop realm, they can be a means for asserting control over one's iden-tity. These roles are fluid, and many rappers shift between these different personas or combine them. For example, Snoop Dogg represents himself as both a gangsta and a pimp. I will focus on the roles of the gangsta and the hustler, as they are both very common within the rap sphere, and Young Jeezy relies on a combination of these roles in his performed identity.

One of the most prominent personas adopted by rappers is that of the gangsta. The image of the gangsta was popularized in the late 1980s and early 1990s, especially on the West Coast. This role was "drawn from the real-life gang battles over economic control of drug markets in communi-ties from Los Angeles to Seattle" (Perry 2004, 131). Early gangsta rappers include Ice-T and N.W.A.—a more recent example is 50 Cent. The role of the gangsta rapper was initially extremely political, rooted in a social cri-tique of white power and the economic disparities between people of dif-ferent races in the United States.[12] Many of these critiques were directed at the police and the justice system—for example, N.W.A.'s "Fuck tha Police" (1989).[13] The persona of the gangsta falls into the broader category of "real-ity rap," which includes any type of rap music whose themes "undertake the project of realism . . . which in this context would amount to an epistemo-logical/ontological project to map the realities of (usually black) inner-city life."[14] Many rappers strive to illustrate the hardships of life in poor, urban neighborhoods, as well as continued racism in the United States.

The genre of reality rap also includes the figure of the hustler, which as Perry has observed, has been more common on the East Coast and in the southern United States than on the West Coast. This figure differs from the gangsta in that he has no gang affiliation, and his goal is to overcome the limitations of his social class (Perry 2004, 132). Representations of the hustler persona are exemplified by artists such as Scarface and Rick Ross, whose song "Hustlin'" contrasts the wealth of South Beach, Florida, with the "real" Miami, where, as the song's hook reiterates, "Everyday we hustlin'." Ross constructs a narrative of upward mobility achieved by illegal activities with lyrics such as "I'm in the distribution" and "We never steal cars, but we deal hard."[15] With the hustler persona, the acquisition of wealth is important, but a connection to the streets or the hood must also be preserved in order to maintain credibility.

MALE VOCAL EXPRESSION

How are these aspects of masculinity reflected in rap's musical practices? How does music, and specifically the voice, participate in the construction of identities in hypermasculine texts? I propose that the voice is essential in constructing MCs' performed identities as well as in conveying specific meanings to audiences. Important aspects of rap vocal practice include quality (resonance, timbre, color) and techniques of lyric delivery (flow, tempo, articulation, declamation, pronunciation), as well as register, range, pitch, and intonation. These elements all factor into rap's conventions, which can signify a variety of characteristics, including aggression, toughness, confidence, braggadocio, sexual assertiveness, and seduction. Performers use a combination of these techniques to convey meanings in their performances. I will focus on the conventions that signify aggression, toughness, and confidence, which are most relevant to the personas of the gangsta and hustler.

Flow

Rappers' flows are one of the most important aspects of their performance. Flow is typically defined as the MCs' rhythmic delivery of the lyrics.[16] In the first extensive monograph on rap's musical workings, *Rap Music and the Poetics of Identity*, Adam Krims proposes a methodology for interpreting MCs' flows. Krims outlines three primary styles of flow: "sung" rhythmic style, "percussion-effusive" style, and "speech-effusive" style.[17] In sung rhythmic style, the rhythms and rhymes tend to be similar to those of many sung styles of pop and rock music. Characteristics of the sung rhythmic style include strict couplet groupings, rhythmic repetition, on-beat accents, and regular on-beat pauses. Percussion-effusive and speech-effusive styles both have a tendency "to spill over the rhythmic boundaries of the meter, the couplet, and, for that matter, of duple and quadruple groupings in general" (Krims 2000, 50). This transgression of rhythmic boundaries is accomplished in a number of ways, including staggering of the syntax or rhymes, uneven subdivision of the beat, repetition of off-beat accents, and the use of polyrhythms.[18] Speech-effusive and percussion-effusive styles differ in that speech-effusive delivery and enunciation is closer to spoken language, whereas percussion-effusive delivery is closer to vocal percussion. Krims notes that these styles of flow exist along a spectrum and that the categories overlap in various ways. For example, rappers might alternate between speech-effusive and percussion-effusive styles even within the same song.

Vocal Quality

A rough, gritty vocal quality is perceived as a desirable feature in rap music. A rough quality can contribute to a hard, edgy sound, which, when combined with appropriate lyrics and imagery, helps to characterize a rapper as tough and masculine. Some rappers have capitalized on their low-pitched, rough vocal timbres; examples are Lil'Jon and Young Jeezy. This effect can be enhanced through specific techniques in the delivery, such as producing the sound gutturally, in the throat, and using harder attacks on syllables. A rough vocal quality is sometimes, but not always, tied to aggression, a further signifier of masculinity in rap. Thus, register, timbre, quality, and articulation can all contribute to an MC's musical performance of toughness.

Tempo and Linguistic Ability

Lyrical prowess and rapid lyrical delivery are also signifiers of masculinity and are often used to signal aggressiveness. The speed of lyric delivery is often a marker of both style and competence since the ability to rap with great speed requires exceptional skill. Some rappers known and admired for their rapid-fire flows are Twista,[19] Busta Rhymes, Krayzie Bone, Shawnna, Eminem, and Ludacris, to name a few. In contrast, other rappers have developed a more relaxed style with a slower speed of delivery, such as T. I. and Baby Boy da Prince. A slower flow still requires a skilled rhythmic delivery in order for the rapper to be respected; however, it can convey a very different affect. For example, a slower flow might be considered "chill" and relaxed, portraying an air of confidence on the part of the rapper.[20] However, even a slower flow can be interpreted as aggressive when it is delivered with a rough timbre, a loud dynamic, or a great deal of intensity.

Confidence is one of the main criteria of maleness that occurs in all genres of rap. Confidence is tied to braggadocio and is often associated with a somewhat slower-paced delivery and lyrical themes of wealth, power, and importance within the community. A rapper with extreme confidence, who demonstrates verbal prowess through impressive flows and clever rhymes, is said to have swagger. A good example is T. I.'s song "Swagger Like Us" (2008), featuring Kanye West, Jay-Z, and Lil Wayne. The lyrics assert that to have swagger you must be well-dressed, financially secure, successful, powerful, "real," and, most importantly, demonstrate exemplary skill as an MC.

Production

Production techniques such as voice doubling also help MCs perform masculinity. Voice doubling is one means of "thickening" a recorded voice, which is a very common technique in both pop and hip-hop that gives the voice a larger-than-life sound. There are two methods of achieving this effect: the first is to record two separate tracks (called "double-tracking"), and the second is to use delay (called "doubling echo").[21] The thicker voice created by doubling gives the impression of strength and power. The technique of voice doubling can, therefore, act as a signifier of masculinity, contributing to an MC's aggressiveness and/or confidence: he dominates the music's texture with his voice.

In practice, these aspects of an MC's vocal delivery tend to overlap, and several are often used simultaneously. In the following analysis of Young Jeezy's "Soul Survivor," I demonstrate how some of these vocal practices are used in the production of meanings.

YOUNG JEEZY: "SOUL SURVIVOR"

Young Jeezy broke out into the mainstream in 2005 with the release of two albums: a solo album entitled *Thug Motivation 101* as well as a self-titled album with the group Boyz n da Hood. Young Jeezy had been active in the Atlanta rap community for several years before his major-label debut. His achievements include the creation of Corporate Thugz Entertainment and the distribution of independent albums and mix tapes, including his debut album *Thuggin' under the Influence* (2001) and *Come Shop wit' Me* (2003).[22] Young Jeezy's music often deals with themes of crime, poverty, and life in the hood, which connect to aspects of his personal biography.[23] His years spent in the Southern drug trade gave him the necessary street credibility to go along with his skills as an MC. He embodies the persona of a gangsta or hustler, which is clearly articulated in songs such as "Gangsta Music," "Don't Get Caught," and "Trap or Die."[24] These themes are maintained in the two albums that follow *Thug Motivation 101*, which are *The Inspiration: Thug Motivation 102* (2006) and *The Recession* (2008). *The Recession* shifts toward political lyrics as Young Jeezy tackles issues such as the current economic climate and the election of President Obama. Jeezy does not abandon his hustler persona on *The Recession*, however, and his political commentary is delivered from within this social and cultural position.[25]

The song "Soul Survivor" from *Thug Motivation 101* is an excellent example of how Young Jeezy marries rough, raw-sounding vocals to narratives of life in the hood. "Soul Survivor" was the second single from the album, reaching number four on the Billboard Hot 100 chart, and number one on the Hot R&B/Hip-Hop chart. The song features Akon, a hip-hop singer who has been featured as a guest artist on countless rappers' tracks.[26] Akon's criminal history, including a stint in jail, provides him with credibility in the rap sphere. This aspect of his identity comes to the forefront in "Soul Survivor," complementing Young Jeezy's performed identity.

The song's form is fairly standard: introduction, chorus, verse 1, chorus, verse 2, chorus, verse 3, bridge, chorus. A slow introduction of sustained string chords leads into Akon's introduction of himself and Young Jeezy, a customary act in many rap songs. The main percussive beat then enters the musical texture (0:27), setting a moderate 4/4 tempo. The entrance of the beat signals the beginning of the chorus, sung by Akon. The lyrics of the chorus (shown below) encapsulate many of the song's themes, including drug trafficking and surviving life in the hood. The words in parentheses are interjections by Young Jeezy.

Chorus

(1) If you lookin' for me I'll be on the block
(2) With my thang cocked possibly sittin' on a drop (Now)
(3) 'Cause I'm a rida (Yeah)
(4) I'm just a Soul Survivor (Yeah)
(5) 'Cause er'body know the game don't stop
(6) Tryin' to make it to the top 'fore your ass get popped (Now)
(7) If you a rida (Yeah)
(8) Or just a Soul Survivor

More specifically, the song's chorus describes a man waiting for a drug deal to go down, with his "thang," meaning gun, at the ready. The lyrics refer to the continuing "game" of life, business, and trying to get ahead in a life of crime without getting killed. The lyric "soul survivor" implies that you have to be tough to survive in this environment. It can also be interpreted as a play on the cliché "sole survivor" (meaning the last one standing). The spelling of "soul" implies a link to the soul music tradition. Many rap artists link themselves to older African American musical traditions through lyric and musical references; Demers 2003 offers an excellent discussion of this convention.

Akon sings the introduction and chorus in his signature style, blending a soulful melody with his unique vocal timbre. His smooth vocal delivery is in tune; he uses a moderate range, fairly soft articulation, and sustains many of his pitches. His vocal quality is starkly contrasted by that of Young Jeezy, who enters in the first verse (0:50). Jeezy's rapped vocals are extremely rough and low-pitched. The first verse opens with the following lyrics:

Verse 1 (0:50)

(1) Tonight I can't sleep, we livin' in hell (Yeah)
(2) First they give us the work, then they throw us in jail (Ayy)
(3) Road Trip, I'm trafficking in the white
(4) Please Lord don't let me go to jail tonight (Yeah)
(5) Who Me? I'm a Soul Survivor
(6) Ask about 'em in the street, the boy Jeez a rida (Jeez a rida)
(7) A hundred grand on my wrist, yeah life sucks
(8) Fuck the club, dawg, I rather count a million bucks (Ayy)

With these lyrics, Jeezy describes living in the hood as hell and notes the paradox of selling drugs to whites and then getting jailed by them (the reference to "trafficking in the white" can also be interpreted as cocaine distribution). This kind of social commentary enters into many "us vs. them" dialogues typical of gangsta rap, referring to the racial inequities in many urban American neighborhoods.

Young Jeezy's masculinity is constructed in this first verse by his narrative of urban, inner-city life and his role as a hustler. Musically, his masculinity is reinforced by his rough, gritty, aggressive vocal delivery. His rhythmic delivery is in some ways representative of the slower-style flow that is associated with some Southern rappers, such as T. I.[27] This type of slow, drawn-out flow is sometimes referred to as "lazy," especially in performances that employ less breath support, making the lyric delivery sound lethargic. Jeezy's flow is slow but energetic rather than lazy. Jeezy's vocals are set against a repeated melodic eighth-note pattern, which is combined or alternated with a chordal sixteenth-note pattern. Most of his vocal accents coincide with quarter-note beats, but his phrasing is irregular. For example, sometimes he begins a line before the hypermetric downbeat, ahead of the accompaniment (for example, lines 2 and 4 of verse 1), and other times he starts his line after the downbeat (for example, lines 3 and 5 of verse 1). This type of delivery is an example of Krims's category of speech-effusive flow. Jeezy does, however, use matching end rhymes in couplets, as is typical of sung flow.

Jeezy emphasizes certain words by accelerating the airflow. For example, on the word "life," at the penultimate line of verse 2 (shown below), he slides into the word, pushing the airflow toward the center of the word.

Verse 2 (1:37)

   (1) Another day, another dolla (dolla)
   (2) Same block, same nigga, same part, same green
   (3) I guess we got the same dreams (Ayy)
   (4) Or is it the same nightmares (nightmares)
   (5) We let the doves do it for us, we don't cry tears (That's right)
   (6) Real niggaz don't budge
   (7) When Mail Man got his time he shot birds at the judge (Yeah)
   (8) I'm knee deep in the game
   (9) So when it's time to re-up, I'm knee deep in the cane (Damn)
  (10) Real talk, look, I'm tellin' you man (tellin' you man)
  (11) If you get jammed up don't mention my name
  (12) Forgive me Lord—I know I ain't livin' right
  (13) Gotta feed the block, niggaz starvin', they got appetites (Ayy)
  (14) And this is er'day, it never gets old (Old)
  (15) Thought I was a juvenile stuck to the G-Code (Yeah)
  (16) This ain't a rap song, nigga this is my life (this is my life)
  (17) And if the hood was a battlefield then I'd earn stripes (Yeah)

The syllable "life" is held for a slightly longer duration than most other words in the song. This accentuation draws attention to the realistic aspect of the song. As noted earlier, narratives of black urban life are characteristic of reality rap, which is one reason why artists' biographies are so important in establishing their credibility. The sense of authenticity is reinforced by phrases such as: "My biography, you damn right, the true story," toward the end of the third verse:

Verse 3 (2:45)

   (1) Gotta watch er' move 'cause them eyes be on you (eyes be on you)
   (2) Gotta drive real cool when them pies be on you (pies be on you)
   (3) Just because we stack paper and we ball outrageous (ball outrageous)
   (4) Them alphabet boys got us under surveillance (Ayy)
   (5) Like animals, they lock us in cages

(6) The same nigga that's a star when you put 'em on stages
(7) I ain't cheat, played the hand I was dealt
(8) Tried to tax the grand pearl when I got it myself
(9) (Let's get it) No nuts, no glory (no glory)
(10) My biography, you damn right, the true story (Yeah)
(11) Set the city on fire, and I didn't even try (try)
(12) Run these streets all day, I can sleep when I die (Ayy)

Jeezy also accentuates words by dragging out the vowel sound—for example, in the word "dreams" at the end of verse 2, line 3, "I guess we got the same dreams." This phrase is paired with line 4, "Or is it the same nightmares." The word "nightmares" is emphasized through repetition created by delay, a production technique rather than a vocal one. The pairing of "dreams" and "nightmares" through their emphasis draws the listener's attention to them. The meaning of these lines is best understood in the context of the preceding phrases, "Another day, another dolla / same block, same nigga, same part, same green," which suggest a reinterpretation of the "American dream." These men are trying to change their social situation and move beyond their class boundary through illegal ventures, which is how the dream becomes a nightmare. These lyrics typify the hustler persona that Young Jeezy embodies.

Another type of vocal emphasis employed by Young Jeezy is an upward or downward inflection at the end of a word. For example, the word "judge," at the end of verse 2, line 7, ends with a downward inflection. This draws attention to the line of text, which describes violence against a member of the judicial system, a typical narrative of reality rap. Similarly, lines 3–6 in the third verse end with an upward inflection. This segment of lyrics comments on the social positioning of the black male as both a thug and superstar, placed in the public eye for the purpose of white spectatorship. Ed Guerrero has discussed the prevalence of these two images of black masculinity in American media: "On the one hand, we are treated to the grand celebrity spectacle of black male athletes, movie stars, and pop entertainers doing what all celebrities are promoted as doing best, that is, conspicuously enjoying the wealth and privilege that fuel the ordinary citizen's material fantasies. Yet in simultaneous contrast to this steady stream of glamour and glitz . . . we are also subjected to the real-time devastation, slaughter, and body-count of a steady stream of faceless black males on the 6 and 11 o'clock news."[28] Hip-hop unifies these two images into a single picture of the black male superstar as thug. Young Jeezy clearly articulates this critique with the above lyrics, underscoring their importance through an upward vocal inflection that sounds both questioning and incredulous, thus challenging this social contradiction.

All of these forms of accentuation add to the intensity of Young Jeezy's vocal delivery, as well as to the rawness and, perhaps, the perceived "realness," of his sound. He expresses his emotional state and frustrations with his life through his vocal delivery in subtle ways. For example, his delivery of line 11 of verse 2, "If you get jammed up don't mention my name," sounds as if it is delivered through gritted teeth: the airflow is coming through a smaller space, and his pronunciation is less clear. The phrase almost comes out as a growl: he sounds angry and threatening. This is immediately contrasted with the following line, "Forgive me Lord, I know I ain't livin' right," which, due to the pitched inflection of certain words, such as "Lord," as well as longer rhythmic durations, is closer to a sung line than the majority of his phrases.[29]

The rough quality of Young Jeezy's voice is amplified through voice doubling. Both techniques of doubling discussed earlier, double-tracking and doubling echo (a minimal delay), are used in this song. For the most part, Jeezy's voice is centered in the mix, but at certain moments, the doubled voice is split-panned left and right, clearly revealing the two tracks. This process also gives the impression that the voice is coming at you from both sides, dominating the musical texture. An example of this panning can be heard during the chorus, as Young Jeezy interjects with "yeah."

As noted above, the contrast between Akon's and Jeezy's voices also emphasizes the roughness and grittiness of Jeezy's vocal timbre. In addition to the introduction and chorus, Akon is featured in the bridge (3:21). His voice is doubled in the bridge and a lower octave added, making his voice sound very thick, adding emphasis to his lyrics at this climactic moment. The lyrics of the bridge reinforce the criminal status of their personas ("you can find me on the street disobeyin' the law"), as well as their connection to the streets ("thoroughbred from the streets"). This particular moment is intensified by the opening up of Akon's vocal range and a more expressive melody, a series of ascending lines. It is not only the contrast of sections, from verse to chorus to bridge, that highlights the distinction between their voices, but also the contrast is present within the sections, as Jeezy continually interjects utterances while Akon is singing; sometimes these are short and clipped, and other times they are drawn out. For example, after the line "Cause I'm a rida" in the chorus, Jeezy says "yeah," leaning into the vowel sound, stretching it out, thus creating a strong emphasis. As is the case with all of the interjections, Jeezy's voice is low and rough and also doubled, intensifying the effect of heaviness or thickness.

In "Soul Survivor," Jeezy performs his race and masculinity through both lyric and vocal strategies. The song's lyrics describe the struggles of life in the hood, including getting caught up in a life of crime in order to survive. The lyrics depict the performative identity that Young Jeezy has constructed for himself of a thug or hustler, an identity reinforced by the artist's personal biography. Young Jeezy's performed persona as a tough, black man is also bolstered by musical elements, such as his rough, low-pitched, aggressive vocal quality, reinforced by double-tracking and by the contrast with Akon's smoother, sung vocal presentation. The meaning of the lyrics is reinforced by his various techniques of vocal emphasis, which include durational accentuation, diction, breath support, and pitch inflection. A reading of this song that combines interpretation of the lyrics and vocal delivery, as well as considering how the artist works within rap's conventions, helps us to better understand the meanings conveyed and how he constructs his identity.

Vocal performance is as important as lyrics and image for asserting one's maleness in the rap sphere. Attitude, aggression, hardness, and confidence are necessary traits for almost any rapper.[30] The best way for a rapper to display these traits is through a skilled delivery. Male rappers perform their masculinity in a variety of ways, and rappers have their own unique styles of delivery. Yet there are certain established conventions of masculinity, including rough vocal quality, verbal speed and prowess, and confidence. Ultimately, many aspects of performance contribute to a rapper's racial and gendered identity: persona, image, lyrics, musical background, and delivery.

This article has provided a brief exploration of how black masculinity is constructed in rap performance. Specifically, it offers perspectives on how gendered and raced meanings can be produced through musical techniques, as well as lyrics and image. In particular, I focused on the ways in which vocal techniques can contribute to the overall meaning and message of the lyrics. By following established musical conventions, rappers such as Young Jeezy reinforce the raced and gendered norms of the rap sphere. Mainstream rap conventions call for a particular version of black, urban masculinity in which men are dominant, powerful, and confident, and heterosexual norms are strictly maintained. The analytic techniques used in this case study of "Soul Survivor" are applicable to many other rap artists. The approaches to vocal practice, music-text relation, and the construction of raced and gendered identities can also be applied to other popular music styles and genres.

NOTES

1. For example, see Perry 2004, chapter 5, and Baldwin 2004.

2. Women's role in rap music is complex, and we must consider how women are depicted in the lyric and visual narratives of men's songs and music videos, as well as how female rappers choose to represent themselves. Due to rap's male exclusivity, constructions of female rappers' identities are intimately connected to conventions of masculinity. I will not delve into this issue in this paper, but I am currently working on a monograph that explores these gender roles in more detail. For further reading on female rappers, see Perry 2004, chapter 6; Pough 2004; Keyes 2002, chapter 7; and Rose 1994, chapter 5.

3. These masculine stereotypes are also present in various underground rap scenes, but there tends to be a wider variety of themes and images expressed in underground hip-hop than in the dominant culture of mainstream rap.

4. A distinction can be drawn between the hood and the ghetto based on socioeconomic factors. While the term "hood" is generally used to refer to an urban neighborhood, the term "ghetto" is used to describe an urban area of social and cultural segregation, driven primarily by economic factors.

5. Jeffrey Ogbar has discussed this phenomenon in Ogbar 2007, 26–27. A prime example of this mentality can be seen in the lyrical themes of 50 Cent's album *Get Rich or Die Trying*.

6. According to Jhally, the control over images of black masculinity primarily belongs to the white men who hold the majority of power in our current media empires.

7. In the film *Dreamworlds 3*, Jhally (2007) discusses the system of images present in rap videos. I extend this system of images to include all aspects of rap performance and promotion.

8. MCs who fall outside of these norms (for example, women, people of different ethnicities, homosexuals), must negotiate these conventions in their performances.

9. Weakness is associated with femaleness or homosexuality, which are gender and sexual identities that are positioned below male heterosexuality in rap's social hierarchy.

10. For example, rappers such as Missy Elliott, Lil' Kim, Eve, Trina, and Shawnna all assert a tough, aggressive persona; however, at other times, they display a more sensitive side, as in Missy's "Teary Eyed" (2005) and Eve's "Love is Blind" (1999).

11. Perry (2004) discusses these roles in chapter 5.

12. Gangsta rap is still political, but its driving force has become economic; the genre has been thoroughly incorporated into the mainstream, and its commercialization has somewhat softened its potential for political impact. The dominant themes that characterized gangsta rap at its inception are still being employed by current artists but within the context of the larger mainstream rap community.

13. For more on gangsta rap, see Dyson 1996 and Quinn 2005.

14. Krims 2000, 70. Krims has delineated a genre system for rap, including the genres of reality rap, mack rap, party rap, and jazz/bohemian rap.

15. For further discussion of Rick Ross, see Ogbar 2007, 26.

16. The term "flow" is used by those within the rap community, as well as by rap scholars. A definition of flow is given in Krims 2000, 15.

17. Krims 2000, 49–52. An important point that Krims addresses is the fact that many fans, MCs, and producers talk about flow and are aware of nuances between different artists, geographical locations, and time periods; however, there is not a commonly accepted vocabulary with which to discuss flows. As a result, the vocabulary that Krims develops is not one used by rap fans, artists, and producers.

18. These techniques are explored and analyzed in detail in Adams 2009.

19. Twista is short for "Tongue Twister," his MC name, which is representative of his fast-paced rhymes.

20. An example of such confidence is T. I.'s hit song "Whatever You Like" (2008), in which he seduces a woman by telling her that he can provide her with anything she could possibly desire.

21. My knowledge of voice doubling has been enhanced by conversations with James Law, sound technician at the University of Ottawa, School of Music.

22. *Thuggin' under the Influence* was released under the name Lil' J. *Come Shop wit' Me* was the first album Young Jeezy released using his current name; his birth

name is Jay Jenkins. For more information on Young Jeezy's early career as a local entrepreneur and MC in Atlanta, see Reid 2005 and Kellman 2008.

23. Biographical information on Young Jeezy, particularly with reference to his childhood, can be found in Thompson 2005.

24. Jeezy often uses the terms "gangsta" and "hustler" when addressing his peers and sometimes uses them interchangeably, conflating these two archetypes. For example, in the song "Gangsta Music," he states, "This is gangsta music," followed almost immediately by the phrase "This is hustler music" in the song's chorus.

25. Jeezy's hustler persona is demonstrated by the inclusion of songs such as "Hustlaz Ambition" and "Amazin'" on the album.

26. Akon is featured as a singer on tracks by Eminem, Bone Thugs and Harmony, Three 6 Mafia, Wyclef Jean, and Kardinal Offishall, just to name a few. Akon holds a unique position in the mainstream rap sphere because he has made a name for himself primarily as a hip-hop singer rather than an R&B or pop singer, who is simply featured on rappers' tracks.

27. Not all Southern rappers are associated with a slower speed of delivery, however—as a counterexample, Ludacris typically has a very fast-paced delivery.

28. Guerrero 1994, 183. Perry also discusses this issue, commenting on Guerrero's critique (2004, 121).

29. Here I am not referring to a "sung flow" as described by Krims but, rather, something that is much closer to the sustained pitches of a sung melodic line.

30. Many rappers also emphasize sexuality and seduction in their performance. A discussion of these vocal conventions is outside the scope of this paper but is part of my ongoing research.

DISCOGRAPHY

Boyz n da Hood. *Boyz n da Hood*. Bad Boy, 2005.
Elliott, Missy. *The Cookbook*. Atlantic, 2005.
Eve. *Ruff Ryders' First Lady*. Interscope, 1999.
50 Cent. *Get Rich or Die Trying*. Universal, 2003.
N.W.A. *Straight Outta Compton*. Priority Records B000003B6J, 1989.
Ross, Rick. *Port of Miami*. Universal, 2006.
T. I. *Paper Trail*. Atlantic, 2008.
Young Jeezy. *Come Shop wit' Me*. Corporate Thugz Entertainment, 2003.
Young Jeezy. *The Inspiration: Thug Motivation 102*. Def Jam, 2006.
Young Jeezy. *Let's Get It: Thug Motivation 101*. Def Jam, 2005.
Young Jeezy. *The Recession*. Def Jam, 2008.
Young Jeezy (Lil' J). *Thuggin under the Influence*. Corporate Thugz Entertainment, 2001.

REFERENCES

Adams, Kyle. 2009. On the metrical techniques of flow in rap music. *Music Theory Online* 15, no. 5.

Baldwin, Davarian L. 2004. Black empires, white desires. In *That's the joint! The hip-hop studies reader*, ed. Murray Forman and Mark Anthony Neal, 159–76. New York: Routledge.

Demers, Joanna. 2003. Sampling the 1970s in hip-hop. *Popular Music* 22, no. 1: 41–56.

Dyson, Michael Eric. 2006. *Between god and gangsta rap: Bearing witness to black culture*. New York: Oxford University Press.

Guererro, Ed. 1994. The black man on our screens and the empty space in representation. In *Black male: Representations of masculinity in contemporary American art*, ed. Thelma Golden and Jean-Michel Basquiet, 181–90. New York: Whitney Museum of American Art.

hooks, bell. 1994. Feminism inside: Toward a black body politic. In *Black male: Representations of masculinity in contemporary American art*, ed. Thelma Golden, 127–40. New York: Whitney Museum of American Art.

———.1995. Performance practice as a site of opposition. In *Let's get it on: The politics of black performance*, ed. Catherine Ugwu, 210–21. London: Institute of Contemporary Arts.

Hurt, Byron. 2006. *Beyond beats and rhymes*. Northampton, MA: Media Education Foundation.

Jhally, Sut. 2007. *Dreamworlds 3: Desire, Sex, and Power in Music Video*. Northampton, MA: Media Education Foundation.

Kellman, Andy. 2008. Young Jeezy biography. Allmusic. http://www.allmusic.com/cg/amg.dll?p=amg&sql=11:jxfixq9ald0e~T1.

Keyes, Cheryl L. 2002. *Rap music and street consciousness*. Urbana: University of Illinois Press.

Krims, Adam. 2000. *Rap music and the poetics of identity*. New York: Cambridge University Press.

Ogbar, Jeffrey O.G. 2007. *Hip-hop revolution: The culture and politics of rap*. Lawrence: University Press of Kansas.

Perry, Imani. 2004. *Prophets of the hood: Politics and poetics in hip hop*. Durham, NC: Duke University Press.

Pough, Gwendolyn D. 2004. *Check it while I wreck it: Black womanhood, hip-hop culture, and the public sphere*. Boston: Northeastern University Press.

Quinn, Eithne. 2005. *Nuthin' but a "G" thang: The culture and commerce of gangsta rap*. New York: Columbia University Press.

Reid, Shaheem. 2005. Young Jeezy. MTV News. http://www.mtv.com/news/yhif/young_jeezy.

Rose, Tricia. 1994. *Black noise: Rap music and black culture in contemporary America*. Hanover, NH: Wesleyan University Press.

Thompson, Bonsa. 2005. I'm a king. *XXL*. http://www.xxlmag.com/Features/2005/oct/jeezy/index.html.

15

Crunkology: Teaching the Southern Hip-Hop Aesthetic

Ali Colleen Neff

> Many underclass black people who do not know conventional aesthetic theoretical language are thinking critically about aesthetics. The richness of their thoughts is rarely documented in books. . . . We must not deny the way aesthetics serves as the foundation for emerging visions. It is, for some of us, critical space that inspires and encourages artistic endeavor.
>
> —bell hooks, *Yearning: Race, Gender, and Cultural Politics*, 112

Southern hip-hop, more a widespread stylistic practice than a specific musical genre, emerged in the popular consciousness in the early oughts, wrapped with layers of history, signified meaning, and heavy diamond pendants. Arising from the milieu of Southern black vernacular traditions and the vamps of global trends, crunk has, in the popular realm, become synonymous with overproduced, gimmicky commercial Southern rap productions even as it retains a dynamic and deeply signified set of meanings within its local contexts. Crunk draws from a deep well of Afro-diasporic vernacular traditions, including trickster tales, children's rhyming games, the blues, and collaborative improvisation, as well as from a shifting intercultural vocabulary. According to my own fieldwork in the Mississippi Delta and throughout the South, crunk is a subsonic bass line, a rocking dance, a call-and-response freestyle, a coordinated and clean outfit, a flat black car exterior, a "hard" aesthetic, a state of intoxication, or a trademarked energy drink. And although the crunk pop-cultural movement originated in a region young residents lovingly call the "Dirty South," it intersects with myriad global expressive forms and has in the last decade shape-shifted into trap music, jook and buck dancing, hyphy, underground techno, and screwed and chopped styles (these genres refer to regional youth dance and music movements in conversation with crunk from Atlanta, Memphis, Oakland, Baltimore, and Houston, respectively). Like most American popular music, crunk lyrics are devoted to a spectrum of feelings and actions, from family and dreams of mobility to the politics of sex and the law.

THE PROJECT

In 2007–08, the international popularity of Southern hip-hop was reaching a peak as my own research interests were emerging at a disciplinary and methodological crossroads. As a PhD student in cultural studies, I had the opportunity to assist in teaching courses in Southern music and the hip-hop aesthetic (under the mentorship of William R. Ferris and Mark Anthony Neal, respectively) before taking on my first independently taught cultural-studies course. Inspired by bell hooks's exploration of the intellectual work of black cultural practitioners in her book *Yearning: Race, Gender, and Cultural Politics*, I sought to engage the creative work—lyrical, material, performative, aesthetic, conversational, sermonic—of hip-hop artists and their surrounding communities as intellectual texts, posed in conversation with academic discourses and pop criticism (hooks 1990). The crunk cultural movement formed around a musical core and offered a complex object of cultural study. To develop this first undergraduate course in hip-hop studies at my Southern university, I invested my graduate coursework in critical pedagogy in assembling a syllabus for an upper-level undergraduate class in contemporary hip-hop, which was offered in fall 2008 as Crunkology: The Southern Hip-Hop Aesthetic, a special-topics section of an upper-level communications-studies media and culture cluster. I drew from my experience as a hip-hop turntablist and music critic to consider a variety of multimedia resources, including classic hip-hop albums, blues documentaries, and popular-music magazines, as well as from my own ethnographic research. In the complexities of this music and its decade-long movement through the popular milieu, I found an opportunity to bring together critical questions in the relationship of the musical elements of sound, lyrics, dance, and production to social and political movements under the rubric of the shape-shifting, complex, and phenomenally popular body of work put forward by young music artists of the American South.

Anchored in the heavy bass and forceful lyrics of crunk, our course materials connected musical practices and unfolding hip-hop discourses to recent media events. For instance, the congressional hearings on hip-hop lyrics (*From Imus to Industry: The Business of Stereotypes and Degrading Images*) in the spring of 2007 represented the (re)eruption of discourses surrounding love and theft, blame and pity, and naturalized xenophobia that trouble the relationships between mainstream misunderstandings of African American culture and emergent black creativities. After sports announcer Don Imus, in the course of announcing a Rutgers women's basketball game, labeled team members a group of "nappy-headed hos," Imus defended his gratuitous and violent language as a harmless parroting of hip-hop slang for black women's bodies. His camp pointed a finger at Southern hip-hop as the cause of his racist and sexist remarks about women athletes of color as the popular media called a series of black rappers to defend their art in reference to Imus's comments (David Carr, "Networks Condemn Remarks by Imus," *New York Times*, April 7, 2007). This swift defense deflected attention from the degrading nature of everyday popular speech toward a series of black hip-hop artists, who, in fact, had no involvement in Imus's transgression. The music made an easy target. Immediately, the world of popular music was invoked in the debates as talk show hosts, talking heads, and congressional representatives called dozens of black, male hip-hop artists to the stand (women were largely excluded from the conversation). For crunk artist David Banner of Jackson, Mississippi, the overwhelming media attention to the decontextualized verbal texts of his songs failed to engage the rich textures of his art and that of his peers. "Have you ever *listened* to my music?" the artist asked his inquisitors at the hearings. "I call my music a bible with a Playboy cover." Banner insisted that, in critically engaging the ugly lexicons of American classism, sexism, and racism, his own self-described "horror music" conceals a series of communicative tools by which young, black Southern people can recognize and effect change upon their own precarious socioeconomic circumstances. Meanwhile, Banner's music pumps from the trunks of thousands of young people in Mississippi as it forges an aesthetic space for community action and personal contemplation. Banner's lyrics, enmeshed in the surging bass of his chosen genre, address his home state's legacies of racial violence, soaring poverty, and spiritual devotion even as they encourage listeners to shake the Saturday-night dance floor.

Although upon engaged listening, the verbal texts of crunk can themselves reveal a wealth of cultural understanding, the aesthetic textures of the music also provide a critical space for other kinds of signifying (voice, rhythm, dance, visual aesthetics), and the incorporation of traditional cultural elements complicate and negotiate the music's surface meanings. Banner's use of an acoustic blues guitar sample from the Delta, for instance, or the use of earth-shaking bass registers to signify the mobility enabled by car ownership offer significant critiques of the socio-aesthetic status quo. By introducing the concept of signifying practices into media and cultural studies via the complexities of emergent musical movements, we unpack the slippages in encoding and decoding described by Stuart Hall at the outset of the Birmingham school project, which was foundational to the contemporary formation of the discipline of cultural studies: "The meaning of a cultural form and its place or position in the cultural field is not inscribed inside its form. Nor is its position fixed once and forever. . . . The meaning of a cultural symbol is given in part by the social field into which it is incorporated, the practices with which it articulates and is made to resonate" (Hall 1981, 235).

Popular music represents an important cultural field through which we can begin to answer Hall's call for deep contextualization in cultural studies. The introduction of diaspora studies, folklore, popular music, and race and gender studies in the form of blues and diaspora scholarship to college curricula in the 1960s and 1970s opened up critical space for the presence of unconventional ways of knowing in the college classroom (to echo the bell hooks quote that begins this chapter). Just as blues and jazz curricula allowed the discourses of black aesthetics to influence the intellectual life of the post-Vietnam War academy, the reemergence of hip-hop into the mainstream offers contemporary scholars the opportunity to do critical work at the intersections of race, gender, sexuality, and the complicated formations of class that result from the confluence of region, family history, the prison-industrial complex, vocational castes, and education in the "Dirty South." Work on crunk music can be done in continuity with rich literatures on the blues and black aesthetics—from Angela Davis and Amiri Baraka to Mark Anthony Neal and Albert Murray—that are largely neglected in the contemporary cultural-studies classroom. Rather than attempt to juxtapose cultural studies and music in the classroom as an alternative to media studies, we recognize and explore the historical enmeshment of culture and media with musical practices.

Popular music, particularly in its underground and subaltern strains, offers an under-examined complex of understandings—bodily, intellectual, traditional, emergent, sublime—that can radically speak across boundaries of difference. Because academic work is so often focused on verbal or visual texts, the ambivalent, conflicting, and hidden meanings that infuse musical aesthetics are habitually overlooked in the classroom, and the performative use of burlesque, satire, circumlocution, sensory communication, signifying, and strategic (mis)representation become analytically flattened. Loved or hated but never ignored, the dynamic cultural practices that converge in the space of Southern hip-hop are undeniably powerful. In taking the music seriously, we came to understand the richness of the critical aesthetic discourses that are taking place both across the surface of the social landscape and in its "Dirty Southern" underground. Further, we challenged ourselves to imagine how new movements in popular music hold political weight through their verbal, performative, and aesthetic engagement with critical cultural discourses.

CRUNKOLOGY: THE COURSE

Above all, the crunkology course focused on the music-in-context: the rich aesthetic practices that infuse the everyday lives of young people in the contemporary "Dirty South" and beyond. In practice, we sought to expand the frame of academic popular-music studies (which are often heavily biased toward linear rock-history classes) and engage Southern hip-hop in its intertextual richness, using multidisciplinary tools to excavate its cultural meanings and practices. As we unpacked the complex power relations that run through hip-hop practice and representation, we deepened our understandings of the cultural discourses present in everyday life by tuning into the intellectual work of cultural practitioners beyond the academy. Thanks to the popularity of the musical subject matter with college students and their generational peers, we found further analytical complexity in mining students' personal engagements with the musical movement, whether close, distant, or ambivalent. For the second half of the semester, the students had the opportunity to choose texts and topics for class discussion. The favorite videos, magazine criticisms, and personal hip-hop recordings my undergraduates introduced demonstrate the velocity with which popular music moves in global contexts even as it articulates to particular scenes and genres. Further, the emergence of discourses in the realm of Southern hip-hop over the course of the semester (such as the sudden popularity of gender-queer, retro Tampa booty-bass act Yo! Majesty or the appearance of a series of Southern rap songs praising candidate Obama) allowed us to think about the contingency of genre and the "changing same" of popular signs, symbols, and sounds. Through this attention to the ever-moving discourses constituted by and constitutive of popular music, we reconceptualized our social world both in terms of its persistent structural inequalities and as a set of transformative cultural practices that are persistently countered, negotiated, and put into disequilibrium by the creative work of Southern hip-hop artists. In contextualizing the emergence of new genres in their cultural contexts, we recognized music's subterranean political features as such.

Even as musical pedagogues continue to search desperately for ways to speak past hegemonic understandings in the academy, crunk artists advocate for their communities, redistribute resources, and create radical social space through their art. Southern hip-hop is a vital object of study for upper-level popular music, folklore, cultural studies, and media undergraduates and offers an ideal space for interdisciplinary work and performative class projects. The centrality of questions of race and representation to the crunk genre pushed the students to analyze the complexities of difference through which they turn to the rich body of black aesthetic literature. The overall arc of this class involved a movement from basic themes and engagements with the crunk/pop formation to more complex, dialectic understandings of black-Atlantic aesthetic practice. We explored the communities that comprise the heavily signified "Dirty South," using this subaltern national term itself to illuminate the complexities of musical genre and the ways in which musical practitioners organize their work. We examined the ruptures between crunk aesthetic practices and their representations in the media in order to problematize the binaries (mind/body, insider/outsider, positive/negative, etc.) that often occlude mainstream understandings of what the music *does*.

The course also allowed for a series of guest lecturers and media showings, which explored the many issues that intersect in the emergence of a new musical scene. Collaboration with my faculty advisors and intellectual mentors was key to the success of my implementation of the course, and Neal and Ferris were able to connect their own work in black-Atlantic music to the issues surrounding crunk in a series of guest lectures, which also included Mississippi Delta hip-hop artist Jerome "TopNotch the Villain" Williams and Piedmont blues artist James "Boo" Hanks. Our department generously placed our class in the basement theatre of the media studies building so that our in-class musical examples could find their fullest performative volume.

Challenges

My own investment in hip-hop pedagogy comes from both my interest in teaching a popular music with a focus on its intersecting culture and my desire to intervene in the exclusion of unconventional, everyday, and community-based intellectual work from the academy. As a longtime hip-hop fan and practitioner, I am committed to representing the music at its most powerful and to making legible the importance of underground aesthetic practices to social discourse. In her work on critical pedagogy, Cheryl Johnson illustrates the ways in which students may immediately identify instructors in terms of our most apparent subject positionalities, judging accordingly with which kinds of expertise we can and cannot speak (Johnson 1994). The object of multicultural education is to move beyond the standpoints of race/class/gender subjectivities and into the liminal spaces of experimentation and collaboration. My experience as a 30-something, Midwestern, white woman with a longstanding involvement in the world of hip-hop allowed me to use my own subjectivity to foreground the complexity of Southern hip-hop as an intellectual and affective engagement by exploring the question of how music both dissolves and makes anew concepts of group, style, and self. The multifaceted nature of hip-hop and its diverse practitioners allows students to question the discourses that locate young black artists as distinct and "different" subjects within a singular "authentic" hip-hop identity that can be accessed by outsiders who perform the right kind of "cool." Instead of assuming a series of static hip-hop subjectivities, we ask how and why this music is created by—and resonates with—a wide series of publics and contexts.

Drawing from contemporary work in critical pedagogy, we employed an intertextual, poly-vocal, and performative approach to learning that mirrors Southern hip-hop as an object of study. As a classroom alternative to a linear dialogic approach in which variegated voices alternate between viewpoints, Linda Flower (2003) proposes a transformative approach, a collaborative tapestry of dynamic understandings. Our own subjectivities became teachable and performative elements in the course as we considered the rich field of Southern hip-hop fans and practitioners. We consider the possibility that my undergraduate students, poised at the threshold of the world of professional work and self-presentation, may become preoccupied with their own visible subjectivities, such as race and gender, and those of their classmates, in reference to course discussions and materials. The heightened affective atmosphere raised by coursework on difference and inequality—elements that are omnipresent in the world of popular music—provide a rich and productively uncomfortable setting in the classroom. Crunkology, on its surface a radical departure from established academic topics, brings to light a series of oblique and unexamined representations of emergent black-Atlantic expressive culture that line social science and humanities curricula. It is a space of performance and play in which students can try on critiques and rhetorical stances rather than root themselves in the omnipresent liberal/conservative divide. Much of the music's power comes from its complex negotiations with sensitive issues. The major lyrical and aesthetic themes of Southern hip-hop involve capital redistribution, financial desires, love and sex, radical leisure and aesthetics, self-representation, and "Dirty Southern" nationalism; these work directly and indirectly on the deepest and most political ruptures in global capitalist modernity. The lyrical tropes of race, gender, and violence that simultaneously appeal to and disgust some listeners are only part of the story, but they remain difficult issues to work through and justly so.

In my experience with the course, our most challenging moments were those in which my students and I clearly experienced the perpetuation of damaging sexist, violent, materialistic, or other negative stereotypes in hip-hop performance even as we unpacked them. We began our engagement with these materials by contextualizing these hip-hop performances within larger structures of dominance, inequality, and violence articulated throughout popular culture. Because I teach at a public university in the South, most of my students had grown up with this music and shared linguistic, socioeconomic, generational, and stylistic contexts with the artists we studied in the class. Together, we remained aware that as rappers, DJs,

dancers, viewers, concertgoers, critics, and fans, we ourselves participate in
the construction of Southern hip-hop and that our critical work had the
potential not only to act upon common-sense understandings of the music
but also to push boundaries and present performative challenges to the
cultures that surround crunk. We considered ourselves not as critics outside
of the cultural field but as practitioners within it and entertained the idea
that even in our best-informed critical representations, we simultaneously
participate in the perpetuation of certain elements of the social status quo.
Our best work arose from these complex and difficult considerations.

Coursework

For this course, students kept weekly blog entries, linked to the course
website via their own name or a self-created pen name. They were expected
to show knowledge of course terminology and concepts in their thinking
and writing for the blogs (as well as on the midterm and final exams).
Rather than *project* certain "readings" onto their object(s) of study, students
were asked to *pose questions* about what the artist might be signifying and
why, as they drew from classic texts on black aesthetics, record reviews, in-
class lectures, and recordings as critical resources. Students were encouraged
to suggest interpretive possibilities rather than decode "true" meanings as
they explored what kind of work the art of crunk, and the diverse cultural
practices that converge within it, does in terms of its action upon the social
domain. By sharing their blogs, students were able to exchange insights and
challenges in their critical thinking on race, gender, regionalism, and the
idea of the popular. Students might unpack the essentialisms involved in
the construction of stereotypical authenticity as it intersects with hip-hop's
ambivalent call to "keep it real" through a blog assignment concerning
the construction of hip-hop's "ATL" in relationship to the city of Atlanta.
Through the public project of culture blogging, students came to recognize
their own cultural performances outside of the classroom as a series of
engagements with critical public discourses in conversation with their studies. Blogs were evaluated according to their critical engagement with course
keywords and issues and students were encouraged to experiment with the
conventional academic writing style. Some students chose to retain the
academic or analytical voices with which they were most comfortable; others patterned their writing on the musical, poetic, narrative, or other styles
drawn from their extracurricular interests and creative communities.

The final essay for the course involved students' making a mix-tape com-
pilation of songs tracing a particular discourse through Southern hip-hop
and its related genres, accompanied by an essay describing the themes involved in their choices. These ranged from studies of blues samples in popular crunk songs to the arc of auto-tune technologies and the rise of New
Orleans "sissy rap." At the close of the course, student evaluations were

overwhelmingly positive and highlighted the value of working through difficult issues in critical cultural studies by focusing on the complexity and multivalence of the subject matter.

Key Questions for the Study of Musical Culture

Our crunkology course successfully drew from the power of an emerging musical movement to gain critical access to deeper currents of difference, inequality, creativity, and aesthetics that line cultural studies of popular music. My upper-level undergraduate students celebrated the opportunity to bring the aesthetic and poetic world of popular hip-hop into conversation with their intellectual work in the classroom. Ultimately, we found that these artistic and critical worlds are deeply enmeshed for the practitioners, fans, and communities that intersect in crunk practices. According to my students, the opportunity to engage everyday life and popular movements was invaluable. One of my students, a major in psychology, is using our coursework to develop performance therapies for at-risk youth; another has designed a high-school curriculum focused on issues in Southern hip-hop. A third student, now graduated, is making a career in the hip-hop music industry and uses our critical work in the course to foster community outreach for her record label. Two students have applied to graduate programs in cultural studies, for which they will further explore questions of race and/or gender representation in black popular culture. Another has shown early success as a music producer.

Although the international-market popularity of Southern hip-hop has waned considerably in the past 18 months, a series of key questions for the study of musical movements-in-cultural-context undergirded our work in crunkology and offer a foundation for new courses in emerging popular musics. These include:

- Who identifies and defines any particular musical genre or scene? How is the commercial genre definition accepted or contested by creative communities, practitioners, or fans?
- Who counts as a practitioner, collaborator, and/or distributor of any particular musical genre? Who consumes the music and through what channels?
- What other social, political, and cultural movements intersect in the emergence of this musical genre?
- What kinds of gendered, youth, queer, or other minority participation is involved in a particular musical scene? Are there unseen communities or practitioners at the sites of the music's creation, origin, and practice?
- What are some of the key subjectivities (class, region, race, gender, age, religion) that are central to popular understandings of a particular

genre? How are these subjectivities recreated and/or complicated by the practitioners themselves?

- What are possible correspondences or disconnections between what musical artists mean to say (through their aesthetic, poetry, style, and performance) and popular interpretations of what they mean?
- How are the emergence and spread of this genre historicized in the popular media, and how do these narratives compare to those of the artists themselves?
- What kinds of cultural sampling, intermixing, fusion, and syncretizing contribute to the singularity of this genre?
- How is the mass-cultural narrative of this genre or scene similar to or different from the trajectory of other musical genres?
- How can we use our understanding of this genre to imagine new movements in popular music?
- How might an understanding of the contextualizing questions above help us to reimagine and mine the complexity of particular musical artists, albums, and performances?

The deeply contextual study of musical movements allows students to bring their affective, creative, and community involvements into conversation with their intellectual work in the academy. By taking the music seriously, students were both able to engage musicians and producers as unconventional intellectuals and to understand their own intellectual work in terms of its extension beyond the classroom. Undergraduate students, poised at the intersection of youth culture and intellectual maturity, find exciting critical possibilities as they explore the questions of what the music does, for whom, and what kinds of possibilities it holds.

SYLLABUS EXCERPT AND SAMPLE LESSON PLANS

The brief description below outlines the basic research questions and objectives of the course. The lesson plans that follow, excerpted from the syllabus and annotated in italics, deal with the critical framing of the course through the first week of class meetings: the delineation of the object of study, the establishment of my own pedagogical performance and the classroom community, the foundations of a basic vocabulary for unpacking Southern hip-hop, and a modeling of course discussion styles that will facilitate complex and nuanced conversations later in the course. They can also be used as a short unit on Southern hip-hop for an upper-level popular music, cultural studies, or media studies course or adapted to an area-studies course in American or Southern cultural or literary studies.

SYLLABUS EXCERPT FOR CRUNKOLOGY: THE SOUTHERN HIP-HOP AESTHETIC

COURSE DESCRIPTION

In this course, we will use critical keywords and concepts in cultural studies to unpack the global Southern hip-hop phenomenon in order to better understand how "underground" communities of practice engage the popular market. In doing so, we will also imagine what new cultural movements, inspired by the success of artists from the "Dirty South," are on the global horizon. We will ask what makes this music so powerful and what this power says about communities that are often misrepresented in the popular media.

COURSE OBJECTIVES

Students will be able to:

- Understand the complex of meaning inherent in Southern hip-hop practice
- Be able to apply Michael Eric Dyson's concept of cultural complexity to Southern hip-hop
- Be able to identify and describe the texts and contexts of a given performance
- Allow for possibilities of meaning in Southern hip-hop rather than provide "translations"
- Think critically about how we approach everyday cultural representations
- Further develop a public critical writing voice
- Identify intellectual discourses taking place outside of the academy and engage these discourses in their academic work
- Have a grounding in the history of Southern and diasporic oral-musical practices
- Grasp unit keywords
- Be able to discuss challenging issues in the representations of difference in Southern hip-hop
- Be able to critically unpack a Southern hip-hop album, artist, and/or song

BLOGS

You will be chronicling your work through course blogs and will have an entry due each week to comprise the bulk of your course grade for written work. You will set up a blogger account as your personal course blog, linked into this course homepage (www.blogger.com). You will either write under your own or a self-chosen "pen name" and develop a blog on Southern hip-hop, which you will maintain weekly throughout the duration of this course. You can write on any element of

(continued)

SYLLABUS EXCERPT FOR CRUNKOLOGY:
THE SOUTHERN HIP-HOP AESTHETIC (*continued*)

the Southern hip-hop aesthetic you like—including its non-Southern variants—but you must engage our course key concepts, discussions, and materials for the week. Each entry should be 300–400 words long. You may also publish extra posts if you like. I will know (and keep confidential, if you prefer) whose blog is whose and hand out a schedule for blog-entry due dates on our first day of class. You will learn to perform public cultural criticism: to learn how to critically unpack culture and to communicate your work to a wider audience. Weekly blog assignments will be posted on our course website. A major goal of this assignment is to help you develop a public critical writing voice.

CLASS 1: MAPPING THE PROJECT

Today, we'll introduce ourselves to each other and talk about our plans for the course. Please be prepared to share your experience with crunk, your interests in studying the topic, and how these studies might fit into your future plans. I'll give a brief overview of how we will frame our study of crunk this semester and what my expectations are in terms of your participation and coursework. We'll also work together to trace some of the themes in Goodie Mob's 1996 song "Soul Food," connecting them to our work for this semester.

Critical Issues:

What brings us into this conversation?
What is our object of study? Crunk, hip-hop, the "Dirty South"?
What is our project in this course?
What does it mean to study "the popular"?
How does this tie into our work in the academy?
What tools will we use for our analysis?

Required Readings and Media:

Rubin Whitmore II (Director): Goodie Mob, "Soul Food" Video
(Lyrics to song distributed in class and available through course website)
As you listen to the song and read the lyrics, pay attention to what elements stand out most to you. Is it the overall story? A particular verse? The samples and voices? The personalities of the rappers themselves? The visuals in the video?

Recommended Readings and Media:

Cheryl L. Keyes, "At the Crossroads: Rap Music and its African Nexus," *Ethnomusicology* 40, no. 2 (1996): 223–48.

Class proceedings: I will introduce the class by playing the Goodie Mob video for "Soul Food" and handing out lyric sheets for the students to follow along. Because the course is grounded in the music of the South, I will offer a song that, in its warm sample, distinctive voices, and confessional lyrics, illustrates the affective depth of the crunk aesthetic. When the song ends, I'll introduce myself, my research, and experience to the class. I will then ask students to introduce themselves to the rest of the class but to frame their introductions in terms of their interest in the subject matter rather than the usual trope of name, year, and major.

I will then explain how this class came about and offer my vision of the course as a think tank for intellectual work on a genre so often represented as anti-intellectual. I'll briefly connect our coursework to emerging themes in the fields of communication, media, performance, and cultural studies as well as contemporary public discourses. I'll discuss the syllabus and the assignment structure, emphasizing the importance of class attendance and discussion. I'll also explain how students can use the syllabus to map their intellectual work, engaging the keywords and concepts and critical questions for each week as they work through the reading materials and media. We'll spend the last few minutes of class sharing our thoughts and experiences with Goodie Mob's song. How does it fit into what we think of crunk? What are some popular perceptions of the music?

CLASS 2: FRAMING THE DIALOGUE

We'll move into talking about some of the "common sense" understandings of Southern hip-hop and consider alternative approaches to unpacking hip-hop practice, specifically by attending to our affective involvement with the music and the critical methodologies that we will develop throughout this course. We'll reference the writing of 19-year-old female crunk artist Kimyata Dear and critical hip-hop discourses outlined by Greg Tate and discuss the representations and negotiations we see in the video of the 2007 congressional Imus hearings. We'll frame our discourse and dialogue for this semester by addressing the fact that we are dealing with challenging issues, language, and social realities in this course. We will consider the ways in which we can work through these issues in partnership with our classmates and engage uncomfortable material and discussions through constructive criticism, critical thinking, and intellectual generosity. Rather than arguing rhetorically from stances with which we agree or disagree, we will think about ways to collaboratively contextualize and complicate our course materials. We'll talk about how we can represent and work through these issues outside the classroom as well.

Critical Issues:

How can we talk about uncomfortable or charged issues in this course?
What does "common sense" say about crunk?

(continued)

SYLLABUS EXCERPT FOR CRUNKOLOGY: THE SOUTHERN HIP-HOP AESTHETIC (*continued*)

What can be gained by using critical analytical tools? By tuning into our affective engagements with the music?
Who are we as students and as people-in-the-world?
What kinds of participation in Southern hip-hop do we practice?
How do we present work that includes critical reflection and our affective involvement?
Ways of knowing: affect and intellect in partnership

Required Readings and Media:

Greg Tate, "Hiphop Turns 30: Whatcha celebratin' for?" *Village Voice*, December 28, 2004.
Yata Dear, "About Yata" (unpublished personal essay on course website).
  Congressional Hearings on Hip-Hop in response to Don Imus: Testimony by Dyson, Banner, and Masta P (videos available online as produced by Dan Manatt at www.politicstv.com, September 27, 2007).
  As you read or experience these materials, please note what aspects of hip-hop are at play in each representation and which are not emphasized.

Recommended Readings and Media:

Linda Flower, "Talking across Difference: Intercultural Rhetoric and the Search for Situated Knowledge," *College Composition and Communication* 55, no. 1 (September 2003): 38–68.
  Class proceedings: Students will be familiar with the critical questions for this class session through our course website. I'll start class at the board, asking students to list the popular perceptions or "common sense" understandings of Southern hip-hop. I'll then begin a second list, asking students to suggest alternative representations that arise in our assigned readings and media materials for the day. I will illustrate the value of Michael Eric Dyson's use of rhetorical criticism (communication-studies students should be familiar with this) and Tate's use of journalistic cultural criticism to illuminate hip-hop understandings. We'll talk about the characteristics of crunk aesthetics (hard, horror) and affects (creativity, enjoyment) as described by David Banner and Kimyata Dear and the importance of affect to our conversation. This part of the lesson is geared toward opening up some of the critical issues in crunkology and allows students to begin to speak about issues in Southern hip-hop in the classroom space without asking them to take larger public analytical risks in our earliest conversations.
  I'll use David Banner's description of signified crunk "performativity" as "horror music" to move into questions of how we will address "horror topics" in this class. With Flower's description of situated knowledge and intellectual collaboration in mind, I'll explain that I myself have difficulty in knowing how to deal with some

of these controversial issues in class and that this discomfort and uncertainty is part of what makes the music so powerful (referring back to Dyson). I'll explain that the most successful discussions of these topics are ones that trouble rhetorical binaries and engage culture in its complexity. I'll ask students to regard their own work in this class and that of their classmates as a process of working through these complexities in order to find new ones and describe the work of intellectual generosity in the classroom, regarding the ruptures between our own understandings and those of our peers as an opportunity for inquiry, contextualization, and collaboration. I'll also invite students to meet with me anytime to speak about any of these issues in confidence.

I have chosen these relatively short reading and viewing materials as samples of contemporary discourses on Southern hip-hop that can reasonably be studied during the first week of school. Tate's piece offers a nuanced and personal engagement with current conversations about the future of the hip-hop genre, while Yata writes as a practitioner for whom crunk provides a critical space for aesthetic practice and self-representation. The 10-minute segment of the congressional hearings on the Imus controversy (which became an institutional conversation on the possibility of banning artists from using certain words in their music) features Michael Eric Dyson speaking on the importance of understanding artistic complexity over value judgments and David Banner describing his perceptions of the power of his own music.

CLASS 3: BRIDGING THE GAPS

Today, we will begin to outline our object of study. We'll talk first about the sounds and styles we associate with crunk music and Southern hip-hop more generally and then think about what practices are involved in crunk creativity. We'll talk about the "Dirty South" as a self-defined diasporic nation and develop a basic vocabulary for talking about the importance of crunk styles and practices in wider global cultural trends. We'll talk about what Dyson's speech before Congress means: for a piece of art to be complex rather than positive or negative. We'll then extend the blurring of that binary to consider the other binaries that come into play in "common sense" understandings of crunk music, practitioners, and style.

Critical Issues:

   Centering the "Dirty South"
   Positive/Negative/Complex (Dyson)
   Highbrow/Lowbrow/Popular
   Inside/Outside/Creativity
   Mind/Body/Voice
   Tradition/Product/Practice
   Representations

(continued)

**SYLLABUS EXCERPT FOR CRUNKOLOGY:
THE SOUTHERN HIP-HOP AESTHETIC (*continued*)**

Required Readings and Media:

W. E. B. Du Bois, "Of Beauty and Death," Chapter 9 in *Darkwater: Voices from within the Veil.*

Recommended Readings and Media:

Raymond Williams, *Keywords: A Vocabulary of Culture and Society,* definitions of "culture" and "the popular."
Richard Wright, "How 'Bigger' was Born" (1940).

Class proceedings: I will begin the class by asking students to list similarities and differences between the "South" and the "Dirty South," writing responses on the board as we go. Rather than counterpose the "Dirty South" in a binary opposition with the South, I will illustrate its self-representation (I'll address the idea of representation here) as a diasporic space of complexity, where Du Bois's beauty and death are engaged in critical conversation. I'll explain that crunk music is created for popular listeners as well as local audiences and ask students to keep in mind the idea that crunk practitioners position themselves on the boundaries between the binaries. I'll work through the binaries listed above, one by one, writing the list out on the board as I explain how these concepts undergird crunk practice.

I will then explain to students why I chose Du Bois's essay to open our conversation about crunk aesthetics. Referring to Dyson's paradigm of complexity, I'll talk about Du Bois's use of the repulsive, the ugly, and the horrible to make meaningful art. Students will be invited to share their own thoughts on the possible connections between Du Bois's description of black verbal art in the age of Jim Crow and contemporary crunk formations (including Goodie Mob's song from the first class). By framing our object of study in terms of its continuities with other black intellectual and artistic movements, I will set the tone for the remainder of our coursework.

ANNOTATED COURSE REFERENCES

Literary Sources

Alexander, Bryant K. 2005. Embracing the teachable moment: The black gay body in the classroom as embodied text. In *Black queer studies,* ed. E. Patrick Johnson and Mae Henderson, 249–65. Durham, NC: Duke University Press.

This piece offers insight into how we as teachers might recognize our bodily presence as a classroom text, an invitation to pedagogical performativity and contextualization that I can use to illustrate difficult issues in crunk subjectivities and representation (recognizing my pedagogical subjectivity as a white, female, middle-class hip-hop DJ and fan, while entertaining the complexity of polyvalent investments in the social).

Asante, Molefi Kete. 1987. African American orature and context. In *The Afrocentric idea*, 83–95. Philadelphia: Temple University Press.
   Asante introduces the concept of *nommo* or the Afro-diasporic power of the word through which transcendence and power are created from below.

Baldwin, Davarian. 2004. Black empires, white desires: The spatial politics of identity in an age of hip-hop. In *That's the joint! A hip-hop studies reader*, ed. Murray Forman and Mark Anthony Neal, 159–176. New York: Routledge.
   This piece addresses questions of consumption and the hip-hop gangsta's redistribution of wealth and offers an excellent contextualization for the work of David Banner.

Bobo, Jacqueline. 1995. *Black women as cultural readers*. New York: Columbia University Press.
   Selections from this book help students to imagine a series of interpretive communities (beyond the more visual/vocal MTV/BET consumers) as the audience for Southern hip-hop. Particularly, Bobo's work helps us to better understand black women as deeply engaged participants in the world of Southern literature and hip-hop, whose critiques of its styles and lyrics come from a deep investment in its artistic and cultural possibilities.

Bourdieu, Pierre. 2007. *Outline of a theory of practice*. Cambridge: Cambridge University Press.
   Bourdieu brings Marxist structuralism and rich ethnographic understandings of expressive culture together in his development of a language of practice. I will frame this course primarily in terms of crunk aesthetic practices rather than its objects or products.

Cobb, William Jelani. 2008. The New South's capital likes to contradict itself. *Washington Post*, July 13.
   This news feature explores the contradictory narratives of Atlanta both as capital of the Antebellum Old South and the hip-hop loving New South of Crunk.

Dear, Yata. "About Yata."
   This is a short biographical piece of writing from one of my main consultants in the Mississippi Delta, 19-year-old rap artist Kimyata "Yata" Dear. Yata is a member of DA F.A.M. (For all Mississippi), a crunk outfit of five young people in Clarksdale. Yata is the only female member of the group, and she uses her time behind the mic to represent the experiences of young women in the Deep South. For Yata, who has survived very difficult circumstances and became a mother just after her 18th birthday, hip-hop is a creative medium for her hopes and dreams, for representations of herself and her community, and a place where she can express the challenges of being a woman and a mother in an economically ravaged region: "Yata is a part of me that's able to speak on life in a creative way, which people would not only understand but they are able to rock, feel, hear, enjoy and want to hear more about how I feel on certain situations of life." Not only are women's voices rarely heard in popular representations of hip-hop, few women

are able to achieve wide recognition as performing artists. Meanwhile, thousands of women and girls write and record rhymes independently.

Du Bois, W. E. B. 1920. Of beauty and death. In *Darkwater: Voices from within the veil*, 130–44. New York: Harcourt, Brace, and Howe. Repr., New York: Schocken Books, 1969.

This piece offers an ideal starting point for our discussion of the aesthetics, complexities, and power of Southern hip-hop. Du Bois's discussions of beauty and death here illustrate Dyson's call for complex artistic work. Du Bois illustrates how the affective ambiguities of Jim Crow life can only be fully illustrated through the aesthetic power of the word. Further, Du Bois makes plain the fallacies behind mainstream rejection of the ugly: "So strong is the spell of beauty that there are those who, contradicting their own knowledge and experience, try to say that all is beauty. They are called optimists, and they lie." DuBois connects the sensory power of ugliness to the negotiations of the Jim Crow system, in which beauty can never be fulfilled.

This piece is critical to getting students used to thinking beyond genre at the outset of the class. Students also have an opportunity to understand Du Bois's own use of ugliness as an expressive practice to negotiate the realities of life in the segregated South. Students will be asked to make connections between Du Bois's message and use of poetic style and those of Southern hip-hop artists in order to illustrate the continuities of the "Dirty South" and other diasporic traditions of the word. Further, Du Bois's piece describes the traps of binary thinking and engages the key dialectic concepts of positive/negative/complex, highbrow/lowbrow/popular, inside/outside/creativity, mind/body/voice. I will highlight the sensory elements of this piece as an engagement with aesthetic subject matter.

Durham, Meenakshi Gigi, and Douglas Kellner. 2005. *Media and cultural studies: KeyWorks.* 2nd ed. Boston: Blackwell.

This media and cultural studies reader provides a foundation for connecting Southern hip-hop practices and contemporary theories in media studies.

Dyson, Michael Eric. 2003. *Open Mike: Reflections on philosophy, race, sex, culture, and religion.* New York: Basic Civitas Books.

Dyson's discussion of "gangsta" rap and American culture as a complex set of cultural practices here remains largely unexplored in contemporary hip-hop research. Dyson's gangsta rappers are artists with agency who negotiate—sometime successfully, other times less so—the structures of inequality.

Ferris, William R. 1979. *Blues from the Delta.* Garden City, NY: Anchor.

Ferris' extensive ethnographic work in the worlds of the Mississippi and Memphis blues throughout the 1960s and 1970s illustrates the traditional enmeshment of blues song with radio announcing, spoken-word poetry, children's song, gospel and spiritual song, and vocal improvisation. His thick descriptions unfold in the space of blues house parties and street-side improvised "raps" from which Southern hip-hop draws its style.

Flower, Linda. 2003. Talking across difference: Intercultural rhetoric and the search for situated knowledge. *College Composition and Communication* 55, no. 1: 38–68.

This article explores the importance of intercultural communication as a tool for contextualizing course issues. Flower uses critical race theory to discuss the importance of the contexts that shape perspectives on contentious topics and the language in which they are shared or kept silent. Rather than adapt a linear poly-vocal approach in which variegated voices alternate between viewpoints, Flower proposes a transformative approach, a collaborative tapestry of dynamic understandings: a poly-vocal teaching methodology that allows potentially polarizing class topics to become sites of inquiry, transformation, and teamwork. Students who in one sense disagree become, in the spirit of intellectual generosity, partners in exploring multiple potential meanings and ways of working through a particular song, artist, performance, or event. Students will recognize that knowledge is always situated and partial and that a rich series of contextual considerations enables us to engage cultural studies in its complexity.

Forman, Murray, and Mark Anthony Neal. 2004. *That's the joint! A hip-hop studies reader.* New York: Routledge.

Forman and Neal's anthology compiles and historically frames dozens of important works in critical hip-hop studies, each of which helps to contextualize and unpack various aspects of the development of current hip-hop styles. For our crunkology course, I selectively assigned pieces from the book according to the emergence of challenging issues that demanded further critical unpacking, including authenticity, racialized language, women's hip-hop participation, and conspicuous consumption.

Gaunt, Kyra D. 2004. Translating double dutch to hip-hop: The musical vernacular of black girls' play. In *That's the joint! A hip-hop studies reader,* ed. Murray Forman and Mark Anthony Neal, 251–63. New York: Routledge.

This piece comes into play later in the semester in a unit on gender and Southern hip-hop communities of practice, but it also theoretically undergirds my early work in the course by expanding the rubric of who counts as a hip-hop practitioner despite media overrepresentations of criminal crunk masculinities.

Gilroy, Paul. 2000. *Against race: Imagining political culture beyond the color line.* Cambridge, MA: Harvard University Press.

Gilroy's work conceptualizes race and the arts of the black diaspora as creative (rather than reactive or strictly resistant) aesthetic worlds. Rather than conceive of black music as a function of blackness, Gilroy describes the positive processes of transformation and world-creation behind hip-hop culture.

Gwaltney, John Langston. 1980. *Drylongso: A self-portrait of black America.* New York: Random House.

This excellent polyvalent ethnography illustrates the creativity and depth of African American self-representations. This ethnographic technique is one we return to throughout the class as we look beyond statistics and media tropes to attend to the ways in which hip-hop practitioners craft a fuller portrait of the "Dirty South."

Hall, Stuart. 1981. Notes on deconstructing the popular. In *People's history and socialist theory,* ed. Raphael Samuel, 227–39. London: Routledge.

Hall's work allows for studies of the popular that are dynamic, contested, and contingent. Communication is a complex of shifting, inclusive textualities and contexts.

———, ed. 1997. *Representation: Cultural representations and signifying practices.* London: Sage.

Hall's textbook on the poetics and politics of sociocultural representation, penned by cultural studies scholars, is a generous resource for teaching cultural studies and media. Hall's own chapter on the spectacle of the "other" is accessible and useful, particularly in its discussion of stereotyping as a representational practice. He delineates practices of essentialism, reductionism, naturalization, and binary organization that will help students identify and analyze the political elements of media representations of crunk. Hall also discusses the affective engagements that undergird cultural representations: desire, fantasy, fetishism, and disavowal all intersect with the political to form the social. Hall considers representations that cross intertextual and contextual boundaries, from visual arrangements in museum exhibits to the parsing of ethnographic material through mediated representational practices. The critical content of the book is clear and accessible, and Hall's work is ideal for teaching undergraduate students basic cultural- and media-studies keywords and concepts.

Hebdige, Dick. 1981. *Subculture: The meaning of style.* New York: Routledge.
This piece encourages students to consider the materiality, intertextuality, and signifying potential of musical practice.

hooks, bell. 1990. An aesthetic of blackness: Strange and oppositional. In *Yearning: Race, gender, and cultural politics*, ed. bell hooks, 103–14. Boston: South End.
A brilliant exploration of the complex aesthetic practices of the black-Atlantic diaspora and the organic intellectual work that makes this creativity possible (quoted on the homepage of the course website and at the beginning of this chapter).

Johnson, Cheryl L. 1994. Participatory rhetoric and the teacher as racial/gendered subject. *College English* 56, no. 4: 409–19.
This article opens up questions of pedagogical subjectivity and the teaching of subjectively coded materials. Drawing from Toni Morrison's work on participatory "call-and-response" authorship and readership, Johnson illustrates the ways in which students may immediately identify instructors in terms of our most apparent subject positionalities, judging accordingly with which kinds of expertise we can and cannot speak. Not only is this piece useful in thinking about professional boundaries and student expectations of expertise and authority, but also it helps to contextualize the potential positions of students of color, who might too easily be expected to take intellectual responsibility for a class on Southern hip-hop. Although no clear solution to the problem of projected subjectivities in the classroom exists, Johnson suggests that we allow ourselves to take on the "painful" position of the cultural pedagogue, allowing the space for problematic and teachable subjective encounters to unfold.

Jones, LeRoi (Amiri Baraka). 1963. *Blues people: Negro music in white America.* New York: W. Morrow.

Baraka's radical recontextualization of the blues continues to inspire research on the continuities and life-affirming elements of black-Atlantic creativity. His articulation of black nationalist aesthetics continues to be valuable to alternative, diasporic understandings of musical practice rather than mainstream linear narratives.

Kelley, Robin D. G. 2004. Looking for the "real" nigga: Social scientists construct the ghetto. In *That's the joint! A hip-hop studies reader*, ed. Murray Forman and Mark Anthony Neal, 15–42. New York: Routledge.

This piece excavates the history behind academic representations of pathos in the expressive culture of the American underclass. Kelley suggests that the neoliberal social sciences have constructed black culture as a monolith of authenticity, describing the world of this "other" as "nihilistic, dysfunctional, and pathological." Kelley suggests that by tuning into black hybridity, style, and aesthetics, intellectual work on black expressive culture can more fully engage the complex social practices in which the "underclass" is participating. He also suggests that we gravely underestimate the global practices of black artists who utilize multicultural elements in their work. This article and Kelley's larger body of work were extremely influential in my development of this course. Kelley breaks open academic hegemony by using the emic tools of black aesthetics to analyze the work of black-Atlantic artists, which can be seen in this light as creative, life-affirming, and emergent rather than pathological or reactive.

Keyes, Cheryl L. 1996. At the crossroads: Rap music and its African nexus. *Ethnomusicology* 40, no. 2: 223–48.

Rather than narrativizing hip-hop roots in linear terms of its origins and development or extenuations, Keyes describes the African nexus of rap, in which new cultural movements are inspired by a series of distinctive diasporic practices. In the wake of recent postmodern studies of the digital sample and popular narratives of hip-hop pathology, Keyes examines the interplay of diasporic aesthetics (she chooses "funk" as a core term) and improvisatory energy in the space of practice. She specifically addresses the interplay between underground/folk creativity and popular commercialization, arguing that the former responds to and stays a perpetual step ahead of the latter through processes of creativity and stylistic change. Keyes' piece is written in accessible language and makes a strong and clear argument for the re-centering of hip-hop studies from the commercial object to the space of community practice. She uses the visual metaphor of the diasporic crossroads to reflect the intersection of tradition and emergence in black aesthetic practice, which in turn recalls *nommo*, or the ritual use of the emergent word to create power from below. I recommend reading this piece for the first class in crunkology, especially for students unfamiliar with hip-hop history.

———. 2004. Empowering self, making choices, creating spaces: Black female identity via rap music performances. In *That's the joint! A hip-hop studies reader*, ed. Murray Forman and Mark Anthony Neal, 265–76. New York: Routledge.

In this piece, Keyes suggests a series of ways in which women find empowerment in the performance of hip-hop as they engage with the music in a number of important ways.

Levine, Lawrence W. 1974. *Black culture and black consciousness: Afro-American folk thought from slavery to freedom.* New York: Oxford University Press.

This piece provides the theoretical underpinnings that connect crunk practices to other dynamic forms of verbal creativity.

Lipsitz, George. 2001. *American studies in a moment of danger.* Minneapolis: University of Minnesota Press.

Lipsitz's piece illustrates the fundamental ruptures in the construction of essentialized American subjectivities. This is especially useful in discussing the global multicultural aesthetics that line crunk practice and using intersections of class and race to open up narrow understandings of who can participate in crunk creativity, analysis, and fandom and why.

Madison, D. Soyini. 2005. *Critical ethnography: Method, ethics, and performance.* Thousand Oaks, CA: Sage.

Madison's theoretically grounded handbook of ethics, methodologies, and practices of cultural representation can be used very successfully with undergraduate students.

Mitchell-Kernan, Claudia. 1990. Signifying. In *Mother wit from the laughing barrel: Readings in the interpretation of Afro-American folklore,* ed. Alan Dundes. Jackson: University of Mississippi Press.

In an alternative discourse on complexity and meaning, Mitchell-Kernan explores organic intellectual understandings of traditional symbolic verbal practices.

Morrison, Toni. *Beloved.*

Morrison's work offers a rich perspective on the historical engagement of black women of the American South with the structures of inequality often critiqued by crunk artists. Morrison's cultural criticism and radical re-historicization of the plantation South contextualizes the black arts as spaces of creativity, agency, and activism. Even as the voices of women are often marginalized within the genre of crunk, they are critical to discourses of Southern political, social, and cultural transformation.

Murray, Albert. 1976. *Stomping the blues.* New York: McGraw-Hill.

Murray, an Alabama cultural journalist and blues fan, has created an excellent resource for demonstrating the historical work of Southern aesthetic practitioners in combating stereotypes of Southern black creativity as reactive or pathological.

Neal, Mark Anthony. 2008. A love supreme? John Coltrane, Lil Wayne and the post-trauma blues. Critical Noir blog, *Vibe,* July 29. http://newblackman.blogspot.com/2008/07/post-trauma-blues-john-coltrane-vs-lil.html.

Neal's deeply critical public intellectual work on black aesthetics in this article (as well as those listed below) encourages students to engage the very real political possibilities of academically grounded pop criticism. Further, Neal's writing style draws both from a legacy of black public intellectual discourse and the hip-hop lexicon, demonstrating the critical potential of hip-hop poetics.

Neff, Ali Colleen. 2009. *Let the world listen right: the Mississippi Delta hip-hop story.* Jackson: University Press of Mississippi.

My five years of ethnographic work with freestyle hip-hop artists and their surrounding communities in the Mississippi Delta explores the personal engagement
of Delta hip-hop artists Jerone "TopNotch the Villain" Williams and Kimyata
"Yata" Dear with both their local traditional music communities and the expanding world of popular Southern rap.

Pough, Gwendolyn D. 2007. *Home girls make some noise! Hip-hop feminism anthology.*
Mira Loma, CA: Parker.
This anthology was a core resource for the development of this class—particularly the gender unit—and highlights the critical work of women who both love
hip-hop and are critical of its gendered practices.

Roberts, John W. 1989. *From trickster to badman: The black folk hero in slavery and
freedom.* Philadelphia: University of Pennsylvania Press.
Roberts's folkloristic study traces the element of badness, in relationship to
black masculinities, from the trickster tales of Africa and through the oppres-
sive culture of the plantation and contemporary film and music. This piece is
especially useful in historically grounding students' understandings of hip-hop
masculinity.

Rose, Tricia. 1994. *Black noise: Rap music and black culture in contemporary America.*
Middletown, CT: Wesleyan University Press.
By framing her germinal hip-hop study in terms of aesthetic community practices, Tricia Rose opens up the boundaries of the "popular" to include underground and subaltern creativity, a major theme in the crunkology class.

Sanneh, Kelefa. 2006. New Orleans hip-hop is the home of gangsta gumbo. *New
York Times*, April 23.
Sanneh's article describes the historic rise of New Orleans hip-hop in terms of
its enmeshment with regional folkways and expressive culture. The piece helps
students to contextualize the synthesis of crunk as a larger regional and global
phenomenon with particular state and city cultural scenes and movements.

Sarig, Roni. 2007. *Third coast: OutKast, Timbaland, and how hip-hop became a Southern
thing.* Cambridge, MA: Da Capo.
Written by an Atlanta cultural journalist, *Third Coast* is the only historically
grounded full-length text exploring Southern hip-hop. Although Sarig does not
strongly differentiate local and commercial aspects of crunk practice, his is a pop-
ular-historical look at the movement of the commercial hip-hop industry through
the subregional scenes of the South. Sarig does an excellent job of excavating the
details of a largely undocumented (in the dominant sense) musical movement,
drawing from hundreds of interviews with otherwise commercially uncelebrated
crunk practitioners. His work is especially useful in enumerating the myriad cultural influences that differentiate the signature sounds of one city from those of
the next, identifying the influential work of particular master practitioners along
the way. The largely historical and interview-based (rather than ethnographic or
practice-driven) book provides a touchstone for Southern hip-hop history and
encourages students to critically unpack the linear narrative that drives the book
from 1980s Miami to contemporary Houston.

Tate, Greg. 2004. Hiphop turns 30: Whatcha celebratin' for? *Village Voice*. December 28.

Tate offers a trenchant and creative analysis of the current state of hip-hop affairs in this piece. Tate references Southern hip-hop only obliquely, implicating it in his critique of the newest wave of criminalized rap without directly railing against its play with aesthetics of badness and masculinity. As a practitioner, Tate foregrounds issues of multiple signification and aesthetics that thicken the hip-hop message even as he calls its practitioners to task for playing to mainstream social desires. Tate's hip-hop is less the popular linear hip-hop narrative (from "real" to "commercial" or "corrupt") and more an exploration of his own ambivalent involvement in a musical form that simultaneously struggles against stereotype and, in its most careless strains, reifies it. In a Southern hip-hop course, the piece offers an opportunity for creative critical contextualization. It's a tactical, liminal stance that allows Tate to see the music from multiple angles at once—a valuable model for complex intellectual work in hip-hop that is accessible to students as they develop their own critical styles.

Wiegman, Robyn, Wahneema Lubiano, and Michael Hardt. 2007. In the afterlife of the Duke case. *Social Text* 93, 25, no. 4: 1–16.

This piece highlights a series of publics to which college educators are (or are not) held accountable. It is especially useful to the crunkology course, which is designed to bridge artistic, popular, and academic discourses on inequality and social structure.

Williams, Raymond. 1976. *Keywords: A vocabulary of culture and society.* London: Croom Held.

This foundational work in cultural studies helps students to imagine the complexity of key course concepts, including definitions of "culture" (which he defines as one of the most complicated words in the English language) and "the popular."

Wimsatt, William Upski. 1994. Wigger: Confessions of a white wannabe. *Chicago Reader* 33, no. 40 (July).

Students can consider the discourses that underlie exceptionalist white involvement in black music.

Wright, Richard. 1940. How "Bigger" was born. *Saturday Review*, June 1.

Wright's description of the creativity behind the amoral character Bigger Thomas ties into class discussions of performativity, trope, artistic agency, and *nommo*: "I don't know if *Native Son* is a good book or a bad book. And I don't know if the book I'm working on now will be a good book or a bad book. And I really don't care. The mere writing of it will be more fun and a deeper satisfaction than any praise or blame from anybody."

Multimedia Sources

African Hip Hop Radio. www.africanhiphop.com.

This website is an excellent source for students to explore emerging global music of the black diaspora as well as consider the flexibility of American hip-hop genre in the global context. The site contains articles and links as well as a series of podcasts showcasing new music from young Africans.

Banner, David. *Mississippi: The Album.* Universal Music Group, 2003.
An excellent, complex album that contains both the surface "gangsta" tropes for which hip-hop is critiqued and riveting hip-hop ballads that directly address the suffering of the agrarian poor.

Frere-Jones, Sasha, and Jake Paine. 2008. Lil Wayne: Best rapper alive? *National Public Radio*, June 18. www.npr.org/templates/story/story.php?storyId=91621901.
This 28-minute piece on the merits of Lil Wayne pits Frere-Jones, a *New Yorker* pop music critic, against hip-hop critic Paine in a debate concerning the merits and the authenticity of the lyrics and aesthetics of Lil Wayne's groundbreaking 2008 album.

Goodie Mob. *Soul Food.* LaFace Records, 2006. Video directed by Rubin Whitmore II.
Atlanta's Goodie Mob, one of the first nationally recognized Southern hip-hop acts outside of Miami, released a series of records centered on the delineation of a particularly Southern set of hip-hop practices and aesthetics drawn from the traditional elements of the blues, folk life, and regional creativity. In this song, the group (who helped coin the term "Dirty South") uses soul food as a metaphor for the nourishments of community and tradition. Here, soul food is a comforting salve for the pain of unfulfilled desires for freedom from the realities of contemporary debt peonage in the "Dirty South." They use the metaphor here in continuity with black literary tropes that demonstrate the ability of poor Southern blacks to transcend systems of institutionalized lack by creating sustenance from leftover scraps. The song also exhibits a meta-narrative feature through which Goodie Mob's lyrics and aesthetics are posed as nourishing elements of Southern culture. In another signified lyrical theme, Goodie's soul food is simultaneously organic, cooked down home, and commercial—made from heavily advertised junk food.

How Crunk. http://howcrunk.com.
A "cyberlore" list of stereotypical crunk traits that invites visitors to participate in a test of their ability to perform elements of crunk style. It provides a quick lesson in surface representations of crunk for students.

Hurt, Byron. 2006. *Hip-hop: Beyond beats and rhymes.* Media Education Foundation.
This documentary offers Hurt's personal narrative of investment in and alienation from media depictions of hip-hop masculinities (including those of the artists themselves), a stance that encourages students to attend to both critical viewpoints and affective involvements in course topics.

Lil' Wayne. *Tha Carter III.* Cash Money Records, 2008.
Wayne's sixth studio album was released and reached triple platinum the summer before our course began; the complex production values, vocal delivery, and poetry of the album as well as the contextual interviews and performances of the artist himself provide a touchstone for understanding the complexity of Southern hip-hop. Featuring a series of crunk producers and collaborators and a combination of carefully wrought and freestyled verse, the album allows students to consider the relationship of emerging music to traditional vocal and poetic styles

as well as the importance of Wayne's local (New Orleans) political context and expressive culture to his contemporary sound.

Marshall, Wayne. Selections from Wayne and Wax blog. wayneandwax.com.
    Marshall provides an exemplary, critically grounded website concerning Jamaican dancehall and related musics. The students draw from his work in order to understand both the enmeshment of global dance music with crunk and to engage the possibility of intellectual work on complex, problematic, and often critically misunderstood music.

U.S. Congress. 2007. Subcommittee on Commerse, Trade, and Consumer Protection. *From Imus to industry: The business of stereotypes and degrading images.* 110th Cong., September 24. (Videos available online as produced by Dan Manatt at www.politicstv.com, September 27, 2007).
    The 2007 Don Imus controversy inspired new iterations of mainstream criticism of Southern hip-hop culture. Scholar Michael Eric Dyson and rappers Master P and David Banner were interviewed by the Congressional Committee on Trade and Commerce (led by Illinois Congressman and former Black Panther Bobby Rush) about the use of violent and "misogynistic" language and images in hip-hop. Tellingly, both rappers brought to the hearings are from the Deep South, and although Master P adopts a revisionist conservative line concerning hip-hop lyricism, the trio managed to eloquently address issues of representation, embodiment, performativity, and complexity in hip-hop practice. Students watch a 10-minute clip of these hearings for our second class and discuss the attempts of Southern hip-hop artists to craft alternative representations of themselves in the mainstream. This clip contains Michael Eric Dyson's resonant thesis about artistic complexity over value judgments, as well as Banner's explanation of mainstream misrepresentations of his own hip-hop activism. Banner insists that the congresspersons who criticize his art have only partially listened to his lyrics, rather than engaging them in context.

16

Mashup Poetics as Pedagogical Practice[1]

Wayne Marshall

Combining the vocals and backing tracks of what are usually rather disparate songs—often cognitively dissonant if sonically consonant—mashups explicitly embody musical collisions. Although many offer simple delights in their whimsical recontextualizations, bringing together unlikely collaborators through some clash of genre, mood, or theme, others seem to suggest a more pointed cultural critique. In doing so, such mashups have inspired me to consider and to explore the mashup aesthetic and procedure as pedagogical tools.

Most mashups truck in irony and nostalgia: the pleasant swirl of memories and associations triggered by the juxtaposition of two well-worn but formerly unassociated songs. Implicit flaunting of copyright or the integrity of a musical work notwithstanding, for many listeners and producers, mashups are quite apolitical. They're just plain fun. Even in seemingly straightforward cases, however, the meanings mashups might make frequently transcend the simply silly or comically consonant. When we hear more pathos in pop songstress Christina Aguilera's vocals if she's singing over the Strokes' garage-rock power chords rather than bubblegum beats or when we fixate on the cartoonish qualities of rapper 50 Cent's macho image as he's rapping over Queen's arena-rock kitsch, we discover correspondences, connotations, and critical readings of performances that we may not have given a second thought—or even a first listen.

It is the mashup's ability to produce such intensely audible and even pleasurable forms of critique, folding musical analysis into musical experience (not to mention embracing contemporary forms and technologies), that I wish to consider in this essay. After a brief discussion of mashup poetics, I will present a couple of examples of my own making.

In addition to offering what might be taken as an approach for making sense of mashups and other contemporary musical or, more broadly, audio-visual products of their ilk—for video footage, video games, and the like are also being mashed up these days—I hope to demonstrate how the mashup might function as a tool of music theory and of musicological pedagogy more generally, not to mention a kind of playful, provocative, publicly engaged scholarship.

MASHUP POETICS

In the last few years, mashups have exploded in popularity as they have exploded, or perhaps simply exposed, commonplace ideas about popular music and consumption practices, digital technology and intellectual property, and the sanctity of the recorded performance as a "complete" and finished work. Critical interventions masquerading as simple pleasures, mashups emerged precisely at the moment that digital technologies enabled them. As "bedroom producers" suddenly had the tools—and, thanks to peer-to-peer networks, the source materials—to play with pop music and to share their creations with a global audience, they turned consumption into production, conjuring Frankenstein versions from the scrap heap of commodity culture.[2] The example that perhaps brought mashups into public discourse more than any other is Danger Mouse's *Grey Album* (2004), which deftly combined vocals from rapper Jay-Z's *Black Album* (2003) with backing tracks constructed from portions of the Beatles' eponymous album popularly known as the *White Album* (1968). Served a cease-and-desist order by EMI, supported by massive online civil disobedience, and profiled in the *New Yorker* and other prominent publications, Danger Mouse quickly became a poster boy for the genre.[3]

Assembled from fragments of the Beatles' music, Danger Mouse's cut-and-pasted collages on the *Grey Album* depart from a certain kind of mashup orthodoxy, often glossed as "A+B" to describe the large chunks of sound typically put together; nevertheless, the underlying philosophy came through loud and clear, and the cleverness and execution of the concept won over legions of listeners and prospective producers. Around the same time, such popular websites as Get Your Bootleg On, served as outlets and networking spaces for mashup enthusiasts, and increasing attention in mainstream and Internet media brought the genre wider attention and acclaim.[4] Even major record labels, for all their cease-and-desist orders, embraced the mashup, officially releasing and sometimes commissioning mashup-style remixes of their artists' recordings as well as encouraging the practice as a form of "viral" marketing for new releases through such social networking sites as MySpace. Although the heyday of the mashup in its most recognizable and orthodox form may already be behind us, the genre's radical recontextualizations have indelibly shaped popular music aesthetics as a generation of producers and consumers, whose roles increasingly blur into each other, have come to hear such unauthorized remixes as quotidian features of the pop landscape.

MASHUP PEDAGOGY

I was initially struck by the mashup's potential to do more than ironically juxtapose disparate musical works or portions thereof when I heard Eminem rapping over a Britney Spears backing track. Appearing to take Eminem up on his sarcastic request to "sit me here next to Britney Spears," the maker of the mashup did just that, overlaying the accompaniment to Spears's "Oops! . . . I Did It Again" with Eminem's a cappella vocals from "The Real Slim Shady"—both released in 2000 and both top 10 radio hits in the United States.[5]

To be sure, this particular mashup delights in its ironic collision of two seemingly distant songs and performers, but, as I realized while I listened and grinned and considered it, "Oops! . . . The Real Slim Shady Did It Again" offers more than simple pleasures. The aural equivalence it poses presents a powerfully audible critique of Eminem's self-conscious posturing, especially in "The Real Slim Shady," as an anti-teenybopper. As the rapper appears to follow formulaic bridges running up to big schmaltzy choruses, the alignment underscores the utter lack of distance between Eminem and one of his favorite targets. Drawing attention to the pre-fab pop-ness of Eminem's song craft, the mashup essentially calls him on his bluff: "Slim Shady doth protest too much, methinks," it seems to wink in its deft marriage of the rapper and his pop doppelgänger.

It was while acting as a participant-observer at clubs in Boston and on the musical blogosphere that I began to notice the subtle pedagogical potential, and the parallel poetics, of the mashup. Through direct juxtaposition, mashups seem to have the power to shape, with potent immediacy, one's sense of how musical style articulates ideas about community, tradition, influence, and interaction. Such musical procedures reimagine the world of the social through the evocative, sensual terms of the sonic. As such, mixes and mashups, especially when explicitly conceived as cultural critique, would thus seem to embrace the insight that, as Michael Bull and Les Back argue, "Thinking with our ears offers an opportunity to augment our critical imaginations" (Bull and Back 2003, 2).

To mix in, or mash up, Richard Taruskin's voice as well, I was struck repeatedly while hearing mashups in clubs and through my computer speakers, by how, as he once put it, "good performers can teach receptive scholars a great deal" (Taruskin 1983, 63). Appreciating the power of such technologically mediated manipulations of prerecorded music to engender a certain kind of critical reflection and an analytical mode of reception, I began to consider ways that I might bring my ethnomusicological expertise to bear on my productions and performances and vice versa. I started to borrow tricks and techniques from mashup producers in order to advance what I like to call "musically-expressed ideas about music."[6] In some sense, then, what I propose here is not so much an imposition of musicological method on mash culture, but a recognition and embrace of the ways the two can work in dialogue, with music scholars highlighting the cultural work that mashups do as we employ these very forms to share our perspectives on music's social and cultural significance—perhaps even issuing in the process a creative challenge to producers to consider the forms and meanings of their mashups beyond clever or purely pleasurable correspondences in title, theme, tempo, rhythm, or key.

Just as music notation and transcription facilitate the work of music scholars researching traditions that themselves employ notation, today's worldwide web of musical interaction might be fruitfully interpreted and expressed through the very tools that artists and audiences are using to create and engage music. Music technologies in the age of digital production offer unprecedented possibilities, as Christopher Small might say, for us to music about music (1998). We would do well, I contend, to investigate the possibilities. But enough discussion and justification for now—allow me to offer some examples.

"BIG GYPTIAN"

The first "pedagogical mashup" I would like to present for your consideration combines "Khosara," a mid-20th century hit in the Arab world sung by Egyptian singer and icon Abdel Halim Hafez, with Jay-Z's "Big Pimpin'," a globally popular hip-hop track released in 1999 that employs a sample of a recording of "Khosara" as part of its accompaniment.[7] An imagined musical reconciliation of sorts, the mashup poses questions about the two songs' copyright dispute, their ability to highlight and reinterpret each other's features, and, among other things, the connections between pimp fantasies and U.S. foreign policy. That the two possess an inherently musical connection, of course, is what motivated the mashup in the first place. Interestingly enough, it was the process of putting them together that later suggested to me a number of critical correspondences.[8]

Listening to the recordings together in this manner, a variety of interesting effects seems to emerge. In an attempt to share and explicate these, I will employ the first person plural ("we") to encourage readers to listen along with me.[9] Among other things, we get to hear more of the original than the simple but central two-measure loop that Jay-Z's producer, Timbaland, extracted for "Big Pimpin'." We, thus, get a better sense of how the two-bar motif figures in Baligh Hamdi's composition; moreover, we become better equipped to appreciate the sonic inspiration at work in Timbaland's production. More mundanely, but not unimportantly, hearing the original, at least for the legions of listeners more familiar with the Jay-Z song, helps to foreground its Egyptian and Arabic qualities. This simple fact might serve to mitigate the Orientalist tendency to hear the "exotic" loop as emanating from Bollywood or Bali—two "other" places erroneously cited as sources for the Jay-Z song in journalistic accounts of "Big Pimpin'."[10] At the same time, we are not only prompted to hear the "Big Pimpin'" instrumental in a new light, understanding what Timbaland fastened onto and why, but also we are simultaneously cued to attend to "Khosara" with enhanced appreciation for the recurring but less frequently repeated motif. Further, we come to focus on how Timbaland's production actually departs from the original composition: rather than returning periodically to mark the form, the two-measure antiphonal phrase now undergirds the entire song, shifting the emphasis toward rhythmic repetition and revelation (rather than harmonic motion) and bass frequencies, among other musical dimensions. Hence, listening to the source alongside and against the sample-based treatment offers us new ways of hearing both.

While some of these new ways of hearing "Khosara" and "Big Pimpin'" demand a degree of active listening, some of the other meanings we might make of the mashup result from active, if not activist, production choices I made. For instance, just as Timbaland musically recontextualizes "Khosara" with his savvy sampling, my mashup semantically recontextualizes "Big Pimpin'" so that rather than supporting an endorsement of exploiting women as sex-workers, Timbaland's breezy beat, now thickened by the winds and strings of the original, instead primarily accompanies the mournful, melismatic singing of Abdel Halim Hafez. Sentiments such as "what a shame, what a shame, behind you neighbor, my eyes are crying" take on new significance in this context, especially for Arabic-fluent listeners, many of whom were appalled by the use of a beloved song as a vehicle for braggadocio and vulgar misogyny. Feeling fairly disgusted myself by most of the lyrics in "Big Pimpin'," I excised all but what I could hear (and, hence, willfully misconstrue) as potentially redeemable moments in Jay-Z's performance. Hence, "love em, leave em" becomes simply "love em," repeated for emphasis. Or, refitted to a musical context that is now explicitly Arab, a line about transforming impoverished women into attractive employees—"take em out the hood, keep em looking good"—suggests quite another set of possible interpretations. We could, for instance, now hear Jay-Z critiquing conservative Islam's call for women to wear veils, or, with a stretch of imagination, we might hear him assailing the interrogation techniques so powerfully symbolized by the hooded prisoners at Abu Ghraib. With a little creative transposition, Jay-Z reemerges, in a duet with Abdel Halim Hafez, as either a liberal (if imperialist) defender of women's rights or as an anti-imperialist, anti-war critic of U.S. conduct. Whether he is any of these things is, of course, immaterial to the open, imaginative exercise animating this mashup in particular and, as I have argued above, mashups more generally.

"THE LION SLEEPS TONIGHT"

The other example I will offer here brings together four versions of the same composition. Originally titled "Mbube" as sung by Solomon Linda and His Evening Birds in South Africa in 1939, many listeners know it better as "Wimoweh" or "The Lion Sleeps Tonight." The story of the song and its various versions is a long and complicated one, and it brings to the fore issues of appropriation and exploitation in an age of global circulation, commerce, and asymmetrical power relationships.[11] My desire here, in mashing up three covers by the Weavers (1951), Yma Sumac (1952), and the Tokens (1961) with the Linda original, is to highlight the accumulated resonances across all the versions and to note the song's strikingly resilient features.

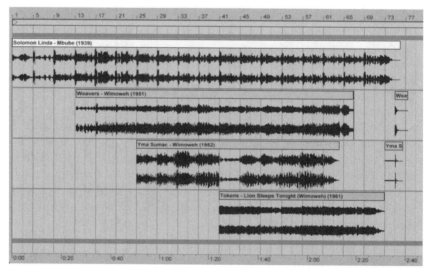

Figure 16.1.   Screenshot of "The Lion Sleeps Tonight" as assembled using Ableton Live. The numbers at the top refer to measures, at the bottom to seconds. The four recordings, represented by waveforms depicting left and right channels, are layered and edited as shown here.

As with "Big Gyptian," however, I am also responsible for some rather purposeful musical tampering here. I have altered the keys and tempos of the Weavers', the Tokens', and Yma Sumac's versions in order to "discipline" them to the original—in an act of symbolic musical retribution, if you will—though I also maintain a degree of dissonance in the mashup in order to underscore the conflict of this long, tortuous story of a popular song.[12]

For me, the gradual layering of new versions in this mashup mirrors the accretion of meanings, money, and—depending on where you stand—injustices that have piled up over time and over dozens of repeat performances. This "mirroring," however, better resembles a grossly proportioned (fun?)house of mirrors than a purely reflective surface. The composition seeps through the mix, but in the end, it sounds like quite a musical mess, which seems an appropriate analog to the messy story of circulation and appropriation the mashup is meant to restage.

AUDIBLE ANALYSES

If such mashups as I've discussed here—and "musically-expressed ideas about music" more generally—remain an underdeveloped area of musical analysis, music theory, and ethno/musicological method, it will be, I suspect, due to such resilient impediments as disciplinary orthodoxies, institutional barriers, and publishing norms, as well as the fact that the tools that make such an approach possible have only recently become widely available and accessible to those outside the realm of elite electronic music production. I strongly believe, however, that the benefits of embracing these tools and approaches at this moment far outweigh the potential perils of going against the grain of convention with regard to notions of music scholarship and pedagogy, not to mention musical ownership and fair use. Because such a practice can produce "musical examples" that are at once analytically interesting and aesthetically compelling, the contexts for which they are suitable extend beyond the classroom to the radio, the club, and the Internet, among other nontraditional venues for teaching and thinking about music. In ways I have tried to outline here, mashups possess a special capacity for imparting the theories and concepts of our disciplines through a mode of discourse more accessible to those unfamiliar with our various specialized lexica.

For all these reasons, then, those of us who are committed to sharing our perspectives with the wider world might consider various forms of musically expressed ideas about music in order to advance our fields amid the sea changes of the digital age. Colliding composition and publication, performance and pedagogy, parody and academic privilege, such mashup methods may raise questions, or at least eyebrows, as they challenge various norms of scholarship and copyright, but their value for hearing, teaching, and theorizing about music is, as I hope I have demonstrated, immediately audible.

NOTES

1. An earlier version of this text was delivered as part of the SMT Committee on Diversity Special Session on November 4, 2006, at the joint annual meeting of the American Musicological Society and the Society for Music Theory in Los Angeles.

2. It is no coincidence that the rise of the mashup coincides with the fall of Napster and the proliferation of similar services that allowed users to share and trade songs, a cappellas, and instrumentals—not to mention the software, such as Sony's Acid Pro, which made it rather easy to combine such recordings (i.e., to mash them up).

3. Despite its contested legality, the *Grey Album* can be downloaded and listened to via bit torrent technology. See the page hosted at http://www.illegal-art.org/audio/grey.html.

4. See http://www.gybo5.com; given the site's various iterations, however, a search for "GYBO" or "Get Your Bootleg On" may be necessary to locate the latest version.

5. Because of the illicit, unauthorized nature of many mashups, it is difficult to point the reader to a stable audio file of "Oops! . . . The Real Slim Shady Did It Again." However, a search for the title on the Internet should turn up several instances for listening. I have also created a page at http://wayneandwax.com/?page_id=2744 where I will attempt to host more permanently the works to which I make reference in this chapter.

6. For an elaboration on what I mean by "musically expressed ideas about music," see http://wayneandwax.blogspot.com/2006/04/musically-expressed-ideas-about-music.html, a blog post that reprints a paper I delivered at the spring 2006 meeting of the New England Chapter of the Society for Ethnomusicology.

7. To read further about the sample in question, see http://wayneandwax.com/?p=180.

8. See http://wayneandwax.com/?p=2731 in order to listen to "Big Gyptian" and to read my initial explication of the track, as well as some of the commentary it generated. Or see http://wayneandwax.com/?page_id=2744 for a collection of stable links to all the music and online content discussed in this essay.

9. Obviously, the listening process is an extraordinarily complex and, in some sense, necessarily idiosyncratic endeavor. So it is something of a conceit to assume that the meanings that reveal themselves to me would be available to others. See Steven Feld's "Communication, Music and Speech about Music" (1984) for a detailed examination of listening and semiotics.

10. See, for example, Tarek Atia's "Pimpin' a Classic" (2000) in the Egyptian newspaper *Al-Ahram Weekly* (http://weekly.ahram.org.eg/2000/484/cu2.htm), which cites such cases of mistaken identity with no little contempt for their ignorance. This conflation of Eastern or other sites more generally perceived as exotic is a classic problem of what Edward Said famously dubbed Orientalism (1978).

11. Rian Malan's exposé in *Rolling Stone* (2000) offers a detailed account of the song and its travels.

12. See http://wayneandwax.com/?p=2716 in order to listen to "The Lion Sleeps Tonight" and to read my initial explicatory text. Or, once more, go to http://wayne-andwax.com/?page_id=2744 for a collection of stable links to all the music and online content discussed in this essay.

REFERENCES

Atia, Tarek. 2000. Pimpin' a classic. *Al-Ahram Weekly* 484, June 1–7.

Bull, Michael, and Les Back, eds. 2003. Introduction: Into sound. In *The audio culture reader*, 1–24. Oxford: Berg.

Feld, Steven. 1984. Communication, music and speech about music. *Yearbook for Traditional Music* 16:1–18.

Malan, Rian. 2000. In the jungle. *Rolling Stone* 841, May 25.

Marshall, Wayne. 2005. Big Gyptian. September 19. http://riddimmethod.net/?p=23.

——. 2006. The lion sleeps tonight. April 13. http://riddimmethod.net/?p=88.

——. 2006. Musically-expressed ideas about music. April 13. http://wayneandwax.blogspot.com/2006/04/musically-expressed-ideas-about-music.html.

——. 2007. Gyp the system. September 12. http://wayneandwax.com/?p=180.

——. 2009. Mashup pedagogy. December 23. http://wayneandwax.com/?page_id=2744.

Said, Edward. 1978. *Orientalism*. New York: Vintage.

Small, Christopher. 1998. *Musicking: The meanings of performing and listening*. Hanover, NH: Wesleyan University Press.

Taruskin, Richard. 1983/1995. On letting the music speak for itself. In *Text and act: Essays on music and performance*, 51–66. Oxford: Oxford University Press.

Index

317

About the Authors

Bret Aarden has a PhD in music theory from Ohio State and teaches music at New College of Florida. His research interests include music cognition and systematic musicology. He has published in *Music Theory Online* and *Computing in Musicology* and presented at national and international music cognition conferences.

Brent Auerbach is assistant professor of music theory at the University of Massachusetts, Amherst. His research concerns Schoenbergian theory, Brahms, counterpoint, and expanding the role of technology in music theory pedagogy. He has papers published and forthcoming in *The Journal of Music Theory*, *Music Theory Online*, and *Gamut*.

Nicole Biamonte holds a PhD in music theory from Yale University and currently teaches at McGill University. She is the author of articles on vernacular music in *Music Theory Online* and *Music Theory Spectrum* and a chapter in the collection *Rush and Philosophy* and serves on the editorial board of *Music Theory Online*.

Benjamin Bierman, an assistant professor at John Jay College, CUNY, has essays in *Jazz Perspectives* and *The American Music Review*. Upcoming publications include *Think Jazz* for Pearson Education and an essay in *The Cambridge Companion to Duke Ellington*. Bierman is a composer, trumpeter, and bandleader in New York City.

Mathonwy Bostock attended Westfield State College in Massachusetts where he studied music history. He is now finishing doctoral studies in music theory at the University of Massachusetts, Amherst. He also teaches music theory at Holyoke Community College in Holyoke, Massachusetts. His other interests include mathematical logic and philosophy.

Lori Burns is professor of music and vice dean of research for the Faculty of Arts at the University of Ottawa. Her work on popular music has been published in leading journals, edited collections, and in monograph form (*Disruptive Divas*, Routledge Press).

Tamar Dubuc holds a master of arts in musicology from the University of Ottawa. Her research concentrates on the study of Nueva Canción Chilena and the embodied subjectivity as resonant quality of the popular music artifact. Tamar is currently coauthoring an article on co-subjectivity with Dr. Burns and Dr. Lafrance.

James A. Grymes is associate professor of musicology and coordinator of undergraduate studies in music at the University of North Carolina at Charlotte. He received his PhD in historical musicology from the Florida State University and is a leading authority on the life and works of Ernst von Dohnányi.

James R. Hughes was involved in a wide variety of musical activities while earning a BA in mathematics from the Catholic University of America and a PhD in mathematics from Brandeis University. Currently on the faculty at Elizabethtown College, he continues to explore connections between mathematics and music.

Kathleen Kerstetter is assistant professor of music at Mount Olive College, in North Carolina. Previously, she taught general and instrumental music in south Florida for more than a decade. She has spoken nationally and internationally about technology in the music classroom, and has published articles in *Music Educators Journal* and *General Music Today*.

Marc Lafrance is an assistant professor of sociology at Concordia University. Lafrance has published widely on media representations of gender, sexuality, race, and ethnicity in the context of contemporary popular culture. His work has appeared in journals like *Body and Society* and *Popular Music and Society*.

Heather MacLachlan received her PhD from Cornell in 2009 and is assistant professor of ethnomusicology at the University of Dayton. Her research focuses primarily on music making among Burmese people, both in Burma and in the diaspora. She has previously published articles in *Asian Music*, *American Music*, and the *Journal of New York Folklore*.

Victoria Malawey is assistant professor of music at Kenyon College. Her research interests include song analysis, popular music, pedagogy, gender studies, and composition. Her PhD dissertation, "Temporal Process, Repetition, and Voice in Björk's *Medúlla*," won the Dean's Dissertation Prize at the Jacobs School of Music at Indiana University in 2009.

Wayne Marshall is an ethnomusicologist, blogger, DJ, and occasional mashup-maker with a keen interest in how technologies inform musical production and circulation. Currently a Mellon Fellow at MIT, he's writing a book on music, social media, and digital youth culture. Recently, Marshall co-edited and contributed to *Reggaeton* (Duke 2009).

Ali Colleen Neff is a musician and ethnographer whose folklore MA work is now a full-length book: *Let the World Listen Right: The Mississippi Delta Hip-Hop Story* (University Press of Mississippi). She is currently conducting fieldwork toward her PhD in Cultural Studies (UNC) with women hip-hop artists and traditional musical practitioners of Senegal.

Nancy Rosenberg received her AB in music and comparative literature from Brown University and holds an MA in musicology and a DMA in music education from Boston University. She maintains an active career as a composer, musical director, and vocalist, and currently teaches at Brown University and Emerson College.

Keith Salley received his BM in jazz guitar from the University of Memphis and his MA from Tulane University, where he wrote a thesis on harmonic substitution in jazz. He holds a doctorate in music theory with a cognate in jazz performance from the University of Oregon. Today, he is the coordinator of music theory at the Shenandoah Conservatory in Winchester, Virginia.

Hope Munro Smith is assistant professor of music at CSU Chico, where she teaches courses in world music and music history. She earned her PhD in ethnomusicology from the University of Texas at Austin. Her work has appeared in *Latin American Music Review*, *Latin American Research Review*, and *Ethnomusicology*.

Karen Snell graduated from the University of Western Ontario, Canada, in 2007 with a PhD in music, majoring in music education. She has more than eight years of public-school teaching experience and several years of university teaching experience at Boston University. Her main teaching and research interests are in popular music and the philosophy of music education.

Alyssa Woods holds a PhD in music theory from the University of Michigan and currently teaches at the University of Ottawa and Carleton University. Her research focuses on issues of gender, race, and sexuality in popular music. She has published in *Music Theory Online* and is writing a monograph on raced and gendered meaning in rap vocal practice based on her dissertation research.

DATE DUE